Map V

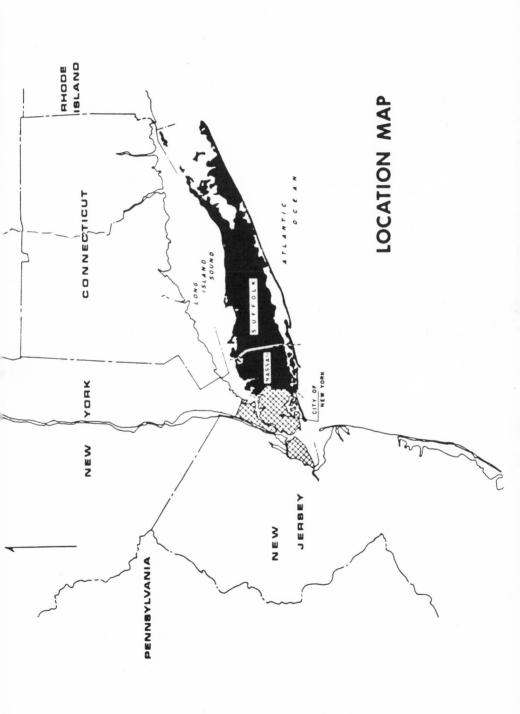

LOCATION MAP

Long Island Gazetteer

Long Island Gazetteer

A Guide to Current and
Historical Place Names

KARL H. PROEHL
AND
BARBARA A. SHUPE

Publishers
New York

First Edition

Library of Congress Cataloging in Publication Data

Proehl, Karl H.
  Long Island gazetteer.

  Bibliography: p.
  Includes index.
  1. Long Island (N.Y.)—Gazetteers. I. Shupe,
Barbara, 1941-   II. Title.
F127.L8P95   1984   917.47'21'00321   84-811
ISBN 0-935912-15-0

Published in the United States of America by
LDA Publishers Bayside, N.Y. 11361

CONTENTS

LIST OF MAPS

v

PREFACE

This publication concerns itself with the location of Long Island place names. While map librarian at the State University of New York at Stony Brook, I realized the importance of having an extensive list of place names, especially of this historically rich region. A project was initiated to establish a reference tool for the Map Library at Stony Brook which would provide locational and other information concerning Long Island place names. The project was nearing its "end" when the idea sprang forth that a gazetteer in published format would be fitting. This idea, however, was almost dashed when it was realized that I'd created a monster of sorts—a few thousand cards with inconsistencies in entries and countless other shortcomings. Add to this the fact that I relocated to Pennsylvania State University as the map librarian at its Pattee Library. Fortunately, Barbara Shupe succeeded me as map librarian at Stony Brook and she realized the importance of this gazetteer. Her conscientious editing and information standardizing found on the following pages made this publication possible.

This gazetteer consists of approximately 3,700 names of physical features, political divisions, and populated places; historical as well as current names are included. Each entry is documented so that one may be able to obtain additional information by either locating the place on a map or researching it in a publication. Variant spellings and historical names were included in the entry along with the source when such information was available.

Although this is the first gazetteer of Long Island to be made available to the public that approaches comprehensiveness, it is not yet a complete listing of Long Island names. The compilation of names is an ongoing and a never ending process. Place names are too numerous and evasive, especially the historical and locally unofficial names. It is, however, an initial attempt at thoroughness and should provide a ready reference tool leading to locational information for most place names on Long Island, present and past. Hopefully, this gazetteer will provide a springboard for more in depth study into place names of Long Island.

Karl H. Proehl
Map Librarian
Pennsylvania State University
University Park, Pennsylvania

ACKNOWLEDGEMENTS

For their encouragement and support, the authors would like to thank, the Library Faculty and Staff at the State University of New York at Stony Brook, especially John Brewster Smith, Dean and Director of Libraries; Barbara Brand, Head of the Reference Department; Irvin Kron, Head of Government Documents; and Evert Volkersz, Special Collections Librarian; and, at Pennsylvania State University Libraries, Rosanna Allen, Chief, Humanities and Social Sciences Division; Dave Adams, cartographer, the Maps Section Staff, Amelia Harding, Hilary Truscott, Allison Hutchison and Alston Turchetta, also, manuscript typists, Karen Chaberek and Elizabeth Roberts.

INTRODUCTION

LONG ISLAND PLACE NAMES

Place names on Long Island, like those of any other geographical region, originated because of our need to distinguish one place from others. Each place name constitutes some sort of geographical entity: political-administrative areas, populated places, or physical features. These geographical entities are closely, indeed inseparably, associated with the history of the area possessing those names. Place names, by virtue of their mere existence, tend to become "historical markers" conveying to later generations the record of human activities (Flick, p. 293). They reflect political issues, offer insights in regard to cultural development, denote the earliest settlers, trace settlement patterns, provide a sort of "who was who" in an area at a given time, or may even create images of past landscapes. Martha Flint writes:

> . . . the names of Long Island possess a value of more than passing interest, faithfully recording as they do, the successive conditions of a varied civilization, Indian, Dutch, and English, of which her narrow territory has been the scene. Many names have been lost . . . but enough remain, not only to preserve a lingering echo of the sonorous Indian speech, and to stamp upon the land the names, the faith, or the ideals of her early settlers, but like the fragmentary bone from which an extinct saurian can be reconstructed and classed, to give curious insight into the simple life of those early times (Flint, p. 60).

Place names do not remain static. They evolve historically, their origins and forms closely associated with the language of those people who occupy the land (Orth, p. 5). It is a universal practice for each successive group to supplant the existing names with those of their own choosing or modify them to suit their own needs (Flick, p. 294). They seldom, however, erase all the names of the previous civilization. Thus, one finds on Long Island many place names which are of English origin, a good number of Indian names, and a few Dutch names.

Place naming on Long Island began with the Algonquian Indians. Most of their names are descriptive of the place to which they were affixed (Trumbull, p. 4). They refer to topography or some feature of the natural environment; references to vegetation and especially to water features are to be found throughout Long Island. Algonquian place names have proven to be realistic designations, coming as close to the bare facts as their language would permit (Flick, p. 298). These names, when recorded and translated correctly, are meaningful words. Each name is complete within itself (Trumbull, p. 48). It consists of a specific word—that which distinguishes the place from other places within the immediate vicinity—and usually a generic term, indicating a geographic feature (e.g., hill, river, tract of land). Comparative terms like big and little, great and small, long and short, old and new are commonly used in order to provide a more descriptive image of the area (Flick, p. 297). The name Connetquot, for example, means at a long tidal river; all the elements are found in this one word. On a current map this body of water is labelled Connetquot River, providing some redundancy—"at a long tidal river" river.

Many Indian names were preserved because of the fact that the new settlers bought land gradually and in small quantities from the Indians (Beauchamp, p. 227). The descriptions of land grants and localities were taken from the known Indian place names due to the absence of ready-made names by the settlers in their newly acquired land (Flick, p. 299). A number of Indian place names have survived to the present day for the continual purpose of identifying places and features; many superseded names, however, have been successfully recorded by W. W. Tooker in his noteworthy publication *Indian Place Names on Long Island*; but unfortunately, many other Indian names have been lost forever.

Indian names created many linguistic problems for the settlers. Authors previously noted—Tooker, Huden, Trumbull and Beauchamp—all brought to the forefront in their writings a sense of dismay concerning the spelling and translation of Indian names. The Indian language had a variety of speech sounds that lack English equivalents; this resulted in crude approximations of the original pronunciation of many words. It was not uncommon for the Englishman to substitute for an Indian name an English word which resembled it in sound (Flint, p. 62). Huden writes:

Native languages were very difficult for . . . [the] colonists, most of whom were not the best penmen—nor, in many cases, even masters of English usage. Many Indian locatives were first heard from terrified, unwilling lips by prejudiced Puritans—circumstances hardly conducive to linguistic clarity! It is not surprising then, that the colonist who spelled his own name six or eight different ways should employ a half-dozen variant spellings of a [native] term in a single document (Huden, p. ix).

Tooker provides the reader of his book with approximately 500 names; practically every one of these place names has variant spellings. Wyandance, for example, is recorded as having ten variant spellings between 1642 and 1659: Weandance, Wiantanse, Wiantance, Weyrinteynich, Wyandance, Wyandack, Wayandancy, and Waiandance (Tooker, pp. 294-295). According to John Huden in *Indian Place Names of New England*, this is a relatively small number of variant spellings. He listed fifty such spellings derived from various documents in regard to the name Lake Winnepesaukee; this he considered a selective list with possibly fifty more variants for the same body of water (Huden, p. 6). George Stewart wrote later that the name Winnepesaukee had approximately 132 variant spellings, possibly holding the record (Stewart, 1975, p. 152). The end result, in many cases, is incorrect translations from these phonetically spelled words. As Trumbull writes:

> . . . that every letter or sound had its value,—if, in the analysis of a name, it becomes necessary to get rid of a troublesome consonant or vowel by assuming it to have been introduced 'for sake of euphony,'—it is probable that the interpretation so arrived at is *not* the right one (Trumbull, p. 46).

The inability to communicate effectively with one another also resulted in many place names lacking substantive meaning or any meaning at all. Misunderstandings have given birth to many place names. It was realized later, for instance, that numerous Indian names which were recorded in town records proved not to be answers relating to the question concerning the name of a particular place or physical feature, but instead possibly a personal name was recorded because the native thought this was what the colonist had requested (Huden, p. 3). One of the most amusing stories concerning place names is about a surveyor and an Eskimo in the northern frontier.* The surveyor had already completed his mapping task and only needed a few place names for reference purposes. At one point they were overlooking a large body of water and spotted two islands which were situated close to one another. The surveyor asked his Eskimo friend for the name of the first island; the Eskimo replied and the surveyor carefully recorded the response. He then asked for the name of the other island; again the Eskimo responded and the surveyor made sure he wrote it down. The map eventually found its way through the printing press and the place names remained intact. It was later noted that the names for those two islands looked atypical in comparison to other local place names. It was revealed on further investigation that the literal translation of the name for the first recorded island was "I don't know" and that of the second island, "I don't know that either!"

The Dutch occupied the western half of Long Island during the first half of the 17th century. Contemporary maps from the time period reflect many Dutch names and Indian place names adopted to Dutch orthography (Flick, p. 302). The Dutch were extremely fond of transferring their homeland names to Long Island: Breukelen, Nieuw Utrecht, Nieuw Amersfoort, and Vlissengen to name a few. Many Dutch names also described the location of a settlement. Armbruster writes:

> These names . . . generally point out some peculiar feature of the ground, which served as a landmark. Thus the present Flatlands was called "bouwery," or district of Achtervelt, i.e., the bowery or plantation in the rear, meaning in the rear of the hills, from achter, behind, and feld, field.

---

*I remember coming across this story in late 1974. I unfortunately forgot not only to cite the source, but also made no effort to record the story. Hence, the above account is a second-generation story; it may be altered, but in essence is correct.

One of the landmarks considered by the Dutch of the greatest importance, was a forest of fir trees . . .The wooded ridges on the northern border of the Town of New Utrecht, caused no doubt the application of the name Grenewijck to this region, from grene (fir) and wijck (quarter, district, refuge, retreat) . . .Several other localities received their names from this same word "grenen" as Greenpoint, from grenen punt or grenen hout-punt. Grenen Berghen, the hills forming the boundary line between the Towns of Newtown and New Lots, were anglicized into Green Hills or Cypress Hills; the cemeteries located upon them, viz., Cypress Hills and the Cemetery of the Evergreens, are translations of the original Dutch name, both having the same meaning (Armbruster, p. 19).

The eventual domination by the English, politically and linguistically, resulted in the changing of important Dutch place names—Midwout to Flatbush, Amersfoort to Flatlands, Middleburgh to Newtown, and Rustdorp to Jamaica. An example of this is found in the name change from New Amersfoort to Flatlands. The town of Nieuw Amersfoort, named for the place in the province of Utrecht (Holland), was eventually matched with Vlacklands, the Flatlands of the English. In 1801, however, a legislative enactment decreed that the town would be known as Flatlands (Flint, p. 88). The Anglicizing of many other Dutch names also took place—Vlissengen to Flushing, Breukelen to Brooklyn, and Waale Boght to Wallabout Bay. English authorities, however, permitted the Dutch to retain most of their minor place names (Flick, p. 305), but these names did not survive much longer than those which were changed or Anglicized.

Since the onslaught of the English settlers from England and New England, the English language, and what eventually became known as American-English, greatly influenced and constituted a substantial majority of the place names on Long Island. The section on classification of place names provides examples of the types of names brought into existence by the English-speaking settlers. Flick notes that

> . . . the 7,000 place names in New York [State] may be divided into the fol-lowing approximate groups: French 250, or 3 per cent; German 300, or 4 per cent; borrowed outright from the Old World and from Latin America 450, or 6 per cent; Indian 500, or 7 per cent; Dutch 1,000, or 14 per cent; and English, Scotch, Irish and Welsh, 4,500 or 64 per cent (Flick, pp. 328-329).

He also noted that Suffolk County consisted of Old World names (2 per cent), Indian names (20 per cent), and English names (74 per cent). This is indic-ative of Long Island as a whole.

CLASSIFICATION OF PLACE NAMES

Indian and Dutch place names stressed descriptive elements in identifying places. The English, however, named places for their impressions of the natural environment, their experiences encountered within an area, and to a great extent in honor of individuals and other places. They were also very good at coining words, which according to the late George Stewart, defied the venerable dictum that "every place-name has a meaning" (Stewart, 1975, p. 140). Most of the place names in this gazetteer fall into one of the following categories: descriptive, associative, transfer, commemorative and possessive, or miscellaneous names.

DESCRIPTIVE NAMES

These names identify places by noting some characteristic of the place, past or present. The name may indicate shape (Long Island), size (Great Peconic Bay), composition (Rocky Point), color (Red Hook), number (Threemile Harbor), common occurrence (Huntington*), or location (East Setauket). Indian and Dutch place names are mainly descriptive as mentioned above. Many of the Indian place names are still appropriate today: Connetquot (a long tidal river), Yaphank (on the river bank), and Aquebogue (at the head of the bay) to name a few. Others, however, are now merely names which indicate, in a quiet manner, past landscapes. An amusing comment was made by Tooker (p. xxiii) when informed that the meaning of an Indian place name does not really apply to the locality now bearing the name. His rebuttal was, "Why should it apply, after a lapse of two and a half centuries or more?" This is true of Dutch names as well. Midwout—later changed by the English to Flatbush—suggested an area surrounded by woods, and Boswijck (Bushwick) meant a town in the woods.

The descriptive category also contains many English-origin place names. Most of these names are straightforward, especially with the addition of generic terms such as hill, creek, neck, town or city.† A glance at a map will afford the onlooker with many names which express some sort of descriptive information. The most numerous are of the dimensional (shape and size) and locational type; the former is usually applied to physical features (e.g., Little Neck, Great Gull Island, Short Beach) while the latter tends generally to be applied to populated places. Big and little, great and small, long and short are commonplace. It also

*"The name of the town originated from the fact that [during the] first purchase a neck of land was reserved by the Indians for the purpose of hunting . . . Hence, the name Huntington, i.e., the hunting-town" (Armbruster, p. 33).

†These terms can offer added information besides noting whether the name refers to a physical feature or populated place. An example is creek. The name creek was usually given to streams running into small salt-water inlets; brooks, on the other hand, noted fresh water streams (Hale, p. 159).

seems from the map that we are inundated with North's, East's, South's, and West's preceding a primary name, along with the lower's, upper's, center's, middle's, head's, and possibly a few more locational descriptives. There exists, for instance, a Centereach, Centerport, Centerville, Centre Island, Middleville, Middle Island, Middle Village, and a Medford which presently or sometime in the past indicate(d) populated places in relation to other places which surround(ed) them.

Locational descriptive names must be put in proper perspective, geographically and historically. Many of these names are relative to the local area rather than their spatial relations to Long Island. Middle Village received its name from its geographical position between Williamsburg and Jamaica (Ross, v. 1, p. 547). The North Sea, for example, was applied to two bodies of water. This place name was used by the inhabitants of the town of Southampton in referring to the Peconic Bay area, while the inhabitants of the town of Southold applied the same name to Long Island Sound (Pelletreau, v. 2, pp. 331 and 417). It becomes clear why the community of North Sea in the town of Southampton bears its name. Another place name which must be looked at in the historical sense is the town of Southold. Southold is the northernmost town on Long Island. Bayles writes:

> The settlers at first gave it the name of Northfleet, and afterward it was called the South Hold by the authorities of the colony of New Haven, which name appears to have been suggested by the fact that they had gained a *hold* upon the land which lay over on the *south* of them (Bayles, p. 361).

Usually a name with a locational descriptive is adjacent to the main place name. One expects to find West Hempstead west of Hempstead, South Ozone Park south of Ozone Park, East Setauket east of Setauket, and North Amityville north of Amityville, or at least relatively so. But East Marion is an exception, since there is no Marion on Long Island, nor has there ever been a place called Marion on Long Island. So, why East Marion? East Marion was formerly called Rocky Point and the people of the community in the 1850's applied for a post office under that name. There was, however, a Rocky Point post office already in existence in the State of New York. This necessitated another name. Warren Griffins, who was an admirer of General Francis Marion (the "Swamp Fox"), suggested the name of Marion (Yeager, p. 140). There was, as it turned out, a community in upstate New York by the name of Marion and it had a post office. So for some reason they attached the locational descriptive, East. But why East? East Marion in Suffolk County is east of Marion in Wayne County, but it is further south than it is east, so why not South Marion? Besides, Francis Marion was from the South (South Carolina)! Or why not Marionville or Marionton—no Marionvilles or Mariontons existed in New York at that time—or Swampy Marion, or Foxy Marion, or . . . It is easy to criticize the naming of a place. One should, however, take into consideration that the main reason for having place names is to distinguish one place from others; and, the name East Marion, does definitely distinguish it from other places.

ASSOCIATIVE NAMES

These names do not offer any actual description but are identified and associated geographically with other places within the immediate vicinity (Stewart, 1975, p. 98). There is a body of water named Threemile Harbor; nearby is a community named Threemile Harbor. The name of Mount Sinai (formerly Old Man's*) is also applied to the harbor, Mount Sinai Harbor (formerly Old Man's Harbor). In the town of East Hampton there is a hilly area called Shinnecock Hills. The Indian name Shinnecock, however, means "a level country" which contradicts the generic term hills. The name Shinnecock was first applied to the plains area to the south of the hills (Tooker, p. xxiii). Since its first application, the name has been used to identify, within the immediate area, a body of water, an inlet, and a peninsula as well as the hills. One finds in the vicinity of Prospect Park such associative names as Park Slope, Eastern Parkway, Parkville, and Borough Park. And finally, it was the practice of the settlers on the south shore, eastern side of Long Island to name the necks of land after the names of the creeks which bordered them on the east (French, p. 631). Many of the names remain intact (Sampawams Neck and Sampawams Creek) while others have changed (Oquenock Neck and Tues Creek). A look at a map will afford one with numerous examples of associative names.

TRANSFERRED NAMES

Names transferred from one geographical area to another are common on Long Island. Westbury, for instance, derives its name from Westbury, Wiltshire, England, which was the birthplace of Henry Willis who was one of the first settlers in Westbury (Pelletreau, v. 2, p. 124). Bohemia receives its name from the Kingdom of Bohemia. A group of Bohemian (Czech) families from Prague purchased land in the southeastern part of the town of Islip (Bailey, v. 1, p. 333). Names for political-administrative areas are usually derived from other places. Examples are Suffolk, Nassau, Islip, Southampton, East Hampton, Flushing (anglicized from the Dutch place name, Vlissingen), and New Utrecht (formerly a town in Kings). The prefix "new" is used to designate the offshoots from other places, like New Suffolk and New Hyde Park. A less understandable prefix is

---

*When the community applied for a post office, the postal authorities declined to accept the name, Old Man's. It was necessary, therefore, to send to Washington another name. The new postmaster's wife opened her Bible at random and laid down her knitting needle on the page; the needle was pointing at the name, Mt. Sinai (Stevens, p. 54).

"old"—Old Bethpage, Old Westbury, and Old Brookville. Biblical and ancient places are also found on Long Island—Babylon, Mount Sinai, Jericho, and Jerusalem (now Wantagh).

COMMEMORATIVE AND POSSESSIVE NAMES

Commemorative names in honor of a person or group, and possessive names which identify a place with a person, especially an owner, are numerous on Long Island. Commemorative names are usually applied to populated places while possessive names tend generally to be applied to phy. ical features. Smithtown is named after Richard "Bull" Smith; Roosevelt, Port Jefferson, and Port Washington are named after presidents; Hicksville is named after Elias Hicks; East Marion, as mentioned earlier, is named after the "Swamp Fox," Francis Marion; and, Hallet's Cove was named after its first proprietor. A strange thing happened to Hallet's Cove. Its name was changed to Astoria in honor of John Jacob Astor. The people of the community decided to make the name change at the time of incorporation with the hope that the community would secure a gratuity for a seminary from J. J. himself. The people, however, were disappointed when Astor only donated $100 (French, p. 548fn). Astor said later, when approached on the matter, that there was already a city named Astoria and one was enough (Ross, v. 1, p. 570).

Commemorative names are also derived from the names of Indian tribes: Canarsie, Merrick, Manhassett, Matinecock, Montauk, Patchogue, Rockaway, and Setauket to name a few. Usually the names for an area denote the name of the tribe which occupied the land at one time. One exception is that of Manhasset. Manhasset is a neck of land on the north shore of Nassau County; the indian tribe named Manhassett however, occupied Shelter Island. Royalty is also recognized on Long Island—Kings and Queens Counties in honor of King Charles II and his wife.

Many physical features are named for or by their owners. One example is Gibbs Pond, so named because the owners of the land surrounding and including the pond were named Gibb. Possessive names are abundant on Long Island—Gardiners Island, Hewlett Neck, Phillips Point, Reeves Bay, Hart Cove, Willett's Creek, and Smith Lake to name just a few. It is not uncommon to look at detailed maps of an area representing different time periods and surmise from them who possibly owned the land by just noting the name changes of a particular physical feature. One such example is East Island in Nassau County, previously named Woolsey's Island and later Butler's Island after the former owners, Benjamin Woolsey and John Butler (Cocks, p. 2).

MISCELLANEOUS NAMES

A few more categories exist into which place names may be classified—incident names, folk etymology, mistaken names, and controversial place names. Names from these categories, however, are not all that numerous on Long Island and are therefore placed in this miscellaneous category.

An incident name is one which arises from a particular event or happening at that place. A few incident names on Long Island are Scuttlehole, Pantigo, Toilsome, Hardscrabble, Mount Misery, and Good Ground. Punks Hole is another incident name. Tooker writes:

> Punk was a name given by the Indians to a fungous growth found on old oak trees and stumps . . . The traditional origin of Punk's Hole is that an early settler became lost in the woods, and was able to locate himself only by these growths on some old trees in a hollow. On being asked where he had been, he replied, "At Punk's Hole" (Tooker, p. 199).

Conscience Point, which is on the west side of North Sea Harbor, had been a landing place for the early settlers. One of the women on debarking from the ship remarked "For conscience sake, I'm on dry land once more" (Adams, p. 51fn). Bread and Cheese Hollow can be considered another incident name. The hollow is located between Fort Salonga and Commack on the border between the towns of Huntington and Smithtown. Tradition has it that the name of the hollow is derived from the meal that Richard Smith had on the day he took his famous bull ride (Langhans, p. 6). Another incident-derived name is Dosoris. Benjamin Woolsey acquired a tract of land which had been bequeathed to his wife by her father. Woolsey named the property Dos-Oris—*Dos Uxoris,* a dowry (Ross, v. 1, p. 137).

Another category of names are folk-etymology names. These are names which have been altered from original names. This is common practice whenever two languages are involved and one of them is superseding the other (e.g., English and the Algonquian languages). Phonetic spelling, as noted earlier, resulted in many names which were grossly different from and lacked the meaning of the original names. Lake Success is derived from "Sacut" (an outlet of a pond); the name change might have been due to a deflection in sound (Thompson, v. 2, p. 60). Instead of an Indian name, Syosset evolved from the Dutch word "Schouts," meaning a sheriff. What occurred was a change in spelling from Schouts, Schout, Siocits, Syocits to Syosset (Tooker, pp. 255-256.) Phonetic spelling not only resulted in many names which became different and lacked the meaning of the original name, but in some cases also led to a very unappealing name. The name change of Mosquito Cove to Glen Cove is one such story. The residents surely thought that the name Mosquito Cove was a misnomer for the beautiful area. Thompson writes that,

> The name by which the settlement had been so long distinguished seemed

to the inhabitants so disagreeable that on the 4th of February, 1834, it was changed to the more inviting and romantic designation [of Glen Cove] (Thompson, v. 1, p. 503).

The word Mosquito actually evolved phonetically from Mosquetah which takes its name from the meadows bordering the cove (Tooker, p. 145). The errant spelling lent itself to "a most misleading and slanderous name." (Flint, p. 62).

The next category is one of mistaken names. Local inhabitants in the nineteenth century, as mentioned earlier, would apply for the establishment of a post office. The people, or at least one person, would send a name or list of names to Washington. These names were frequently indecipherable or nearly so, or possibly spelled incorrectly in the first place (Stewart, 1975, p. 152). Thus a clerk in Washington would enter into the books the official name of the community. In 1836 when a post office was to be established in what is now Sayville, the secretary of the organizing committee blundered in spelling the chosen name of Seville and made it Sayville (Bailey, v. 1, p. 331 and Pelletreau, v. 2, p. 251). The name of Sayville was officially recognized in Washington and the community on Long Island received a mistaken name.

The last category consists of controversial names, considered controversial because there is disagreement as to the origin of these names. Gravesend is one such example. This place, according to one source, was settled by the English who emigrated from a place of that name in England to New England and then to Long Island (Barber, p. 236). Another source believes that the name was derived from s'Gravesende after the place in Holland (Ross, v. 1, p. 354). And finally, Armbruster noted another possible source of origin:

> On the Long Island shore the sand is of a grayish color, and this fact may have led the settlers to name this shore, "Graauwezande," or Grauesand, as the name is often written in old documents i.e., "Grayishsand" (Armbruster, p. 24).

The origin of the name for the town of Hempstead is another controversial one. Thompson derived it from the English town of the same name, while some believed that the name was taken from the Dutch word *Heemstede* which means homestead (Thompson, v. 2, p. 3 and Armbruster, p. 30).

COMMENTS ON LONG ISLAND PLACE NAMES

The following two lengthy statements provide a fitting example of contrasting points of view concerning Long Island place names. Commenting first is Benjamin Thompson, Long Island historian and resident, who lived from 1784 to 1849; his remarks are taken from *A History of Long Island*. Thompson writes:

> . . . we cannot help expressing our sincere regret, at the disposition so pre-

valent in the present day, for changing the names of places; many of those adopted being remarkable for little else, than their singularity and inappropriateness. In a historical and economical view, this passion for change is much to be lamented, as leading in the end to confusion and uncertainty.

Old names, like old friends, should not be changed for light and transient causes, much less from mere whim and caprice, the consequences of which will, at a future period, be attended with more serious evils than are now contemplated, by those concerned in this useless innovation.

It is also equally to be regretted, that the original Indian and Dutch names, had not been more religiously preserved, as they were very generally distinguished for their propriety and fitness, when fully understood.

Thus Hallett's Cove, named in honor of the first proprietor, has given place to the unmeaning designation of Astoria; Cow Neck, celebrated for its fine pasture lands, has become, by some strange metamorphosis, Manhasset, the name of an Indian tribe, once inhabiting Shelter Island; Success, which should have satisfied the most fastidious, has been changed to the more charming designation of Lakeville*; Musketo Cove, probably from some fancied irritation, has obtained the very romantic appellation of Glen Cove; Cow Harbor, conveying the humiliating idea that the people fed mostly on milk, has become North Port; Drown Meadow, which had become a considerable place, notwithstanding its unpleasant name, has acquired the more patriotic cognomen of Port Jefferson; Old Man's has gone to the Holy Land, for the name of Mount Sinai, and the snug little village of Oyster Ponds, is now more classically denominated, Orient (Thompson, v. 2, p. 302).

Approximately 100 years later came remarks by William O. Stevens, an Anglophile, who toured Long Island and recorded the following comments which ended up in his publication entitled *Discovering Long Island*.

As we scan the map, leaving for the moment the lines of red and blue for the places they lead to, the wayfarer is immediately struck by the amazing names of Long Island towns. Of course there are, anywhere in America, the Indian names. Those on the Long Island area are not so bad as they might be, but they are not all of honeyed sweetness to the ear. Names Quogue, Aquebogue, Patchogue and Cutchogue; stating that they all rhyme with "fog."

Others, which may be hybrid English and Indian, are worse. Consider

---

*Lakeville was later changed to Lake Success.

Speonk, Yaphank, or Sweezy, for instance. Then in plain, unmistakable English behold Scuttlehole, Hardscrabble and Barnes' Hole. It must be very embarrassing for dwellers in those parts. For example, when an Englishman writes a letter from his country place the address at the top of his note paper reads something impressive like this: The Lindens, Upper-Chipping-Wobbley by Woking, Hants. Imagine answering your English friend by heading a letter with "Quoque," "Speonk," "Yaphank," or "Barnes' Hole"! It's just another of those cases where the poor American would be drowned in a wave of inferiority, and the letter would never be written.

Of course there are plenty of other names that suggest the homeland, such as the Hamptons, Devon, Southold and Suffolk. Then there is a rather unusual assortment of Biblical names, the most inspiring of which is Babylon. Considering the remarks made in Holy Writ on the manners and morals of the original Babylon, especially the phrases used by the author of "Revelation," it is hard to understand how any group of pious English settlers should have chosen such a name. Or maybe they weren't as pious as we think.

But these Puritans who came over from New England lacked imagination, or at any rate a feeling for beauty in nomenclature. Some of the worst of the names have been changed by a more aesthetic later generation. For example, "Cow Neck" is now "Manhasset"; "Skunk's Misery"—fancy that one—is now "Malvern"; "Punk's Hole" has become Manorville"; and "Mosquito Cove" is "Glen Cove." But we still have Great Hog Neck, which isn't pretty; and Great Neck, also, which has inspired its obvious pathological quip (Stevens, pp. 9-10).

LOCATIONS OF PLACE NAMES

A place name study naturally lends itself to proper location. There are a number of ways of specifying location. The approach used in this gazetteer is to provide locational information at three levels:

Administrative location: county—town
Relative location: in the general direction of another place name
Specific location: the use of geographical coordinates

Each level serves a purpose. Administrative location pertains to political boundaries. It gives the user an immediate mental image as to the general whereabouts of a place name. This type of information in the case of the place name Bohemia is cited Suffolk—Islip; this indicates that the community of Bohemia is in Suffolk County and in the town of Islip. To facilitate location and avoid con-

xxii

fusion, county and town designations refer to present county and town boundaries.

The most common method of expressing location is to identify one place in relation to another place (Bohemia is in the southeast part of the town of Islip), or to identify a place which is adjacent to it (Bohemia is east of Central Islip). Relative location, as it is known, was used in patent statements and in county and town histories.

The most precise way of indicating location is through the use of geographical coordinates which describe the position of a physical feature or populated place in such terms that its unique position with respect to other places is made known. The coordinates for Bohemia are Latitude 40° 46′ 30″ North and Longitude 73° 6′ 45″ West. Large scale topographic maps published by the U.S. Geological Survey were used to obtain the geographic coordinates for the places in this study. See the following section entitled "Place Names and Maps" for further information.

POLITICAL DIVISIONS OF LONG ISLAND

The political makeup of Long Island began in the mid-1600s. The first divisions to take form were towns. The "first generation towns" in the eastern part of Long Island were established as independent units and had no political alliance with one another, although they all recognized the authority of New England (Dyson, p. 15). These towns were Southold, Southhampton, East Hampton, Huntington, Brookhaven, and Smithtown. Riverhead (formed from Southold), Shelter Island (politically independent from Southold), Islip, and Babylon (formed from Huntington) were later designated towns.

The western part of Long Island was under Dutch domination during the period 1620-1664. The West India Company recommended that its settlers should establish "towns, villages and hamlets as the English are in habit of doing" (Wilson, p. 26). The result was the eventual establishment of the Five Dutch Towns: Breukelen (Brooklyn), Midwout (Flatbush), New Amersfoort (Flatlands), New Utrecht, and Boswyck (Bushwick). These towns were formed into one administrative district in 1661 (Flint, p. 78). Two towns were later formed from these Five Dutch Towns: Williamsburg (from Bushwick) and New Lots (formerly the eastern part of Flatbush). The town of Gravesend was settled by the English with permission from the Dutch authorities.

An organized attempt does not seem to have been made by the Dutch authorities to colonize the area which is now occupied by the counties of Nassau and Queens (Flint, p. 116). The authorities did not establish this area in a forthright manner, as they did with the Five Dutch Towns. What simply occurred was that English settlers lived under Dutch rule. The first settlements in the area were known as the "English Towns" of Hempstead, Flushing, Newtown, and

Jamaica. The town of Oyster Bay, however, proved to be the most disputed town between the English and Dutch governments. The early town boundaries in Kings and Queens counties are shown on Map I.

When the English finally gained total dominance in 1664, larger political divisions were established on Long Island. The first of these divisions were called "ridings." Long Island was divided into three ridings, constituting Yorkshire, which occupied the following areas:

West Riding: the present Kings County, the town of Newtown (and Staten Island; in 1675 Staten Island was separated from West Riding).

North Riding: the towns of Hempstead, Oyster Bay, Flushing, and Jamaica (and the present Westchester County).

East Riding: the present Suffolk County.

The ridings were short lived and were abolished in 1683. Long Island was then redivided into three counties: Kings, Queens, and Suffolk. There has been only one change since the inception of counties on Long Island, the incorporation of Nassau County in 1899. This was brought about by the creation of Greater New York City, which took in Kings County and the western part of Queens. The eastern part of Queens chose to become a separate county rather than a part of New York City, and was named Nassau County.

The dates of settlement, patent, and administrative establishment or recognition for each of the counties and towns on Long Island are illustrated in Table I.

PLACE NAMES AND MAPS

Maps are an important form of communication in the compilation and study of place names. They are important in that they serve as an alternate means of representing information. Maps are visual messages which not only identify information, which is the common bond among all forms of communication, but more importantly, locate information as well. They are the most effective means of recording and communicating locational information. Maps put information in its place.

Maps provide an overview of an area and, at the same time, show selected information about that area. This is done by first reducing (scaling) the area down to an adequate size for the purpose of observation and comprehension; the second stage is translating the information derived from documented sources (e.g., surveys, histories, statistical tables, gazetteers) into visual form. The result is a form of communication which provides a frame of reference and a means of summarizing information in comprehensible form. Information is shown simultaneously. It's information at a glance. A map provides for a consistent whole which allows one an introductory look at the mapped area, then leads one to

xxiv

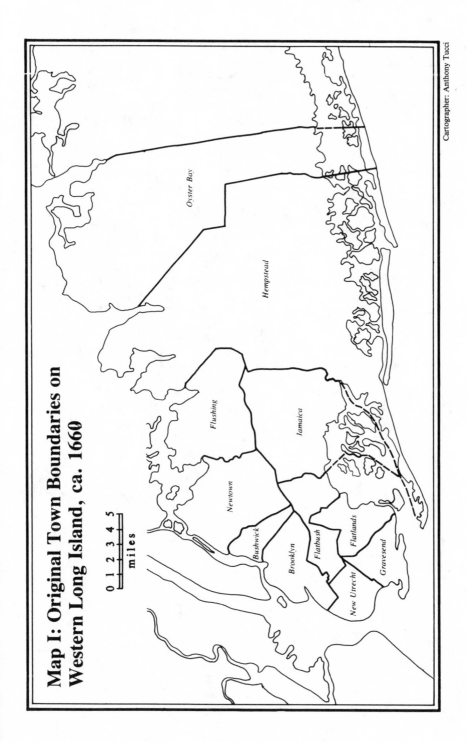

Map I: Original Town Boundaries on Western Long Island, ca. 1660

0 1 2 3 4 5
miles

Oyster Bay

Hempstead

Flushing

Jamaica

Newtown

Bushwick

Brooklyn

Flatbush

Flatlands

New Utrecht

Gravesend

Cartographer: Anthony Tucci

TABLE I

County-Town	Settled	Patent	Established/ Recognized	Comments
Kings County			1683	Became identical with the City of Brookyn in 1896; became part of Greater New York City in 1898; named a borough in 1898.
Bushwick	1638	1666	1788	It remained associated with other towns until 1708; included the town of Williamsburg until 1840; consolidated and incorporated into the City of Brooklyn in 1854.
Brooklyn	1625	1667	1788	It consolidated and incorporated the towns of Bushwick and Williamsburg (1854), New Lots (1886), Flatbush, New Utrecht and Gravesend (1894), and Flatlands (1896); in 1898 named the Borough of Brooklyn.
Flatbush	1651	1652	1788	Included the town of New Lots until 1852; incorporated into the City of Brooklyn in 1894.
Flatlands	1636	1667	1788	Incorporated into the City of Brooklyn in 1896.
Gravesend	1643	1645	1788	Incorporated into the City of Brooklyn in 1894.
New Lots			1852	Formed from the town of Flatbush in 1852; incorporated into the City of Brooklyn in 1886.
New Utrecht	1654	1662	1788	Incorporated into the City of Brooklyn in 1894.
Williamsburg			1840	Formed from the town of Bushwick in 1840; incorporated into the City of Brooklyn in 1854.
Nassau County			1899	Formed from Queens County in 1899.
Hempstead	1643	1644	1788	Included the town of North Hempstead up to 1784; name changed to South Hempstead, 1784-1792; name of Hempstead readopted in 1792.

TABLE I (Cont.)

County-Town	Settled	Patent	Established/Recognized	Comments
North Hempstead	1640		1788	Formed from the town of Hempstead in 1784.
Oyster Bay	1640	1667	1788	Lloyd Neck was made part of the town in 1788, but became incorporated with the town of Huntington in the late 1800's.
Queens County			1683	Included the area of Nassau County until 1899; became a borough in 1898.
Flushing	1643	1645	1788	
Jamaica	1656	1660	1788	
Newtown	1651	1652	1788	Part of this town was set off in 1870 and incorporated a city under the name of Long Island City.
Suffolk County			1683	
Babylon			1872	Formed from the town of Huntington in 1872.
Brookhaven	1655	1666	1788	
East Hampton	1655	1666	1788	
Huntington	1653	1666	1788	Included the town of Babylon until 1872.
Islip	1666	1697	1788	Organized as a town in 1720.
Riverhead			1792	Formed from the town of Southold in 1792.
Shelter Isl.	1652	1666	1788	Its government was united with Southold until 1730 when the island was organized as a town.
Smithtown	1663	1677	1788	
Southampton	1640	1676	1788	
Southold	1640	1676	1788	Included the town of Riverhead until 1792.

Note: In 1788 the towns which were established at that time were recognized by the laws of the newly established State of New York (Armbruster, p. 18).

locate selected information of particular interest, and finally the map serves as a summary by showing how that information relates to the whole area.

Putting information in its place and showing it at a glance is important in the study of place names. Whether one is reading a county history or going through an alphabetical listing of place names in a gazetteer, maps provide a visual sense of place. It's a concrete image which provides for proper orientation and adds structure to what has been written or arranged in alphabetical order. Most local histories, for example, are written with relative location as the only means of specifying location. The following abbreviated paragraph is an example of a typical travelogue approach, leading the reader from one place to another while describing the local area.

> About a mile northwest of Ponquogue, on Smith's Creek, is a settlement of eighteen houses called Springville. This is on the west side of the penin-sula . . .Still further up, and on the creek which forms the western bound-ary of the peninsula, and gives the locality its name, is the hamlet of Tian-na, containing fourteen houses. This is about a mile southwest of the vill-age centre of Good Ground (Bayles, pp. 320-321).

Although this statement provides an accurate account of the area, the locational information slowly loses its importance because the whole picture is given in a piecemeal manner. Constructing a mental image of the area would be difficult from this travelogue approach. The map on p. xxix covers the same area and allows the reader to follow the author's account while maintaining the total picture.

This frame of reference provides a setting which shows the interrelationship among those places mentioned in Bayles' statement. The map information also adds substantially to the description by revealing the nature of the surrounding area: topography, water features, transportation network, and dwellings. Al-though this U.S. Geological Survey topographic map was published 29 years after Bayles' publication, many of the place names remain in use. Bayles, how-ever, in a following paragraph, mentioned the communities of Red Creek and Hubbardtown which are not on the map. Using the relative location provided in the description, it was easy to approximate the geographic location of these former communities, especially with the supporting evidence provided by the map—the locations of Red Creek Pond and Hubbard Creek. The map thereby serves as an effective means of determining locations of historical place names.

Current large-scale topographic maps published by the U.S. Geological Sur-vey reflect an accurate representation of the area and can provide the best means of locating and/or plotting information derived from other sources. Stand-ardized symbols are used to depict over 200 different cultural and physical fea-tures. A topographic map could, therefore, be used to locate a site through prop-er interpretation of the description given in a written account, provided that a subsequent man-made feature, such as a housing development, did not erase all

Map II

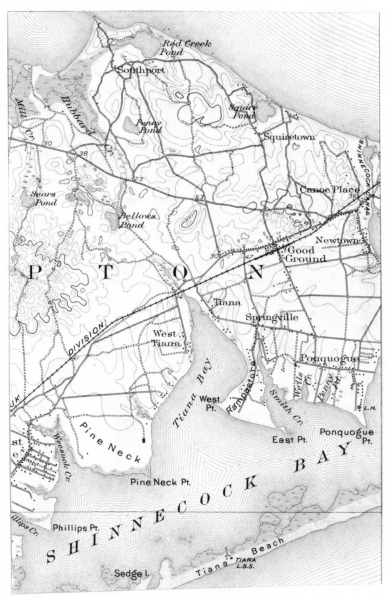

Portion of Riverhead Quad, 15 ′, 1903

traces of the past landscape. These USGS maps can also be used with contemporary maps of given time periods in order to determine the locations of historical names. This is another advantage of using maps in place name studies because information can be transferred from one map to another. One must, of course, be cognizant of the fact that earlier maps are not as accurate as the present-day USGS topographic maps. There is also a high degree of reliability in the accuracy of place names on the current maps (Raitz, p. 35). Place names are verified through field checks and through numerous other sources before they are placed on the map. The U.S. Geological Survey has published topographic maps of Long Island since the 1890s and place name changes are reflected on these maps. The section of the New York State topographic index which includes the map sheets covering Long Island.

A topographic quadrangle is cited in most place name entries in this gazetteer. The cited quadrangle is the map sheet upon which the name will appear. If it is an historical place name, an asterisk (*) will precede the quadrangle name indicating that the *place* is (was) located on the map sheet, but that the *name* will not appear.

More information concerning these topographic maps and other types of maps can be obtained from the National Cartographic Information Center (NCIC). The Center provides a national information service to make cartographic data of the United States more accessible to the public. NCIC collects and organizes descriptive information about maps and related cartographic materials and provides ordering assistance.
Write to:

National Cartographic Information Center
U.S. Geological Survey
507 National Center
Reston, VA 22092

REFERENCES

Adams, James T. *History of the Town of Southampton.* Bridgehampton, NY: Hampton Press, 1918.

Armbruster, Eugene L. *Long Island: Its Early Days and Development.* New York: The Brooklyn Daily Eagle, 1914.

Bailey, Paul, ed. *Long Island: A History of Two Great Counties, Nassau and Suffolk.* 3 vols. New York: Lewis Historical Publishing Company, [1949].

Barber, John W., and Howe, Henry. *Historical Collections of the State of New York.* 1841. Reprint. Port Washington, NY: Kennikat Press, 1970.

Bayles, Richard M. *Historical and Descriptive Sketches of Suffolk County.* Port Jefferson, NY: By the Author, 1874.

Beauchamp, William M. "Aboriginal Place Names of New York," *New York State Museum Report* 60 (1906) 5-333.

Cocks, George William. "Old Matinecock," *The Nassau County Historical Journal* 22 (Fall 1961) 1-11.

Dyson, Verne. *Anecdotes and Events in Long Island History.* Port Washington, NY: Ira J. Friedman, 1969.

Flick, Alexander, ed. *History of the State of New York.* Vol. 10. Port Washington, NY: Ira J. Friedman, 1962.

Flint, Martha B. *Early Long Island; A Colonial Study.* New York: G. P. Putnam's Sons, 1896.

French, John H. *Gazetteer of the State of New York.* 10th ed. Syracuse, NY: R. P. Smith, 1860.

Hale, Edward Everett, Jr. "Dialectical Evidence in the Place-Names of Eastern New York," *American Speech* 5 (December 1929) 154-167.

Huden, John C. *Indian Place Names of New England.* Contributions from the Museum of the American Indian Heye Foundation, Vol. 18. New York: Museum of the American Indian Heye Foundation, 1962.

Langhans, Rufus B. *Place Names in the Town of Smithtown: Their Location and Meaning.* Smithtown Library-Handley Series No. 2. Smithtown, NY: Smithtown Library, 1961.

Manley, Seon. *Long Island Discovery.* Garden City, NY: Doubleday & Company, 1966.

Orth, Donald J. *Dictionary of Alaska Place Names.* U.S. Geological Survey Professional Paper 567. Washington, D.C.: Government Printing Office, 1967.

Pelletreau, William S. *A History of Long Island.* Vol. 2. New York: Lewis Publishing Company, 1903.

Raitz, Karl. "Ethnic Settlements on Topographic Maps," *Journal of Geography* 72 (November 1973) 29–40.

Ross, Peter. *A History of Long Island.* Vol. 1. New York: Lewis Publishing Company, 1903.

Spafford, Horatio G. *A Gazetteer of the State of New York.* Albany, NY: B. D. Packard, 1824.

Stevens, William O. *Discovering Long Island.* New York: Dodd, Mead & Co., 1939.

Stewart, George R. *American Place-Names.* New York: Oxford University Press, 1970.

Stewart, George R. *Names on the Globe.* New York: Oxford University Press, 1975.

Thompson, Benjamin F. *The History of Long Island.* 2 vols. New York: Gould, Banks & Co., 1843.

Tooker, William W. *The Indian Place-Names on Long Island and Islands Adjacent.* New York: G. P. Putnam's Sons, 1911.

Trumbull, J. Hammond. "The Composition of Indian Geographical Names, Illustrated from the Algonkin Languages," *Collections of Connecticut Historical Society* 2 (1870) 3–50.

Wilson, Rufus R. *Historic Long Island.* New York: Berkeley Press, 1902.

Yeager, Edna H. "Some Long Island Patriots," *Long Island Forum* 39 (July 1976) 134–141.

GUIDE TO USE

ENTRIES
All entries are arranged alphabetically. Cross references are provided from historical names to names in current use, and from alternate names and variant spellings. The following elements are used to describe the place names, although not all elements were available or necessary for each entry:

> **PLACE NAME**
> Type of feature or place
> Administrative location; relative location; geographic coordinates
> Source—of the name if it does not appear on a USGS quadrangle map
> Historical—former name(s) with a citation to locate the source(s)
> Variations—variant spelling(s) followed by citation(s)
> Quadrangle map—name of the USGS 7.5′ quadrangle map upon which the name may be found; each quadrangle covers 7.5 minutes of latitude and 7.5 minutes of longitude.
> *Quadrangle map—name of the USGS 7.5′ quadrangle upon which the place may be located, but no name appears

REFERENCES
Citations in the entries are keyed to the bibliography which is geographically arranged. Each citation in the place name entries is in parentheses and includes:
Author's last name
The number of the citation in the bibliography
Additional bibliographic information necessary
  for locating the reference

ABBREVIATIONS AND SYMBOLS
Most abbreviations and symbols will be readily understood. Exceptions are:
AMS Army Map Service
ca.   about
fn   footnote
quad quadrangle
*   place is located on, but name does not
      appear on the quadrangle map
x   separates latitude coordinates from
      longitude coordinates

Acabonack Harbor;
41°0′50″x72°7′40″
Gardiners Island West Quad (7.5′)

ACABONACK HARBOR
Physical feature
Suffolk—East Hampton; E of
Threemile Harbor;
41°1′40″x72°8′30″
Gardiners Island West Quad (7.5′)

ABETS CREEK
Physical feature
Suffolk—Brookhaven; W of Bellport,
flows into Patchogue Bay;
40°44′55″x72°58′40″
Bellport and Howells Point Quads
(7.5′)

ABRAMS LANDING
Physical feature
Suffolk—East Hampton; S side of
Napeague Bay, ENE of Amagansett;
40°59′35″x72°6′25″
Napeague Beach Quad (7.5′)

ACABONACK
Physical feature—neck—historical
Suffolk—East Hampton; land and
meadows adjoining Gardiners Bay;
ca. 41°2′15″x72°10′
Source: (Tooker 44, pp. 1–2)
Variations: Occabonack,
Accobannocke, Accaboneck,
Occobonak, Ackobonuk,
Ackabonuk, Accaponack, etc. (Ibid.)
*Gardiners Island West Quad (7.5′)

ACABONACK CLIFF
Physical feature
Suffolk—East Hampton; SE of

ACCABONAC
see
SPRINGS
Source: (Manley 30, p. 38)

ACCOBAUKE BROOK
see
BEAVERDAM CREEK
Suffolk—Southampton
Source: (Beauchamp 7, p. 290)

ACCOMBOMMOK
Community—historical
Suffolk—East Hampton; on
Montauk Peninsula
Source: (Tooker 44, p. 2)
*Montauk Point Quad (7.5′)

ACCOMPSETT
see
NESAQUAGE ACCOMPSETT
Source: (Tooker 44, pp. 3, 158)

ACHABACHAWESUCK CREEK
see
WEESUCK CREEK
Source: (Tooker 44, pp. 3–4)

ACHTERWELT
Locality—historical
Kings; farmland "after" or
"beyond" the Great Flats
Source: (Bryant 55, p. 106)

ACOMBAMACK NECK
Physical feature—historical
Suffolk—Brookhaven; E of
Patchogue Bay;
40°44'45"x73°57'10"
Source: (Tooker 44, p. 4)
Variations: Occambamack,
Ockanbamack, Combamack (Ibid.)
*Howells Point and Bellport Quads
(7.5')

ACOMBOMACK
see
BELLPORT
Source: (Bailey 19, vol. 1, p. 251)

ADDITIONS POINT
Physical feature—historical
Suffolk—Southold; SSW of Dam
Pond, E of East Marion;
ca. 41°7'50"x72°20'
Source: (Ullitz 164, plate 12)
*Orient Quad (7.5')

ADELPHI
Community
Kings; N of Flatbush, E of South
Brooklyn; 40°41'x73°57'45"
Brooklyn Quad (7.5')

AGAWAM
see
SOUTHAMPTON
Source: (Flint 26, p. 74)

AGAWAM LAKE
Physical feature
Suffolk—Southampton; S of the
village of Southampton;
40°52'30"x72°23'40"
Historical: Town Pond (Pelletreau 38,
p. 307)
Variations: Agawom, Lake Agawam
(Tooker 44, p. 5)
Shinnecock Inlet and Southampton
Quads (7.5')

AHAQUATUWAMUCK
see
SHELTER ISLAND
Source: (Tooker 44, p. 6)

AIRPORT POND
Physical feature
Suffolk—East Hampton; S part of
Gardiners Island;
41°3'50"x72°5'50"
Gardiners Island East Quad (7.5')

ALBERTS LANDING
Physical feature
Suffolk—East Hampton; E of the
village of East Hampton;
41°0'12"x72°7'10"
Gardiners Island East Quad (7.5')

ALBERTSON
Community
Nassau—North Hempstead; S-
central part of the town, N of
Mineola; 40°46'30"x73°38'45"
Sea Cliff Quad (7.5')

ALCOTTS POND
Physical feature
Suffolk—Southampton; SW of

East Quogue;
40°50'10"x72°35'30"
Quogue Quad (7.5')

ALDEN MANOR
Community
Nassau—Hempstead; NW part of
the town, S of Floral Park;
40°41'30"x73°43'
Lynbrook Quad (7.5')

ALDER ISLAND
Physical feature
Nassau—Hempstead; N of Point
Lookout and Jones Inlet;
40°36'x73°35'
Jones Inlet Quad (7.5')

ALEWIFE BROOK
Physical feature
Suffolk—East Hampton; E side
of Northwest Harbor;
41°2'3"x72°14'35"
Gardiners Island West Quad (7.5')

ALEWIFE POND
Physical feature
Suffolk—East Hampton; E of
Northwest Harbor, SW of the North-
west Woods; 41°1'55"x72°13'50"
Historical: Ely Brook (U.S. 167, Map
T-72), Cedar Pond (U.S. 5, List No.
5904, p. 37)
Variations: Alewine Pond, Alewive
Pond, Alwive Pond (Ibid.)
Gardiners Island West Quad (7.5')

ALLENS POINT
Community—historical
Queens (Nassau)—Oyster Bay; NE
part of Mill Neck; 40°54'x73°32'30"
Source: (Hyde 147)
*Bayville Quad (7.5')

ALLENS POINT
Physical feature
Nassau—Oyster Bay; NE point of
Mill Neck; 40°54'5"x73°32'30"
Source: (Hyde 147)
*Bayville Quad (7.5')

ALLENWOOD
Community
Nassau-North Hempstead; S
of the village of Great Neck;
ca. 40°47'30"x73°43'10"
Source: (Rand 154, 1977, p. 380)
Also known as Great Neck
Gardens (Ibid.) and (Hagstrom
140, 1978, p. 24)
*Sea Cliff Quad (7.5')

ALLEY
Physical feature—landing—
historical
Queens; between Little Neck and
Flushing; ca. 40°46'x73°45'20"
Source: (Gordon 11, p. 635)
*Flushing Quad (7.5')

ALLEY CREEK
Physical feature
Queens; flows into the S part of
Little Neck Bay, SE of Little
Neck; 40°46'x73°45'20"
Flushing and Sea Cliff Quads (7.5')

AMAGANSETT
Community
Suffolk—East Hampton; E of the
village of East Hampton;
40°58'25"x72°9'
Historical: Indian Well Plain
(Tooker 44, pp. 7–8)
East Hampton Quad (7.5')

AMAGANSETT BEACH
Physical feature
Suffolk—East Hampton; S of
Amagansett, E of the village
of East Hampton;
40°47'45"x72°8'
East Hampton Quad (7.5')

AMERICAN VENICE
Community—historical
Suffolk—Babylon; S part of
Copiague Neck;
ca. 40°40'x73°22'35"
Source: (Macoskey 29, p. 47) and
(Hyde 148)
* Amityville Quad (7.5')

AMERSFORT MEADOWS
Physical feature—historical
Kings; presently part of SE
Canarsie; no longer exists;
ca. 40°38'x73°53'40"
Source: (Walling 172)
*Brooklyn Quad (7.5')

AMESFORD
see
FLATLANDS
Town
Source: (Gordon 11, p. 497)

AMITY CHANNEL
Physical feature
Nassau—Oyster Bay; ESE part of
South Oyster Bay;
40°37'50"x73°26'15"
Amityville Quad (7.5')

AMITY HARBOR
Community
Suffolk—Babylon; SW part of the
town, S of Copiague;

40°39'45"x73°24'
Amityville Quad (7.5')

AMITYVILLE
Village
Suffolk—Babylon; SW part of the
town, W of Copiague;
40°40'40"x73°25'
Historical: Huntington West Neck
South (Bailey 19, vol. 1, p. 380),
West Neck
(French 10, p. 636fn)
Amityville Quad (7.5')

AMITYVILLE CREEK
Physical feature
Suffolk—Babylon; flows N to S
through the central part of
Amityville into the Great
South Bay; 40°39'30"x73°24'50"
Amityville Quad (7.5')

ANCHANNOCK
see
ROBINS ISLAND
Source: (Tooker 44, pp. 9–11)

ANCLE SEA
Community—historical
Nassau—Hempstead; in the
vicinity of East Rockaway;
ca. 40°38'x73°39'
Source: (Macoskey 29, p. 47)
*Lynbrook Quad (7.5')

ANENDESAK NECK
see
EATONS NECK
Physical feature
Source: (Tooker 44, p. 11)

ANNUSKEMUNNICA CREEK
see

CARLLS RIVER
Source: (Sammis 104, p. 252)

ANOCK CREEK
Physical feature—historical
Suffolk—Southampton; SE side of
Atlanticville (East Quogue);
ca. 40°50′10″x72°34′25″
Source: (Tooker 44, p. 11)
*Quogue Quad (7.5′)

ANUSKKUMMIKAK NECK
see
LITTLE EAST NECK
Source: (Tooker 44, pp. 12-14)

APACUCK POINT
Physical feature
Suffolk—Southampton; NE side of
Moriches Bay, S of Westhampton;
40°48′10″x72°40′10″
Source: (Hagstrom 141, 1979, p. 64)
*Eastport Quad (7.5′)

APAQUOGUE
Community
Suffolk—East Hampton; SW of the
village of East Hampton;
40°56′30″x72°12′30″
Historical: Lily Pond (Tooker 44,
p. 15)
Variations: Appaquogue, Apoquogue
(Ibid.)
East Hampton Quad (7.5′)

APAUCOCK CREEK
see
BEAVERDAM CREEK
Source: (Tooker 44, p. 14)

APOCOCK
Tract of land—historical
Suffolk—Southampton; E of

Beaverdam Creek, tract of upland
and meadow at or near
Westhampton; ca. 40°49′x72°39′
Source: (Tooker 44, p. 14)
Variations: Apocuck, Appocock,
Apocock, Apockac (Ibid.)
*Eastport Quad (7.5′)

APPLETREE NECK
Physical feature
Suffolk—Islip; SW part of the
town, S of Brightwaters;
40°41′45″x73°16′
Historical: Saghtekoos, Sagtakos,
Sattock's, Saghtecoos, (Tooker 44,
pp. 223-224)
Bay Shore West Quad (7.5′)

APPOPOTTAMAX CREEK
Physical feature—historical
Suffolk—Islip; in Bay Shore
Source: (Tooker 44, pp. 15-16)

AQUEBOGUE
Community
Suffolk—Riverhead; NW of Flanders
Bay, W of South Jamesport;
40°56′50″x72°37′20″
Historical: Ocquebauck (Tooker 44,
p. 16), Upper Aquebogue (U.S. 170,
Chart No. 115, 1855), East River-
head (Pelletreau 38, p. 399)
Mattituck and Riverhead Quads (7.5′)

AQUEBOGUE
Tract of land—historical
Suffolk—Riverhead; land and
meadows on the N side of
Flanders Bay, although the same
name was afterwards bestowed on
meadows at Flanders in
Southampton:
40°56′30″x72°51′

Source: (Tooker 44, p. 16)
Variations: Occabock, Occabauk,
Agabake, Ocquebauk, Ahkobauk,
Ackqueboug, Aucquobouke,
Hauquebaug, Occaquabauk, etc.
(Ibid., p. 17), Occapogue
(Beauchamp 7, p. 218)
*Wading River Quad (7.5 ')

AQUEDUCT
Community—historical
Queens; SE of Woodhaven, W of
Jamaica South and Springfield;
ca. 40°40 'x73°49 '50 "
Source: (Brooklyn Quad, 15 ', 1897)
*Jamaica Quad (7.5 ')

ARACA NECK
see
WEST NECK
Physical feature—historical
Suffolk—Babylon
Source: (Tooker 44, p. 18)

ARASECOSEAGGE
see
LITTLE EAST NECK
Source: (Tooker 44, pp. 18–19)

ARESHUNK NECK
Physical feature—historical
Suffolk—Brookhaven; S part
of Center Moriches, bordered on the
W by Senix Creek and on the E
by Areskonk Creek;
40°47 '15 "x72°48 '
Source: (Tooker 44, pp. 19–20)
Variations: Arescunk, Aresunk,
Warishone (Ibid.)
*Moriches Quad (7.5 ')

ARESKONK CREEK
Physical feature
Suffolk—Brookhaven; flows into
the NW side of Moriches Bay, S
of Center Moriches;
40°47 '10 "x72°47 '50 "
Historical: Ruscocunks
(Tooker 44, p. 217)
Variations: Areskond, Areshunk
(Ibid.)
Moriches Quad (7.5 ')

ARGO VILLAGE
Community
Nassau—Hempstead; in the
vicinity of Elmont
Source: (Rand 154, 1977, p. 380)
*Lynbrook Quad (7.5 ')

ARGYLE LAKE
Physical feature
Suffolk—Babylon; N side of the
village of Babylon, in Memorial
Park; 40°41 '40 "x73°19 '45 "
Historical: mistakenly labeled
Memorial Pond (Bay Shore West
Quad, 7.5 ', 1954), Blythbourne
Lake (Sammis 104, p. 249)
*Bay Shore West Quad (7.5 ')

ARHAKAAMUNK
see
CRAB MEADOW
Physical feature
Source: (Tooker 44, pp. 20–21)

ARLYN OAKS
Community
Nassau—Oyster Bay; SE of
Massaspequa Park;
ca. 40°39 '30 "x73°29 '
Source: (Rand 154, 1977, p. 380)
*Amityville Quad (7.5 ')

ARRASQUAUG BROOK
Physical feature—historical
Queens (Nassau)—Oyster Bay; forms
part of the W boundary of South
Oyster Bay; ca. 40°39'x73°29'15"
Source: (Tooker 44, pp. 21-22).
Also known as Passaqueung and
Minell's Creek (Ibid., pp. 178-179)
*Amityville Quad (7.5')

ARSHAMONAQUE
Community
Suffolk—Southold; W of Pipes
Cove and Greenport, E of
Hashamomuck Pond;
41°5'25"x72°23'30"
Variations: Harshamomgue, Hasha-
momuk, Arshamomaque (Tooker
44, pp. 23, 69)
Southold Quad (7.5')

ART VILLAGE
Community
Suffolk—Southampton; W of the
village of Southhampton;
40°53'x72°25'30"
Southampton Quad (7.5')

ARTIST LAKE
Community—historical
Suffolk—Brookhaven; near Artist
Lake, E side of Middle Island;
40°53'x72°55'45"
Source: (Macoskey 29, p. 48)
*Middle Island Quad (7.5')

ARTIST LAKE
Physical feature
Suffolk—Brookhaven; E of Middle
Island; 40°53'5"x72°55'50"
Historical: Glover's Pond (Bayles
93, p. 262), Curran's Pond
(Thompson 41, vol. 1, p. 436),

Corwin's Pond (Bayles 95, p. 50)
Middle Island Quad (7.5')

ARVERNE
Community
Queens: SW part of Queens, SE
side of Jamaica Bay, W of
Edgemere;
40°35'15"x73°47'50"
Historical: Arverne By The Sea
(Hyde 147)
Far Rockaway Quad (7.5')

ARVERNE BY THE SEA
see
ARVERNE
Source: (Hyde 147)

ASAWSUNCE
Physical feature—swamp—
historical
Suffolk—Brookhaven; S of
Yaphank, on the Yaphank Creek;
ca. 40°47'x72°54'
Source: (Tooker 44, pp. 22, 167)
Variations: Oosunk, Oosence
(Ibid.)
*Bellport Quad (7.5')

ASHAMOMUCK
see
CRAB MEADOW
Physical feature
Source: (Tooker 44, p. 23)

ASHAROKEN
Village
Suffolk—Huntington; N of
Northport Bay;
40°55'40"x73°21'30"
Northport Quad (7.5')

**ASHAROKEN BEACH
SAND HOLE**
Physical feature—cove
Suffolk—Huntington; N of
Northport, SW of the community of
Crab Meadow;
40°55′30″x73°20′20″
Northport Quad (7.5′)

ASHAWAGH
Track of land—historical
Suffolk—East Hampton; between the
branches of Hands Creek, W of
Threemile Harbor; 41°1′x72°12′25″
Source: (Tooker 44, p. 23). Also
known as Ashowale (Ibid.)
*Gardiners Island West Quad (7.5′)

ASHFORD
see
SETAUKET
Community
Source: (Flint 26, p. 74)

ASHOWALE
see
ASHAWAGH
Source: (Tooker 44, p. 23)

ASPATUCK RIVER
Physical feature
Suffolk—Southampton; flows into
the W part of Quantuck Bay, NE of
Westhampton Beach;
40°48′30″x72°37′40″
Variations: Aspatatuck,
Assopatuck, Assapatuck
(Tooker 44, pp. 24–25)
Eastport Quad (7.5′)

ASSASQUAGE CREEK
Physical feature—historical
Suffolk—Riverhead; near

Jamesport, name means Great
Meadow Creek, possibly present
day East Creek;
ca. 40°56′10″x72°34′20″
Source: (Tooker 44, pp. 25–26)
*Mattituck Quad (7.5′)

ASSAWANAMA
Physical feature—pond—
historical
Suffolk—Huntington; NW side of
Eatons Neck;
ca. 40°57′x73°24′5″
Source: (Tooker 44, p. 26)
*Lloyd Harbor Quad (7.5′)

ASSOP'S STALK
see
ASSUPS NECK
Source: (Pelletreau 38, p. 336)

ASSUPS NECK
Physical feature—historical
Suffolk—Southampton; present
site of the village of Quogue,
ENE of Quantuck Bay;
40°49′x72°36′30″
Source: (Tooker 44, pp. 26–27)
Also known as Assop's Stalk
(Pelletreau 38, p. 336)
Variations: Assops, Assoops,
Assup (Tooker 44, p. 27)
*Quogue Quad (7.5′)

ASTORIA
Community
Queens; NW side of Queens, N
of Long Island City;
40°46′15″x73°55′45″
Historical: Sunswick, Hallets
Cove (French 10, p. 548fn),
Jacques Farm (Flint 26, p. 69)
Central Park Quad (7.5′)

ATHSCAR
Physical feature—stream—
historical
Suffolk—Islip; flowed from Deer
Swamp into Orowoc Creek;
ca. 40°43'50"x73°13'45"
Source: (Tooker 44, p. 28)
*Bay Shore East Quad (7.5')

ATLANTIC AVENUE
Community—historical
Nassau—Hempstead; in the
vicinity of Oceanside and
Rockville Centre
Source: (Macoskey 29, p. 48)

ATLANTIC BASIN
Physical feature
Kings; on Buttermilk Channel,
W side of Kings, NW part of
Red Hook;
40°41'x74°0'45"
Jersey City Quad (7.5')

ATLANTIC BEACH
Village
Nassau—Hempstead; SW side of the
town, S of Lawrence;
40°35'15"x73°43'30"
Lawrence Quad (7.5')

ATLANTICVILLE
see
EAST QUOGUE
Source: (Bayles 93, p. 318)

ATLANTIQUE
Community
Suffolk—Islip; on Fire Island,
E of Fair Harbor, SW of Seaview;
Seaview;
40°38'30"x73°10'5"
Bay Shore East Quad (7.5')

ATLANTIQUE BEACH
Physical feature
Suffolk—Islip; on Fire Island,
SE of Fair Harbor, SW of
Seaview;
40°38'20"x73°10'25"
Bay Shore East Quad (7.5')

AUBURNDALE
Community
Queens; SE of Flushing, SW of
Bayside; 40°45'45"x73°47'30"
Source: (Ricard 86, p. 6) and
(Rand 154, 1979, p. 380)
*Flushing Quad (7.5')

AUKABOG
Locality—historical
Suffolk—Southampton; in
Flanders, in the vicinity of
Goose Creek;
ca. 40°54'15"x72°36'30"
Source: (Tooker 44, p. 167).
Also known as Omkalog (Ibid.)
*Mattituck Quad (7.5')

AUSTEN'S POND
see
GOLDFISH POND
Source: (Adams 92, p. 7)

AVON LAKE
Physical feature
Suffolk—Babylon; central part
of the village of Amityville;
40°40'30"x73°24'50"
Amityville Quad (7.5')

AWEEKSA BROOK
see
AWIXA CREEK
Source: (Tooker 44, p. 28)

AWEEKSA NECK
see
AWIXA NECK
Source: (Tooker 44, p. 28)

AWIXA CREEK
Physical feature
Suffolk—Islip; flows into Great
Cove, E of Bay Shore, SW of Islip;
40°43'10"x73°14'
Historical: Aweeksa Brook (Tooker
44, p. 28),
Cagoqunk Creek (Ibid., pp. 30-31),
Kahaijongh Brook (Ibid., p. 76)
Bay Shore East Quad (7.5')

AWIXA NECK
Physical feature—historical
Suffolk—Islip; S part of Bay
Shore; bordered on the E by
Awixa Creek and on the W by
Penataquit Creek;
40°43'x73°14'15"
Source: (Tooker 44, p. 28)
Variation: Aweeksa Neck (Ibid.)
*Bay Shore East Quad (7.5')

BABYLON
Town
Suffolk; SW part of the county
Historical: Huntington South,
part of the town of Huntington
until 1872
(Bailey 19, vol. 1, p. 337)
Amityville, Huntington, Greenlawn
and Bay Shore West Quads (7.5')

BABYLON
Village
Suffolk—Babylon; E part of the town,
E of Lindenhurst; 40°42'x73°20'
Historical: Huntington South, South
Huntington (Bailey 19, vol. 1, pp.
363-364), New Babylon (Pelletrau
38, p. 193), South Huntington
(Chace 127), Red Hook (Flint 26,
p. 69)
Bay Shore West Quad (7.5')

BABYLON COVE
Physical feature
Suffolk—Islip, Babylon; on the Great
South Bay, S of West Islip, SE of the
village of Babylon;
40°41'x73°18'40"
Bay Shore West Quad (7.5')

BAES JURIAEN'S HOEK
Physical feature—marsh—historical
Kings; E end of Strom Kill
(Gerritsen Creek);
ca. 40°36'15"x73°55'15"
Source: (Dilliard 23, p. 74)
*Coney Island Quad (7.5')

BAISLEY POND
Physical feature
Queens; in Baisley Pond Park, SW of
Locust Manor, SE of Jamaica;
40°40'40"x73°47'10"
Historical: Jamaica Pond
(Walling 172)
Jamaica Quad (7.5')

BAITING HOLLOW
Community
Suffolk—Riverhead; N part of the
town, NW of the community of
Riverhead; 40°57'30"x72°44'20"
Historical: Fresh Ponds (Bailey 19,
vol. 1, p. 184)
Riverhead Quad (7.5')

BAITING HOLLOW STATION
see
CALVERTON
Source: (Bailey 19, vol. 1, p. 194)

BAITING PURCHASE
Tract of land—historical
Suffolk—Huntington; NW part of
Babylon town, formerly Huntington
town, and SW part of the town
of Huntington
Source: (Bailey 19, vol. 1, p. 360)

12

BALD HILL
Physical feature
Suffolk—Brookhaven; S of Selden,
 NE of Farmingville;
 40°50'35"x73°1'25"
Patchogue Quad (7.5')

BALD HILL
Physical feature
Suffolk—Southampton; W side of
 the town, SW of the community
 of Riverhead;
 40°52'50"x72°42'40"
Riverhead Quad (7.5')

BALD HILLS
see
FARMINGVILLE
Source: (Bayles 93, p. 267)

BALDWIN
Community
Nassau—Hempstead; central part of
 the town, W of Freeport;
 40°39'20"x73°36'40"
Historical: Baldwinville, Mileburn
 (Walling 172), Milburn (Macoskey
 29, p. 57)
Freeport Quad (7.5')

BALDWIN BAY
Physical feature
Nassau—Hempstead; ESE of Baldwin
 Harbor, S of Freeport;
 40°37'45"x73°35'30"
Freeport and Jones Inlet Quads (7.5')

BALDWIN HARBOR
Community
Nassau—Hempstead; S-central part of
 the town, SW of Freeport,
 E of Oceanside;

40°38'15"x73°36'30"
Freeport and Jones Inlet Quads (7.5')

BALDWINVILLE
see
BALDWIN
Source: (Walling 172)

BALL ISLAND
Physical feature—historical
Nassau—Hempstead; SW part of East
 Bay, N of Big Crow Island,
 no longer exists;
 40°37'55"x73°32'20"
Source: (Hempstead Quad, 15', 1897)
*Freeport Quad (7.5')

BANK PLAZA
Community
Nassau—Hempstead; in the vicinity
 of Merrick
Source: (Rand 154, 1977, p. 380)
*Freeport Quad (7.5')

BANNISTER BAY
Physical feature
Nassau—Hempstead; SW of
 Lawrence, along the course
 of Bannister Creek;
 40°36'15"x73°43'55"
Source: (U.S. 5, List No. 8101, p. 12)
*Lawrence Quad (7.5')

BANNISTER CREEK
Physical feature
Nassau—Hempstead; flows through
 the W part of Lawrence into the
 W side of Reynolds Channel;
 40°35'45"x73°44'10"
Lawrence Quad (7.5')

BAR BEACH
Community—historical
Nassau—North Hempstead; W side
of Hempstead Harbor;
40°49′45″x73°39′20″
Source: (Macoskey 29, p. 48)
*Sea Cliff Quad (7.5′)

BAR BEACH
Physical feature
Nassau—North Hempstead; on
Manhasset Neck, W side of
Hempstead Harbor;
40°49′45″x73°39′15″
*Sea Cliff Quad (7.5′)

BARBADOES BASIN
Physical feature
Queens; SE side of Jamaica Bay,
NW of Arverne;
40°35′30″x73°48′30″
Far Rockaway Quad (7.5′)

BARCELONA NECK
Physical feature
Suffolk—East Hampton; E of Sag
Harbor, SE of North Haven
Peninsula; 41°0′30″x72°15′45″
Historical: Roussel's Neck (U.S.
167, Map T-72), Russell's Neck
(Tooker 44, p. 29)
Greenport Quad (7.5′)

BARCELONA POINT
Physical feature
Suffolk—East Hampton; E side of the
town, NE of Sag Harbor, NW point
of Barcelona Neck;
41°0′35″x72°15′50″
Greenport Quad (7.5′)

BARKER POINT
Physical feature
Nassau—North Hempstead; NW
point of Manhasset Neck, N of Kings
Point; 40°50′55″x73°44′20″
Variations: Barkers Point (Hagstrom
140, 1978, p. 22)
Sea Cliff Quad (7.5′)

BARKER'S ISLAND
see
RAM ISLAND
Suffolk—Southampton
Source: (Pelletreau 38, p. 289)

BARKERS POINT
Community—historical
Nassau—North Hempstead; NW
side of Manhasset Neck;
40°50′55″x73°44′20″
Source: (Macoskey 29, p. 48)
*Sea Cliff Quad (7.5′)

BARKERS POINT
Physical feature
see
BARKER POINT
Source: (Hagstrom 140, 1978, p. 22)

BARLEYFIELD COVE
Physical feature
Suffolk—Southold; in Block Island
Sound, E side of Fishers Island,
SW of East Harbor;
41°16′40″x71°57′10″
Mystic Quad (7.5′)

BARLOW POND
Physical feature
Suffolk—Southold; central part of
Fishers Island; 41°16′15″x71°59′30″
Mystic Quad (7.5′)

14

BARNES HOLE
Community
Suffolk—East Hampton; NE of the
village of East Hampton;
41°0'x72°7'55"
Gardiners Island West Quad (7.5')

BARNES LANDING
Community
Suffolk—East Hampton; E of the
village of East Hampton, SE of
Threemile Harbor and Acabonack
Harbor; 41°0'20"x72°7'30"
Gardiners Island West Quad (7.5')

BARNUM ISLAND
Community
Nassau—Hempstead; in the vicinity
of Island Park, ESE of Island Park;
40°36'x73°39'10"
Source: (Macoskey 29, p. 48) and
(Hagstrom 140, 1973, p.33)
*Lawrence Quad (7.5')

BARNUM ISLAND
Physical feature—historical
Nassau—Hempstead; S of East
Rockaway, N of Long Beach;
40°36'x73°39'10"
Source: (Hempstead Quad, 15', 1897)
*Lawrence Quad (7.5')

BARNUM POND
Physical feature—historical
Nassau—Hempstead; E side of
Uniondale along the East Meadow
Brook, S of Front Street;
40°42'30"x73°34'45"
Source: (Hempstead Quad, 15', 1897)
*Freeport Quad (7.5')

BARNUMS CHANNEL
Physical feature
Nassau—Hempstead; S of Oceanside,
NE of Island Park, N of Garrett
Marsh; 40°36'45"x73°38'20"
Lawrence Quad (7.5')

BARREN ISLAND
see
CONEY ISLAND
Physical feature
Source: (Manley 30, p. 32)

BARTEAU'S CREEK
see
YAPAHANK CREEK
Source: (Bailey 19, vol. 1, p. 255)

BARTLETT
Community—historical
Suffolk—East Hampton;
the Amagansett vicinity
Source: (Macoskey 29, p. 48)

BASKET NECK
Physical feature—historical
Suffolk—Southampton; SW side of
Remsenburg, E of Seatuck
Cove; 40°48'30"x72°43'
Source: (Pelletreau 38, p. 342)
*Eastport Quad (7.5')

BASS CHANNEL ISLAND
Physical feature—marsh island
Queens; Jamaica Bay, W of
Far Rockaway, SW of Motts
Point; 40°36'40"x73°46'40"
Source: (Brooklyn Quad, 15', 1897)
*Far Rockaway Quad (7.5')

BASS CREEK
Physical feature—historical
Suffolk—Shelter Island
Source: (Tooker 45, p. 56)
*Greenport Quad (7.5')

BASS CREEK
Physical feature—historical
Suffolk—Smithtown; flowed into
the NW part of Nissequogue
River, NNW of San Remo;
40°54'x73°13'45"
Source: (Langhans 98, p. 5)
*Saint James Quad (7.5')

BASSALONA
Physical feature—high sandy
bluffs—historical
Suffolk—East Hampton; the bluffs of
Barcelona Neck, formerly Russell's
Neck; 41°0'45"x72°15'40"
Source: (Tooker 44, p. 29)
*Greenport Quad (7.5')

BATH
see
BATH BEACH
Source: (Beers 117, p. 24)

BATH BEACH
Community
Kings; SW part of Kings, S of New
Utrecht; 40°36'15"x74°0'30"
Historical: Bath (Beers 117, p. 24)
The Narrows Quad (7.5')

BAXTER ESTATES
Village
Nassau—North Hempstead; on
Manhasset Neck, N of Port
Washington, NE of Manhasset
Bay; 40°50'x73°42'
Sea Cliff Quad (7.5')

BAXTER POND
Physical feature
Nassau—North Hempstead; W side of
Manhasset Neck, Baxter Estates
vicinity; 40°50'x73°41'50"
Sea Cliff Quad (7.5')

BAY COLONY
Community
Nassau—Hempstead; S-central
part of the town, W of Baldwin
Bay; 40°37'45"x73°35'45"
Freeport Quad (7.5')

BAY OF FAR ROCKAWAY
see
EAST ROCKAWAY INLET
Source: (Hyde 147)

BAY OF FUNDY
Physical feature
Nassau—Hempstead; S of Pine Marsh
and Pettit Marsh, NE of Alder
Island; 40°36'45"x73°33'45"
Jones Inlet Quad (7.5')

BAY PARK
Community
Nassau—Hempstead; S of
East Rockaway, N of Hewlett
Bay; 40°38'x73°40'20"
Lynbrook Quad (7.5')

BAY POINT
Community
Suffolk—East Hampton; in
the Sag Harbor Cove vicinity;
41°00'20"x72°18'40"
Greenport Quad (7.5')

BAY POINT
Physical feature
Suffolk—East Hampton; projects
into Sag Harbor Cove,
S of North Haven Peninsula;
41°00'20"x72°18'40"
Historical: part of Hagonock
(Hyde 147)
Greenport Quad (7.5')

BAY POOSE
see
SEAPOOSE
Source: (Adams 92, p. 18)

BAY RIDGE
Community
Kings; W side of Kings, NW of
New Utrecht; 40°38'15"x74°1'
Jersey City Quad (7.5')

BAY RIDGE CHANNEL
Physical feature
Kings; W side of Kings, W of
Bay Ridge; 40°39'30"x74°1'40"
Jersey City Quad (7.5')

BAY SHORE
Community
Suffolk—Islip; W side of town;
40°43'30"x73°15'
Historical: Sodom, Mechanicsville
(Bailey 19, vol. 1, p. 327)
Penataquit (Ibid.) and (Tooker 44,
pp. 188-189), Mechanicsville
(U.S. 170, Chart No. 119, 1844)
Bay Shore East and Bay Shore West
Quads (7.5')

BAY SHORE BROOK
see

LAWRENCE CREEK
Suffolk—Islip
Source: (Tooker 44, p. 46)

BAY TERRACE
Community
Queens; in the vicinity of
Flushing
Source: (Rand 154, 1977,
p. 380)
*Flushing Quad (7.5')

BAY VIEW PARK
Community—historical
Suffolk—Brookhaven; in
the Port Jefferson area
Source: (Macoskey 29, p. 49)
*Port Jefferson Quad (7.5')

**BAYARD CUTTING
ARBORETUM**
State Park
Suffolk—Islip; on the Connetquot
River, S of the
Connetquot River State
Park, E of East Islip;
40°44'10"x73°9'55"
Bay Shore East and Central
Islip Quads (7.5')

BAYBERRY DUNES
Community
Suffolk—Brookhaven; on
Fire Island, S of Patchogue
Bay; 40°41'30"x72°59'20"
Howells Point Quad (7.5')

BAYBERRY POINT
Physical feature
Suffolk—Islip; on the Great
South Bay, SE of Bay Shore
and Great Cove, S of Islip;

40°42'30"x73°13'20"
Bay Shore East Quad (7.5')

BAYLAWN
Community—historical
Suffolk—Babylon; E side of Amity
Harbor; 40°39'50"x73°23'10"
Source: (Ullitz 165, plate 1)
*Amityville Quad (7.5')

BAYPORT
Community
Suffolk—Islip; E of Sayville, SW
of Patchogue; 40°44'20"x73°3'
Historical: Mid-Road Ville (Chace
127), Middle Road (Bailey 19, vol.
1, p. 333)
Sayville Quad (7.5')

BAYSIDE
Community
Queens; E of Flushing, NE part of
Queens; 40°46'10"x73°46'45"
Flushing Quad (7.5')

BAYSIDE PARK
Community
Suffolk—Babylon; SW part
of the town, S part of Amityville;
40°39'30"x73°25'5"
Source: (Hagstrom 141, 1979, p. 32)
*Amityville Quad (7.5')

BAYSWATER
Community—historical
Queens; W side of Far Rockaway,
E of Norton Basin;
40°36'15"x73°46'
Source: (Hyde 147)
*Far Rockaway Quad (7.5')

BAYVIEW
Community
Suffolk—Southold; on Great Hog
Neck, S of the community of
Southold; ca. 41°2'15"x72°24'30"
Source: (Hagstrom 141, 1979, p. 67)
*Southold Quad (7.5')

BAYVILLE
Village
Nassau—Oyster Bay; N side
of town, on Oak Neck;
40°54'30"x73°34'
Bayville Quad (7.5')

BEACH CHANNEL
Physical feature
Queens; SW side of Jamaica
Bay, N of Belle Harbor and
Seaside; 40°35'x73°50'
Far Rockaway Quad (7.5')

BEACH HAMPTON
Community
Suffolk—East Hampton; S of
Napeague Bay, E of Amagansett;
40°58'40"x72°6'20"
Napeague Beach Quad (7.5')

BEACH POND
Physical feature
Suffolk—Southold; central
part of Fishers Island;
41°16'10"x71°58'45"
Mystic Quad (7.5')

BEACH THATCH
Physical feature—marsh island
Suffolk—Babylon; S side of
the town, E of West Gilgo Beach;
40°37'20"x73°23'40"
West Gilgo Beach Quad (7.5')

18

BEACON HILL
Community
Nassau—North Hempstead;
E side of Manhasset Neck, N
of Port Washington;
40°49'30"x73°40'15"
Source: (Macoskey 29, p. 49)
and (Hagstrom 140, 1978, p. 19)
*Sea Cliff Quad (7.5')

BEACON HILL
Physical feature
Nassau—North Hempstead; E side
of Manhasset Neck, E of Baxter
Estates; 40°49'35"x73°40'15"
Source: (Walling 172)
*Sea Cliff Quad (7.5')

BEAVER BROOK
Physical feature
Nassau—Oyster Bay; flows into
Beaver Lake from Shu Swamp and
Lower Francois Pond and Upper
Francois Pond within the vicinity
of the village of Mill Neck;
40°52'45"x73°34'
Historical: Papa-quatunk,
Papequtunck, Beaver Swamp River
(Cocks 70, pp. 5–6)
Bayville and Hicksville Quads (7.5')

BEAVER DAM POND
Physical feature
Suffolk—Southampton; N of
Westhampton Beach;
40°49'30"x72°49'45"
Variation: Beaver Lake (Hagstrom
141, 1979, p. 64)
Eastport Quad (7.5')

BEAVER LAKE
Physical feature
Nassau—Oyster Bay; S of Oak Neck

and Bayville, W of Mill Neck;
40°53'x73°34'
Bayville Quad (7.5')

BEAVER SWAMP HOLLOW
Physical feature—historical
Queens (Nassau)—Oyster Bay;
area from the W side of Mill Neck,
S to Brookville;
ca. 40°52'x73°34'10"
Source: (Cocks 70, p. 6)
*Hicksville Quad (7.5')

BEAVER SWAMP HOLLOW
Village
see
BROOKVILLE
Source: (Flint 26, p. 67)

BEAVER SWAMP RIVER
see
BEAVER BROOK
Source: (Cocks 70, p. 6)

BEAVERDAM
see
WESTHAMPTON
Source: (Pelletreau 38, p. 340)

BEAVERDAM COVE
Physical feature
Suffolk—Southampton; E
side of Moriches Bay;
40°48'20"x72°40'
Source: (Hagstrom 141, 1952, p. 46)
*Eastport Quad (7.5')

BEAVERDAM CREEK
Physical feature
Suffolk—Brookhaven; flows
into the N part of Bellport
Bay, through the community

of Brookhaven;
40°45'35"x72°55'20"
Bellport Quad (7.5')

BEAVERDAM CREEK
Physical feature
Suffolk—Southampton; flows into the
NE side of Moriches Bay, through
part of Westhampton;
40°48'30"x72°40'
Historical: Apocock Creek
(Tooker 44, p. 290), Apaucock Creek
(Ibid., p. 14), Accobauke Brook
(Beauchamp 7, p. 209)
Eastport Quad (7.5')

BEDELL CREEK
Physical feature
Nassau—Hempstead; SSE part of
Oceanside, flows into Garrett Lead;
40°37'30"x73°37'30"
Lynbrook, Lawrence and Jones Inlet
Quads (7.5')

BEDELLTOWN
Community—historical
Queens (Nassau)—Oyster Bay; W of
Bethpage
Source: (Beers 117, p. 131)

BEDFORD
see
BEDFORD-STUYVESANT
Source: (U.S. 5, List No. 8101, p. 12)

BEDFORD PARK
Community
Suffolk—Islip; NE of Central Islip;
40°48'30"x73°10'10"
Source: (Hagstrom 141, 1969, p. 39)
*Central Islip Quad (7.5')

BEDFORD PASS
Physical feature—historical
Kings; E of Eastern Parkway, W of
East New York;
ca. 40°40'30"x73°55'15"
Source: (Luke 79, p. 128)
*Brooklyn Quad (7.5')

BEDFORD REEF
Physical feature
Suffolk—Southold; E of Plum
Island in Block Island Sound;
41°11'x72°9'
Plum Island Quad (7.5')

BEDFORD-STUYVESANT
Community
Kings; between Fort Greene and
Broadway Junction;
40°41'x73°56'30"
Source: (U.S. 5, List No. 8101, p. 12)
Historical: Formerly separately
named Bedford and Stuyvesant
(Brooklyn Quad, 7.5', 1967)
*Brooklyn Quad (7.5')

BEECHHURST
Community
Queens; N part of Queens, E of
Whitestone, N of Flushing;
40°47'30"x73°48'20"
Flushing Quad (7.5')

BEEKMAN BEACH
Physical feature
Nassau—Oyster Bay; S part of the
shoreline of Oyster Bay Harbor,
NW shoreline of the community of
Oyster Bay; 40°52'40"x73°32'35"
Bayville Quad (7.5')

BEIXEDON ESTATES
Community
Suffolk—Southold; E of the
  community of Southold;
41°4'x72°24'40"
Southold Quad (7.5')

BELLAIRE
Community
Queens; NE side of Queens, SW of
  Floral Park, E of Hollis;
40°42'35"x73°45'
Historical: Brushville (Ricard 86,
  p. 7)
Jamaica and Lynbrook Quads (7.5')

BELLE CREST
Community
Suffolk—Huntington; N side of East
  Northport; 40°53'x73°20'
Source: (Hagstrom 141, 1969, p. 34)
*Northport Quad (7.5')

BELLE CROFT
Community
Suffolk—Brookhaven; Port Jefferson
  Station area
Source: (Macoskey 29, p. 49)
*Port Jefferson Quad (7.5')

BELLE HARBOR
Community
Queens; SW part of Queens and
  Jamaica Bay, SW of Far Rockaway;
40°34'40"x73°51'
Far Rockaway Quad (7.5')

BELLE TERRE
Village
Suffolk—Brookhaven; E of Port
  Jefferson Harbor, located on Mount
  Misery; 40°57'30"x73°4'

Historical: Oak Wood (Chace 127)
Port Jefferson Quad (7.5')

BELLEROSE
Community
Queens; W of New Hyde Park, NE of
  Queens Village; 40°43'35"x73°43'
Source: (Hagstrom 140, 1978, p. 26)
*Lynbrook Quad (7.5')

BELLEROSE
Village
Nassau—Hempstead; NW part of the
  town, W of Floral Park;
40°43'15"x73°43'
Lynbrook Quad (7.5')

BELLEROSE TERRACE
Community
Nassau—Hempstead; NW part of
  the town, W of Floral Park;
40°43'20"x73°43'30"
Lynbrook Quad (7.5')

BELLMORE
Community
Nassau—Hempstead; E of Freeport
  and Merrick, W of Seaford;
40°40'x73°31'30"
Historical: New Bridge (Walling 172),
  Little Neck (French 10, p. 547)
Freeport Quad (7.5')

BELLMORE CREEK
Physical feature
Nassau—Hempstead; flows into East
  Bay, SE part of Bellmore;
40°38'30"x73°31'5"
Freeport Quad (7.5')

BELLOWS POND
Physical feature
Suffolk—Southampton; W of

Hampton Bays;
40°52'50"x72°33'40"
Mattituck Quad (7.5')

BELLPORT
Village
Suffolk—Brookhaven; S-central
part of the town, E of Patchogue;
40°45'30"x72°56'30"
Historical: Acombomack,
Occumbomuck (Bailey 19, vol. 1,
pp. 251, 258), Occombomock
(Beauchamp 7, p. 218)
Bellport and Howells Point Quads
(7.5')

BELLPORT BAY
Physical feature
Suffolk—Brookhaven; E part
of the Great South Bay;
40°45'x72°55'
Bellport and Howells Point
Quads (7.5')

BELLPORT STATION
see
NORTH BELLPORT
Source: (Moriches Quad, 15', 1903)

BELLVIEW BEACH
Physical feature
Suffolk—Brookhaven; S side of
Central Moriches, NW shoreline of
Moriches Bay; 40°47'x72°47'15"
Moriches Quad (7.5')

BELMONT LAKE
Physical feature
Suffolk—Babylon; N part of
Belmont Lake State Park, SE of
Wyandanch; 40°44'x73°20'30"
Bay Shore West Quad (7.5')

BELMONT LAKE STATE PARK
Suffolk—Babylon; between West
Babylon and North Babylon;
40°43'x73°20'20"
Bay Shore West Quad (7.5')

BENEDICTS CREEK
see
MILL CREEK
Physical feature
Suffolk—Southampton—Mecox Bay
Source: (Adams 92, p. 18)

BENNET'S POINT
see
LONG ISLAND CITY (part of)
Source: (Flint 26, p. 72)

BENNETT'S POINT
see
HUNTER'S POINT
Source: (Ricard 86, p. 10)

BENNETTS POINT
Physical feature
Kings—The Narrows; S of Bay
Ridge, NW of New Utrecht;
40°38'x74°2'20"
Source: (Walling 172)
*Jersey City Quad (7.5')

BENS POINT
Physical feature
Suffolk—Southold; SW tip of
Orient Beach; 41°7'42"x72°16'
Orient Quad (7.5')

BENSONHURST
Community
Kings; SW part of Kings, N of
Coney Island, W of Gravesend;
40°36'15"x73°59'30"
Coney Island Quad (7.5')

BERGEN BASIN
Physical feature
Queens—Jamaica Bay; N of Jamaica
Bay, W of JFK International
Airport; 40°39'30"x73°49'30"
Historical: Bergen Creek
(Brooklyn Quad, 15', 1897),
Bergens Creek (Jamaica Quad, 7.5',
AMS, 1947)
Jamaica Quad (7.5')

BERGEN BEACH
Community
Kings; SE side of Kings, E of
Flatlands; 40°37'x73°54'15"
Historical: Winippauge, Wimbaccoe
(Tooker 44, p. 288), Bergens Island
(Walling 172)
Coney Island Quad (7.5')

BERGEN CREEK
see
BERGEN BASIN
Source: (Brooklyn Quad, 15', 1897)

BERGEN PARK
Community
Suffolk—Huntington; W side of
Huntington Station;
40°51'x73°25'50"
Source: (Rand 154, 1977, p. 381)
*Huntington Quad (7.5')

BERGENS CREEK
see
BERGEN BASIN
Source: (Jamaica Quad, 7.5', AMS,
1947)

BERGENS ISLAND
see
BERGEN BEACH
Source: (Walling 172)

BERLIN
Community—historical
Queens—Newtown (town); W side of
the town, S of Laurel Hill
Source: (Beers 117, p. 52)

BERRIANS ISLAND
Physical feature—historical
Queens—East River; NW of Bowery
Bay and Steinway, SW of Rikers
Island; 40°47'10"x73°54'
Source: (Walling 172)
*Central Park Quad (7.5')

BETHPAGE
Community
Nassau—Oyster Bay; central part of
the town, NW of Farmingdale;
40°44'x73°29'
Historical: Central Park
(Metropolitian 81) and (Hempstead
Quad, 15', 1897)
Variation: Bethphage (French 10,
p. 551fn)
Amityville and Huntington Quads
(7.5')

BETHPAGE STATE PARK
Nassau—Oyster Bay; E side of the
town, N of Farmingdale, S of
Plainview; 40°45'x73°27'30"
Amityville and Huntington Quads
(7.5')

BETTS CREEK
Physical feature
Kings; E part of Kings, flows into
Old Mill Creek;
40°39'20"x73°51'45"
Jamaica Quad (7.5')

BEVER POND
see
JAMAICA
Community
Source: (Flint 26, p. 71)

BIG CHANNEL
Physical feature
Kings; W side of Jamaica Bay, W of
Ruffle Bar; 40°36'x73°52'20"
Far Rockaway Quad (7.5')

BIG CROW ISLAND
Physical feature
Nassau—Hempstead; SW of East Bay,
W of Cuba Island, E of Pettit Marsh;
40°37'15"x73°32'30"
Freeport and Jones Inlet Quads (7.5')

BIG FISH CREEK
Physical feature
Suffolk—Brookhaven; flows into the
NE part of Bellport Bay;
40°46'x72°53'25"
Bellport Quad (7.5')

BIG FISH CREEK POND
Physical feature
Suffolk—Brookhaven; NE of Bellport
Bay, S of Shirley;
40°46'25"x72°52'50"
Bellport Quad (7.5')

BIG FISHKILL CHANNEL
Physical feature
Kings; W side of Jamaica Bay;
40°36'15"x73°51'45"
Far Rockaway Quad (7.5')

BIG FRESH POND
Physical feature
Suffolk—Southampton; NW of the

village of Southampton;
40°55'10"x72°25'10"
Historical: Missipaug (Tooker 44,
p. 136)
Southampton Quad (7.5')

BIG HASSOCK
Physical feature
Nassau—Hempstead; NE side of
Lawrence, SW of Brosewere Bay;
40°36'20"x73°42'25"
Lawrence Quad (7.5')

BIG MUCKS CREEK
Physical feature
Queens; E side of Jamaica Bay,
between Jo Co Marsh and Silver
Hole Marsh; 40°36'30"x73°48'
Far Rockaway Quad (7.5')

BIG REED POND
Physical feature
Suffolk—East Hampton; on Montauk
Peninsula, NE of Lake Montauk,
NW of Oyster Pond;
41°4'37"x71°54'40"
Historical: Reed Pond (Montauk
Quad, 15', 1904)
Montauk Point Quad (7.5')

BILL'S COVE
see
TUTHILL COVE
Source: (U.S. 5, List No. 5904, p. 38)

BILTMORE SHORES
Community
Nassau—Oyster Bay; S-central
side of Massapequa, S of
Massapequa Lake;
40°39'55"x73°28'
Amityville Quad (7.5')

BIRCH CREEK
Physical feature
Suffolk—Southampton; S of
Flanders Bay, E of Flanders;
40°54'30"x72°35'25"
Historical: Suggamuck Creek (Tooker
44, p. 251)
Mattituck Quad (7.5')

BIRCHWOOD
see
NORTH ROCKVILLE CENTRE
(part of)
Source: (Rand 154, 1977, p. 381)

BLACK BANK MARSH
Physical feature—marsh island
Kings, Queens; in Jamaica Bay, W
of Rulers Bar Hassock;
40°37'20"x73°50'
Far Rockaway Quad (7.5')

BLACK BANKS HASSOCK
see
**NORTH BLACK BANKS HAS-
SOCK or SOUTH BLACK BANKS
HASSOCK**
Source: (U.S. 5, List No. 8101,
p. 13)

BLACK BANKS ISLAND
Physical feature—marsh island
Nassau—Hempstead, Oyster Bay;
SW of South Oyster Bay, E of South
Line Island; 40°37'x73°29'
West Gilgo Beach Quad (7.5')

BLACK MARSH
Physical feature—historical
Suffolk—East Hampton; part of the
E shoreline of Threemile Harbor;
41°1'x72°10'50"
Source: (U.S. 167, Map T-72)
*Gardiners Island West Quad (7.5')

BLACK POINT
Physical feature
Queens; on Grassy Bay, NW point
of Broad Creek Marsh;
40°37'55"x73°48'25"
Source: (Jamaica Quad, 7.5', AMS,
1947)
*Jamaica Quad (7.5')

BLACK POINT
Physical feature
Queens; on Jamaica Bay, E side of
Jo Co Marsh, W of Inwood;
40°36'50"x73°46'55"
Far Rockaway Quad (7.5')

BLACK POND
Physical feature
Suffolk—Southampton; N of
Bridgehampton;
40°57'x72°17'50"
Sag Harbor Quad (7.5')

BLACK WALL CHANNEL
Physical feature
Kings; SE Kings, W side of
Jamaica Bay; 40°36'30"x73°50'10"
Far Rockaway Quad (7.5')

BLACK WALL MARSH
Physical feature—marsh island
Queens; SW part of Queens and
Jamaica Bay, NE of Ruffle Bar;
40°36'25"x73°50'
Historical: Black Well Marsh
(Brooklyn Quad, 15', 1897)
Far Rockaway Quad (7.5')

BLANCHARD LAKE
Physical feature
Suffolk—Huntington; N part of
Northport, W of Crab Meadow, E of
Northport Basin;

40°55′25″x73°53′50″
Source: (Hagstrom 141, 1979, p. 23)
Historical: The Cove, Round Swamp
(Sammis 104, p. 181)
*Northport Quad (7.5′)

BLISSVILLE
Community
Queens; SE side of Long Island City
Source: (Rand 154, 1977, p. 381)
Variation: Bliss (Beers 117, pp. 40, 42)
and (Rand 154, 1977, p. 381)
*Brooklyn Quad (7.5′)

BLUE POINT
Community
Suffolk—Brookhaven; SW of
Patchogue, E of Sayville;
40°44′30″x73°1′40″
Historical: Manowtasquott (Tooker 44,
p. 100), Manowtussquott (French 10,
p. 634fn)
Sayville Quad (7.5′)

BLUE POINT
Physical feature
Suffolk—Brookhaven; on the Great
South Bay, S of Blue Point, SE of
Sayville; 40°43′50″x73°2′
Sayville Quad (7.5′)

BLUE POINT BAY
see
PATCHOGUE BAY
Source: (Overton 37, p. 17)

BLUE POINT BEACH
Physical feature
Suffolk—Brookhaven; E of Blue
Point, NW side of Patchogue Bay,
40°44′50″x73°1′35″
Sayville Quad (7.5′)

BLUFF POINT
Physical feature
Suffolk—Huntington; SE side of
Northport Bay;
40°54′40″x73°21′35″
Northport Quad (7.5′)

BLUFF POINT
Physical feature
Suffolk—Southampton; in Upper Sag
Harbor Cove, W of Sag Harbor,
40°59′40″x72°18′25″
Sag Harbor Quad (7.5′)

BLYDENBURG'S LANDING
see
THE LANDING
Community
Source: (Langhans 98, pp. 13–14)
and (Pelletreau 38, p. 211)

BLYDENBURG'S MILLS
see
NEW MILLS
Source: (Bayles 93, pp. 191–192)

BLYDENBURGH'S POND
see
NEW MILLPOND
Source: (Langhans 98, p. 17)

BLYTHEBOURNE
see
BOROUGH PARK
Source: (Brooklyn Quad, 15′, 1897)

BLYTHBOURNE LAKE
see
ARGYLE LAKE
Source: (Sammis 104, p. 249)

BOGGY SWAMP
Physical feature—historical
Nassau—Oyster Bay; in Glen Cove,
in the vicinity of Dosoris Pond;
ca. 40°53′50″x73°37′20″
Source: (Coles 73, p. 11)
*Bayville Quad (7.5′)

BOHEMIA
Community
Suffolk—Islip; SE part of Islip town,
W of Patchogue;
40°46′30″x73°6′45″
Patchogue Quad (7.5′)

BOMBAY HOOK
Physical feature
Kings; SW point of Red Hook, in the
vicinity of Erie Basin;
ca. 40°40′x74°1′40″
Source: (Ratzer 155)
*Jersey City Quad (7.5′)

BONAIRE
Community—historical
Suffolk—Brookhaven; in the vicinity
of Patchogue
Source: (Macoskey 29, p. 49)
*Patchogue Quad (7.5′)

BONDYQUOGUE
see
PONQUOGUE
Source: (Tooker 44, pp. 29, 192–193)

BOOMERTOWN
see
SAINT JAMES
Source: (Langhans 98, p. 5)

BOROUGH PARK
Community
Kings; W side of Kings, SW of

Flatbush; 40°38′x74°0′
Historical: Blythebourne
(Brooklyn Quad, 15′, 1897)
Brooklyn and Jersey City Quads (7.5′)

BOSTWICK BAY
Physical feature
Suffolk—East Hampton; NE side of
Gardiners Island; 41°7′x72°7′40″
Variations: Bostwicks, Bostick,
Bostic (Tooker 44, p. 29)
Gardiners Island West Quad (7.5′)

BOSTWICK CREEK
Physical feature
Suffolk—East Hampton; NE side of
Gardiners Island;
41°6′20″x72°7′35″
Gardiners Island East and Gardiners
Island West Quads (7.5′)

BOSTWICK POINT
Physical feature
Suffolk—East Hampton; N tip of
Gardiners Island;
41°7′27″x72°7′50″
Gardiners Island West Quad (7.5′)

BOSWYCK
see
BUSHWICK
Source: (Wilson 51, p. 27)

BOUTON'S POINT
Physical feature—historical
Suffolk—Huntington; at the entrance
of Huntington Harbor, possibly
Sandy Point;
ca. 40°54′25″x73°26′5″
Source: (Valentine 111, p. 75)
*Lloyd Harbor Quad (7.5′)

BOWERY BAY
Community
see
NORTH BEACH
Source: (Ricard 86, pp. 12-13)

BOWERY BAY
Physical feature
Queens; S of Rikers Island Channel,
NW part of Queens, S of
Rikers Island;
40°46'40"x73°53'20"
Central Park Quad (7.5')

BOWLING GREEN
Community
Nassau—Hempstead; S of
New Cassell, SW of Hicksville;
40°44'30"x73°33'10"
Source: (Hagstrom 140, 1973, p. 40)
*Freeport Quad (7.5')

BOWMAN'S POINT
see
CHICKEN POINT
Source: (Ross 158)

BRANCH BROOK
see
NORTHEAST BRANCH
Source: (Langhans 98, pp. 5, 24)

BRANT POINT
Physical feature
Queens; SE side of Jamaica Bay,
NW of Arverne;
40°35'55"x73°48'15"
Far Rockaway Quad (7.5')

BREAD AND CHEESE HOLLOW
Physical feature—historical
Suffolk—Smithtown, Huntington;

an area N of Commack and S of
Fort Salonga, on the border
between Smithtown and Huntington;
40°54'x73°17'45"
Source: (Langhans 98, p. 6)
*Northport Quad (7.5')

BREAD SPRINGS
Physical feature
Nassau—Oyster Bay; W side of
Farmingdale, SW of Bethpage
State Park; 40°44'5"x73°27'40"
Amityville Quad (7.5')

BREEZY POINT
Community
Queens; W of the community of
Rockaway Point, S of Rockaway
Inlet; 40°33'30"x73°55'30"
Coney Island Quad (7.5')

BREEZY POINT
Physical feature
Queens; N of the community of
Rockaway Point, W of Roxbury;
40°33'35"x73°55'45"
Coney Island Quad (7.5')

BRENCK-LANDT
see
BROOKLYN
Borough
Source: (French 10, p. 367fn)

BRENTWOOD
Community
Suffolk—Islip; SW of
Lake Ronkonkoma,
S of Smithtown; 40°47'x73°14'
Historical: Modern Times (French 10,
p. 637)
Central Islip and Greenlawn Quads
(7.5')

BRESLAU
see
LINDENHURST
Source: (Bailey 19, vol. 1, p. 364)

BRESLAU GARDENS
Community
Suffolk—Babylon; NW side of the
town, NW of Lindenhurst, E of
Maywood; 40°43′20″x73°24′35″
Source: (Hagstrom 141, 1969, p. 28)
*Amityville Quad (7.5′)

BREUKELEN
Community—historical
Kings; in the vicinity of Red Hook;
ca. 40°40′30″x 74°0′35″
Source: (Armbruster 53, p. 9).
Earlier called Meryckawick (Ibid.)
Also a variant spelling of Brooklyn
(Bryant 55, p. 107)
*Jersey City Quad (7.5′)

BREWSTER'S BROOK
see
MOTTS BROOK
Source: (Shaw 106, p. 211)

BRIAR PARK
Community
Nassau—Hempstead; in the
vicinity of North Wantagh
Source: (Rand 154, 1977, p. 381)
*Freeport Quad (7.5′)

BRICK KILN
Tract of land—historical
Suffolk—Brookhaven; W side of
Port Jefferson Harbor;
ca. 40°57′15″x73°5′
Source: (Bayles 93, p. 249)
*Port Jefferson Quad (7.5′)

BRICK KILN CREEK
Physical feature
Suffolk—Islip; S of Oakdale, flows
into Nicoll Bay;
40°43′45″x73°7′30″
Source: (Geographia 139, p. 23)
Historical: Essachias (Tooker 44, p. 63)
*Bay Shore East Quad (7.5′)

BRICKYARD POINT
Physical feature
Nassau—Oyster Bay; on Oyster Bay
Harbor, SW point of Centre Island,
E of Mill Neck; 40°53′x73°32′
Historical: Soper's Point (Walling 172)
Bayville Quad (7.5′)

BRICKYARD POND
Physical feature
Suffolk—Southold; W-central part
of Fishers Island, SE of West
Harbor; 41°16′x71°59′35″
Mystic Quad (7.5′)

BRIDGE BRANCH
Physical feature
Suffolk—Smithtown; a branch of the
Nissequogue River, SW of the
community of Smithtown, flows into
the NW side of New Millpond;
40°50′45″x73°14′
Source: (Langhans 98, p. 6)
*Central Islip Quad (7.5′)

BRIDGE HAVEN
Community—historical
Nassau—Hempstead; between
Seaford (Jerusalem South) and
Merrick; ca. 40°40′x73°32′
Source: (French 10, p. 547)
*Freeport Quad (7.5′)

BRIDGEHAMPTON
Community
Suffolk—Southampton; S of Sag
  Harbor, NE of Mecox Bay;
  40°56'15"x72°18'20"
Historical: Feversham (Flint 26, p. 69),
  BullHead (French 10, p. 639fn),
  Bull head (Adams 92, p. 133),
  Northampton (Cary 126)
Sag Harbor Quad (7.5')

BRIDGEHAMPTON
Locality—historical
Suffolk—Southampton; extending
  from East Hampton to the W part
  of Mecox Bay
Source: (French 10, p. 638fn)

BRIDGEHAMPTON BAY
see
SAG HARBOR
Source: (Adams 91, p. 148)

BRIGHTON BEACH
Community
Kings; SW part of Kings, E of
  Coney Island;
  40°34'30"x73°57'30"
Coney Island Quad (7.5')

BRIGHTWATERS
Village
Suffolk—Islip; W of Bay Shore,
  N of Appletree Neck;
  40°43'x73°16'
Bay Shore West Quad (7.5')

BRIGHTWATERS CANAL
Physical feature
Suffolk—Islip; SE part of
  Brightwaters; 40°42'15"x73°15'
Historical: John Moby Creek

(Babylon Quad, 15', 1903)
Bay Shore West Quad (7.5')

BROAD CHANNEL
Community
Queens; S-central part of
  Jamaica Bay, N of Holland;
  40°36'15"x73°49'15"
Far Rockaway Quad (7.5')

BROAD CHANNEL
Physical feature
Nassau—Hempstead; ENE of
  Lawrence Marsh, W of Black Banks
  Hassock; 40°36'10"x73°41'
Lawrence Quad (7.5')

BROAD CHANNEL
Physical feature
Queens
see
EAST BROAD CHANNEL
Source: (U.S. 5, List No. 8101, p. 13)

BROAD CREEK CHANNEL
Physical feature
Nassau—Hempstead; flows between
  Cuba Island and Big Crow Island,
  S part of East Bay;
  40°37'30"x73°32'
Freeport and Jones Inlet Quads (7.5')

BROAD MEADOWS POINT
Physical feature—historical
Suffolk—Riverhead; W side of
  Flanders Bay; ca. 40°55'x72°37'
Source: (Tooker 44, p. 129)
*Mattituck Quad (7.5')

BROADE HAVEN
see
BROOKHAVEN
Town
Source: (Untitled 171)

BROADWATER COVE
Physical feature
Suffolk—Southold; W of
  Little Peconic Bay, N
  of Cutchogue Harbor;
41°0'50"x72°27'
Southold Quad (7.5')

BROADWAY-FLUSHING
Community—historical
Queens; E side of Flushing;
  ca. 40°45'45"x73°47'30"
Source: (Ricard 86, p. 8)
*Flushing Quad (7.5')

BROADWAY JUNCTION
Community
Kings; NW of East New York,
  S of Ridgewood;
40°40'40"x73°54'15"
Brooklyn Quad (7.5')

BROOKFIELD
Community—historical
Queens (Nassau)—Hempstead
Source: (French 10, p. 547)

BROOKFIELD
Suffolk—Brookhaven
see
YAPHANK
Source: (French 10, p. 634fn)
  and (Burr 124)

BROOKHAVEN
Community
Suffolk—Brookhaven; NE
  of Bellport, W of Shirley;
40°46'40"x72°55'
Historical: Fire Place
  (Bayles 93, p. 274)
Bellport Quad (7.5')

BROOKHAVEN
Community—historical
see
MIDDLE ISLAND
Community
Source: (Bayles 95, p. 49)

BROOKHAVEN
Town
Suffolk; central part of the county
Historical: Proposed names for the
  town were Cromwell Bay, Setauket,
  Setaulcott, and Ashford (Bailey 19,
  vol. 1, pp. 260, 256), Broade Haven
  (Untitled 171), Selasacott (Tooker 44,
  p. 234)
Saint James, Central Islip, Sayville,
  Patchogue, Port Jefferson, Middle
  Island, Howells Point, Pattersquash
  Island, Moriches and Wading River
  Quads (7.5')

BROOKHAVEN BAY
see
NICOLL BAY
Source: (Chace 127)

**BROOKHAVEN NATIONAL
LABORATORY**
U.S. Reservation
Suffolk—Brookhaven; N of Shirley,
  E of Middle Island;
  ca. 40°52'30"x72°52'30"
Historical: Camp Upton Military
  Reservation (Bellport Quad, 7.5',
  AMS, 1944), (Middle Island Quad,
  7.5', AMS, 1947), (Moriches Quad,
  7.5', AMS, 1947), (Wading River
  Quad, 7.5', AMS, 1944)
Bellport, Middle Island, Moriches and
  Wading River Quads (7.5')

BROOKHAVEN STATE PARK
Suffolk—Brookhaven; N part of
the town, N of Brookhaven
National Laboratory, SW of
Wading River;
40°55′x72°52′30″
Source: (Hagstrom 141, 1979, p. 54)
*Middle Island and Wading
River Quads (7.5′)

BROOKLYN
Borough
Kings County—Borough of
New York City; SW part of
Long Island;
40°30′x73°55′
Variations: Bruijkleen,
Breucklen, Breucklyn,
Brychline, Brookland,
Breukelen, Breucklin,
Brucklyn, Broucklyn
Breuckland, Brooklane,
Brookline (Bryant 55, p. 107),
Brenck-landt (French 10, p. 367fn)
Brooklyn Quad (7.5′)

BROOKLYN
Community—historical
Suffolk—Southampton; S of
the community of Riverhead,
S side of the Peconic River
Source: (Bayles 93, p. 299)
*Riverhead Quad (7.5′)

BROOKLYN
Town—historical
Kings; N part of the county,
along New York Bay and the
East River to Newtown Creek
Source: (French 10, pp. 367-372)

BROOKLYN BASIN
Physical feature
Kings; on Gowanus Bay, E of
Erie Basin, S side of Red Hook;
40°40′5″x74°00′30″
Source: (Staten Island Quad, 15′,
1898)
*Jersey City Quad (7.5′)

BROOKLYN HEIGHTS
Community
Kings; NW side of Kings, W of
Fort Greene; 40°41′50″x73°59′35″
Historical: Ihpetonga, Sphetonga
(Tooker 44, pp. 74, 249)
Brooklyn Quad (7.5′)

BROOKLYN MANOR
Community
Queens; W side of Queens, W of
Jamaica; 40°41′50″x73°50′45″
Jamaica Quad (7.5′)

BROOKLYN RESERVOIR
see
RIDGEWOOD RESERVOIR
Source: (Brooklyn Quad, 15′, 1897)

BROOKS POINT
Physical feature
Suffolk—Southold; on Fishers
Island; NE of Chocomount Cove,
41°17′8″x71°58′5″
Mystic Quad (7.5′)

BROOKVILLE
Village
Nassau—Oyster Bay; W-
central part of town, NW
of Hicksville; 40°48'50"x73°33'45"
Historical: Sucos (Tooker 44,
pp. 250-251), Susco's Wigwam,
Pink's Hollow (Flint 26, p. 69),
Wolverhampton, later Wolver
Hollow (Cocks 70, p. 6),
Beaver Swamp Hollow (Flint 26,
p. 67)
Hicksville Quad (7.5')

BROOKVILLE PARK
Community
Suffolk—Islip; in the vicinity
of the community of Islip
Source: (Rand 154, 1977, p. 381)
*Bay Shore East Quad (7.5')

BROSEWERE BAY
Physical feature
Nassau—Hempstead; NW part
of the town, NE part of Lawrence;
40°36'45"x73°42'15"
Lawrence Quad (7.5')

BROWN CREEK
Physical feature
Suffolk—Islip; flows into the
Great South Bay, SE of Sayville;
40°43'25"x73°3'10"
Historical: Terrys Swamp
Creek, Rulands Creek
(Pelletreau 38, pp. 238, 243)
Sayville Quad (7.5')

BROWN POINT
Physical feature
Suffolk—Islip; on the Great South
Bay, SE of Sayville;

40°43'25"x73°4'10"
Sayville Quad (7.5')

BROWN POINT
Physical feature
Suffolk—Riverhead; E of Jamesport,
NW part of Great Peconic Bay;
40°56'50"x72°33'30"
Mattituck Quad (7.5')

BROWNS HILLS
Physical feature
Suffolk—Southold; NE of Orient;
41°9'20"x72°17'40"
Orient Quad (7.5')

BROWNS POINT
Physical feature
Suffolk—Southold; within Long
Beach Bay; 41°7'45"x72°16'50"
Orient Quad (7.5')

BROWNSVILLE
Community
Kings; NE of Flatbush, E side of
Kings; 40°39'40"x73°55'
Brooklyn Quad (7.5')

BRUSH NECK
Physical feature
Suffolk—Southampton; W of Sag
Harbor, middle of Sag Harbor
Cove; 40°59'50"x72°18'50"
Sag Harbor Quad (7.5')

BRUSH NECK
Physical feature—historical
Suffolk—Southampton; S of
Sag Harbor Cove, E of Noyack,
W of Sag Harbor, SW of the
present Brush Neck;
40°59'30"x72°19'10"

Source: (U.S. 167, Map T-71)
*Sag Harbor Quad (7.5')

BRUSH'S CREEK
Physical feature
Suffolk—Southold; NW part
of Great Peconic Bay, SW
of Mattituck;
40°57'20"x72°32'55"
Historical: Laurel Creek
(U.S. 5, List No. 5903, p. 42)
Mattituck Quad (7.5')

BRUSH'S POND
see
MILLERS POND
Suffolk—Smithtown
Source: (Langhans 98, pp. 17–18)

BRUSHVILLE
Queens—SW of Floral Park
see
BELLAIRE
Source: (Ricard 86, p. 7)

BRUSHVILLE
Queens—W of Floral Park
see
QUEENS VILLAGE
Community
Source: (French 10, p. 548fn)

BRUSHY NECK
Physical feature—historical
Suffolk—Southampton; E of
Speonk River, SW of Westhampton;
40°48'20"x72°41'25"
Source: (Bayles 93, p. 313)
*Eastport Quad (7.5')

BRUSHY PLAIN
Physical feature—historical
Suffolk—Southampton; located

in what is now the central part
of the community of Bridgehampton;
ca. 40°56'15"x72°18'20"
Source: (Adams 92, p. 90)
*Sag Harbor Quad (7.5')

BRUSHY PLAINS
Locality—historical
Queens (Nassau), Suffolk—
Oyster Bay, Huntington, Babylon;
E-W tract of land, crossing the
Oyster Bay-Huntington (Babylon)
border, well into Huntington
(Babylon) town
Source: (Burr 124) and (Burr 125)

BRYANT'S LANDING
see
NORTHPORT
Source: (Sammis 104, p. 160)

BUCHANANVILLE
Community—historical
Suffolk—Riverhead
Source: (Pelletreau 38, p. 401)

BUCKRAM
see
LOCUST VALLEY
Source: (Coles 75, pp. 207, 218)
and (Cocks 70, p. 8)

BUDDS POND
Physical feature
Suffolk—Southold; on Shelter Island
Sound, S of Hashamomuck Pond,
NE of Beixedon Estates;
41°4'30"x72°24'15"
Southold Quad (7.5')

BULKHEAD DRAIN
Physical feature—channel
Nassau—Hempstead, Oyster Bay;
on South Oyster Bay; between
North Line Island and Middle Line
Island; 40°37'40"x73°29'
Amityville Quad (7.5')

BULL DITCH
Canal
Suffolk—Islip; flows into
Penataquit Creek, S part of Bay
Shore, N of Great Cove;
40°43'15"x73°14'20"
Bay Shore East Quad (7.5')

BULL HEAD
see
BRIDGEHAMPTON
Community
Source: (Adams 92, p. 133)

BULLHEAD
see
BRIDGEHAMPTON
Community
Source: (French 10, p. 638fn)

BULLHEAD BAY
Physical feature
Suffolk—Southampton; SE side of
Great Peconic Bay;
40°54'40"x72°26'50"
Historical: Long Creek of Seaponack
(Pelletreau 38, p. 289)
Southampton Quad (7.5')

BUNGTOWN
see
COLD SPRING HARBOR
Community
Source: (Overton 37, p. 220)

BUNGY
see
WESTVILLE
Source: (Flint 26, p. 75)

BURGER JORIS KILLS
see
DUTCH KILLS
Physical feature
Source: (Flint 26, p. 70)

BURLEY POND
Physical feature—historical
Queens (Nassau)—Hempstead; NW
of the village of Hempstead,
corner of Fulton and Franklin,
no longer exists;
40°42'30"x73°37'45"
Source: (Walling 172)
*Lynbrook Quad (7.5')

BURNETT CREEK
Physical feature
Suffolk—Southampton; N of
Flying Point, W of Mecox Bay;
40°53'45"x72°21'
Sag Harbor Quad (7.5')

BURYING HILL
Physical feature
Suffolk—Huntington; N side of the
community of Huntington Station;
40°51'30"x73°25'25"
Source: (Overton 37, pp. 142–143)
*Huntington Quad (7.5')

BUSHVILLE
see
QUEENS VILLAGE
Community
Source: (Flint 26, p. 74)

BUSHWICK
Community
Kings; E side of Kings,
 SW of Ridgewood;
 40°41′40″x73°55′10″
Historical: Woodtown (Bayles
 93, p. 16), Boswyck (Wilson 51,
 p. 27)
Brooklyn Quad (7.5′)

BUSHWICK
Town—historical
Kings; in the NE part of the
 county, bounded on the NW by
 the East River, on the E by
 Queens County, and on the S by
 Brooklyn
Source: (Thompson 41, vol. 2,
 p. 159)
Annexed to Brooklyn city in 1854
 (French 10, p. 367)

BUSHWICK CREEK
see
BUSHWICK INLET
Source: (Flint 26, p. 69)

BUSHWICK CROSS ROADS
Community—historical
Kings; E of Williamsburg
Source: (French 10, p. 367)
*Brooklyn Quad (7.5′)

BUSHWICK GREEN
Community—historical
Kings; E of Williamsburg
Source: (French 10, p. 367)
*Brooklyn Quad (7.5′)

BUSHWICK INLET
Physical feature
Kings; on the East River, W side of

Greenport, NW part of Kings;
 40°43′30″x73°57′30″
Historical: Bushwick Creek,
 Norman's Kill (Flint 26, p. 69)
Brooklyn Quad (7.5′)

BUSHWICK JUNCTION
Community
Queens; NW side of Queens,
 S of Maspeth;
 40°42′45″x73°54′45″
Brooklyn Quad (7.5′)

BUSHY NECK
Physical feature—historical
Suffolk—Smithtown; S of Jericho
 Turnpike, E of the Nissequogue
 River, extending to the business
 section of Smithtown;
 ca. 40°51′x73°12′30″
Source: (Langhans 98, p. 6)
*Central Islip Quad (7.5′)

BUTLER'S ISLAND
see
EAST ISLAND
Nassau—Oyster Bay
Source: (Cocks 70, p. 2)

BYRON LAKE PARK
Physical feature
Suffolk—Islip; E side of
 Oakdale, N of Nicoll Bay;
 40°44′15″x73°8′10″
Bay Shore East Quad (7.5′)

CABLES
see
WEST BRIGHTON
Source: (Ross 39, p. 375)

CACHINNCAK BROOK
see
OROWOC CREEK
Source: (Tooker 44, pp. 29–30, 170–172)

CAGOQUNK CREEK
see
AWIXA CREEK
Source: (Tooker 44, pp. 30–31)

CALF CREEK
Physical feature
Suffolk—Southampton; flows into
  the N part of Mecox Bay;
40°54'50"x72°19'50"
Sag Harbor Quad (7.5')

CALF PEN NECK
Physical feature—historical
Suffolk—Southampton; N of Mecox
  Bay, between Hayground Cove and
  Calf Creek; ca. 40°55'x72°20'
Source: (Pelletreau 38, p. 322)
*Sag Harbor Quad (7.5')

CALLAHANS BEACH
Physical feature
Suffolk—Smithtown; on the shoreline
  of Sunken Meadow State Park;
40°55'10"x73°16'30"
Northport Quad (7.5')

CALVERTON
Community
Suffolk—Riverhead; W of the
  community of Riverhead;
40°54'30"x72°44'40"
Historical: Conungum (Tooker 44,
  pp. 49–50), Hulse's Turnout, Baiting
  Hollow Station (Bailey 19, vol. 1,
  p. 194)
Riverhead Quad (7.5')

CALVES NECK
Physical feature—historical
Suffolk—Southold; S of the
  community of Southold;
41°3'30"x72°26'
Source: (Pelletreau 38, p. 418)
*Southold Quad (7.5')

CAMBRIA HEIGHTS
Community
Queens; E side of Queens,
  N of Laurelton, S of Queens Village;
40°41'30"x73°44'30"
Lynbrook Quad (7.5')

CAMMANNS POND
Physical feature
Nassau—Hempstead; S part of
  Merrick;
40°39'10"x73°33'
Freeport Quad (7.5')

38

CAMP HERO
Military Reservation
Suffolk—East Hampton;
on Montauk Peninsula,
W of Montauk Point;
41°4'x71°52'15"
Montauk Point Quad (7.5')

CAMP UPTON MILITARY RESERVATION
see
BROOKHAVEN NATIONAL LABORATORY
Source: (Bellport Quad, 7.5', AMS, 1944), (Middle Island Quad, 7.5', AMS, 1947), (Moriches Quad, 7.5', AMS, 1947), and (Wading River Quad, 7.5', AMS, 1944)

CAMPS POND
Physical feature
Suffolk—Southampton; NW of
  Bridgehampton, S of Noyack Bay;
  40°57'8"x72°21'35"
Sag Harbor Quad (7.5')

CANAAN LAKE
Community
Suffolk—Brookhaven; N of
  Patchogue, near Canaan Lake;
  ca. 40°47'20"x73°1'20"
Source: (Macoskey 29, p. 50)
*Patchogue Quad (7.5')

CANAAN LAKE
Physical feature
Suffolk—Brookhaven; N of
  Patchogue; 40°47'20"x73°1'20"
Patchogue Quad (7.5')

CANAPAUKAH
see
DUTCH KILLS

Physical feature
Source: (Tooker 44, p. 31)

CANARASSET
see
JAMAICA
Community
Source: (Flint 26, p. 71)

CANARSIE
Community
Kings; E side of Kings, NW of
  Jamaica Bay;
  40°38'25"x73°54'15"
Historical: Keskaechqueren
  (Bailey 19, vol. 1, p. 29)
Variations: Conorasset, Canarise,
  Canaryssen, Canause, Canarisea,
  Kanarsingh (Tooker 44, pp. 31-33,
  49)
Brooklyn Quad (7.5')

CANARSIE POL
Physical feature—island
Kings; W side of Jamaica Bay, E of
  Flatlands; 40°37'20"x73°52'20"
Far Rockaway, Jamaica and Coney
  Island Quads (7.5')

CANARSIS MEADOWS
Physical feature—historical
Kings; SE of Canarsie, SW of Fresh
  Creek, no longer exists;
  ca. 40°38'30"x73°53'15"
Source: (Walling 172)
*Brooklyn Quad (7.5')

CANOE PLACE
Community
Suffolk—Southampton; NE of
  Hampton Bays, W of Shinnecock
  Canal; 40°53'15"x72°30'25"

Historical: Merosuck, the Indian name for the isthmus (Tooker 44, pp. 125-126), Niamuck (Ibid., p. 159)
Mattituck Quad (7.5')

CANOE PLACE CREEK
Physical feature—historical
Suffolk—East Hampton; N part of Gardiners Island, flowed into Bostwick Creek, no longer exists; 41°6'22"x72°6'5"
Source: (Gardiners Island Quad, 15', 1903)
*Gardiners Island East and Gardiners Island West Quads (7.5')

CANOE PLACE CREEK
Suffolk—Southampton
see
SHINNECOCK CANAL
Source: (Tooker 44, pp. 105-106)

CANORASSET
see
JAMAICA
Town—historical
Source: (French 10, p. 547fn)

CANTASQUNTAH BROOK
see
NICOLL CREEK
Source: (Tooker 44, pp. 34-35)

CANTIAQUE
Physical feature—point of trees—historical
Nassau—Hempstead, Oyster Bay; on the boundary between the towns of Hempstead and Oyster Bay
Source: (Tooker 44, pp. 34-35)
Variation: Cantiagge (Ibid.)

CAPE RUTH
Physical feature
Queens; E side of Flushing Bay, S of College Point, E of North Beach; 40°46'20"x73°51'
Source: (Harlem Quad, 15', 1897)
*Flushing Quad (7.5')

CAPTAIN FLEET'S NECK
see
LITTLE EAST NECK
Source: (Tooker 44, pp. 12-14)

CAPTAIN KIDD ESTATES
Community
Suffolk—Southold; on Long Island Sound, N of Mattituck; 41°0'30"x72°33'40"
Source: (Hagstrom 141, 1979, p. 66)
*Mattituck Hills Quad (7.5')

CAPTAIN KIDD HOLLOW
Physical feature
Suffolk—East Hampton; W side of Gardiners Island, S of Bostwick Bay; 41°5'43"x72°8'
Gardiners Island West Quad (7.5')

CAPTAIN SMITH'S POINT
see
HAVENS POINT
Source: (U.S. 5, List No. 5904, p. 37)

CAPTAIN'S NECK
Physical feature
Suffolk—Southampton; SW of the village of Southampton, E of Heady Creek; 40°52'5"x72°25'
Source: (Pelletreau 38, p. 292)
*Shinnecock Inlet Quad (7.5')

CAPTREE ISLAND
Physical feature
Suffolk—Babylon, Islip; SW part of
Great South Bay, SW of Bay Shore,
N of Fire Island Inlet;
40°39'x73°16'
Bay Shore West and Bay Shore East
Quads (7.5')

CAPTREE STATE PARK
Suffolk—Babylon, Islip; S half of
Captree Island; 40°38'20"x73°16'
Bay Shore West Quad (7.5')

CARLE PLACE
Community
Nassau—North Hempstead; SE part
of the town, E of Mineola;
40°45'x73°36'45"
Hicksville and Freeport Quads (7.5')

CARLLS RIVER
Physical feature
Suffolk—Babylon; flows through
Babylon into the Great South Bay;
40°41'x73°19'50"
Historical: Annuskemunnica Creek,
West Creek (Sammis 104, p. 252),
Great River (Bayles 93, p. 179)
Variations: Carll River, Carlls Creek
Bay Shore West Quad (7.5')

CARLTON PARK
Community—historical
Suffolk—Islip; in the vicinity of
Islip Terrace; ca. 40°45'x73°11'40"
Source: (Macoskey 29, p. 50)
*Central Islip Quad (7.5')

CARMAN CREEK
Physical feature
Nassau—Oyster Bay; flows on the W
side of Amityville, E of Massapequa

Park, into South Oyster Bay;
40°39'30"x73°26'
Amityville Quad (7.5')

CARMANS
Community—historical
Suffolk—Brookhaven; presently the
W side of the community of Shirley,
E of South Haven;
ca. 40°47'50"x72°52'30"
Source: (Thompson 41, inside cover
map)
*Bellport and Moriches Quads (7.5')

CARMANS RIVER
Physical feature
Suffolk—Brookhaven; flows into the
NE side of Bellport Bay;
40°45'50"x72°53'30"
Historical: Connecticut River
(Chace 127) and (Tooker 44, p. 48),
East Connecticut River, Conitticut
River (Ibid.), Fire Place River
(Thompson 41, vol. 1, p. 437)
Bellport Quad (7.5')

CAROWAY
see
CORAM
Source: (Flint 26, p. 70)

CARPENTER(S) NECK
Physical feature—historical
Nassau—Oyster Bay; on Hempstead
Harbor, W part of Sea Cliff;
40°50'45"x73°38'45"
Source: (U.S. 170, Chart No. 366,
1879 and 1905)
*Sea Cliff Quad (7.5')

CARPENTER POINT
Physical feature
Nassau—Oyster Bay; on Hempstead

Harbor; 40°50'40"x73°39'15"
Sea Cliff Quad (7.5')

CARPENTERSVILLE
Community—historical
Queens (Nassau)—Oyster Bay;
N part of Sea Cliff, S of Glen Cove
Creek; 40°51'10"x73°38'45"
Source: (Walling 172). On the map,
diagonal slashes through each letter;
may have been a place name
mistake
*Sea Cliff Quad (7.5')

CARTWRIGHT ISLAND
Physical feature
Suffolk—East Hampton; S of the SE
part of Gardiners Island, NW of
Napeague Harbor, E of Acabonack
Harbor; 41°1'35"x72°6'15"
Historical: Ram Island (Chace 127)
Gardiners Island East Quad (7.5')

CASCADE LAKES
Physical feature
Suffolk—Islip; S part of Brightwaters;
40°42'45"x73°15'50"
Bay Shore West Quad (7.5')

CASEY POND
Physical feature—historical
Suffolk—East Hampton; N-central
part of Gardiners Island, W of
Eastern Plain Point;
41°5'50"x72°6'10"
Source: (Gardiners Island Quad, 15',
1903)
*Gardiners Island East Quad (7.5')

CASTATEUM
Physical feature—salt meadow—
historical
Kings; in the vicinity of Flatlands;

40°37'15"x73°53'30"
Source: (Tooker 44, p. 35)
Variations: Cashuteyie,
Kaskutensuken (Ibid.)

CATACONNOCK
see
OLD FIELD
Village
Source: (Tooker 44, p. 36)

CATAWAMUCK
see
CRAB MEADOW
Physical feature
Source: (Tooker 44, pp. 20-21, 36)

CATCHAPONACK NECK
Physical feature—historical
Suffolk—Southampton; SW of
Quiogue, E of Westhampton Beach;
40°48'5"x72°38'
Source: (Pelletreau 38, p. 338)
*Eastport Quad (7.5')

CATSJEYICK
see
CUTCHOGUE
Source: (Tooker 44, pp. 56-58)

CATUMB
Physical feature—reef of rocks—
historical
Suffolk; in Long Island Sound,
E end of Fishers Island
Source: (Tooker 44, p. 37)
*Mystic Quad (7.5')

CAUMSETT
see
LLOYD NECK
Source: (Tooker 44, pp. 37-38)

CAUMSETT STATE PARK
Suffolk—Huntington; NW part of
the town, central part of Lloyd
Neck; ca. 40°55′40″x73°28′
Source: (Hagstrom 141, 1979, p. 22)
*Lloyd Harbor Quad (7.5′)

CAUS CUNG QUARAM
see
GREAT EAST NECK
Source: (Tooker 44, p. 38)

CAUSHAWASHA
Physical feature—swamp—historical
Suffolk—Southold; on Hashamomuk
Neck, W of the village of Greenport,
SW of Hashamomuk Pond;
40°4′45″x72°24′30″
Source: (Tooker 44, pp. 38–39)
Variation: Causawashowy (Ibid.)
*Southold Quad (7.5′)

CAVALIER ISLAND
see
DOSORIS ISLAND
Source: (Russell 87, p. 211)

CEDAR BEACH
Community
Suffolk—Southold; S side of Great
Hog Neck; 41°2′x72°23′35″
Source: (Hagstrom 141, 1969, p. 67)
Historical: Cedar Beach Point
(Macoskey 29, p. 50)
*Southold Quad (7.5′)

CEDAR BEACH
Community—historical
Suffolk—Brookhaven; N of Mt.
Sinai Harbor; 40°57′50″x73°2′
Source: (Macoskey 29, p. 50)
*Port Jefferson Quad (7.5′)

CEDAR BEACH
Physical feature
Suffolk—Babylon; S-central shore of
Cedar Island, W of Fire Island Inlet;
40°37′45″x73°21′
Bay Shore West Quad (7.5′)

CEDAR BEACH
Physical feature
Suffolk—Brookhaven; on Long
Island Sound, N of Mt. Sinai
Harbor, NW of Miller Place;
40°57′50″x73°2′
Historical: East Beach, Mount Sinai
Beach (U.S. 5, List No. 5903, p. 42)
Port Jefferson Quad (7.5′)

CEDAR BEACH CREEK
Physical feature—inlet
Suffolk—Southold; SE part of Great
Hog Neck; 41°2′x72°23′40″
Southold Quad (7.5′)

CEDAR BEACH POINT
Community
see
CEDAR BEACH
Suffolk—Southold
Source: (Macoskey 29, p. 50)

CEDAR BEACH POINT
Physical feature
Suffolk—Southold; SE point of
Great Hog Neck; 41°2′x72°23′15″
Southold Quad (7.5′)

CEDAR CREEK
Physical feature
Nassau—Hempstead; flows through
the S part of Seaford into Island
Creek; 40°38′45″x73°30′
Freeport Quad (7.5′)

CEDAR CREST
Community—historical
Suffolk—Southampton; in the
  vicinity of the village of
  Southampton
Source: (Macoskey 29, p. 50)
*Southampton Quad (7.5')

CEDAR CROFT
Community
Suffolk—Huntington; N of
  Greenlawn, S of Centerport;
  40°52'37"x73°22'
Source: (Hagstrom 141, 1969, p. 25)
*Northport Quad (7.5')

CEDAR HILL
Physical feature
Suffolk—Brookhaven; S of Port
  Jefferson; 40°55'50"x73°3'50"
Port Jefferson Quad (7.5')

CEDAR ISLAND
Physical feature
Nassau—Hempstead; S of Hewlett
  Bay, E of North and South Green
  Sedge; 40°36'45"x73°40'45"
Lawrence Quad (7.5')

CEDAR ISLAND
Physical feature
Suffolk—Babylon; SW side of Great
  South Bay, S of Lindenhurst;
  40°38'30"x73°21'
Historical: Screcunkas Island
  (Tooker 44, p. 228)
Bay Shore West Quad (7.5')

CEDAR ISLAND
Physical feature—historical
Suffolk—East Hampton; between
  Cedar Point in Northwest Harbor,
  and Gibsons Beach on Shelter

Island, no longer exists;
41°2'30"x72°16'10"
Source: (Chace 127), (Shelter Island
  Quad, 15', 1904), and (U.S. 167,
  Maps T-69 and T-72)
*Greenport Quad (7.5')

CEDAR ISLAND
Physical feature—spit
Suffolk—Shelter Island; E-central
  Shelter Island, in Coecles Inlet;
  41°4'10"x72°18'
Greenport Quad (7.5')

CEDAR ISLAND COVE
Physical feature
Suffolk—Shelter Island; SE side of
  Coecles Inlet, S of Ram Island;
  41°4'x72°17'40"
Greenport Quad (7.5')

CEDAR ISLAND CREEK
Physical feature
Nassau—Hempstead; E of Lawrence,
  connects Nums Channel and Broad
  Channel between Cedar Island
  Marsh and Cedar Island;
  40°36'24"x73°40'52"
Source: (U.S. 5, List No. 8101,
  p. 12)
*Lawrence Quad (7.5')

CEDAR ISLAND INLET
Physical feature—historical
Suffolk—Islip; SSE of Cedar Island,
  possibly Huntington Gut;
  40°37'50"x73°19'30"
Source: (Osborne 35, p. 89) and
  (Babylon Quad, 15', 1903)
*Bay Shore West Quad (7.5')

CEDAR ISLAND MARSH
Physical feature
Nassau—Hempstead; E of Lawrence,
bounded on the W by Neds Hole
Creek, on the E by Cedar Island
Creek; 40°36'47"x73°41'
Source: (U.S. 5, List No. 8101,
p. 12)
*Lawrence Quad (7.5')

CEDAR MANOR
Community
Queens; E of Jamaica, SW of St.
Albans; 40°41'20"x73°47'30"
Jamaica Quad (7.5')

CEDAR OVERLOOK BEACH
Physical feature
Suffolk—Babylon; SW shoreline of
Cedar Island, W of Fire Island Inlet;
40°38'x73°20'
Bay Shore West Quad (7.5')

CEDAR POINT
Physical feature
Suffolk—East Hampton; N of
Northwest Harbor; 41°2'35"x72°15'
Gardiners Island West and Greenport
Quads (7.5')

CEDAR POND
Physical feature
Suffolk—East Hampton; NE of
Northwest Harbor, NW of
Northwest Woods;
41°2'35"x72°14'20"
Gardiners Island West Quad (7.5')

CEDAR POND
Physical feature
Suffolk—Southampton; part of
Cedar Swamp, S of Riverhead;

40°54'30"x72°40'30"
Riverhead Quad (7.5')

CEDAR POND
Suffolk—East Hampton
see
ALEWIFE POND
Source: (U.S. 5, List No. 5904,
p. 37)

CEDAR SWAMP
Community—historical
Queens (Nassau)—Oyster Bay;
presently the site of Old Brookville;
ca. 40°50'x73°36'15"
Source: (Walling 172)
*Hicksville Quad (7.5')

CEDAR SWAMP
Physical feature
Suffolk—Southampton; S of
Riverhead; 40°54'35"x72°40'30"
Riverhead Quad (7.5')

CEDAR SWAMP CREEK
Physical feature
Nassau—Hempstead; SE of Merrick,
SW of Bellmore;
40°38'40"x73°31'50"
Freeport Quad (7.5')

CEDARHURST
Village
Nassau—Hempstead; SW part of the
town, N of Lawrence;
40°37'x73°43'30"
Lawrence and Lynbrook
Quads (7.5')

CENTER ISLAND POINT
see
ROCKY POINT
Physical feature

Nassau—Oyster Bay
Source: (U.S. 5, Decisions Rendered between July 1, 1940 and June 30, 1941, p. 48)

CENTER MORICHES
Community
Suffolk—Brookhaven; E of Moriches, SE part of the town;
40°48′x72°47′
Moriches Quad (7.5′)

CENTEREACH
Community
Suffolk—Brookhaven; NE of Lake Ronkonkoma; 40°51′30″x73°6′
Historical: New Village (Bailey 19, vol. 1, p. 297) and (Chace 127), West Middle Island (Bayles 93, p. 265)
Patchogue Quad (7.5′)

CENTERPORT
Community
Suffolk—Huntington; N-central part of the town, S of Northport Bay;
40°53′20″x73°22′30″
Historical: Little Cow Harbor (French 10, p. 636fn)
Northport and Lloyd Harbor Quads (7.5′)

CENTERPORT HARBOR
Physical feature
Suffolk—Huntington; SE side of Northport Bay; 40°54′x73°23′
Historical: Little Cow Harbor (Bayles 93, p. 158)
Northport and Lloyd Harbor Quads (7.5′)

CENTERVILLE
Community
Suffolk—Riverhead; NW of Riverhead, SE of Reeves Park;
40°58′x72°41′30″
Riverhead Quad (7.5′)

CENTERVILLE
Community—historical
Queens; in the former town of Jamaica, "adjacent to the trotting course"
Source: (French 10, p. 548)

CENTRAL ISLIP
Community
Suffolk—Islip; SW of Lake Ronkonkoma, E of Brentwood;
40°47′x73°12′
Historical: North Islip (Chace 127) and (French 10, p. 637), Suffolk Station (Bayles 93, p. 206) and (French 10, p. 637)
Central Islip Quad (7.5′)

CENTRAL PARK
see
BETHPAGE
Source: (Metropolitan 81) and (Hempstead Quad, 15′, 1897)

CENTRE ISLAND
Physical feature
Nassau—Oyster Bay; NE side of town, Oyster Bay Harbor vicinity;
40°54′x73°31′15″
Historical: Hog Island (French 10, p. 550fn), Middle Island (Thompson 41, vol. 1, p. 51)
Bayville Quad (7.5′)

CENTRE ISLAND
Village
Nassau—Oyster Bay; occupying all
of Centre Island, NE side of town;
40°54'x73°31'15"
Historical: Hog Island (French 10,
p. 550fn)
Bayville Quad (7.5')

CENTRE ISLAND BEACH
Physical feature
Nassau—Oyster Bay; on Long Island
Sound, NE shore of Oak Neck,
NW of Centre Island;
40°54'45"x73°32'
Bayville Quad (7.5')

CENTRE ISLAND POINT
see
ROCKY POINT
Physical feature
Nassau—Oyster Bay
Source: (U.S. 5, Decisions Rendered
between July 1, 1940 and June 30,
1941, p. 48)

CHAGECHAGON BROOK
Physical feature—historical
Queens (Nassau)—Oyster Bay; flows
from the N part of the village of
Matinecock, ENE of Locust Valley,
through Chagechagon Swamp into
Kantuck Pond;
ca. 40°52'55"x73°34'25"
*Bayville Quad (7.5')

CHAGECHAGON SWAMP
Physical feature—historical
Queens (Nassau)—Oyster Bay;
located in a valley, N of the village
of Matinecock, ENE of Locust
Valley

Source: (Cocks 70, pp. 8-9)
*Bayville Quad (7.5')

CHAMPLIN CREEK
Physical feature
Suffolk—Islip; flows through Islip,
E of East Islip;
40°42'30"x73°12'15"
Historical: Winganhauppauge Brook
(Tooker 44, p. 286), Vail's Brook
(Thompson 42, p. 129)
Bay Shore East Quad (7.5')

CHANNEL POND
Physical feature
Suffolk—Southampton; E of
Southampton village, SW of Mecox
Bay; 40°53'20"x72°20'30"
Sag Harbor Quad (7.5')

CHARLES POINT
Physical feature
Nassau—Hempstead; NE part of
Lawrence Marsh, SE of Lawrence;
40°36'18"x73°41'40"
Lawrence Quad (7.5')

CHARLOTTEVILLE
Community—historical
Queens; N of Locust Grove, W of
Corona, NE of Woodside;
ca. 40°45'15"x73°54'30"
Source: (Cram 132, p. 111)
*Central Park Quad (7.5')

CHASE CREEK
Physical feature
Suffolk—Shelter Island; flows into
the S part of Dering Harbor, E of
Shelter Island Heights;
41°5'x72°21'10"
Greenport Quad (7.5')

CHEBIAKINNAUSUK
Locality—historical
Suffolk—East Hampton; on
Montauk Peninsula, on the north
neck
Source: (Tooker 44, pp. 39–40)
Variation: Chabiakinnauhsuk (Ibid.)
*Montauk Point Quad (7.5')

CHECKACHAGIN BROOK
Physical feature—historical
Queens (Nassau)—Oyster Bay; flowed
NE into Beaver Swamp Creek
(now Beaver Brook) and into Beaver
Lake; ca. 40°53'x73°34'
Source: (Tooker 44, p. 40)
Variations: Chaugreen, Chogorin,
Choggin (Ibid.)
*Bayville Quad (7.5')

CHELTENHAM SPRINGS
Physical feature—historical
Queens; at the head of Flushing Bay;
ca. 40°45'45"x73°50'10"
Source: (French 10, p. 546fn)
*Flushing Quad (7.5')

CHENEY POND
Physical feature
Suffolk—Southampton; S of the
community of Riverhead;
40°54'45"x72°40'30"
Riverhead Quad (7.5')

CHEQUIT POINT
Physical feature
Suffolk—Shelter Island; NW part of
Shelter Island, W side of Dering
Harbor; 41°5'10"x72°21'10"
Historical: Chichwick (Tooker 44,
pp. 40–41)
Greenport Quad (7.5')

CHERRY GROVE
Community
Suffolk—Brookhaven; on Fire Island,
S of Sayville; 40°39'40"x73°5'10"
Historical: Raccoon Woods
(Strong 107, p. 116)
Sayville Quad (7.5')

CHERRY HARBOR
Physical feature
Suffolk—East Hampton; NE side of
Gardiners Bay, W side of Gardiners
Island; 41°5'25"x72°7'
Historical: Sherry Harbor, Home
Harbor (Dyson 24, p. 29)
Gardiners Island East and Gardiners
Island West Quad (7.5')

CHERRY HILL POINT
Physical feature
Suffolk—East Hampton; W tip of
Gardiners Island; 41°5'33"x72°8'23"
Gardiners Island West Quad (7.5')

CHERRY HILL POND
Physical feature
Suffolk—East Hampton; W end of
Gardiners Island, SW of Bostwick
Bay; 41°5'32"x72°8'30"
Gardiners Island West Quad (7.5')

CHERRY POINT
Community
see
GREENPOINT
Source: (Flint 26, p. 71)

CHERRY POINT
Physical feature
Suffolk—East Hampton; N of
Promised Land, W of Napeague;
41°0'30"x72°4'45"
Gardiners Island East Quad (7.5')

48

CHERRY TREE VALLEY
Community—historical
Suffolk—East Hampton; on
Montauk Peninsula, SW of the
community of Montauk, possibly
the present community of Montauk
Beach
Source: (Ullitz 164, index map)
*Montauk Point Quad (7.5 ')

CHESHIRES CREEK
Physical feature
Nassau—Hempstead; E border of
South Line Island, W border of
Black Banks Island; 40°37 'x73°29 '
West Gilgo Beach Quad (7.5 ')

CHICKEN POINT
Physical feature—historical
Nassau—North Hempstead; SE point
of Manorhaven;
40°50 '20 "x73°42 '55 "
Source: (Ross 158). Also known as
Bowman's Point (Ibid.)
*Sea Cliff Quad (7.5 ')

CHIKEMENCHOAKE
see
COCHIMINCHOAKE
Source: (Tooker 44, p. 43)

CHOCOMOUNT
Physical feature—hill
Suffolk—Southold; on Fishers Island,
NW of Barleyfield Cove, N of
Chocomount Beach;
41°16 '50 "x71°57 '50 "
Mystic Quad (7.5 ')

CHOCOMOUNT BEACH
Physical feature
Suffolk—Southold; on Fishers Island,
W of Barleyfield Cove, S of

Chocomount Cove;
41°16 '35 "x71°57 '45 "
Mystic Quad (7.5 ')

CHOCOMOUNT COVE
Physical feature
Suffolk—Southold; N-central coast
of Fishers Island; 41°17 'x71°58 '30 "
*Mystic Quad (7.5 ')

CHOPPAUHSHAPAUGAUSUCK
Locality—historical
Suffolk—East Hampton; S of Lake
Montauk, in the vicinity of Ditch
Plains; 41°2 '40 "x71°55 '
Source: (Tooker 44, pp. 41–42)
*Montauk Point Quad (7.5 ')

CHRISTIAN HILL
see
MUTTONTOWN
Source: (Pelletreau 38, p. 154)

CHRISTIAN HOOK
see
OCEANSIDE
Source: (U.S. 170, Chart No. 119,
1844), (Walling 172), and
(Hempstead Quad, 15 ', 1897)

CHRISTIANPOL MARSH
Physical feature
Kings; W side of Jamaica Bay, E of
Canarsie Pol; 40°37 'x73°51 '50 "
Far Rockaway Quad (7.5 ')

CILLINGWORTH
see
KILLINGWORTH
Source: (Pelletreau 38, p. 148)

CINDER CREEK
Physical feature
Nassau—Hempstead; flows into
  Reynolds Channel, S of Parsonage
  Island, between Ingraham Hassock
  and Cinder Island;
  40°35'30"x73°37'
Jones Inlet Quad (7.5')

CINDER ISLAND
Physical feature—marsh island
Nassau—Hempstead; S of Middle
  Bay, SE of Oceanside, NE of Lido
  Beach; 40°36'x73°36'40"
Jones Inlet Quad (7.5')

CLAM CREEK
Physical feature
Suffolk—Brookhaven, Southampton;
  flows into Moriches Bay, S of Swan
  Island and Seatuck Cove;
  40°46'30"x72°43'35"
Eastport Quad (7.5')

CLAM HOLLOW
Physical feature—historical
Suffolk—Brookhaven; midway
  between Bellport and the
  community of Brookhaven;
  ca. 40°46'15"x72°55'10"
Source: (Shaw 106, p. 211)
*Bellport Quad (7.5')

CLAM ISLAND
Physical feature—peninsula
Suffolk—Southampton; S of Noyack
Bay, W of Noyack;
  40°59'40"x72°21'50"
Sag Harbor Quad (7.5')

CLAM POND
Physical feature
Suffolk—Islip; on Fire Island, E of

Saltaire, S of the Fire Islands;
  40°38'20"x73°11'30"
Historical: Saltaire Harbor
  (Hyde 148)
Bay Shore East Quad (7.5')

CLARENCEVILLE
see
RICHMOND HILL
Source: (Ricard 86, p. 13)

CLARKS CREEK
see
NARRASKATUCK CREEK
Source: (U.S. 5, Decisions Rendered
  between July 1, 1940 and June 30,
  1941, p. 38)

CLAY PITS
see
EAST NORTHPORT
Source: (Bailey 19, vol. 1, p. 356)
  and (Chace 127)

CLAY POINT
Physical feature
Suffolk—Southold; N-central part of
  Fishers Island; 41°16'50"x71°59'30"
Mystic Quad (7.5')

CLEAR CREEK
see
VALLEY STREAM
Physical feature
Source: (Cram 132, p. 111)

CLEAVES POINT
Physical feature
Suffolk—Southold; NE of Greenport;
  41°6'45"x72°20'35"
Greenport Quad (7.5')

CLINKTOWN
see
EAST ROCKAWAY
Source: (Flint 26, p. 73)

CLINT DARLING'S SWAMP
see
LAKE McKINLEY
Source: (Langhans 98, p. 13)

CLINTON BAY
see
FLUSHING BAY
Source: (Flint 26, p. 71)

CLINTONVILLE
see
WHITESTONE
Source: (French 10, p. 546fn)

CLOCKS CREEK
see
NARRASKATUCK CREEK
Source: (U.S. 5, Decisions Rendered between July 1, 1940 and June 30, 1941, p. 38)

CLOWESVILLE
Community—historical
Queens (Nassau)—North Hempstead; in the vicinity of Mineola
Source: (French 10, p. 550)

COATSVILLE
Community—historical
Suffolk—Brookhaven; S of Medford, N of Patchogue; ca.
40°48'45"x73°00'25"
Source: (Rand 153, pp. 89–94)
*Patchogue Quad (7.5')

COBB
Community
Suffolk—Southampton; E of Southampton, W of Mecox Bay;
40°54'5"x72°21'20"
Historical: Cobs Pound, Chestnut Pound (Tooker 44, pp. 42–43)
Sage Harbor Quad (7.5')

COBBLE HILL
Physical feature—historical
Kings; W side of Brooklyn Heights;
40°41'40"x73°59'50"
Source: (Ratzer 155). Also known as Ponkiesberg (Stiles 66, vol. 1, p. 252)
*Brooklyn Quad (7.5')

COCHIMINCHOAKE
Physical feature—island—historical
Suffolk—Brookhaven; in Moriches Bay, S of East Moriches, no longer an island; 40°47'30"x72°45'
Source: (Tooker 44, pp. 43, 83–84). Also known as Chikemenchoake, Kitchaminchok, Moriches Island (Ibid.)
*Eastport and Moriches Quads (7.5')

COCKLE HARBOR
see
COECLES INLET
Source: (Burr 124)

COCK'S NECK
Physical feature—historical
Suffolk—Southold; NW of Mattituck; 41°0'x72°33'30"
Source: (U.S. 167, Map T-55)
*Mattituck Hills Quad (7.5')

COECKLES HARBOR
see

COECLES INLET
Source: (U.S. 5, List No. 6802,
p. 18)

COECLES INLET
Physical feature
Suffolk—Shelter Island; NE side of
Shelter Island; 41°4'15"x72°18'15"
Variations: Cocckles Harbor, Cockles
Harbor, Coeccles Harbor, Coeckles
Harbor, Cockles Harbor, Coecle
Harbor Inlet, Coecles Harbor Inlet,
Coecles Harbor, Coeclis Inlet (U.S.
5, List No. 6802, p. 18), Cockle
Harbor (Burr 124)
Greenport Quad (7.5')

COEKWAS CREEK
Physical feature—historical
Queens; in the vicinity of Far
Rockaway
Source: (Tooker 44, pp. 44–45, 51–52)
Variation: Copwax (Ibid.)
*Far Rockaway Quad (7.5')

COE'S HOOK
Community—historical
Queens (Nassau)—Hempstead;
E of Christian Hook (Oceanside),
SE of Baldwinville (Baldwin);
40°38'30"x73°36'
Source: (Walling 172)
*Freeport Quad (7.5')

COLD SPRING
see
COLD SPRING HARBOR
Community
Source: (Northport Quad, 15',
1901)

COLD SPRING BAR BEACH
see
COLD SPRING BEACH
Source: (Huntington Quad, 7.5')

COLD SPRING BEACH
Physical feature—spit
Nassau—Oyster Bay; between Cold
Spring Harbor and Inner Harbor;
40°52'x73°28'
Source: (U.S. 5, List No. 7403,
p. 21). Also know as Cold Spring Bar
Beach (Huntington Quad, 7.5')
*Huntington Quad (7.5')

COLD SPRING GUT
Physical feature—historical
Suffolk, Nassau—Huntington, Oyster
Bay; inlet between Cold Spring
Harbor and Inner Harbor;
40°52'x73°27'50"
Source: (Valentine 50, p. 99)
*Huntington Quad (7.5')

COLD SPRING HARBOR
Community
Suffolk—Huntington; W-central part
of the town; 40°52'x73°27'30"
Historical: Bungtown (Overton 37,
p. 220), Cold Spring (Northport
Quad, 15', 1901), Nachaquatuck
(French 10, p. 636fn)
Huntington Quad (7.5')

COLD SPRING HARBOR
Physical feature
Suffolk, Nassau—Huntington, Oyster
Bay; NW side of the town of
Huntington and NE side of the
town of Oyster Bay;
40°53'45"x73°29'
Historical: Wauwepex (Bayles 93,
p. 139)
Lloyd Harbor Quad (7.5')

COLD SPRING HARBOR STATION
Community
Suffolk, Nassau—Huntington, Oyster
Bay; S of Cold Spring Harbor;
40°50′x73°27′30″
Huntington Quad (7.5′)

COLD SPRING POND
Physical feature
Suffolk—Southampton; SE of Great
Peconic Bay, W of Southampton;
40°54′x72°27′30″
Southampton Quad (7.5′)

COLD SPRING RIVER
Physical feature
Suffolk, Nassau—Huntington, Oyster
Bay; flows into St. Johns Lake and
Cold Spring Harbor;
40°50′40″x73°27′30″
Source: (Valentine 50, p. 99)
*Huntington Quad (7.5′)

COLD SPRING TERRACE
Community
Suffolk—Huntington; W of
Huntington Station, S of Cold
Spring Harbor;
ca. 40°50′20″x73°27′30″
Source: (Rand 154, 1977, p. 382)
*Huntington Quad (7.5′)

COLLEGE POINT
Community
Queens; NW side of Queens, E of
Rikers Island; 40°47′15″x73°50′45″
Historical: Tue's Neck, Tew's Neck,
Strattonport, Lawrence's Neck
(Ricard 86, p. 8)
Flushing Quad (7.5′)

COLLEGE POINT
Physical feature
Queens; NW side of the community
of College Point;
40°47′40″x73°51′10″
Historical: Wigwam Swamp (Flint
26, p. 69), Lawrences Neck (French
10, p. 546fn), Stevens Point (Bailey
19, vol. 1, p. 39)
Flushing Quad (7.5′)

COLONELS ISLAND
Physical feature
Suffolk—Southampton; near the
mouth of the Peconic River, E of
the community of Riverhead;
40°55′x72°38′10″
Riverhead Quad (7.5′)

COLONIAL MANOR
Community—historical
Suffolk—Babylon; in the vicinity of
the village of Babylon
Source: (Macoskey 29, p. 50)
*Bay Shore West Quad (7.5′)

COLONIAL SPRINGS
Community
Suffolk—Babylon; N part of the
town, NW of Wyandanch;
ca. 40°45′30″x73°23′
Source: (Northport Quad, 15′, 1901)
and (Hagstrom 141, 1969, p. 28)
*Huntington Quad (7.5′)

COLUMBIA GROVE
Physical feature—swamp—historical
Suffolk—Huntington; SW side of
Lloyd Neck; ca. 40°54′40″x73°29′
Source: (U.S. 170, Chart No. 367,
1916)
*Lloyd Harbor Quad (7.5′)

COLUMBUSVILLE
Community—historical
Queens; E of Maspeth, N of Middle
Village; ca. 40°43′40″x73°53′50″
Source: (Brooklyn Quad, 15′, 1897)
*Brooklyn Quad (7.5′)

COMAC
see
COMMACK
Source: (Tooker 44, p. 45)

COMAC HILLS
Physical feature
Suffolk, Nassau—Babylon, Oyster
Bay; WNW of Farmingdale;
40°45′x73°27′
Source: (Pelletreau 38, p. 155)
*Amityville and Huntington
Quads (7.5′)

COMETICO
Community
see
GREENLAWN
Source: (Flint 26, p. 71)

COMETICO
Physical feature
see
OLD FIELD POINT
Source: (Tooker 44, p. 45)

COMMACK
Community
Suffolk—Huntington, Smithtown; on
the border of the towns of
Huntington and Smithtown;
40°50′30″x73°18′
Variations: Comac, Comack,
Winnecomac, Winnecomak,
Winecomack, Weno Comack,
Wenecomack, Wenea-Commack

(Tooker 44, pp. 45, 288–289)
Greenlawn Quad (7.5′)

COMPAWAMS CREEK
see
LAWRENCE CREEK
Suffolk—Islip
Source: (Tooker 44, pp. 91–92)

COMPOWAMS NECK
Physical feature—historical
Suffolk—Islip; S side of the village
of Brightwaters, NW of Great Cove;
40°42′20″x73°15′15″
Source: (Tooker 44, pp. 46–47) and
(Chace 127). Also known as
Manetuck Neck (Tooker 44,
pp. 91–92)
Variations: Compowis,
Compauwams and Compowms
(Ibid.)
*Bay Shore West Quad (7.5′)

COMPTON PARK
Community
Nassau—Hempstead; East Rockaway
vicinity; ca. 40°38′x73°41′
Source: (Macoskey 29, p. 51)
*Lynbrook Quad (7.5′)

CONCHS HOLE POINT
Physical feature
Queens; SE part of Jamaica Bay,
NE of Arverne, S of Jo Co Marsh;
40°36′10″x73°47′15″
Far Rockaway Quad (7.5′)

CONEGUMS CREEK
see
REEVES CREEK
Source: (Tooker 44, pp. 47–48)

CONETQUOT
see
GREAT RIVER
Suffolk—Islip
Source: (Bailey 19, vol. 1, p. 324)

CONEY ISLAND
Community
Kings; SE part of Kings, S of
Bensonhurst; 40°34'30"x74°0'
Coney Island and The Narrows
Quads (7.5')

CONEY ISLAND
Physical feature
Kings; SE side of Kings;
40°34'30"x73°59'45"
Historical: a series of little islands
which had many names, Narrioch,
Pine Island, Guisbert's Island,
Plumb Island, Pelican Island, and
Barren Island (Manley 30, p. 32),
Scheyer's Island (Flint 26, p. 70),
Equendito (Tooker 44, pp. 62-63)
Coney Island and The Narrows
Quads (7.5')

CONEY ISLAND CREEK
Physical feature
Kings; flows into Gravesend Bay,
N of Coney Island;
40°34'45"x73°59'25"
Coney Island Quad (7.5')

CONGDONS CREEK
Physical feature
Suffolk—Shelter Island; central part
of Shelter Island, SW part of
Coecles Inlet; 41°4'x72°19'
Historical: Dennis Creek (Ullitz 164,
plate 13)
Greenport Quad (7.5')

CONGDONS POINT
Physical feature
Suffolk—Shelter Island; central
Shelter Island, SW part of Coecles
Inlet; 41°4'5"x72°18'40"
Greenport Quad (7.5')

CONITTICUT RIVER
see
CARMANS RIVER
Source: (Tooker 44, p. 48)

CONKLIN POINT
Physical feature
Suffolk—Islip; S point of Okenok
Neck, E of Babylon Cove;
40°41'x73°16'45"
Bay Shore West Quad (7.5')

CONKLING POINT
Physical feature
Suffolk—Southold; S of Pipes Cove,
NE of Southold Bay;
41°4'45"x72°22'25"
Greenport and Southold Quads (7.5')

CONKLING'S POND
Physical feature—historical
Suffolk—Smithtown; N part of San
Remo, no longer exists;
ca. 40°53'40"x73°13'25"
Source: (Langhans 98, p. 7)
*Saint James Quad (7.5')

CONNARIE SEE
see
JAMAICA BAY
Source: (Tooker 44, p. 32)

CONNECTICOTT
see
SOUTH HAVEN
Source: (Thompson 41, vol. 1,
p. 437)

CONNECTICUT RIVER
see
CARMANS RIVER
Source: (Chace 127) and
(Tooker 44, p. 48)

CONNETQUOT PARK
Community—historical
Suffolk—Islip; in the vicinity of East
Islip
Source: (Macoskey 29, p. 51) and
(Hyde 147)
*Bay Shore East Quad (7.5')

CONNETQUOT RIVER
Physical feature
Suffolk—Islip; flows into the Great
South Bay, E side of Islip;
40°43'30"x73°8'15"
Historical: West Connecticut,
Conetquot Brook, Nicoll's River
(Tooker 44, p. 48), Great River
(U.S. 6, 1977, p. 213), Quonettquott
(Tooker 44, p. 208)
Bay Shore East Quad (7.5')

**CONNETQUOT RIVER STATE
PARK**
Suffolk—Islip; central part of the
town, NE of East Islip, W of
Bohemia; 40°45'x73°9'
Source: (Hagstrom 141, 1979, p. 41)
*Bay Shore East and Central Islip
Quads (7.5')

CONOE LAKE
Physical feature
Suffolk—Riverhead; N of Calverton;
40°54'40"x72°45'5"
Wading River Quad (7.5')

CONORASSET
see
CANARSIE
Source: (Tooker 44, p. 49)

CONSCIENCE BAY
Physical feature
Suffolk—Brookhaven; W of Strongs
Neck and Port Jefferson Harbor,
N of Setauket; 40°57'30"x73°7'20"
Historical: Oldsfield Bay (Flint 26,
p. 73)
Port Jefferson and Saint James
Quads (7.5')

CONSCIENCE POINT
Physical feature
Suffolk—Southampton; in North Sea
Harbor; 40°56'20"x72°25'
Southampton Quad (7.5')

CONSELYEAS POND
Physical feature
Queens; E side of Queens, SW part
of Rosedale; 40°39'30"x73°44'45"
Lynbrook Quad (7.5')

CONSTIBLES NECK
Physical feature
Suffolk—Brookhaven; E of
Pattersquash Creek, N of Narrow
Bay and Pattersquash Island;
40°45'30"x72°50'15"
Source: (Strong 107, p. 116)
*Moriches Quad (7.5')

CONUNGUM
see
CALVERTON
Source: (Tooker 44, pp. 49-50)

56

COOKIE HILL
see
WHITESTONE
Source: (French 10, p. 546fn)

COOKS CREEK
Physical feature—historical
Suffolk—Southampton; NE side of
Mecox Bay, SE of Calf Creek;
ca. 40°54′45″x72°19′45″
Source: (Adams 92, p. 18)
*Sag Harbor Quad (7.5′)

COOPER BLUFF
Physical feature
Nassau—Oyster Bay; NE part of the
town, NW of Cold Spring Harbor;
40°53′40″x73°29′45″
Lloyd Harbor Quad (7.5′)

COOPERS HILLS
see
MATTITUCK HILLS
Source: (U.S. 167, Map T-55)

COOPER'S NECK
Physical feature
Suffolk—Southampton; SW of the
village of Southampton;
40°52′5″x72°24′15″
Source: (Pelletreau 38, p. 292)
*Shinnecock Inlet Quad (7.5′)

COOPERS NECK POND
Physical feature
Suffolk—Southampton; S of the
village of Southampton;
40°52′x72°24′10″
Shinnecock Inlet Quad (7.5′)

COOSPUTUS NECK
Physical feature
Suffolk—Brookhaven; one of the

smaller necks of land into which
Mastic Neck is divided
Source: (Tooker 44, p. 50)
*Moriches Quad (7.5′)

COPECES
see
SAMMYS BEACH
Source: (Tooker 44, p. 50)

COPIAGUE
Community
Suffolk—Babylon; W of Lindenhurst,
E of Amityville; 40°41′x73°24′
Historical: East Amityville, Great
Neck (Bailey 19, vol. 1, p. 385)
Amityville Quad (7.5′)

COPIAGUE NECK
Physical feature
Suffolk—Babylon; on the Great
South Bay, S-central part of the
town, S of Lindenhurst;
40°40′x73°22′45″
Variations: Copiag, Coppiage,
Copyag, Cuppuauge (Tooker 44,
pp. 50-51)
Amityville and Bay Shore West
Quads (7.5′)

COPPAUHSHAPAUGANSUK
Tract of land—historical
Suffolk—East Hampton; SE of
Montauk Harbor;
ca. 41°2′40″x71°53′45″
Source: (Pelletreau 38, p. 371)
*Montauk Point Quad (7.5′)

COPROG NECK
Physical feature—historical
Suffolk—Babylon; S side of
Lindenhurst, E of Copiague Neck,
W of Little Neck;

ca. 40°40′5″x73°22′25″
Source: (Thompson 42, p. 128)
*Bay Shore West Quad (7.5′)

COPWAX CREEK
see
COEKWAS CREEK
Source: (Tooker 44, pp. 44–45, 51–52)

CORAM
Community
Suffolk—Brookhaven; NE of Lake
  Ronkonkoma, NW of Yaphank;
  40°52′x73°0′
Variations: Corum, Wincoram,
  Moncorum (Tooker 44, pp. 52–53),
  Caroway (Flint 26, p. 70)
Bellport Quad (7.5′)

CORAM HILL(S)
Community
Suffolk—Brookhaven; S of Coram,
  W of Gordon Heights;
  40°51′x72°58′30″
Source: (Hagstrom 141, 1965, p. 49)
  and (Tooker 44, pp. 52–53)
*Bellport Quad (7.5′)

CORCHAUGE
Tract of land—historical
Suffolk—Southold; area surrounding
  the community of Cutchogue
Source: (Tooker 44, pp. 56–58)

COREY CREEK
Physical feature
Suffolk—Brookhaven; flows into the
  NW part of Patchogue Bay, E of
  Blue Point; 40°44′40″x73°1′45″
Sayville Quad (7.5′)

COREY CREEK
Physical feature—inlet
Suffolk—Southold; flows into the
  Little Peconic Bay; 41°2′x72°25′30″
Southold Quad (7.5′)

COREY POND
Physical feature
Suffolk—Brookhaven; E side of the
  town, SE of Lake Panamoka;
  40°55′x72°50′40″
Wading River Quad (7.5′)

CORMORANT POINT
Physical feature
Suffolk—Southampton; NW part of
  Shinnecock Bay, N of Ponquogue;
  40°52′27″x72°29′30″
Shinnecock Inlet Quad (7.5′)

CORN CREEK
Physical feature—historical
Queens (Nassau)—Oyster Bay; W
  side of Mill Neck Creek, SW of
  Bayville; 40°53′45″x73°34′30″
Source: (Cocks 70, p. 5)
*Bayville Quad (7.5′)

CORNBURY
see
LITTLE NECK
Community
Queens
Source: (Ricard 86, p. 12)

CORNEILLE ESTATES
Community
Suffolk—Islip; on Fire Island, W of
  Ocean Beach, S of Heckscher State
  Park; ca. 40°38′35″x73°9′35″
Source: (Hagstrom 141, 1979, p. 42)
*Bay Shore East Quad (7.5′)

CORNELIUS POINT
Physical feature
Suffolk—Shelter Island; N part of
  Shelter Island, NE of Dering
  Harbor; 41°3'15"x72°22'15"
  Greenport Quad (7.5')

CORNELL CREEK
Physical feature—historical
Queens; no longer exists, presently
  the S side of JFK Airport;
  ca. 40°38'40"x73°48'50"
Source: (Brooklyn Quad, 15', 1897).
  Also known as Duryea's Creek
  (Walling 172)
*Jamaica Quad (7.5')

CORNELLS POND
Physical feature
Nassau—Hempstead; in Valley
  Stream State Park, E side of Valley
  Stream; 40°40'10"x73°41'50"
Source: (Walling 172)
*Lynbrook Quad (7.5')

CORONA
Community
Queens; NW side of Queens, S of
  Flushing Bay; 40°45'x73°51'45"
Historical: West Flushing (Ricard 86,
  p. 8)
Flushing Quad (7.5')

CORTLANDT PATENT
Tract of land—historical
Suffolk—Islip; on Appletree Neck;
  ca. 40°42'x73°16'
Source: (Bayles 93, p. 198)
*Bay Shore West Quad (7.5')

CORWIN'S POND
see
ARTIST LAKE
Source: (Bayles 95, p. 50)

COSTEYICK
A place of uncertain location, Dutch
  word
Source: (Tooker 44, p. 53)

COTSJEWAMINCK
see
SHELTER ISLAND
Source: (Tooker 44, p. 53)

COVE BROOK
Physical feature—historical
Nassau—Oyster Bay; SW side of
  Cove Neck, flowed into The Cove
  and Oyster Bay Harbor;
  ca. 40°52'25"x73°30'10"
Source: (Overton 37, p. 318)
*Hicksville and Huntington Quads
  (7.5')

COVE NECK
Physical feature
Nassau—Oyster Bay; NE part of the
  town; 40°53'15"x73°30'
Bayville and Lloyd Harbor Quads
  (7.5')

COVE NECK
Village
Nassau—Oyster Bay; on Cove Neck,
  NE part of the town;
  40°53'15"x73°30'
Bayville and Lloyd Harbor Quads
  (7.5')

COVE POINT
Physical feature
Nassau—Oyster Bay; on Oyster Bay
  Harbor, NE point of Cove Neck, E
  of Centre Island;
  40°53'30"x73°30'35"
Bayville Quad (7.5')

COW BAY
Physical feature
see
MANHASSET BAY
Source: (Bailey 19, vol. 1, p. 443)

COW BAY
Village
see
PORT WASHINGTON
Source: (Bailey 19, vol. 1, p. 444)

COW HARBOR
see
NORTHPORT
Source: (Tooker 44, pp. 20, 37–38, 77) and (Bailey 19, vol. 1, p. 340)

COW MEADOW PRESERVE
Physical feature—marsh island
Nassau—Hempstead; SE of Freeport, W of Fighting Island;
40°38'x73°34'15"
Variation: South Cow Meadow (Hagstrom 140, 1965, p. 50)
Freeport Quad (7.5')

COW NECK
Community
see
MANHASSET
Source: (Flint 26, p. 72)

COW NECK
Physical feature
Nassau—North Hempstead
see
MANHASSET NECK
Source: (Tooker 44, p. 95) and (U.S. 170, Chart No. 116, 1855)

COW NECK
Physical feature
Suffolk—Southampton; E of Great

Peconic Bay, SW of Little Peconic Bay; 40°56'x72°26'30"
Southampton Quad (7.5')

COW NECK POINT
Physical feature
Suffolk—Southampton; SE of Robins Island, E of Great Peconic Bay; 40°56'43"x72°26'40"
Southampton Quad (7.5')

COW NECK VILLAGE
see
PORT WASHINGTON
Source: (Flint 26, p. 74)

COW YARD
Physical feature—beach
Suffolk—Southampton; E of Flanders, SE Flanders Bay shoreline;
40°54'40"x72°34'
Mattituck Quad (7.5')

COWAMOKE
see
FRESH POND
Physical feature
Suffolk—Smithtown
Source: (Tooker 44, pp. 53–54)

CRAB CREEK
Physical feature
Suffolk—East Hampton; SW side of Shelter Island, SW side of West Neck; 41°3'x72°22'15"
Greenport Quad (7.5')

CRAB MEADOW
Community
Suffolk—Huntington; NE part of the
town, N of Northport;
40°55′30″x73°20′
Variation: Waterside Park (Rand 154,
1977, p. 382)
Northport Quad (7.5′)

CRAB MEADOW
Physical feature
Suffolk—Huntington; NE side of
town, NE of Northport;
40°55′30″x73°19′30″
Historical: Arhakaamunk,
Katawamac (Tooker 44, pp. 20–21),
Ashamomuck (Ibid., p. 23),
Catawamuck (Ibid., p. 36)
Northport Quad (7.5′)

CRAFFORD
see
JAMAICA
Community
Source: (Ricard 86, p. 11)

CRANBERRY HOLD
Physical feature—marsh
Suffolk—East Hampton; W of Lazy
Point, S of Hicks Island;
ca. 41°0′5″x72°3′55″
Source: (Rattray 102, p. 102)
*Gardiners Island East Quad (7.5′)

CRANBERRY POND
Physical feature
Suffolk—Brookhaven; E of South
Manor; 40°51′45″x72°46′45″
Moriches Quad (7.5′)

CRANBERRY POND
Physical feature
Suffolk—Brookhaven, Riverhead; E

side of Brookhaven town, S of
Lake Panamoka;
40°54′50″x72°50′30″
Wading River Quad (7.5′)

CRANBERRY RIVER
Physical feature
Suffolk—Brookhaven; flows into the
Peconic River, S of Calverton;
40°54′20″x72°44′45″
Riverhead Quad (7.5′)

CRANE NECK
Physical feature
Suffolk—Brookhaven; NE of
Smithtown Bay, N of Stony Brook;
40°57′40″x73°9′
Saint James Quad (7.5′)

CRANE NECK POINT
Physical feature
Suffolk—Brookhaven; on Long
Island Sound, NW of Stony Brook,
W of Old Field; 40°58′x73°9′35″
Saint James Quad (7.5′)

CRAWFORD
see
JAMAICA
Town—historical
Source: (French 10, p. 547fn)

CREEDMOOR
Community—historical
Queens; SE part of the former town
of Flushing; ca. 40°43′30″x73°44′
Source: (Hempstead Quad, 15′,
1897) and (Hyde 147)
*Lynbrook Quad (7.5′)

CRESCENT BEACH
Physical feature
Suffolk—Huntington; part of the

N shoreline of East Neck;
40°54'30"x73°24'
Lloyd Harbor Quad (7.5')

CRESCENT BEACH
Physical feature
Suffolk—Shelter Island; W part of
Shelter Island; 41°4'50"x72°21'50"
Greenport Quad (7.5')

CRIPPLEBUSH
Community—historical
Kings; N of Bedford, W of
Bushwick;
ca. 40°42'x73°57'
Source: (Stiles 66, vol. 1, p. 381)
*Brooklyn Quad (7.5')

CROMMEGOUW
see
GARDINER'S BAY
Source: (Tooker 44, p. 175)

CROMWELL BAY
Community
see
SETAUKET
Community
Source: (Thompson 41, vol. 1,
p. 433)

CROMWELL BAY
Physical feature
see
SETAUKET HARBOR
Source: (Flint 26, p. 74)

CROOKED CREEK
Physical feature
Nassau—Hempstead; SE of
Lawrence, extends SW from Post
Lead to Reynolds Channel;

40°36'30"x73°43'07"
Lawrence Quad (7.5')

CROOKED DITCH
Physical feature—inlet
Suffolk—Islip; SW part of Heckscher
State Park, E of the mouth of
Quintuck Creek;
40°42'15"x73°10'30"
Source: (Town of Islip 163)
*Bay Shore East Quad (7.5')

CROOKED LEAD
Physical feature—channel
Nassau—Hempstead; between Cuba
Island and Middle Island;
40°37'30"x73°31'30"
Jones Inlet Quad (7.5')

CROOKED POND
Physical feature
Suffolk—Southampton; S of Sag
Harbor; 40°58'x72°17'40"
Sag Harbor Quad (7.5')

CROOKED ROW
An infamous name for Long Island;
so called because of growth of
piracy and privateering on Long
Island, due to the long seacoast
which was adapted to illicit practices
Source: (Bailey 19, vol. 1, p. 77)

CROW HEAD
Physical feature—bluff
Suffolk—East Hampton; W part of
Gardiners Island, SW of Bostwick
Bay; 41°6'5"x72°8'25"
Gardiners Island West Quad (7.5')

62

CROW INLET
Physical feature—historical
Nassau—Hempstead; inlet into Broad
Channel, SE of Lawrence;
ca. 40°35'x73°41'20"
Source: (Osborne 35, p. 89)
*Lawrence Quad (7.5')

CROW ISLAND LEAD
Physical feature—channel
Nassau—Hempstead; borders the S
side of Big Crow Island,
N boundary of West Crow Island
and Middle Crow Island;
40°37'x73°32'50"
Jones Inlet Quad (7.5')

CROW SHOAL
Physical feature
Suffolk—East Hampton; in
Gardiners Bay, NE of Threemile
Harbor; 41°4'40"x72°10'
Gardiners Island West Quad (7.5')

CROWN VILLAGE
Community
Nassau—Oyster Bay; W of
Amityville, SE of Massapequa Park;
ca. 40°40'25"x73°26'55"
Source: (Rand 154, 1977, p. 382)
*Amityville Quad (7.5')

CRUIKSHANK'S POND
Physical feature
Suffolk—Smithtown; W of
Hauppauge, S of New Millpond;
40°49'35"x73°13'15"
Historical: Green Gate Pond
(Langhans 98, p. 7)
Central Islip Quad (7.5')

CRYDERS POINT
Physical feature

Queens; NW of Little Bay, NE side
of Beechhurst; 40°47'40"x73°47'45"
Flushing Quad (7.5')

CRYSTAL BROOK
Community
Suffolk—Brookhaven; NE of Port
Jefferson, W of Mount Sinai;
40°57'x73°2'30"
Port Jefferson Quad (7.5')

CRYSTAL BROOK
Physical feature—historical
Suffolk—Brookhaven; flowed into
the SW side of Mount Sinai Harbor;
40°57'15"x73°2'40"
Source: (Tooker 44, p. 164). Also
known as Nonowantuck Creek
(Ibid.)
*Port Jefferson Quad (7.5')

CRYSTAL BROOK HOLLOW
Physical feature
Suffolk—Brookhaven; E of Port
Jefferson, W of Mount Sinai;
40°56'50"x73°2'30"
Port Jefferson Quad (7.5')

CUBA
Locality—historical
Suffolk—Huntington; S of
Greenlawn, NW of Elwood;
ca. 40°51'20"x73°21'45"
Source: (Bayles 93, p. 166)
*Greenlawn Quad (7.5')

CUBA ISLAND
Physical feature
Nassau—Hempstead; S of East Bay,
E of Big Crow Island;
40°37'x73°31'45"
Freeport and Jones Inlet Quads (7.5')

CUFFERS BEACH
Physical feature—historical
Suffolk—East Hampton; possibly the
S shoreline of Northwest Harbor;
41°00'40"x72°15'
Source: (U.S. 167, Map T-72)
*Greenport and Gardiners Island
West Quads (7.5')

CULLODEN POINT
Physical feature
Suffolk—East Hampton; N of the
community of Montauk, NW side
of North Neck; 41°4'15"x71°57'37"
Montauk Point Quad (7.5')

CUM CITY
Community—historical
Suffolk—Riverhead; N of Jamesport,
E of Northville;
ca. 40°57'45"x72°35'
Source: (Ullitz 164, index map)
*Mattituck Quad (7.5')

CUMSEWOGUE
Farming area—historical
Suffolk—Brookhaven; in the area
presently known as Port Jefferson
Station; ca. 40°55'50"x73°3'
Source: (Tooker 44, pp. 54–55)
Variation: Cumsewage (Ibid.)
*Port Jefferson Quad (7.5')

CUPSAGE
Locality—historical
Suffolk—Southampton; S of
Eastport on Great South Beach;
ca. 40°46'30"x72°43'30"
Source: (Tooker 44, pp. 55–56)
Variations: Capsoge, Copsoage, Cup
Soak Gutt, Cupsoge, Cupsouge,

Cupsawege (Ibid.)
*Eastport Quad (7.5')

CUPSOQUE BEACH
Physical feature
Suffolk—Brookhaven; E of Moriches
Inlet, on the Atlantic Ocean, SE
part of the town; 40°46'10"x72°44'
Eastport Quad (7.5')

CUPTWANGE
Tract of land—historical
Suffolk—Southampton; on Fire
Island, SW side of town, S of Swan
Island; ca. 40°46'20"x72°43'25"
Source: (Thompson 41, vol. 1,
p. 418)
*Eastport Quad (7.5')

CURRAN'S POND
see
ARTIST LAKE
Physical feature
Source: (Thompson 41, vol. 1,
p. 436)

CUTCHOGUE
Community
Suffolk—Southold; N of Great
Peconic Bay; 41°00'40"x72°29'10"
Variations: Catsjeyick, Catsjaock,
Carchake, Corchake, Corchauge,
Curchaug, Kachogue, etc.
(Tooker 44, pp. 56–58)
Southold Quad (7.5')

CUTCHOGUE HARBOR
Physical feature
Suffolk—Southold; N of Robins
Island; 41°00'x72°27'50"
Southold and Southampton Quads
(7.5')

CUTCHOGUE STATION
Community
Suffolk—Southold; NW of
 Cutchogue; 41°1′20″x72°29′50″
Southold Quad (7.5′)

CUTSGUNSUCK
Locality—historical
Suffolk—Smithtown; NE of Saint
 James, in the vicinity of Mills Pond;
 ca. 40°53′50″x73°9′
Source: (Pelletreau 101, p. 30)
*Saint James Quad (7.5′)

CUTSGUNSUCK
Physical feature
see
STONY BROOK
 Physical feature
 Source: (Tooker 44, pp. 58–59)
 and (Langhans 98, p. 7)

CUTTINGS CREEK
Physical feature—historical
Suffolk—Southampton; flows into
 Quantuck Bay, possibly Quantuck
 Creek; ca. 40°49′x72°37′20″
Source: (Tooker 44, p. 202)
*Quogue Quad (7.5′)

CUTUNOMACK
see
KETANOMOCKE
 Source: (Tooker 44, pp. 59, 79)

CYPREE AVENUE
Railroad Station—historical
Queens; near the Kings County line,
 in the vicinity of Woodhaven;
 ca. 40°41′30″x73°52′15″
Source: (French 10, p. 548)
*Jamaica Quad (7.5′)

CYPRESS HILLS
Community—historical
Kings; NE part of the town of New
 Lots; ca. 40°41′15″x73°52′15″
Source: (French 10, p. 373)
*Jamaica Quad (7.5′)

DARLINGTON
Community—historical
Suffolk—Smithtown; W side of
 Nissequogue River, SSE of San
 Remo; 40°53'15"x73°12'30"
Source: (Langhans 98, p. 7) and (U.S.
 170, Chart No. 116, 1855)
Variation: Darling's Hollow
 (Langhans 98, p. 7)
*Saint James Quad (7.5')

DAVES CREEK
Physical feature
Suffolk—Southampton; flows into
 Shinnecock Bay, SE part of East
 Quogue; 40°50'10"x72°34'30"
Quogue Quad (7.5')

DAVID'S POINT
Physical feature
Suffolk—Brookhaven; NW side of
 Moriches Bay, S of Center
 Moriches; 40°47'x72°47'
Moriches Quad (7.5')

DAVIS CREEK
Physical feature
Suffolk—Southampton; flows from
 Turtle Cove to North Sea Harbor;
 40°56'40"x72°24'30"
Southampton Quad (7.5')

DAVIS PARK
Community
Suffolk—Brookhaven; on Fire Island,
 S of Patchogue, E of Fire Island
 Pines; 40°41'x73°00'30"
Sayville and Howells Point Quads
 (7.5')

DAYTON ISLAND
Physical feature
Suffolk—East Hampton; NE side of
 Threemile Harbor, S of The Flats;
 41°1'35"x72°11'
Gardiners Island West Quad (7.5')

DAYTON'S BROOK
see
MOTTS BROOK
Source: (Shaw 106, p. 211)

DAYTON'S SWAMP
Physical feature—historical
Queens (Nassau)—Oyster Bay; W of
 Oak Neck and Bayville;
 40°54'25"x73°35'30"
Source: (Cocks 70, p. 3)
*Bayville Quad (7.5')

DEAD HORSE BAY
Physical feature
Kings; E of Sheepshead Bay, SW of
 Floyd Bennett Field;
 40°35'x73°54'5"
Coney Island Quad (7.5')

DEAD HORSE INLET
see
GERRITSON INLET
Source: (U.S. 170, Chart No. 369,
 1908)

DEB'S INLET
see
EAST ROCKAWAY INLET
Source: (Pearsall 84, p.79)

DEEP CREEK
Physical feature
Kings; SW of Floyd Bennett Field,
E of Sheepshead Bay;
40°35'10"x73°54'10"
Coney Island Quad (7.5')

DEEP CREEK
Suffolk—Riverhead
see
TERRYS CREEK
Source: (U.S. 5, List No. 5903,
p. 44)

DEEP CREEK MEADOW
Physical feature—marsh island
Nassau—Hempstead; NNW of Jones
Beach State Park, SE of Big Crow
Island; 40°36'30"x73°31'10"
Jones Inlet Quad (7.5')

DEEP HOLE
Community—historical
Suffolk—Riverhead; S of Baiting
Hollow, NE of Calverton;
ca. 40°56'15"x72°43'45"
Source: (Hyde 147)
*Riverhead Quad (7.5')

DEEP HOLE
Suffolk—Huntington
see
WOOD HOLLOW
Source: (Sammis 104, p. 182)

DEEP HOLE CREEK
Physical feature
Suffolk—Southold; flows into Great

Peconic Bay, E of Mattituck;
40°59'10"x72°30'30"
Mattituck Quad (7.5')

DEEP HOLLOW
see
WOOD HOLLOW
Source: (Sammis 104, p. 182)

DEEP POND
Physical feature
Suffolk—Riverhead; NW side of the
town, SE of Wading River;
40°56'10"x72°50'
Wading River Quad (7.5')

DEER PARK
Community
Suffolk—Babylon; E of Wyandanch,
SE of Half Hollow Hills;
40°45'30"x73°19'45"
Greenlawn Quad (7.5')

DEER RANGE PARK
see
HECKSCHER STATE PARK
Source: (Macoskey 29, p. 51)

DEER SWAMP
Physical feature—historical
Suffolk—Islip; in the Orowoc Creek
vicinity; ca. 40°43'55"x73°13'45"
Source: (Tooker 44, p. 28)
*Bay Shore East Quad (7.5')

DEERFIELD
Community
Suffolk—Southampton; N of Water
Mill; 40°56'5"x72°21'50"
Sag Harbor Quad (7.5')

DEER'S HOLE
Physical feature—pond—historical
Suffolk—Southampton; SSE of
Crooked Creek;
40°57'40"x72°17'30"
Source: (Adams 92, p. 17)
*Sag Harbor Quad (7.5')

DELAFIELD POINT
Physical feature
Suffolk—Brookhaven; N of Forge
Point, W side of Forge River, W of
Old Neck; 40°47'x72°49'20"
Moriches Quad (7.5')

DEMOCRAT POINT
Physical feature
Suffolk—Babylon; W point of Fire
Island; 40°37'30"x73°18'30"
Bay Shore West Quad (7.5')

DENNIS CREEK
see
CONGDONS CREEK
Source: (Ullitz 164, plate 13)

DENTON HILLS
Community
Suffolk—Huntington; NW of
Centerport, S of Huntington Beach;
ca. 40°53'x73°23'
Source: (Hagstrom 141, 1965, p. 19)
*Lloyd Harbor and Northport Quads
(7.5')

DENTONS MILL POND
Physical feature—historical
Kings; in the vicinity of Gowanus
Canal, W of Park Slope;
40°40'25"x73°59'50"
Source: (Field 138)
*Brooklyn Quad (7.5')

DENYSE'S FERRY
see
FORT HAMILTON
Source: (Overton 37, p. 39)

DERING HARBOR
Physical feature
Suffolk—Shelter Island; N part of
Shelter Island; 41°5'40"x72°20'35"
Greenport Quad (7.5')

DERING HARBOR
Village
Suffolk—Shelter Island; N side of
the Island, NE of Shelter Island
Heights; 41°5'35"x72°20'25"
Historical: Manhasset (Mackoskey 29,
p. 56)
Greenport Quad (7.5')

DERING POINT
Physical feature
Suffolk—Shelter Island; NW Shelter
Island, W of the village of Dering
Harbor; 41°5'42"x72°20'55"
Historical: Locust Point (Bayles 93,
p. 398)
Greenport Quad (7.5')

DEVON
Community
Suffolk—East Hampton; S of
Napeague Bay, E of Amagansett;
40°59'30"x72°6'30"
Napeague Quad (7.5')

DIAMOND SHOALS
Physical feature—marsh island
Nassau—Oyster Bay; in South Oyster
Bay, E of South Line Island, SW
corner of the town;
40°37'20"x73°28'30"
West Gilgo Beach Quad (7.5')

DICKEPECHEGANS
see
DIX HILLS
Physical feature
Source: (Tooker 44, pp. 59–60)

DICKERSON CHANNEL
Physical feature
Suffolk—Islip; in the Great South
Bay, NE of Captree Island, S of
Bay Shore; 40°40′x73°15′
Bay Shore East and Bay Shore West
Quads (7.5′)

DICKERSON CREEK
Physical feature
Suffolk—Shelter Island; S part of
Shelter Island, on West Neck
Harbor; 41°3′x72°20′20″
Greenport Quad (7.5′)

DIKER MEADOW
Physical feature—historical
Kings; in Dyker Beach Park, E of
Fort Hamilton, NW of New Utrecht
Source: (Walling 172)
*The Narrows Quad (7.5′)

DISMAL
Locality—historical
Suffolk—Southold; in the vicinity of
Greenport
Source: (Beauchamp 7, p. 211)
*Greenport Quad (7.5′)

DITCH PLAINS
Community
Suffolk—East Hampton; on
Montauk Peninsula, S of Lake
Montauk; 41°2′25″x71°55′
Montauk Point Quad (7.5′)

DIVINITY HILL
Community
Suffolk—East Hampton; SW of East
Hampton; 40°56′45″x72°12′30″
East Hampton Quad (7.5′)

DIVISION CREEK
Physical feature—historical
Suffolk—Islip; E of the mouth of
Champlin Creek, W of Quintuck
Creek, S of East Islip;
40°42′30″x73°12′
Source: (Pelletreau 38, facing p. 243)
*Bay Shore East Quad (7.5′)

DIVISION POND
Physical feature
Suffolk—Southampton; SE of
Flanders Bay; 40°53′5″x72°34′
Mattituck Quad (7.5′)

DIX HILLS
Community
Suffolk—Huntington; S-central part
of the town, SW of Commack;
40°49′x73°21′
Greenlawn Quad (7.5°)

DIX HILLS
Physical feature
Suffolk—Huntington; S-central part
of the town; 40°49′x73°21′
Historical: Dickepechegans (Tooker
44, pp. 59–60)
Variations: Dicketheyans,
Dichpechegans (Ibid.)
Greenlawn Quad (7.5′)

DOCTOR HOLE HASSOCK
Physical feature—marsh island—
historical
Queens; in Jamaica Bay, E of
Canarsie Pol, N of Christianpol

Marsh; 40°36'x73°51'50"
Source: (Brooklyn Quad, 15', 1897)
*Coney Island and Far Rockaway
Quads (7.5')

DODGES INLET
Physical feature—historical
Nassau—North Hempstead; E side of
Manhasset Bay, N of Port
Washington; 40°50'x73°42'20"
Source: (Ross 158)
*Sea Cliff Quad (7.5')

DODGES ISLAND
Physical feature—peninsula—
historical
Nassau—North Hempstead; SE of
Manorhaven, NW of Port
Washington; 40°50'5"x73°42'30"
Source: (Ross 158)
*Sea Cliff Quad (7.5')

DOMINE'S HOECK
see
LONG ISLAND CITY
Source: (Flint 26, p. 72)

DOMINIES HOOK
see
HUNTERS POINT
Source: (French 10, p. 549fn)

DOOLEY'S BAY
Physical feature—historical
Kings; in the vicinity of Dead Horse
Bay and Gerritsen Inlet;
ca. 40°35'x73°54'40"
Source: (Ross 39, p. 377)
*Coney Island Quad (7.5')

DOS UXORIS
see

DOSORIS ISLAND
Source: (Cocks 70, p. 3)

DOSORIS
Community—historical
Queens (Nassau)—Oyster Bay; S of
Dosoris Island, formerly West
Island, and West Pond;
40°53'10"x73°38'40"
Source: (Walling 172)
*Bayville Quad (7.5')

DOSORIS ISLAND
Physical feature
Nassau—Oyster Bay; NW side of the
city of Glen Cove;
40°53'30"x73°38'20"
Historical: West Island (Walling 172),
Cavalier Island (Russell 87, p. 211),
Dos Uxoris (Cocks 70, p. 3), one of
the two Matinecock Islands (Cocks
70, p. 2)
Mamaroneck Quad (7.5')

DOSORIS POND
Physical feature—inlet
Nassau—Oyster Bay; NW part of the
town, N of the city of Glen Cove;
40°53'40"x73°38'
Historical: Powell Pond (Coles 73,
p. 8)
Bayville and Mamaroneck Quads
(7.5')

DOUGHEY CREEK
Physical feature—historical
Queens; N of Jamaica Bay, E of
Bergens Creek, no longer exists,
presently part of Bergen Basin;
40°39'30"x73°48'20"
Source: (Jamaica Quad, 7.5', AMS,
1947)
*Jamaica Quad (7.5')

DOUGLASTON
Community
Queens; NE part of Queens, E of
Flushing, S of Great Neck;
40°46'10"x73°44'30"
Historical: Marathon (Ricard 86,
p. 8) and (Walling 172)
Sea Cliff Quad (7.5')

DOWNS CREEK
Physical feature
Suffolk—Southold; N of Great
Peconic Bay, W of New Suffolk;
41°00'x72°29'45"
Southold and Southampton Quads
(7.5')

DOXEYS CREEK
see
JOBS CREEK
Source: (Adams 92, p. 18)

DOXSEE NECK
Physical feature—historical
Suffolk—Southampton; E side of
Mecox Bay;
ca. 40°54'10"x72°18'35"
Source: (Adams 92, p. 29)
*Sag Harbor Quad (7.5')

DOXSEE'S COVE
see
GREAT COVE
Source: (Chace 127)

DOXSEE'S CREEK
see
OROWOC CREEK
Source: (Bayles 93, p. 213)

DRISCOLL'S POINT
see

NICOLL POINT
Source: (Cram 131, p. 31)

DROWN MEADOW BAY
see
PORT JEFFERSON HARBOR
Source: (Untitled Map 171)

DROWN'D MEADOW HARBOR
see
PORT JEFFERSON HARBOR
Source: (Burr 124) and (Smith 162)

DROWNED MEADOW
see
PORT JEFFERSON
Source: (Tooker 44, pp. 246–247)
and (Burr 124)

DROYERS DITCH
see
DYOGERS CREEK
Source: (Brooklyn Quad, 15', 1897)

DRYERS NECK
Physical feature—historical
Suffolk—Brookhaven; SW side of
Port Jefferson Harbor, the village
of Poquott occupies the neck;
40°57'10"x73°5'15"
Source: (U.S. 170, Chart No. 116,
1914). Also known as Van Brunt's
Neck (Flint 26, p. 70)
Variation: Dyer's Neck (Ibid.)
*Port Jefferson Quad (7.5')

DUCK CREEK
Physical feature
Queens; E side of Jamaica Bay,
between Duck Creek Marsh and Jo
Co Marsh; 40°37'20"x73°47'30"
Far Rockaway Quad (7.5')

DUCK CREEK MARSH
Physical feature—marsh island
Queens; E side of Jamaica Bay, N of
Jo Co Marsh; 40°37'25"x73°47'30"
Far Rockaway Quad (7.5')

DUCK CREEK POND
Physical feature—historical
Suffolk—East Hampton; E side of
Threemile Harbor, N of the
community of Threemile Harbor;
41°1'15"x72°10'50"
Source: (U.S. 167, Map T-72)
*Gardiners Island West Quad (7.5')

DUCK ISLAND
Physical feature
Suffolk—Huntington; NE side of
Northport Bay, SE of Eatons Neck;
40°55'40"x73°22'45"
Lloyd Harbor Quad (7.5')

DUCK ISLAND BLUFF
Physical feature
Suffolk—Huntington; S side of Duck
Island, NE side of Northport Bay;
40°55'30"x73°22'45"
Lloyd Harbor Quad (7.5')

DUCK ISLAND HARBOR
Physical feature
Suffolk—Huntington; NE part of
Northport Bay; 40°56'x73°23'
Northport and Lloyd Harbor Quads
(7.5')

DUCK POINT
Physical feature
Kings; S tip of Duck Point Marshes,
W side of Jamaica Bay;
40°37'x73°51'40"
Far Rockaway Quad (7.5')

DUCK POINT MARSHES
Physical feature
Kings; NW part of Jamaica Bay,
S of Ozone Park; 40°37'25"x73°51'
Jamaica and Far Rockaway Quads
(7.5')

DUCK POND
Physical feature
Suffolk—Riverhead; SW side of
town, NW of Manorville, W of
Swan Pond; 40°53'48"x72°50'10"
Wading River Quad (7.5')

DUCK POND POINT
Physical feature
Suffolk—East Hampton; N of
Mattituck; 41°2'25"x72°31'10"
Mattituck Hills Quad (7.5')

DUMPLING HILL
Physical feature
Suffolk—Huntington; N part of Dix
Hills, between Greenlawn and
Commack; 40°50'x73°19'30"
Source: (Bailey 19, vol. 1, p. 358)
*Greenlawn Quad (7.5')

DUNEWOOD
Community
Suffolk—Islip; on Fire Island, in the
vicinity of Fair Harbor;
ca. 40°38'25"x73°10'50"
Source: (Rand 154, 1977, p. 383) and
(Hagstrom 141, 1979, p. 42)
*Bay Shore East Quad (7.5')

DUNTON
Community—historical
Queens; SE of Richmond Hill, WSW
of Jamaica; ca. 40°41'45"x73°50'10"
Source: (Brooklyn Quad, 15', 1897)
*Jamaica Quad (7.5')

72

DUNTON LAKE
Physical feature
Suffolk—Brookhaven; W side of
 Bellport; 40°45'15"x72°57'50"
Bellport Quad (7.5')

DURYEA'S CREEK
see
CORNELL CREEK
Source: (Walling 172)

DUTCH KILLS
Community—historical
Queens; N of Newtown Creek;
 ca. 40°44'25"x73°56'45"
Source: (French 10, p. 549)
*Brooklyn Quad (7.5')

DUTCH KILLS
Physical feature—stream
Queens; N branch of Newtown
 Creek, SW of Sunnyside;
 40°44'20"x73°56'45"
Historical: Canapaukah (Tooker 44,
 p. 31), Kanapauka Kills, Burger
 Joris Kills (Flint 26, p. 70)
Brooklyn Quad (7.5')

DUTCH POINT
Physical feature
Nassau—Hempstead; SW tip of
 South Green Sedge, NE of
 Lawrence Marsh;
 40°35'18"x73°41'22"
Lawrence Quad (7.5')

DYER'S NECK
see
DRYERS NECK
Source: (Flint 26, p. 70)

DYKER HEIGHTS
Community
Kings; SW part of Kings, N of New
 Utrecht; 40°37'15"x74°0'50"
The Narrows Quad (7.5')

DYOGERS CREEK
Physical feature—historical
Queens; JFK Airport, NE side of
 Jamaica Bay, no longer exists;
 40°37'55"x73°46'30"
Source: (Jamaica Quad, 7.5', AMS,
 1947). Previously known as Droyers
 Ditch (Brooklyn Quad, 15', 1897)
*Jamaica Quad (7.5')

EAST AMITYVILLE
see
COPIAGUE
Source: (Bailey 19, vol. 1, p. 385)

EAST BAR
see
SHORT BEACH
Suffolk—Smithtown
Source: (Langhans 98, p. 7)

EAGLE ISLAND
Physical feature—historical
Suffolk—Islip; E of Central Islip,
 a neck formed by a branch of the
 Connetquot River, no longer exists;
 ca. 40°47′x73°10′10″
Source: (Pelletreau 38, facing p. 243)
*Central Islip Quad (7.5′)

EAGLE POINT
Physical feature
Suffolk—Southold; N of Long Beach
 Bay; 41°8′15″x72°16′45″
Orient Quad (7.5′)

EAGLES NECK POINT
Physical feature
Suffolk—Southold; NE of Long
 Beach Bay; 41°8′12″x72°15′45″
Orient Quad (7.5′)

EAST ALDER ISLAND
Physical feature
Nassau—Hempstead; E of Alder
 Island, W of Meadow Island, N of
 Jones Inlet; 40°36′x73°34′20″
Jones Inlet Quad (7.5′)

EAST BAY
Physical feature
Nassau—Hempstead; SE part of the
 town, S of Merrick and Bellmore,
 SE of Freeport; 40°38′x73°32′
Freeport Quad (7.5′)

EAST BAY
Suffolk—Brookhaven
see
MORICHES BAY
Source: (Chace 127)

EAST BEACH
Physical feature
Nassau—Oyster Bay; on Long Island
 Sound, N of Glen Cove;
 40°53′50″x73°37′30″
Bayville and Mamaroneck Quads
 (7.5′)

EAST BEACH
Physical feature
Suffolk—Brookhaven
see
CEDAR BEACH
Source: (U.S. 5, List No. 5903,
 p. 42)

EAST BEACH
Physical feature
Suffolk—Huntington; SE part of
 Lloyd Neck, on Huntington Bay;
 40°55'10"x73°25'45"
Lloyd Harbor Quad (7.5')

EAST BEACH
Physical feature
Suffolk—Islip; E part of Heckscher
 State Park, W shore of Nicoll Bay;
 40°42'20"x73°8'50"
Bay Shore East Quad (7.5')

EAST BRANCH
Physical feature
Suffolk—Islip; flows into the E side
 of Brown Creek;
 40°44'10"x73°4'30"
Source: (Sayville Quad, 7.5', 1955)
*Sayville Quad (7.5')

EAST BRANCH
Physical feature
Suffolk—Southampton; SE of
 Eastport, flows into Seatuck Cove;
 40°49'x72°43'25"
Variation: East River (Hagstrom 141,
 1979, p. 59)
Eastport Quad (7.5')

EAST BRENTWOOD
Community
Suffolk—Islip; W of Central Islip,
 SW of Hauppauge;
 40°47'30"x73°14'
Central Islip Quad (7.5')

EAST BROAD CHANNEL
Physical feature
Queens; in Jamaica Bay, W of Far
 Rockaway, extends SW from
 Winhole Channel to Beach Channel;

40°36'51"x73°48'30"
Source: (U.S. 5, List No. 8101,
 p. 13)
Historical: Broad Channel (Ibid.)
 and (Far Rockaway Quad, 7.5',
 1969)
*Far Rockaway Quad (7.5')

EAST BROOKLYN
see
WALLABOUT
Source: (French 10, p. 367)

EAST CANAL
Physical feature
Suffolk—Islip; one of 3 man-made
 canals S of Islip, on the Great
 South Bay; 40°42'30"x73°13'
Bay Shore East Quad (7.5')

EAST CHANNEL
Physical feature
Nassau—Hempstead; N of Lido
 Beach, S of Oceanside;
 40°36'x73°37'30"
Lawrence and Jones Inlet Quads
 (7.5')

EAST CHANNEL
Physical feature
Suffolk—Brookhaven; S of Nicoll
 Bay, in the Great South Bay;
 40°40'x73°8'10"
Bay Shore East Quad (7.5')

EAST CHANNEL ISLANDS
Physical feature
Nassau—Hempstead; S of Oceanside,
 E of Island Park;
 40°36'15"x73°37'50"
Lawrence Quad (7.5')

EAST COMMACK
Community
Suffolk—Smithtown; E of Commack,
W of the community of Smithtown;
ca. 40°50′27″x73°16′5″
Source: (Hagstrom 141, 1979,
pp. 36, 38)
*Greenlawn Quad (7.5′)

EAST CONNECTICUT RIVER
see
CARMANS RIVER
Source: (Tooker 44, p. 48)

EAST COVE
Physical feature
Suffolk—Brookhaven; NE part of
Bellport Bay; 40°45′55″x72°53′20″
Bellport Quad (7.5′)

EAST CREEK
Physical feature
Nassau—North Hempstead; N part
Manhasset Neck;
40°52′10″x73°42′45″
Sea Cliff Quad (7.5′)

EAST CREEK
Physical feature
Suffolk—Babylon
see
SAMPAWAMS CREEK
Source: (Rohl 103, p. 259)

EAST CREEK
Physical feature
Suffolk—Riverhead; E of South
Jamesport, NW part of Great
Peconic Bay; 40°56′10″x72°34′20″
Mattituck Quad (7.5′)

EAST CREEK
Physical feature
Suffolk—Southold; S of East
Cutchogue; 41°0′50″x72°28′15″
Southold Quad (7.5′)

EAST CROW ISLAND
Physical feature
Nassau—Hempstead; SE of Big
Crow Island, S of Cuba Island;
40°36′45″x73°31′45″
Jones Inlet Quad (7.5′)

EAST CUTCHOGUE
Community
Suffolk—Southold; NE of
Cutchogue; 41°2′15″x72°28′30″
Southold Quad (7.5′)

EAST ELMHURST
Community
Queens; NW part of Queens, SW of
Flushing Bay; 40°45′45″x73°51′45″
Flushing Quad (7.5′)

EAST FARMINGDALE
Community
Suffolk—Babylon; NE of
Farmingdale;
ca. 40°44′10″x73°25′50″
Source: (Rand 154, 1977, p. 383)
*Amityville Quad (7.5′)

EAST FIRE ISLAND
Physical feature
Suffolk—Islip; in the Great South
Bay, N of Fair Harbor, E of
Captree Island; 40°39′30″x72°11′
Historical: Hollins Island (U.S. 5,
List No. 6301, p. 30)
Bay Shore East Quad (7.5′)

EAST FLATBUSH
Community
Kings; central part of Kings;
40°39'x73°56'
Brooklyn Quad (7.5')

EAST FORT POINT
Physical feature
Suffolk—Huntington; E tip of Lloyd
Neck; 40°55'45"x73°25'45"
Lloyd Harbor Quad (7.5')

EAST FOX CREEK
Physical feature
Suffolk—Babylon; flows through the
central and E part of Cedar Island,
in the SW part of Great South Bay;
40°38'20"x73°20'30"
Bay Shore West Quad (7.5')

EAST GREENLAWN
Community
Suffolk—Huntington; E of
Greenlawn, S of Northport;
ca. 40°52'15"x73°20'55"
Source: (Hagstrom 141, 1979, p. 25)
*Greenlawn Quad (7.5')

EAST HALF HOLLOW HILLS
Community
Suffolk—Huntington; N of Deer
Park; ca. 40°47'x73°20'
Source: (Rand 154, 1977, p. 383)
*Greenlawn Quad (7.5')

EAST HAMPSTEAD
see
EAST HAMPTON
Town
Source: (Faden 136)

EAST HAMPTON
Town
Suffolk; E side of the county, on the
South Fork
Historical: East Hampstead (Faden
136)
Greenport, Sag Harbor, Gardiners
Island West, Gardiners Island East,
East Hampton, Napeague Beach,
and Montauk Point Quads (7.5')

EAST HAMPTON
Village
Suffolk—East Hampton; SW side of
the town, E of Bridgehampton,
W of Amagansett; 40°58'x72°11'30"
Historical: Maidstone (Flint 26,
p. 70)
East Hampton Quad (7.5')

EAST HAMPTON BEACH
Physical feature
Suffolk—East Hampton; SW of East
Hampton village, on the Atlantic
Ocean; 40°56'40"x72°11'45"
East Hampton Quad (7.5')

EAST HARBOR
Physical feature
Suffolk—East Hampton; SE part of
Acabonack Harbor;
41°1'25"x72°8'
Gardiners Island West Quad (7.5')

EAST HARBOR
Physical feature
Suffolk—Southold; E part of Fishers
Island; 41°17'10"x71°56'40"
Mystic Quad (7.5')

EAST HAUPPAUGE
Community
Suffolk—Smithtown; NW of Lake

Ronkonkoma, S of Saint James;
40°50'x73°9'
Central Islip Quad (7.5')

EAST HEMPSTEAD
Community
Nassau—Hempstead; in the vicinity
of Uniondale;
ca. 40°42'10"x73°36'15"
Source: (Rand 154, 1977, p. 383)
*Freeport Quad (7.5')

EAST HIGH MEADOW
Physical feature—marsh island
Queens; E side of Jamaica Bay,
NW of Jo Co Marsh;
40°37'20"x73°48'15"
Far Rockaway and Jamaica Quads
(7.5')

EAST HILLS
Village
Nassau—North Hempstead; E part
of the town, SE of Roslyn;
40°47'30"x73°38'
Sea Cliff Quad (7.5')

EAST HOLBROOK
Community
Suffolk—Islip; S of Holbrook,
SE of Long Island MacArthur
Airport; 40°46'20"x73°4'25"
Source: (Hagstrom 141, 1979, p. 50)
*Patchogue Quad (7.5')

EAST HUNTINGTON
Community
Suffolk—Huntington; N of
Huntington Station;
ca. 40°52'50"x73°24'50"
Source: (Rand 154, 1977, p. 383)
*Lloyd Harbor Quad (7.5')

EAST ISLAND
Physical feature
Nassau—Hempstead; SE of East Bay,
E of Cuba Island and Big Crow
Island; 40°37'x73°30'50"
Freeport and Jones Inlet Quads (7.5')

EAST ISLAND
Physical feature—peninsula
Nassau—Oyster Bay; N part of Glen
Cove; 40°53'55"x73°38'
Historical: One of the two
Matinecock Islands, Meutalear Island,
Woolsey's Island, Butler's Island
(Cock's 70, p. 2), Matinnecock
Island (Thompson 41, vol. 1, p.
495), Morgan Island (Coles 72,
p. 45), Presque Island, Multear
Island (Russell 87, p. 211)
Mamaroneck Quad (7.5')

EAST ISLIP
Community
Suffolk—Islip; SW of Lake
Ronkonkoma; 40°44'x73°11'
Bay Shore East Quad (7.5')

EAST JAMAICA
see
HOLLIS
Source: (Ricard 86, p. 10)

EAST LAKE RONKONKOMA
Community
Suffolk—Brookhaven; S of
Centereach;
ca. 40°49'45"x73°6'15"
Source: (Rand 154, 1977, p. 383)
*Patchogue Quad (7.5')

EAST MARION
Community
Suffolk—Southold; NE of Greenport;
41°7'30"x72°20'30"
Historical: Rocky Point (French 10,
p. 640) and (U.S. 170, Chart No.
(115, 1855), Rocco Point (Burr 124)
Greenport and Orient Quads (7.5')

EAST MARION LAKE
see
MARION LAKE
Source: (Ullitz 164, plate 12)

EAST MASSAPEQUA
Community
Nassau—Oyster Bay; E of
Massapequa Park, W of Amityville;
ca. 40°40'25"x73°26'50"
Source: (Rand 154, 1977, p. 383)
*Amityville Quad (7.5')

EAST MATTITUCK
Community
Suffolk—Southold; E of Mattituck,
NW of Cutchogue;
ca. 41°00'20"x72°31'30"
Source: (Hagstrom 141, 1979, p. 66)
*Mattituck Hills Quad (7.5')

EAST MEADOW
Community
Nassau—Hempstead; NE part of the
town, W of Levittown;
40°42'45"x73°33'20"
Freeport Quad (7.5')

EAST MEADOW
Physical feature—island
Nassau—Hempstead; N of Island
Park; 40°36'45"x73°39'30"
Lawrence Quad (7.5')

EAST MEADOW BROOK
Physical feature
Nassau—Hempstead; flows on the E
side of Uniondale and Roosevelt,
W side of East Meadow, North
Merrick and Merrick;
40°41'x73°34'30"
Freeport Quad (7.5')

EAST MEADOW POND
Physical feature
Nassau—Hempstead; E side of
Freeport, W side of Merrick;
40°39'45"x73°34'
Freeport Quad (7.5')

EAST MIDDLE ISLAND
see
YAPHANK
Source: (Thompson 41, vol. 1,
p. 440)

EAST MILL BASIN
Physical feature
Kings; W of Jamaica Bay, SE
of Flatlands; 40°36'30"x73°54'20"
Coney Island Quad (7.5')

EAST MILLPOND
Physical feature
Suffolk—Brookhaven; E of Mastic,
N of Forge River;
40°48'30"x72°49'50"
Moriches Quad (7.5')

EAST MORICHES
Community
Suffolk—Brookhaven; SE part of the
town, SW of Eastport;
40°48'20"x72°45'
Moriches Quad (7.5')

EAST NECK
Community—historical
Suffolk—Huntington; in the vicinity
of Halesite, on East Neck;
ca. 40°53'15"x73°23'45"
Source: (Macoskey 29, p. 52)
*Lloyd Harbor Quad (7.5')

EAST NECK
Physical feature
Suffolk—Huntington; N-central part
of the town, S of Huntington Bay
and Northport Bay;
40°54'x73°24'30"
Lloyd Harbor Quad (7.5')

EAST NEW YORK
Community
Kings; E side of Kings, N of
Canarsie; 40°40'10"x73°53'30"
Brooklyn and Jamaica Quads (7.5')

EAST NORTHPORT
Community
Suffolk—Huntington; E-central side
of town, NW of Commack;
40°52'x73°20'
Historical: Clay Pit (Bailey 19, vol. 1,
p. 356) and (Chace 127), Larkfield
(Macoskey 29, p. 56) and
(Northport Quad, 15', 1901),
proposed names: Genola and Fair
View (Bayles 93, p. 166)
Greenlawn Quad (7.5')

EAST NORWICH
Community
Nassau—Oyster Bay; N-central part
of the town, S of Oyster Bay;
40°51'x73°32'
Historical: Norwich (French 10,

p. 551), (Burr 125) and (Walling
172)
Hicksville Quad (7.5')

EAST PATCHOGUE
Community
Suffolk—Brookhaven; E of
Patchogue, NW of Bellport;
40°46'x73°00'
Patchogue and Bellport Quads (7.5')

EAST POINT
Physical feature
Suffolk—Southampton; on
Shinnecock Bay, S of Hampton
Bays; 40°50'45"x72°31'10"
Quogue Quad (7.5')

EAST POINT
Physical feature
Suffolk—Southold; E end of Fishers
Island; 41°17'30"x71°55'20"
Mystic Quad (7.5')

EAST POINT
Physical feature
Suffolk—Southold; on Block Island
Sound, E point of Plum Island;
41°11'25"x72°9'45"
Plum Island Quad (7.5')

EAST POND
Physical feature
Queens; on Rulers Bar Hassock in
Jamaica Bay, SW of JFK Airport;
40°37'30"x73°49'22"
Source: (U.S. 5, List No. 8101,
p. 13)
Historical: Swift Creek (Far
Rockaway and Jamaica Quads (7.5')
*Far Rockaway and Jamaica Quads
(7.5')

EAST POND
Physical feature
Suffolk—Islip; N of Oakdale, West
Brook, Middle Brook and
Rattlesnake Brook flow into East
Pond which is connected to
Connetquot River;
40°44'55"x73°8'45"
Central Islip and Bay Shore East
Quads (7.5')

EAST QUOGUE
Community
Suffolk—Southampton; W of
Shinnecock Bay; 40°50'30"x72°35'
Historical: Atlanticville, Fourth Neck
(Bayles 93, p. 318)
Quogue Quad (7.5')

EAST RIDING OF YORKSHIRE
see
YORKSHIRE
Source: (French 10, p. 544fn)

EAST RIVER
Physical feature
Queens, Kings, Bronx, New York
Counties; flows from Long Island
Sound to the Hudson River in
Upper New York Bay, forms the N
Boundary of Queens and NW
boundary of Kings;
40°47'45"x73°52'30"
Central Park and Flushing Quads
(7.5')

EAST RIVERHEAD
see
AQUEBOGUE
Community
Source: (Pelletreau 38, p. 399)

EAST ROCKAWAY
Village
Nassau—Hempstead; SW side of
town, N of Hewlett Bay, W of
Oceanside; 40°38'45"x73°40'10"
Historical: Near Rockaway (Walling
172), Clinktown (Flint 26, p. 73)
Lynbrook Quad (7.5')

EAST ROCKAWAY CHANNEL
Physical feature
Nassau—Hempstead; flows through
the E side of Oceanside into the NE
part of Hewlett Bay;
40°37'20"x73°39'40"
Lawrence and Lynbrook Quads (7.5')

EAST ROCKAWAY INLET
Physical feature
Queens, Nassau—Hempstead; SW
point of the town of Hempstead,
SE point of Queens;
40°35'40"x73°45'
Historical: Bay of Far Rockaway
(Hyde 147), Deb's Inlet (Pearsall 84,
p. 79), Hog Island Inlet (Walling
172)
Lawrence and Far Rockaway Quads
(7.5')

EAST SETAUKET
Community
Suffolk—Brookhaven; S of Setauket
Harbor, W of Port Jefferson;
40°56'30"x73°6'
Port Jefferson Quad (7.5')

EAST SHORE
Community—historical
Nassau—North Hempstead; in the
vicinity of the village of Great Neck;
ca. 40°49'x72°42'50"

Source: (Macoskey 29, p. 52)
*Sea Cliff Quad (7.5')

EAST SHOREHAM
Community
Suffolk—Brookhaven; E of
Shoreham, W of Wading River;
40°57'30"x72°53'15"
Source: (Hagstrom 141, 1979, p. 54)
*Middle Island Quad (7.5')

EAST WILLIAMSBURGH
Community—historical
Queens; NW of Fresh Pond, S of
Maspeth and Linden Hill;
ca. 40°42'45"x73°54'45"
Source: (Brooklyn Quad, 15', 1897)
*Brooklyn Quad (7.5')

EAST WILLISTON
Village
Nassau—North Hempstead; S-central
part of the town, NE of Mineola;
40°45'40"x73°38'15"
Sea Cliff Quad (7.5')

EAST WOODS
see
SYOSSET
Source: (French 10, p. 550fn)

EASTERN PARKWAY
Community
Kings; NE of Flatbush;
40°40'20"x73°56'30"
Brooklyn Quad (7.5')

EASTERN PLAIN
Physical feature
Suffolk—East Hampton; E end of
Gardiners Island, NE of Tobaccolot
Pond; 41°5'50"x72°5'
Gardiners Island East Quad (7.5')

EASTERN PLAIN POINT
Physical feature
Suffolk—East Hampton; E tip of
Gardiners Island;
41°5'50"x72°4'40"
Gardiners Island East Quad (7.5')

EASTERN SHIELD
Eight forts located on Plum Island,
Long Island, Fishers Island,
Gardiners Island and the Gull
Islands for defensive purposes
during the Second World War.
Source: (Dyson 24, p. 121)

EASTPORT
Community
Suffolk—Brookhaven, Southampton;
SE side of the town of Brookhaven,
SW side of the town of
Southampton; 40°49'30"x72°43'30"
Historical: Seatuck (Chace 127),
Moriches Station, Waterville (Bayles
93, p. 280)
Eastport Quad (7.5')

EASTSIDE
Community
Suffolk—East Hampton; S of
Acabonack Harbor;
41°00'15"x72°8'5"
Gardiners Island West Quad (7.5')

EASTVILLE
Community—historical
Suffolk—Southampton; SE side of
the village of Sag Harbor;
40°59'50"x72°29'40"
Source: (Bayles 93, p. 356). Also
known as Snooksville (Ibid.)
*Sag Harbor Quad (7.5')

EATONS MANOR
see
EATONS NECK
Physical feature
Source: (French 10, p. 636fn)

EATONS NECK
Community
Suffolk—Huntington; on Eatons
Neck, N of Northport Bay;
ca. 40°56'25"x73°24'
Source: (Hagstrom 141, 1979, p. 23)
Historical: Valley Grove (Macoskey
29, pp. 52, 63)
*Northport Quad (7.5')

EATONS NECK
Physical feature
Suffolk—Huntington; N-central part
of the town, N of Northport Bay,
E of Lloyd Neck;
40°56'30"x73°23'45"
Historical: Anendesak Neck (Tooker
44, p. 11), Eatons Manor, Gardners
Neck (French 10, p. 636fn)
Variations: Eader Neck, Eaton Neck,
Eaton's Neck (Tooker 44, p. 11)
Lloyd Harbor Quad (7.5')

EATONS NECK BASIN
Physical feature
Suffolk—Huntington; NW side of
Eatons Neck, NE side of
Huntington Bay; 40°57'x73°24'
Source: (U.S. 170, Chart No. 12365,
1979)
*Lloyd Harbor Quad (7.5')

EATONS NECK POINT
Physical feature
Suffolk—Huntington; N point of
Eatons Neck; 40°57'20"x73°24'5"
Lloyd Harbor Quad (7.5')

EBWONS NECK
Physical feature
Suffolk—Brookhaven; N of Narrow
Bay, SW side of Mastic Neck,
bounded on the W by Pattersquash
Creek; 40°45'30"x72°50'30"
Source: (Tooker 44, pp. 60, 289–290).
Also known as Rattlesnake Neck,
Snake Neck (Ibid.)
*Moriches Quad (7.5')

ECHO
see
PORT JEFFERSON STATION
Source: (Setauket Quad, 15', 1904)

ECTOR
Community—historical
Suffolk—Brookhaven; on Fireplace
Neck, SW of South Haven, in the
vicinity of the community of
Brookhaven;
ca. 40°46'15"x72°54'50"
Source: (Pelletreau 38, p. 281)
*Bellport Quad (7.5')

EDENVALE
Community—historical
Suffolk—Brookhaven; E of Bohemia;
ca. 40°45'30"x73°2'30"
Source: (Bayles 93, pp. 207, 268)
*Patchogue Quad (7.5')

EDGEMERE
Community
Queens; SE side of Queens, S of Far
Rockaway; 40°35'40"x73°46'
Historical: New Venice (Ricard 86,
p. 9)
Far Rockaway Quad (7.5')

EDGEMERE INLET
Physical feature—historical
Queens; existed W of Edgemere,
  connected with Norton Basin;
  40°35′45″x73°46′30″
Source: (Osborne 35, p. 90). Also
  known as Wave Crest Inlet
  (Osborne 36, p. 117)
*Far Rockaway Quad (7.5′)

EDGEWOOD
Community
Suffolk—Islip; SW of Brentwood,
  NE of Deer Park;
  ca. 40°46′40″x73°17′15″
Source: (Northport Quad, 15′, 1901)
  and (Hagstrom 141, 1979, pp. 29,
  40)
*Greenlawn Quad (7.5′)

EDWARDS CREEK
Physical feature—historical
Suffolk—Islip; S side of Sayville,
  W of Brown Creek;
  40°43′25″x73°5′
Source: (Pelletreau 38, facing p. 243)
*Sayville Quad (7.5′)

EDWARDS POINT
Physical feature—historical
Suffolk—Islip; on the Great South
  Bay, S of Bayport;
  40°43′45″x73°2′45″
Source: (Chace 127)
*Sayville Quad (7.5′)

EDWARDSVILLE
Community—historical
Suffolk—Brookhaven; NW of
  Patchogue, N of Blue Point;
  40°46′30″x73°2′25″
Source: (Hyde 147)
*Patchogue Quad (7.5′)

EEL CREEK
Physical feature
Nassau—Oyster Bay; E side of Cove
  Neck, flows into Cold Spring
  Harbor; 40°53′5″x73°29′30″
Source: (Lloyd Harbor Quad, 7.5′,
  AMS, 1947)
*Lloyd Harbor Quad (7.5′)

EGG ISLAND
Physical feature—marsh island
Nassau—Hempstead; NE of Deep
  Creek Meadow, NW of Jones
  Beach State Park, W of Green
  Island; 40°37′5″x73°30′50″
Jones Inlet Quad (7.5′)

EGYPT
Locality—historical
Suffolk—Riverhead; S of the
  community of Riverhead
Source: (Bailey 19, vol. 1, p. 187)
*Riverhead Quad (7.5′)

ELDA LAKE
Physical feature
Suffolk—Babylon; NW side of North
  Babylon; 40°43′30″x73°19′50″
Historical: Rod and Reel Pond
  (Babylon Quad, 15′, 1903)
Bayshore West Quad (7.5′)

ELDER ISLAND
Physical feature
Suffolk—Babylon; W side of Great
  South Bay, S of Amity Harbor;
  40°38′40″x73°23′30″
Amityville Quad (7.5′)

ELDERS POINT MARSH
Physical feature—marsh island
Kings; E side of Kings County, NW
 side of Jamaica Bay;
 40°38'x73°51'
Jamaica Quad (7.5')

ELLISON'S POINT
Community—historical
Nassau—Hempstead; in the vicinity
 of Freeport
Source: (Macoskey 29, p. 52)
*Freeport Quad (7.5')

ELLISON'S POINT
Physical feature—historical
Nassau—Hempstead; in Freeport
Source: (Verity 89, p. 202)
*Freeport Quad (7.5')

ELM POINT
Community—historical
Nassau—North Hempstead; N of
 Kings Point, NW side of Great
 Neck; 40°49'x73°45'40"
Source: (Macoskey 29, p. 52)
*Flushing Quad (7.5')

ELM POINT
Physical feature
Nassau—North Hempstead; W part
 of Great Neck, N of the village of
 Kings Point, on Long Island Sound;
 40°49'x73°45'45"
Flushing Quad (7.5')

ELMHURST
Community
Queens; SE of Jackson Heights, NE
 of Maspeth; 40°44'10"x73°53'15"
Historical: Middleburg, New Towne,
 Hastings, Newton (Ricard 86, p. 9)
Brooklyn Quad (7.5')

ELMONT
Community
Nassau—Hempstead; NW part of the
 town, S of Floral Park;
 40°42'x73°43'
Lynbrook Quad (7.5')

ELWOOD
Community
Suffolk—Huntington; E-central part
 of the town, W of Commack;
 40°50'45"x73°20'
Greenlawn Quad (7.5')

ELY BROOK
 see
ALEWIFE POND
 Source: (U.S. 67, Map T-72)

ELY CREEK
Physical feature
Suffolk—Brookhaven; flows into
 Forge River from the E, E of
 Morches; 40°47'40"x72°49'45"
Moriches Quad (7.5')

ELY'S POND
Physical feature
Suffolk—Smithtown; in Hauppauge,
 E of Veteran's Highway, N of
 Town Line Road;
 ca. 40°49'40"x73°11'50"
Source: (Langhans 98, p. 8)
*Central Islip Quad (7.5')

EMORY CREEK
Physical feature
Nassau—Hempstead; flows from W
 to E through the middle of Cow
 Meadow Preserve, SE of Freeport;
 40°37'50"x73°34'5"
Freeport Quad (7.5')

ENAUGHQUAMUCK
Locality—historical
Suffolk—Southampton; on Pikes
  Beach and Westhampton Beach, S
  shoreline of the E half of Moriches
  Bay; ca. 40°47′30″x72°43′
Source: (Tooker 44, pp. 61–62)
*Eastport Quad (7.5′)

ENDEAVOR SHOALS
Physical feature
Suffolk—East Hampton; in Block
  Island Sound, NE of Montauk
  Point; 41°6′x71°50′
Source: (U.S. 170, Chart No. 13209,
  1979)

ENGLISH KILLS
Locality—historical
see
MASPETH
  Source: (French 10, p. 549fn) and
  (Burr 125)

ENGLISH KILLS
Physical feature—creek
Kings; ENE part of Kings, flows into
  Newtown Creek, E of Williamsburg;
  40°43′x73°55′50″
Brooklyn Quad (7.5′)

EQUENDITO
see
CONEY ISLAND
  Physical feature
  Source: (Tooker 44, pp. 62–63)

ERIE BASIN
Physical feature
Kings; E side of Upper Bay, SW of
  Red Hook; 40°40′x74°1′
Source: (Hagstrom 142, 1976, p. 18)
Historical: Vandykes Mill Pond

(Field 138)
*Jersey City Quad (7.5′)

ESCALLOP POND
see
SCALLOP POND
  Source: (Bishop 122)

ESSACHIAS
see
BRICK KILN CREEK
  Source: (Tooker 44, p. 63)

EVERGREEN
see
RIDGEWOOD
  Queens
  Source: (Hagstrom 143)

EXCHANGE POINT
Physical feature
Suffolk—Southampton; SW side of
  Quantuck Bay, S of the mouth of
  Aspatuck River;
  40°48′25″x72°37′35″
Source: (Eastport Quad, 7.5′, AMS,
  1947)
*Eastport Quad (7.5′)

EXECUTION ROCKS
Physical feature
Nassau, Westchester; in Long Island
  Sound, NW of Manhasset Neck,
  W of Glen Cove;
  40°52′45″x73°44′20″
Historical: in Colonial days, named
  for the execution of murderers
  (Tuomey 49, pp. 29–30)
Mamaroneck Quad (7.5′)

Source: (Bailey 19, vol. 1, p. 355)
and (Islip Quad, 30', 1904)

FALSE CHANNEL
Physical feature
Nassau—Hempstead; E boundary of
Pettit Marsh, S of Fighting Island;
40°37'30"x73°33'35"
Freeport Quad (7.5')

FACTORY POND
Physical feature
Nassau—Oyster Bay; E of
Lattingtown, NE of Locust Valley, W
of Mill Neck; 40°53'40"x73°34'40"
Bayville Quad (7.5')

FALSE CHANNEL MEADOW
Physical feature—marsh island
Nassau—Hempstead; SE of Freeport,
S of Merrick, E of False Channel
Marsh;
40°37'40"x73°33'20"
Freeport Quad (7.5')

FAIR HARBOR
Community
Suffolk—Islip; on Fire Island, S of
Five Islands, E of Saltaire;
40°38'20"x73°11'
Bay Shore East Quad (7.5')

FALSE POINT
Physical feature
Suffolk—East Hampton; NW of
Montauk Point, NE of Lake
Montauk; 41°4'35"x71°52'5"
Montauk Point Quad (7.5')

FAIR VIEW
see
EAST NORTHPORT
Source: (Bayles 93, p. 166)

FANNING POINT
Physical feature
Suffolk—Southold; S tip of
Greenport;
41°5'30"x72°21'55"
Greenport Quad (7.5')

FAIRFIELD POND
Physical feature
Suffolk—Southampton; SE of
Bridgehampton; 40°55'x72°16'10"
Sag Harbor Quad (7.5')

FAR POND
Physical feature—inlet
Suffolk—Southampton; NE part of
Shinnecock Bay;
40°52'45"x73°27'20"
Southampton Quad (7.5')

FAIRGROUND
see
HUNTINGTON STATION

FAR ROCKAWAY
Community
Queens; SE part of Queens, SE of
Jamaica Bay; 40°36'x73°46'
Far Rockaway Quad (7.5')

FARM SHOALS
Physical feature
Suffolk—Islip; SW part of Great
South Bay, SE of Captree Island;
40°38'30"x73°12'45"
Bay Shore East Quad (7.5')

FARMERS VILLAGE
Locality—historical
Queens (Nassau)—North Hempstead
Source: (French 10, p. 550)

FARMINGDALE
Village
Nassau—Oyster Bay; E of Bethpage,
W of Wyandanch;
40°44'x73°27'15"
Historical: Hard Scrabble (Flint 26,
p. 70) and (Thompson 41, vol. 1,
inside cover map)
Amityville Quad (7.5')

FARMINGVILLE
Community
Suffolk—Brookhaven; N of
Patchogue, E of Ronkonkoma;
40°50'x73°2'
Historical: Bald Hills (Bayles 93,
p. 267)
Patchogue Quad (7.5')

FARRET'S ISLAND
see
SHELTER ISLAND
Source: (Flint 26, p. 74)

FARRINGTON NECK
see
JESSUP NECK
Source: (U.S. 167, Map T-71)

FARRINGTON POINT
Physical feature—historical
Suffolk—Southampton; E side of
Jessup Neck, formerly Farrington
Neck;
ca. 40°00'x72°22'
Source: (Chace 127)
*Greenport Quad (7.5')

FERNDALE
Community—historical
Suffolk—Islip; in the vicinity
of Central Islip
Source: (Macoskey 29, p. 52)
*Central Islip Quad (7.5')

FERRY BEACH
Physical feature
Nassau—Oyster Bay; NE shoreline
of Oak Neck, NE Oyster Bay
Harbor;
40°54'30"x73°33'
Bayville Quad (7.5')

FEVERSHAM
see
BRIDGEHAMPTON
Community
Source: (Flint 26, p. 69)

FIDDLER'S GREEN
Stagecoach stop—historical
Suffolk—Smithtown; S of Kings
Park, on the road between Head
of the River and Northport;
ca. 40°52'x73°14'35"
Source: (Langhans 98, p. 8)
*Central Islip Quad (7.5')

FIDDLETON
Community—historical
Suffolk—Brookhaven; on Fire
Island, opposite Patchogue;
ca. 40°42'30"x72°57'45"
Source: (Shaw 106, p. 48)
*Howells Point Quad (7.5')

FIER ISLANDS
see
FIRE ISLANDS
Source: (Wittlock 52, p. 165)

FIGHTING ISLAND
Physical feature
Nassau—Hempstead; SE of Freeport,
SW of Merrick;
40°38'x73°34'45"
Freeport Quad (7.5')

FILERS CREEK
Physical feature—historical
Suffolk—Shelter Island; NW of
Majors Harbor; 40°2'30"x72°17'35"
Source: (Pelletreau 38, p. 453)
*Greenport Quad (7.5')

FILERS POND
Physical feature—historical
Suffolk—Shelter Island; SE side of
the Island, NW of Majors Harbor;
41°2'35"x72°17'25"
Source: (Pelletreau 38, p. 453)
*Greenport Quad (7.5')

FINGER ISLAND
Physical feature—historical
Nassau—Hempstead; in Head of Bay,
NE of Northwest Point, SE side of
Head of Bay, no longer exists;
40°37'45"x73°45'5"
Source: (Brooklyn Quad, 15', 1897)
*Jamaica Quad (7.5')

FIRE ISLAND
Physical feature
Suffolk—Babylon, Islip, Brookhaven;
a barrier beach off the S shore of
Long Island, about 30 miles long,
extends from a point S of Babylon
on the W to Moriches Inlet on the
E, shelters Great South Bay and
part of Moriches Bay from the
Atlantic Ocean; 40°38'x73°00'
Historical: Siekrewhacky, Seal Island
(Flint 26, p. 70), Five Islands
(Thompson 41, vol. 1, p. 451),
Great Fier Island (Wittlock 52,
p. 165)
Bay Shore West, Bay Shore
East, Sayville, Howells Point,
Pattersquash Island and Moriches
Quads (7.5')

FIRE ISLAND INLET
Physical feature
Suffolk—Babylon, Islip; SW side of
Great South Bay, S of Captree
Island; 40°38'x73°17'
Historical: Great Gut, Nicoll's Gut,
and Nine Mile Gut (Thompson 41,
vol. 1, p. 451), Great Fier Island
Inlet and Ship Channel (Wittlock
52, p. 165), New Gut (Osborne 35,
p. 90), Gilgo Inlet (Tooker 44,
p. 65)
Bay Shore West Quad (7.5')

**FIRE ISLAND NATIONAL
SEASHORE**
Suffolk—Islip, Brookhaven; on Fire
Island, S of Long Island;
40°39'x73°10'
Bay Shore East and Sayville Quads
(7.5')

FIRE ISLAND PINES
Community
Suffolk—Brookhaven; on Fire Island,
 S of Bayport, SE of Sayville;
 40°40′x73°4′
Sayville Quad (7.5′)

FIRE ISLANDS
Physical feature
Suffolk—Islip; SW part of Great
 South Bay, consisting of West Fire
 Island, East Fire Island, Penny
 Island, Money Island, and the
 Hassock; 40°39′30″x73°11′
Historical: Fier Islands (Wittlock 52,
 p. 165)
Bay Shore East Quad (7.5′)

FIRE PLACE
see
BROOKHAVEN
Community
Source: (Bayles 93, p. 274)

FIRE PLACE BAY
see
PATCHOGUE BAY
Source: (Thompson 41, vol. 1,
 inside cover map)

FIRE PLACE RIVER
see
CARMANS RIVER
Source: (Thompson 41, vol. 1,
 p. 437)

FIREPLACE
Community
Suffolk—East Hampton; NE of
 Threemile Harbor, NW of
 Acabonack Harbor;
 41°2′50″x72°9′15″
Gardiners Island West Quad (7.5′)

FIREPLACE
Locality
see
SOUTH HAVEN
Source: (Flint 26, p. 70)

FIREPLACE NECK
Physical feature
Suffolk—Brookhaven; N of Bellport
 Bay; 40°45′50″x72°54′
Historical: possibly Tarman's Neck
 (Bailey 19, vol. 1, p. 279)
Bellport Quad (7.5′)

FIRST MILL POND
see
ST. JOHNS LAKE
Source: (Valentine 50, p. 98)

FIRST NECK
Physical feature
Suffolk—Southampton; S side of the
 village of Southampton;
 40°52′25″x72°24′
Source: (Pelletreau 38, p. 292)
*Shinnecock Inlet Quad (7.5′)

FIRST PURCHASE
Tract of land—historical
Nassau—Oyster Bay; in the vicinity
 of the community of Huntington;
 ca. 40°52′30″x73°25′
Source: (Bailey 18, p. 8)
*Huntington Quad (7.5′)

FISH COVE
Physical feature
Suffolk—Southampton; SE of North
 Sea Harbor, S of Little Peconic
 Bay; 40°56′10″x72°24′20″
Southampton Quad (7.5′)

FISH CREEK
Physical feature
Suffolk—Southampton; S of Speonk,
  W of Remsenberg;
  40°48′25″x72°43′30″
Source: (U.S. 170, Chart No. 12352,
  1976)
*Eastport Quad (7.5′)

FISH POND
Physical feature—historical
Suffolk—Smithtown; S of Sunken
  Meadow, no longer exists;
  ca. 40°54′15″x73°15′20″
Source: (Langhans 98, p. 8) and
  (Pelletreau 101, p. 325)
*Northport Quad (7.5′)

FISHERMANS BEACH
Physical feature
Suffolk—Southold; NW shore of
  Little Hog Neck;
  41°0′22″x72°27′20″
Southold Quad (7.5′)

FISHERS ISLAND
Community
Suffolk—Southold; W side of Fishers
  Island; 41°15′25″x72°1′25″
New London Quad (7.5′)

FISHERS ISLAND
Physical feature
Suffolk—Southold; NE side of the
  town, in Long Island Sound;
  41°16′x71°58′
Historical: Munnawtawkit (Tooker
  44, pp. 146-147), Vischers Island
  (French 10, p. 639fn), Winthrop's
  Island (Manley 30, p. 220)
New London and Mystic Quads
  (7.5′)

FISHERS ISLAND SOUND
Physical feature
Suffolk—Southold; N of Fishers
  Island, in Long Island Sound;
  41°18′x71°56′30″
New London and Mystic Quads (7.5′)

FISHERS POINT
see
NORTH BEACH
Source: (Ross 39, p. 539)

FISHKILL HASSOCKS
Physical feature—marsh islands
Kings; W side of Jamaica Bay, NW
  of Ruffle Bar; 40°36′30″x73°52′
Far Rockaway Quad (7.5′)

FISH'S POINT
Physical feature—historical
Queens; NW side of Flushing Bay,
  no longer exists due to La Guardia
  Airport; ca. 40°47′10″x73°52′15″
Source: (Tooker 44, p. 219)
*Flushing Quad (7.5′)

FISH-SHAPED PAUMANOK
see
LONG ISLAND
Source: (Coles 20, p. 97)

FIVE DUTCH TOWNS
Towns—historical
Kings; the five towns were Bushwick,
  New Utrecht, Flatlands, Brooklyn,
  and Flatbush.
Source: (Thompson 41, vol. 2, p. 159)

FIVE ISLANDS
see
FIRE ISLAND
Source: (Thompson 41, vol. 1,
p. 451)

FIVE WIGWAMS
Tract of land—historical
Suffolk—Southold; on Hashamomuk
Neck of Pipes Neck
Source: (Tooker 44, pp. 94-95)
*Southold Quad (7.5')

FLAG STATION
Railroad Station—historical
Suffolk—Brookhaven; SW of
Yaphank, E of Plainfield Station,
N of Bellport;
ca. 40°49'15"x72°57'
Source: (Hyde 147)
*Bellport Quad (7.5')

FLAGG BROOK
see
ISLAND SWAMP BROOK
Source: (Coles 73, p. 11)

FLANDERS
Community
Suffolk—Southampton; SW of Great
Peconic Bay, SW of Jamesport;
40°54'30"x72°37'30"
Mattituck and Riverhead Quads
(7.5')

FLANDERS BAY
Physical feature
Suffolk—Southampton; W extension
of Great Peconic Bay, N of
Flanders; 40°55'x72°36'
Historical: Mistaken and labelled
Little Peconic Bay (U.S. 5, List No.

5904, p. 37) and (Thompson 41,
vol. 1, inside cover map)
Mattituck Quad (7.5')

FLANDERS HILL
Physical feature
Suffolk—Southampton; S of
Flanders, W of Hampton Bays
40°52'30"x72°36'30"
Mattituck Quad (7.5')

FLAT CREEK
Physical feature
Nassau—Hempstead; SE of Bellmore,
NE side of East Bay;
40°37'30"x73°30'45"
Freeport Quad (7.5')

FLAT HAMMOCK
Physical feature—island
Suffolk—Southold; N of the W part
of Fishers Island, in Long Island
Sound; 41°17'x72°0'40"
New London Quad (7.5')

FLAT HASSOCK
Physical feature—marsh island—
historical
Queens; in Head of Bay, no longer
exists; ca. 40°38'x73°45'15"
Source: (Brooklyn Quad, 15', 1897)
*Jamaica Quad (7.5')

FLATBUSH
Community
Kings; central part of Kings;
40°39'15"x73°57'30"
Historical: Midwout, Midwood
(French 10, p. 372)
Variations: Vlachtebos, Flackebos,
Flacckebos
Brooklyn Quad (7.5')

FLATBUSH
Town—historical
Kings; central part of Kings
Source: (French 10, p. 372)
*Brooklyn Quad (7.5')

FLATBUSH PASS
Physical feature—historical
Kings; E of Gowanus Bay;
ca. 40°42'20"x73°56'30"
Source: (Luke 79, p. 128)
*Brooklyn Quad (7.5')

FLATLANDS
Community
Kings; SE part of Kings, SE of
Flatbush; 40°37'15"x73°56'
Historical: The Bay (Dilliard 23,
p. 67)
Brooklyn and Coney Island Quads
(7.5')

FLATLANDS
Town—historical
Kings; central part of Kings
Source: (French 10, p. 372fn) Also
known as New Amesfort (Ibid.) and
Amesford (Gordon 11, p. 497)

FLAX POND
Physical feature
Suffolk—Brookhaven; N side of
Crane Neck, N of Stony Brook;
40°57'45"x73°8'30"
Historical: Flax Pond Bay
(Thompson 41, vol. 1, p. 430)
Saint James Quad (7.5')

FLAX POND BAY
see
FLAX POND
Source: (Thompson 41, vol. 1,
p. 430)

FLAX POND GUT
Physical feature
Suffolk—Brookhaven; on Crane
Neck, NE side of Flax Pond,
leading into Long Island Sound;
40°58'x73°8'5"
Source: (Thompson 41, vol. 1, p. 40)
*Saint James Quad (7.5')

FLEET POINT
Physical feature
Suffolk—Babylon; S point of Great
East Neck; 40°40'15"x73°20'30"
Bay Shore West Quad (7.5')

FLEETS COVE
Physical feature
Suffolk—Huntington; NE part of
East Neck, NW of Huntington
Beach; 40°54'10"x73°23'10"
Lloyd Harbor Quad (7.5")

FLEETS NECK
Community
Suffolk—Southold; NW of
Cutchogue Harbor;
41°00'25"x72°28'
Southold Quad (7.5')

FLEETS NECK
Physical feature
Suffolk—Southold; NW of
Cutchogue Harbor;
41°00'25"x72°28'
Historical: Pequash Neck,
Goldsmith's Neck (Tooker 44,
p. 189), Quash Neck
Pelletreau 38, p. 432)
Southold Quad (7.5')

FLEETS NECK
Physical feature—historical
Suffolk—Babylon; S of the village
of Babylon; ca. 40°40'15"x73°20'
Source: (Thompson 42, p. 128)
*Bay Shore West Quad (7.5')

FLEETS POND
see
RED CREEK POND
Source: (Schmersal 105, p. 44)

FLORAL PARK
Village
Nassau—Hempstead; NW part of the
town, W of Garden City;
40°43'15"x73°42'30"
Lynbrook Quad (7.5')

FLORAL PARK CENTER
Community
Nassau—Hempstead; N of Floral
Park, W of New Hyde Park;
40°44'x73°42'30"
Source: (Hagstrom 140, 1973, p. 26)
*Lynbrook Quad (7.5')

FLOWER HILL
Village
Nassau—North Hempstead; S central
part of Manhasset Neck, SE of Port
Washington; 40°48'30"x73°41'
Sea Cliff Quad (7.5')

FLOWERFIELD
Community
Suffolk—Brookhaven; N of Lake
Grove, S of Stony Brook;
40°53'45"x73°8'
Source: (Hagstrom 141, 1979,
pp. 37, 46)
*Saint James Quad (7.5')

FLOWERFIELD
Locality—historical
Suffolk—Smithtown; NE of Saint
James, SE of Head of the Harbor;
40°53'50"x73°9'
Source: (Langhans 98, pp. 7, 18, 64)
Also known as Mill's Pond Village
(Ibid.)
*Saint James Quad (7.5')

FLOYD
Village—historical
Suffolk—Brookhaven; on Mastic
Neck, W side of Forge River, SW
of Moriches, NE of Mastic
Source: (Burr 124)
*Moriches Quad (7.5')

FLOYD POINT
Physical feature
Suffolk—Brookhaven; E point of
Forge Point, W side of Moriches
Bay; 40°45'45"x72°48'50"
Moriches Quad (7.5')

FLOYDS NECK
see
PATTERSQUASH NECK
Source: (Pelletreau 38, p. 264)

FLUSHING
Community
Queens; N part of Queens, N of
Jamaica; 40°46'x73°49'
Historical: Vlissengen, Newark, New-
warke (Ricard 86, p. 9), part of
Flushing was known as Murray
Hill (Ibid., p. 12)
Flushing Quad (7.5')

FLUSHING
Town—historical
Queens; NNE side of Queens

Source: (French 10, p. 546)
*Flushing and Jamaica Quads (7.5')

FLUSHING BAY
Physical feature
Queens; WNW part of Queens, NW
of Flushing; 40°46'40"x73°51'15"
Historical: Clinton Bay (Flint 26,
p. 71
Flushing Quad (7.5')

FLUSHING CREEK
Physical feature
Queens; flows into the S part of
Flushing Bay; 40°45'55"x73°50'30"
Flushing Quad (7.5')

FLUSHING MILL POND
see
MILL CREEK
Queens
Source: (Walling 172)

FLY ISLAND
Physical feature
Suffolk—Huntington; NW part of
Lloyd Neck; 40°56'20"x73°28'55"
Lloyd Harbor Quad (7.5')

FLYING POINT
Community
Suffolk—Southampton; E of
Southampton, W of Mecox Bay;
40°53'40"x72°21'
Sag Harbor Quad (7.5')

FOLESTONE
see
OYSTER BAY
Community
Source: (Flint 26, p. 73)

FOREST HILLS
Community
Queens; W side of Queens, NW of
Jamaica, SE of Elmhurst;
40°43'x73°51'
Historical: Whitepot or Whiteput
(Ricard 86, p. 9) and (Cram 132,
p. 111)
Jamaica Quad (7.5')

FOREST LAKE
see
LAKE RONKONKOMA
Physical feature
Source: (Thompson 41, vol. 1,
p. 448)

FOREST POND
Physical feature
Suffolk—Riverhead; W of Calverton
and Swan Pond, N of Manorville;
40°54'x72°49'10"
Wading River Quad (7.5')

FORGE
Locality—industrial site—historical
Suffolk—Riverhead; in the vicinity of
the village of Sweyze and Lake
Peconic; ca. 40°55'x72°43'45"
Source: (Yeager 114, p. 14)
*Riverhead Quad (7.5')

FORGE MILL POND
Physical feature—historical
Suffolk—Riverhead; in the Peconic
Lake vicinity;
ca. 40°55'x72°43'15"
Source: (Yeager 114, p. 14)
*Riverhead Quad (7.5')

FORGE POINT
Physical feature
Suffolk—Brookhaven; W side of
  Moriches Bay, E of Mastic Beach;
  40°46'x72°49'20"
Moriches Quad (7.5')

FORGE RIVER
Community—historical
Suffolk—Brookhaven; in the vicinity
  of Central Moriches
Source: (Macoskey 29, p. 52)
*Moriches Quad (7.5')

FORGE RIVER
Physical feature
Suffolk—Brookhaven; flows through
  Moriches into the NW side of
  Moriches Bay; 40°46'40"x72°48'50"
Historical: Wegonthotak River and
  Mastic River (Tooker 44, pp. 280,
  114), Swift Stream (Bailey 19, vol. 1,
  p. 272)
Moriches Quad (7.5')

FORKS NECK
Physical feature—historical
Suffolk—Islip; ENE of Sayville,
  bordered on the W by Brown Creek;
  40°44'50"x73°4'30"
Source: (Pelletreau 38, facing p. 243)
*Sayville Quad (7.5')

FORT DIAMOND
  see
FORT HAMILTON
  Military reservation
  Source: (French 10, p. 373fn)

FORT EATON
Military reservation—historical
Suffolk—Huntington; SW part of
  Eatons Neck; ca. 40°55'x73°24'

Source: (Ullitz 164, plate 2)
*Lloyd Harbor Quad (7.5")

FORT GREEN
Military reservation—historical
Kings—town of Williamsburg;
  N part of Fort Greene;
  40°41'55"x73°57'45"
Source: (French 10, p. 369)
*Brooklyn Quad (7.5')

FORT GREENE
Community
Kings; E of Brooklyn Heights;
  40°41'40"x73°58'
Brooklyn Quad (7.5')

FORT HAMILTON
Community
Kings; SW part of Kings, W of
  New Utrecht; 40°37'x74°2'10"
Historical: Najack Bay (Flint 26,
  p. 71)
The Narrows Quad (7.5')

FORT HAMILTON
Military reservation
Kings; SW part of Kings, W of
  New Utrecht; 40°36'30"x74°1'45"
Historical: Naieck (Bryant 55, p. 107),
  Nayack (Tooker 44, p. 155), Fort
  Diamond (French 10, p. 373fn),
  Denyse's Ferry (Overton 37, p. 98)
The Narrows Quad (7.5')

FORT HILL
Community
Suffolk—Huntington; E of
  Huntington, S of Huntington Bay;
  40°52'45"x73°24'40"
Lloyd Harbor Quad (7.5')

FORT HILL
Fort—historical
Suffolk—East Hampton; near Fort
Pond
Source: (Tooker 44, p. 143)
*Montauk Point Quad (7.5')

FORT LAFAYETTE
Fort—historical
Kings; W of Fort Hamilton, in the
Narrows; 40°36'25"x74°2'20"
Source: (Walling 172)
Jersey City Quad (7.5')

FORT NECK
Physical feature
Nassau—Oyster Bay; S part of
Massapequa and Massapequa Park;
40°39'30"x73°27'30"
Amityville Quad (7.5')

FORT NECK
Physical feature—historical
Suffolk—Southold; S of Cutchogue;
ca. 40°59'45"x72°29'40"
Source: (Tooker 44, pp. 190–191).
Also known as Old Field (Pelletreau
38, p. 433)
*Southold and Southampton Quads
(7.5')

FORT POND
Physical feature
Suffolk—East Hampton; E part of
Long Island, E of Montauk;
41°2'30"x71°57'10"
Historical: N part called
Quanuntowunk and the S part
called Konkhunganik (Tooker 44,
pp. 84–85, 203–204)
Montauk Point Quad (7.5')

FORT POND BAY
Physical feature
Suffolk—East Hampton; N of
Montauk; 41°4'x71°57'
Montauk Point Quad (7.5')

FORT ST. GEORGE
Fort—historical
Suffolk—Brookhaven
Source: (French 10, p. 634)

FORT SALONGA
Community
Suffolk—Smithtown, Huntington;
W of Sunken Meadow, E of
Northport; 40°54'45"x73°18'
Historical: Fort Slonga, Slongo
(Langhans 98, p. 8), Freshpond
(Sammis 104, p. 190)
Northport Quad (7.5')

FORT SLONGA
see
FORT SALONGA
(Langhans 98, p. 8)

FORT TERRY
Military reservation
Suffolk—Southold; NE side of Plum
Island; 41°11'x72°11'20"
Source: (Hagstrom 141, 1979, p. 73)
and (Plum Island Quad, AMS,
7.5', 1943)
*Plum Island Quad (7.5')

FORT TILDEN
Military reservation
Queens; SW Queens, E of Rockaway
Point, S of Floyd Bennett Field;
40°33'55"x73°53'15"
Coney Island Quad (7.5')

FORT TOTTEN
Military reservation
Queens; NW side of Little Neck Bay,
 NE of Flushing, N of Bayside;
 40°47'30"x73°46'45"
Flushing Quad (7.5')

FORT WRIGHT
Military reservation
Suffolk—Southold; W end of Fishers
 Island; 41°15'10'x72°2'
Source: (Ullitz 164, plate 7) and
 (Hagstrom 141, 1979, p. 21)
*New London Quad (7.5')

FOSTER MEADOWS
Locality—historical
Nassau—Hempstead; W side of town,
 W of the community of Hempstead;
 ca. 40°43'x73°43'
Source: (Burr 129)
*Lynbrook Quad (7.5')

FOSTERS CREEK
Physical feature
Suffolk—Babylon; flows through the
 S part of Babylon village, E side of
 Little East Neck;
 40°41'x73°19'50"
Bay Shore West Quad (7.5')

FOSTER'S MEADOW
Community—historical
Queens (Nassau)—Hempstead;
 presently part of S Floral Park,
 W of Hempstead;
 ca. 40°42'40"x73°43'20"
Source: (Walling 172)
*Lynbrook Quad (7.5')

FOSTERS MEADOWS
 see
ROSEDALE

Source: (Ricard 86, p. 14) and
 Hempstead Quad, 15', 1897)

FOURTH NECK
Community
 see
EAST QUOGUE
 Source: (Bayles 93, p. 318)

FOURTH NECK
Physical feature—historical
Suffolk—Southampton; W of Pine
 Neck, presently East Quogue;
 40°50'30"x73°34'45"
Source: (Tooker 44, p. 3). Also
 known as Great Fourth Neck
 (Pelletreau 38, p. 316)
*Quogue Quad (7.5')

FOX ISLAND
Physical feature—historical
Nassau—Oyster Bay; N of
 Lattingtown and Frost Creek, W of
 Oak Neck, no longer an island;
 ca. 40°54'x73°36'
Source: (Thompson 41, vol. 1, p. 51)
*Bayville Quad (7.5')

FOX POINT
Physical feature
Nassau—Oyster Bay; N part of the
 town, NE part of Lattingtown;
 40°54'30"x73°35'45"
Bayville Quad (7.5')

FOX POND
Physical feature
Suffolk—Riverhead; N of Manorville,
 between Linus and Sandy Ponds;
 40°53'30"x72°48'40"
Wading River Quad (7.5')

FOXBOROUGH
Community—historical
Nassau—Hempstead; S of Baldwin,
 W of Milburn Creek;
 ca. 40°48'45"x73°36'15"
Source: (Asher 116, p. 25)
*Freeport Quad (7.5')

FOXEN CREEK
Physical feature
Suffolk—Shelter Island; S part of
 Congdons Creek, S of Coecles Inlet;
 41°3'55"x72°18'50"
Source: (Ullitz 164, plate 13)
*Greenport Quad (7.5')

FRANCIS NECK
Physical feature—historical
Suffolk—Brookhaven; S part of
 East Patchogue; 40°45'x73°00'
Source: (Bailey 19, vol. 1, p. 269)
*Patchogue and Bellport Quads (7.5')

FRANKLIN SQUARE
Community
Nassau—Hempstead; NW side of the
 town, W of Hempstead village, S of
 New Hyde Park and Stewart Manor;
 40°42'30"x73°40'50"
Lynbrook Quad (7.5')

FRANKLINVILLE
see
LAUREL
 Source: (U.S. 167, Map T-55),
 (U.S. 170, Chart No. 115, 1855),
 (Chace 127), and (Riverhead Quad,
 15', 1903)

FRANKLINVILLE POND
see
LAUREL LAKE
 Source: (U.S. 167, Map T-55)

FREEKES MILL POND
Physical feature—historical
Kings; in the vicinity of Gowanus
 Canal, W of Park Slope;
 40°40'30"x73°59'30"
Source: (Field 138)
*Brooklyn Quad (7.5')

FREEPORT
Village
Nassau—Hempstead; central part of
 the town, E of Rockville Centre;
 40°39'30"x73°35'
Historical: Raynor South (Gordon 11,
 p. 636), Raynortown (French 10,
 p. 547fn), Raynorville, Hempstead
 South (Pelletreau 38, p. 102)
Freeport Quad (7.5')

FREEPORT CREEK
Physical feature
Nassau—Hempstead; flows along
 the E side of Freeport;
 40°37'50"x73°33'55"
Freeport Quad (7.5')

FREETOWN
Community
Suffolk—East Hampton; N of the
 village of East Hampton;
 40°58'45"x72°11'
East Hampton Quad (7.5')

FRESH CREEK
Physical feature
Kings; flows into the NW side of
 Jamaica Bay; 40°38'10"x73°52'35"
Source: (U.S. 5, List No. 8101, p. 13)
Variations: Fresh Creek Basin (Ibid.)
 and (Brooklyn Quad, 7.5', 1967),
 earlier Fresh Creek (Walling 172)
*Brooklyn Quad (7.5')

FRESH CREEK BASIN
see
FRESH CREEK
Source: (U.S. 5, List No. 8101,
p. 13)

FRESH MEADOWS
Community
Queens; central part of Queens,
W of Queens Village;
40°44'10"x73°47'30"
Jamaica Quad (7.5')

FRESH MEADOWS
Suffolk—East Hampton
see
NAPEAGUE MEADOWS
Source: (U.S. 167, Map T-60)

FRESH POND
Community
Queens; W side of Queens, N of
Ridgewood, S of Maspeth;
40°42'30"x73°54'15"
Brooklyn Quad (7.5')

FRESH POND
Community—historical
Suffolk—Smithtown, Huntington;
NW side of the town of Smithtown,
NE side of the town of Huntington;
ca. 40°55'20"x73°17'55"
Source: (Bayles 93, pp. 164–165)
*Northport Quad (7.5')

FRESH POND
Physical feature
Suffolk—East Hampton; SE of
Napeague Bay, E of Amagansett;
40°59'45"x72°7'
Napeague Beach Quad (7.5')

FRESH POND
Physical feature
Suffolk—East Hampton; in Hither
Hills State Park;
40°1'x72°1'30"
Historical: Nammoneck Lake (Ullitz
165, plate 8)
Gardiners Island East Quad (7.5')

FRESH POND
Physical feature
Suffolk—Huntington; N-central side
of Lloyd Harbor;
40°56'5"x73°27'25"
Lloyd Harbor Quad (7.5')

FRESH POND
Physical feature
Suffolk—Shelter Island; S side of
Shelter Island; 41°3'25"x72°20'15"
Greenport Quad (7.5')

FRESH POND
Physical feature
Suffolk—Southampton; SE of Little
Peconic Bay; 40°58'x72°23'30"
Southampton Quad (7.5')

FRESH POND
Physical feature—historical
Suffolk—Smithtown, Huntington;
NW side of the town of Smithtown,
NE side of the town of Huntington;
40°55'20"x73°17'50"
Source: (Tooker 44, pp. 266–268).
Also known as Cowamoke and
Unshemamuck (Ibid., pp. 53–54,
266–268), and Oshamamucks
(Pelletreau 101, p. 172)
*Northport Quad (7.5')

FRESH POND JUNCTION
Community
Queens; W side of Queens, NE of
  Ridgewood, S of Elmhurst;
  40°42'10"x73°53'30"
Brooklyn Quad (7.5')

FRESH PONDS
see
BAITING HOLLOW
Source: (Bailey 19, vol. 1, p. 184)

FRESHPOND
see
FORT SALONGA
Source: (Sammis 104, p. 190)

FRESHPOND NECK
Physical feature
Suffolk—Huntington; NE part of the
  town, E of Crab Meadow;
  40°55'5"x73°18'15"
*Northport Quad (7.5')

FRIARS HEAD
Physical feature—hill
Suffolk—Riverhead; on the Long
  Island Sound shoreline, NW of the
  community of Riverhead;
  40°58'15"x72°43'35"
Riverhead Quad (7.5')

FROST CREEK
Physical feature
Nassau—Oyster Bay; flows along
  the N side of Lattingtown;
  40°54'05"x73°36'30"
Variation: Also known as Guthries
  Creek (Cocks 70, p. 3) and (U.S. 6,
  1977, p. 201)
Bayville Quad (7.5')

FUNDY CHANNEL
Physical feature
Nassau—Hempstead; NE of Bay of
  Fundy, between Pettit Marsh and
  Jones Island; 40°37'x73°33'20"
Jones Inlet Quad (7.5')

GAINE'S POND
see
HECKSCHER PARK LAKE
Source: (Sammis 104, pp. 40–41)

GALES POND
Physical feature
Suffolk—East Hampton; S part of
Gardiners Island; 41°4′8″x72°5′45″
Gardiners Island East Quad (7.5′)

GARDEN CITY
Village
Nassau—Hempstead; N part of the
town, S of Mineola;
40°43′30″x73°39′
Lynbrook Quad (7.5′)

GARDEN CITY PARK
Community
Nassau—North Hempstead; NW of
Garden City, W of Mineola;
40°44′15″x73°40′
Lynbrook Quad (7.5′)

GARDEN CITY SOUTH
Community
Nassau—Hempstead; S of Garden
City, W of the village of Hempstead;
40°42′30″x73°39′45″
Lynbrook Quad (7.5′)

GARDINERS BAY
Physical feature
Suffolk—East Hampton, Southold;
NW of Gardiners Island, E of
Shelter Island; 41°5′x72°12′
Historical: Crommegrouw (Tooker
44, p. 175)
Gardiners Island West, Gardiners
Island East, and Plum Island Quads
(7.5′)

GARDINERS ISLAND
Physical feature
Suffolk—East Hampton; NE side of
the town, E of Shelter Island, NW
of Montauk; 41°6′x72°6′
Historical: Manchonack, The Isle of
Wight (Tooker 44, pp. 90–91)
Gardiners Island East and Gardiners
Island West Quads (7.5′)

GARDINERS NECK
see
EATONS NECK
Physical feature
Source: (French 10, p. 636fn)

GARDINERS POINT
Physical feature—island
Suffolk—East Hampton; in
Gardiners Bay, N of Gardiners
Island, SE of Plum Island;
41°8′30″x72°8′50″
Plum Island Quad (7.5′)

GARRETT LEAD
Physical feature—channel
Nassau—Hempstead; N of Reynolds
 Channel, E of Garrett Marsh, S of
 Oceanside; 40°36'15"x73°38'
Lawrence Quad (7.5')

GARRETT MARSH
Physical feature—island
Nassau—Hempstead; E of Island
 Park, NE of Long Beach;
 40°36'15"x73°38'30"
Lawrence Quad (7.5')

GARVIES POINT
Physical feature
Nassau—Oyster Bay; SW side of the
 city of Glen Cove, N of Glen Cove
 Creek; 40°51'20"x73°39'10"
Source: (Coles 72, p. 46)
Historical: Sheep Pen Point (Ibid.)
*Sea Cliff Quad (7.5')

GEMECO
see
JAMAICA
Source: (Ross 39, p. 39)

GENISSEE
Physical feature—swamp—historical
Suffolk—Southampton; NW side of
 Sag Harbor, S of Sag Harbor Cove;
 41°00'x72°18'10"
Source: (Tooker 44, pp. 63–64)
*Sag Harbor and Greenport Quads
 (7.5')

GENOLA
see
EAST NORTHPORT
Source: (Bayles 93, p. 166)

GEORGE CAKE
see
GEORGICA
Source: (Tooker 44, pp. 64–65)

GEORGES CREEK
Physical feature
Nassau—Hempstead; flows from
 Marcy Channel to Brosewere Bay,
 E of Hewlett Neck and SW of
 Hewlett Harbor;
 40°37'20"x73°41'45"
Lawrence and Lynbrook Quads (7.5')

GEORGES NECK
Physical feature
Suffolk—Brookhaven; includes East
 Setauket and Poquott;
 40°56'30"x73°5'
Source: (Bailey 19, vol. 1, p. 279)
*Port Jefferson Quad (7.5')

GEORGE'S NECK
Physical feature
Suffolk—Islip; S side of West Islip,
 between Skookwams Creek and
 Willetts Creek; 40°41'15"x73°18'20"
Historical: Go-or-go His Neck,
 Goorgo Neck, St. George's Neck,
 (Tooker 44, pp. 65–66), (Bayles 93,
 p. 209) and (Beers 117, p. 152)
*Bay Shore West Quad (7.5')

GEORGICA
Community
Suffolk—East Hampton; SW part of
 the town, NW of Apaquogue;
 40°56'40"x72°13'15"
Variations: George Cake, Georgika,
 Georgeke, Georgekea, Georgiacy,
 Georgake, Jorgke, Jorgake (Tooker
 44, pp. 64–65)
East Hampton Quad (7.5')

GEORGICA COVE
Physical feature
Suffolk—East Hampton; SW part of
the village of East Hampton, flows
into Georgica Pond;
40°56′x72°13′15″
East Hampton Quad (7.5′)

GEORGICA POND
Physical feature
Suffolk—East Hampton; SW corner
of the town of East Hampton;
40°56′x72°13′45″
East Hampton Quad (7.5′)

GERARD PARK
Community
Suffolk—East Hampton; N of
Acabonack Harbor, SE of Fireplace
and Whispering Woods;
41°2′40″x72°8′45″
Gardiners Island West Quad (7.5′)

GERMAN FLATS
Community—historical
Suffolk—Brookhaven; SE of Floyd
Point and Narrow Bay, W of
Reeves Island;
ca. 40°45′45″x72°47′15″
Source: (Beers 117, p. 161)
*Moriches Quad (7.5′)

GERMANTOWN CROSSING
Community—historical
Suffolk—Brookhaven; in the vicinity
of the community of Rocky Point
Source: (Macoskey 29, p. 53)
*Middle Island Quad (7.5′)

GERRITSEN
Community
Kings; S part of Kings, SE of

Gravesend; 40°35′30″x73°55′45″
Coney Island Quad (7.5′)

GERRITSEN CREEK
Physical feature
Kings; ENE of Gerritsen, S of
Flatlands; 40°35′45″x73°55′30″
Historical: Strom Kill (Bailey 19,
vol. 1, p. 29)
Coney Island Quad (7.5′)

GERRITSEN'S ISLAND
Community
Kings
see
RED HOOK (part of)
Source: (Ratzer 155)

GERRITSON INLET
Physical feature
Kings; S part of Kings, E of Coney
Island, Brighton Beach, and
Manhattan Beach;
40°34′45″x73°54′30″
Historical: Dead Horse Inlet (U.S.
170, Chart No. 369, 1908), Plumb
Inlet (Burr 125)
Coney Island Quad (7.5′)

GIANT BAR MARSH
Physical feature—marsh island
Queens; SW side of Jamaica Bay,
N of Seaside, S of Big Egg Marsh;
40°35′20″x73°49′40″
Far Rockaway Quad (7.5′)

GIBBONS BEND
Physical feature—shoreline—
historical
Suffolk—Shelter Island; SE side of
Shelter Island, ENE of Majors
Harbor; 41°2′30″x72°17′
Source: (Young 115, p. 28)
*Greenport Quad (7.5′)

GIBBS PATENT
Tract of land—historical
Suffolk—Islip; on Winganhauppauge
Neck, bordered on the E by
Champlin Creek and on the W by
Orowoc Creek; ca: 40°43′x73°13′
Source: (Pelletreau 38, p. 242)
*Bay Shore East Quad (7.5′)

GIBBS POND
Physical feature
Suffolk—Smithtown; NW of Lake
Ronkonkoma, E of Nesconset;
40°50′40″x73°8′25″
Source: (Langhans 98, pp. 8–9)
and (Hagstrom 141, 1979, p. 39)
*Central Islip Quad (7.5′)

GIBSON
Community
Nassau—Hempstead; N of Hewlett,
S of Valley Stream;
40°38′45″x73°42′
Source: (Hagstrom 140, 1978, p. 30)
*Lynbrook Quad (7.5′)

GIBSONS BEACH
Physical feature
Suffolk—Shelter Island; SE part of
Shelter Island; 41°2′30″x72°16′50″
Greenport Quad (7.5′)

GILGO BEACH
Community
Suffolk—Babylon; E of West Gilgo

Beach, SW part of the town;
40°37′5″x73°24′
West Gilgo Beach Quad (7.5′)

GILGO GUT
Physical feature—historical
Suffolk—Babylon; in Gilgo State
Park, formerly existed between
Cedar Island and Oak Island;
40°38′x73°19′40″
Source: (Thompson 41, vol. 1,
p. 451). Also known as Huntington
Gut (Ibid.)
*Bay Shore West Quad (7.5′)

GILGO HEADING
Physical feature—inlet
Suffolk—Babylon; SW part of the
town, E of West Gilgo Beach;
40°37′10″x73°24′10″
West Gilgo Beach Quad (7.5′)

GILGO INLET
see
FIRE ISLAND INLET
Source: (Tooker 44, p. 65)

GILGO ISLAND
Physical feature
Suffolk—Babylon; SW part of Great
South Bay, S of Amityville;
40°37′45″x73°24′30″
Amityville Quad (7.5′)

GILGO STATE PARK
Suffolk—Babylon; S half of Cedar
Island; 40°38′x73°20′30″
Bay Shore West Quad (7.5′)

GLEASON POINT
Physical feature
Suffolk—Southampton; NW point of

North Haven Peninsula in Shelter Island Sound; 41°2'5"x72°20' Greenport Quad (7.5')

GLEN COVE
City
Nassau—NW of the town of Oyster Bay, N of Sea Cliff; 40°52'x73°37'15"
Historical: Musketa Cove (Cocks 70, p. 8), Mosquito Cove (French 10, p. 550fn), Muscota, Pembroke, The Place (Flint 26, p. 71), Musquetoe Cove (Burr 125), Red Spring (Macoskey 29, p. 60) and (Hyde 147)
Bayville, Hicksville, Sea Cliff and Mamoronek Quads (7.5')

GLEN COVE
Physical feature
see
MOSQUITO COVE
Physical feature
Source: (U.S. 170, No. 366, 1879 and 1905)

GLEN COVE CREEK
Physical feature
Nassau—Oyster Bay; flows through the W part of the city of Glen Cove, into Hempstead Harbor; 40°51'20"x73°39'
Sea Cliff Quad (7.5')

GLEN HEAD
Community
Nassau—Oyster Bay; SE of Sea Cliff, S of Glen Cove, NW of Old Brookville; 40°50'x73°37'45"
Sea Cliff Quad (7.5')

GLEN OAKS
Community
Queens; NE part of Queens, NW of New Hyde Park; 40°44'30"x73°43'
Sea Cliff and Lynbrook Quads (7.5')

GLEN STREET
see
SEA CLIFF (part of)
Source: (Rand 154, 1977, p. 384)

GLENDALE
Community
Queens; W side of Queens, NW of Jamaica, SW of Forest Hills; 40°42'15"x73°52'
Jamaica and Brooklyn Quads (7.5')

GLENWOOD LANDING
Community
Nassau—Oyster Bay; S of Glen Cove and Sea Cliff, E of Hempstead Harbor; 40°49'50"x73°38'30"
Sea Cliff Quad (7.5')

GLOVER'S POND
see
ARTIST LAKE
Physical feature
Source: (Bayles 93, p. 262)

GOFF ISLAND
see
HICKS ISLAND
Source: (Chace 127)

GOFF POINT
Physical feature
Suffolk—East Hampton;
 N of Napeague Harbor;
 41°1′15″x72°3′25″
Historical: Goffs Island Point
 (Chace 127)
Gardiners Island East Quad (7.5′)

GOFFS ISLAND POINT
 see
GOFF POINT
 Source: (Chace 127)

GOING OVER
Physical feature—ford—historical
Suffolk—Smithtown; in the
 Nissequogue River, where Moriches
 Road ends and Horse Race Lane
 begins; 40°53′55″x73°12′15″)
Source: (Langhans 98, p. 9)
Variations: Old Going, Going Over
 River (Ibid.)
*Saint James Quad (7.5′)

GOLD STAR BEACH
Physical feature
Suffolk—Huntington;
 NW of the community of
 Huntington, on Huntington
 Harbor; 40°53′50″x73°25′50″
Lloyd Harbor Quad (7.5′)

GOLDEN HILL
Physical feature
Suffolk—Smithtown; a hill just N of
 Main Street in Smithtown at the
 intersection of Blydenburgh Avenue
 and Bellemeade Avenue;
 40°51′22″x73°11′25″
Source: (Langhans 98, p. 9)
*Central Islip Quad (7.5′)

GOLDFISH POND
Physical feature
Suffolk—Southampton;
 W of Bridgehampton;
 40°56′30″x72°19′50″
Historical: Austen's Pond (Adams
 92, p. 7)
Sag Harbor Quad (7.5′)

GOLDSMITH INLET
Physical feature
Suffolk—Southold; NW of Peconic,
 NE of Mattituck;
 41°3′10″x72°28′10″
Southhold Quad (7.5′)

GOLDSMITH'S NECK
 see
FLEETS NECK
 Physical feature
 Suffolk—Southold
 Source: (Tooker 44, p. 189)

GONUX
Physical feature—point of land
Suffolk—Southold; on Great
 Hog Neck
Source: (Tooker 44, p. 65)
*Southold Quad (7.5′)

GOOD GROUND
 see
HAMPTON BAYS
 Source: (U.S. 167, Map T-70),
 (Chace 127), and (Macoskey 29,
 p. 53)

GO–OR–GO HIS NECK
 see
GEORGE'S NECK
 Suffolk—Islip
 Source: (Tooker 44, pp. 65–66)
 and (Bayles 93, p. 209)

GOORGO NECK
see
GEORGE'S NECK
Suffolk—Islip
Source: (Tooker 44, pp. 65–66)

GOOSE BAY ESTATES
Community
Suffolk—Southold; in the vicinity
of the community of Southold;
ca. 41°2'35"x72°26'
Source: (Rand 154, 1977, p. 384)
*Southold Quad (7.5')

GOOSE CREEK
Physical feature
Nassau—Hempstead; in the SE part
of town, N of Jones Beach, flows
N of Green Island and S of Low
Island; 40°37'30"x73°30'
Jones Inlet and West Gilgo Beach
Quads (7.5')

GOOSE CREEK
Physical feature
Suffolk—Southampton; flows N into
Flanders Bay, E of Flanders;
40°55'x72°36'
Historical: Nobbs Creek (Tooker 44,
p. 162)
Mattituck Quad (7.5')

GOOSE CREEK
Physical feature—historical
Queens; in Jamaica Bay, N of Rulers
Bar Hassock, no longer exists;
40°38'15"x73°49'20"
Source: (Brooklyn Quad, 15', 1897)
*Jamaica Quad (7.5')

GOOSE CREEK
Physical feature—inlet
Suffolk—Southold; flows into

Southold Bay, NW of Great Hog
Neck; 41°3'x72°25'30"
Southold Quad (7.5')

GOOSE CREEK POINT
Physical feature
Suffolk—Southampton; NE of
Flanders, S of Flanders Bay;
40°55'x72°36'
Mattituck Quad (7.5')

GOOSE ISLAND
Physical feature
Suffolk—Smithtown
see
YOUNGS ISLAND
Source: (Langhans 98, p. 9)

GOOSE ISLAND
Physical feature
Suffolk—Southold; NW side of
Fishers Island, in West Harbor;
41°15'50"x72°0'30"
New London Quad (7.5')

GOOSE ISLAND
Physical feature—marsh island
Nassau—Hempstead, Oyster Bay; on
the W side of South Oyster Bay,
S of Seaford; 40°38'35"x73°29'
Amityville Quad (7.5')

GOOSE ISLAND DRAIN
Physical feature—channel
Nassau—Hempstead, Oyster Bay;
between Great Island Channel and
South Oyster Bay, N of Goose
Island, E of Seamans Island, S of
Seaford; 40°38'45"x73°29'
Amityville Quad (7.5')

GOOSE NECK
Physical feature
Suffolk—Southold; W of Great Hog
Neck, N of Little Peconic Bay;
41°2′45″x72°25′50″
Southold Quad (7.5′)

GOOSE POINT
Physical feature
Suffolk—Brookhaven; on Fire Island
in the Great South Bay, S of
Bellport; 40°43′15″x72°55′20″
Howells Point Quad (7.5′)

GOOSE POND MARSH
Physical feature—marsh island—
historical
Queens; in Jamaica Bay, presently
the S part of Rulers Bar Hassock;
40°36′40″x73°49′20″
Source: (Brooklyn Quad, 15′, 1897)
*Jamaica Quad (7.5′)

GORDON HEIGHTS
Community
Suffolk—Brookhaven; N of
Patchogue, SW of Wading River;
40°51′30″x72°58′
Bellport and Middle Island Quads
(7.5′)

GORE-IN-THE-HILLS
Locality—historical
Suffolk—Brookhaven; SE of
Yaphank, N of Middle Country
Road; ca. 40°40′45″x72°53′45″
Source: (Bailey 19, vol. 1, p. 274)
*Bellport Quad (7.5′)

GOSHEN PURCHASE
Tract of land—historical
Nassau—Oyster Bay; S of Half
Hollow Hills; ca. 40°45′x73°22′30″

Source: (Bailey 18, p. 8)
*Greenlawn Quad (7.5′)

GOULD POND
Physical feature
Suffolk—Brookhaven; N of Lake
Ronkonkoma, SW of Centereach;
40°51′x73°7′15″
Patchogue Quad (7.5′)

GOWANUS
Community—historical
Kings; E of Gowanus Bay;
ca. 40°41′x73°59′40″
Source: (French 10, p. 367)
Variations: Gouwanis, Goujanes,
Coujanes, Cojanes, Cujanes
(Tooker 44, p. 66)
*Brooklyn Quad (7.5′)

GOWANUS BAY
Physical feature
Kings; E side of Upper Bay, W side
of Kings, S of Red Hook, N of Bay
Ridge; 40°39′50″x74°1′
Jersey City Quad (7.5′)

GOWANUS CANAL
Physical feature—creek
Kings; W side of Kings, flows into
Gowanus Bay; 40°40′x74°0′15″
Variations: Kil of Gowanes (Tooker
44, p. 66)
Jersey City Quad (7.5′)

GRANT PARK
Community
Nassau—Hempstead; in the vicinity
of Hewlett
Source: (Rand 154, 1977, p. 384)
*Lynbrook Quad (7.5′)

GRASS HASSOCK
Physical feature—marsh island—
historical
Nassau—Hempstead; no longer an
island, presently in Queens, N of
Negro Bar Channel;
40°36′x73°46′20″
Source: (Brooklyn Quad, 15′, 1897)
*Far Rockaway Quad (7.5′)

GRASS HASSOCK CHANNEL
Physical feature
Queens; SE side of Jamaica Bay, SE
of Jo Co Marsh;
40°36′10″x73°47′20″
Far Rockaway Quad (7.5′)

GRASS ISLAND
Physical feature
Suffolk—Babylon; SW side of Great
South Bay, W of Captree Island;
40°39′10″x73°17′20″
Bay Shore West Quad (7.5′)

GRASS POND
Physical feature
Suffolk—Southampton; W of
Hampton Bays; 40°53′x72°33′30″
Mattituck Quad (7.5′)

GRASSY BAY
Physical feature
Queens; NE side of Jamaica Bay;
40°38′50″x73°49′45″
Jamaica Quad (7.5′)

GRASSY HOLLOW
Physical feature
Suffolk—East Hampton; E of
Northwest Harbor;
40°1′30″x72°13′30″
Gardiners Island West Quad (7.5′)

GRASSY POND
Physical feature
Suffolk—Riverhead; SE side of
town, NW of Manorville;
40°53′40″x72°50′10″
Wading River Quad (7.5′)

GRASSY POND
Physical feature
Suffolk—Smithtown; S side of the
town, W of Hauppauge;
40°49′25″x73°13′50″
Source: (Langhans 98, p. 9)
Central Islip Quad (7.5′)

GRAVELLY HILL
Physical feature
Suffolk—Smithtown; on the
Veteran's Highway, between
Commack and Hauppauge;
ca. 40°49′45″x73°15′
Source: (Langhans 98, p. 9)
*Central Islip and Greenlawn
Quads (7.5′)

GRAVERS KILL
Physical feature—historical
Kings; present site of Atlantic Basin,
no longer exists; 40°41′x74°00′45″
Source: (Ratzer 155)
*Jersey City Quad (7.5′)

GRAVESEND
Community
Kings; SW of Flatlands, E of
Bensonhurst, N of Sheepshead Bay;
40°36′30″x73°57′20″
Coney Island Quad (7.5′)

GRAVESEND
Town—historical
Kings; SE side of the county
Source: (French 10, pp. 372–373)
*Coney Island Quad (7.5 ')

GRAVESEND BAY
Physical feature
Kings; SW side of Kings, SW of
  Bensonhurst, NW of Coney Island;
  40°35 'x74°00 '
Coney Island Quad (7.5 ')

GRAVESEND NECK
Physical feature—historical
Kings; presently part of the
  communities of Sheepshead Bay and
  Gerritsen; 40°35 '15 "x73°56 '15 "
Source: (Tooker 44, pp. 110, 153).
  Also known as Massabarkem and
  Narrioch Neck (Ibid.)
*Coney Island Quad (7.5 ')

GREAT COVE
Physical feature
Suffolk—Islip; NW side of Great
  South Bay, S of Bay Shore;
  40°42 '45 "x73°14 '
Historical: Doxee's Cove (Chace 127)
Bay Shore East Quad (7.5 ')

GREAT COW HARBOR
Physical feature
see
NORTHPORT HARBOR
Source: (Bayles 93, p. 160)

GREAT COW HARBOR
Village
see
NORTHPORT
Source: (French 10, p. 636fn)

GREAT CREEK
see
GREAT NECK CREEK
Source: (Babylon Quad, 15 ', 1903)

GREAT EAST NECK
Physical feature
Suffolk—Babylon; in Great South
  Bay, SW of Babylon, SE of Linden-
  hurst; 40°40 '30 "x73°20 '30 "
Historical: Caus Cung Quaram
  and Guscomquorum (Tooker 44,
  pp. 38, 67–68)
Bay Shore West Quad (7.5 ')

GREAT FIER ISLAND
see
FIRE ISLAND
Source: (Wittlock 52, p. 165)

GREAT FIER ISLAND INLET
see
FIRE ISLAND INLET
Source: (Wittlock 52, p. 165)

GREAT FOURTH NECK
see
FOURTH NECK
Physical feature
Source: (Pelletreau 38, p. 316)

GREAT GULL ISLAND
Physical feature
Suffolk—Southold; in Long Island
  Sound, NE of Plum Island;
  41°12 '10 "x72°7 '10 "
Plum Island Quad (7.5 ')

GREAT GUT
see
FIRE ISLAND INLET
Source: (Thompson 41, vol. 1,
  p. 451)

GREAT HOG NECK
Physical feature
Suffolk—Southold; N of Little
  Peconic Bay; 41°2'30"x72°24'30"
Southold Quad (7.5')

GREAT HOG NECK SOUTH
  see
NORTH HAVEN PENINSULA
Source: (U.S. 167, Map T-71)

GREAT HOLLOW
Physical feature
Suffolk—Smithtown; W of the
  Northeast Branch;
  40°50'x73°16'30"
Source: (Langhans 98, p. 9)
*Greenlawn Quad (7.5')

GREAT ISLAND
Physical feature
Nassau—Hempstead; E of East Bay,
  S of Seaford and Seamans Island;
  40°38'x73°30'20"
Freeport and Amityville Quads (7.5')

GREAT ISLAND
Physical feature
Suffolk—Babylon; W side of Great
  South Bay, SW of Elder Island,
  N of Gilgo Beach;
  40°38'10"x73°24'
Amityville Quad (7.5')

GREAT ISLAND CHANNEL
Physical feature
Nassau—Hempstead; SE side of the
  town, S of Seaford, between
  Great Island and North Line
  Island; 40°38'10"x73°29'30"
Amityville Quad (7.5')

GREAT MEADOW
Physical feature—historical
Suffolk—Southampton; presently the
  NW side of the village of Sag
  Harbor; 41°00'x72°17'40"
Source: (Pelletreau 38, p. 324).
  Also known as Smith's Meadow
  (Ibid.)
*Sag Harbor Quad (7.5')

GREAT MEADOW
Physical feature—historical
Suffolk—Southold; W of New
  Suffolk; 40°59'30"x72°28'40"
Source: (Manley 30, p. 5)
*Southampton Quad (7.5')

GREAT NECK
Community
  see
COPIAGUE
Source: (Bailey 19, vol. 1, p. 385)

GREAT NECK
Physical feature
Nassau—North Hempstead; NW side
  of town, SW of Manhasset Neck;
  40°48'x73°45'
Historical: Madnan's Neck (Tooker
  44, p. 87), Madnack, Madnan's
  Neck, Mad Nan's Neck, Horse
  Neck (Flint 26, p. 71)
Sea Cliff and Flushing Quads (7.5')

GREAT NECK
Physical feature
Suffolk—Babylon; S-central part of
  the town, W of Copiague;
  40°39'45"x73°23'30"
Historical: Tatamuckatakis Neck
  (Tooker 44, pp. 256–257)
Amityville Quad (7.5')

GREAT NECK
Village
Nassau—North Hempstead; central
part of Great Neck;
40°49′15″x73°44′
Sea Cliff and Flushing Quads (7.5′)

GREAT NECK CREEK
Physical feature
Suffolk—Babylon; NW of Great
South Bay, E boundary of Great
Neck, W of Copiague Neck;
40°30′30″x73°22′50″
Historical: Great Creek (Babylon
Quad, 15′, 1903), Tatamuckatakis
Creek (Tooker 44, p. 256)
Variations: Yatamuntatauket,
Yatamontitaheg (Tooker 44, pp.
256-257)
Amityville Quad (7.5′)

GREAT NECK ESTATES
Village
Nassau—North Hempstead; NW side
of the town, SW of Great Neck;
40°47′15″x73°44′
Sea Cliff and Flushing Quads (7.5′)

GREAT NECK GARDENS
see
ALLENWOOD
Source: (Rand 154, 1977, p. 380)
and (Hagstrom 140, 1978, p. 24)

GREAT NECK PLAZA
Village
Nassau—North Hempstead; W side
of town, S of Great Neck and
Kensington; 40°47′20″x73°43′30″
Sea Cliff Quad (7.5′)

GREAT NORTH RIVER
Community
Suffolk—Islip; NE of Islip, E of
Islip Terrace; 40°44′40″x73°10′20″
Bay Shore East Quad (7.5′)

GREAT NOYACK
see
JESSUP NECK
Source: (Pelletreau 38, p. 292)

GREAT PATCHOGUE LAKE
Physical feature
Suffolk—Brookhaven; W side of
Patchogue; 40°46′15″x73°1′35″
Patchogue Quad (7.5′)

GREAT PECONIC BAY
Physical feature
Suffolk—Southampton, Southold;
NW of Southampton, N of
Shinnecock Bay; 40°57′x72°30′
Historical: The Crooked Bay, 'T
Cromme Gouwe, North Sea (Flint
26, pp. 72-73), Rohms Bay
(Untitled Map 171)
Southampton and Mattituck Quads
(7.5′)

GREAT PLAIN
Locality—historical
Suffolk—East Hampton; between
Ditch Plains and Hither Plains;
ca. 41°1′25″x72°56′30″
Source: (Ullitz 164, index map)
*Montauk Point Quad (7.5′)

GREAT PLAYNE
Tract of land—historical
Suffolk—Southampton; E side of
Shinnecock Bay;
ca. 40°52′30″x72°25′

Source: (Pelletreau 38, p. 292)
*Shinnecock Inlet and Sag Harbor
  Quads (7.5')

GREAT POND
Physical feature
Suffolk—East Hampton; S side of
  Gardiners Island;
41°3'35"x72°5'35"
Gardiners Island East Quad (7.5')

GREAT POND
Physical feature
Suffolk—Southold; W of the
  community of Southold;
41°4'x72°27'20"
Southold Quad (7.5')

GREAT POND
Suffolk—East Hampton
see
LAKE MONTAUK
  Source: (U.S. 167, Map T-62),
  (Montauk Quad, 15', 1904) and
  (Chace 127)

GREAT POND
Suffolk—Islip, Smithtown,
  Brookhaven
see
LAKE RONKONKOMA
  Physical feature
  Source: (Langhans 98, p. 13)

GREAT POND
Suffolk—Southampton
see
WILDWOOD LAKE
  Source: (Chace 127)

GREAT RIVER
Community
Suffolk—Islip; SW of Oakdale, W of

Nicoll Bay; 40°43'15"x73°9'30"
Historical: Conetquot, Youngsport
  (Bailey 19, vol. 1, p. 324)
Bay Shore East Quad (7.5')

GREAT RIVER
Suffolk—Babylon
see
CARLLS RIVER
  Source: (Bayles 93, p. 179)

GREAT RIVER
Suffolk—Islip
see
CONNETQUOT RIVER
  Source: (U.S. 6, 1977, p. 213)

GREAT RIVER STATION
Community
Suffolk—Islip; N of Great River,
  SW side of Connetquot River State
  Park; ca. 40°44'25"x73°10'
Source: (Hagstrom 141, 1979, p. 41)
*Bay Shore East Quad (7.5')

GREAT SOUTH BAY
Physical feature
Suffolk—Babylon, Islip,
  Brookhaven; between the S part
  of Long Island and Fire Island,
  E of South Oyster Bay, W of
  Moriches Bay;
40°41'25"x73°6'
Historical: South Sound (Ryder 159)
Amityville, Bay Shore West, Bay
  Shore East, Sayville, Howells Point,
  Pattersquash Island and Moriches
  Quads (7.5')

GREAT SOUTH BEACH
Physical feature
Suffolk—Islip, Brookhaven;
  extending about 30 miles along
  the entire S coast of Fire Island;
  40°38'25"x73°10"
Historical: Matthabanks (Tooker 44,
  p. 120), Pikes Beach, in part,
  sometimes incorrectly called Fire
  Island (U.S. 5, List No. 6301, p. 30)
Bay Shore East, Bay Shore West,
  Sayville, Howells Point,
  Pattersquash Island and Moriches
  Quads (7.5')

GREAT SWAMP
Physical feature—historical
Suffolk—Smithtown; a large swamp
  on the W side of the Nissequogue
  River in the vicinity of what is now
  called The Landing;
  ca. 40°52'x73°11'45"
Source: (Langhans 98, p. 9)
*Central Islip Quad (7.5')

GREAT TANNER NECK
  see
TANNER NECK
  Source: (Pelletreau 38, p. 341)

GREAT THATCH BED
Physical feature—island
Suffolk—Smithtown; in Stony Brook
  Harbor, S of Long Beach; ca.
  40°55'x73°10'30"
Source: (Langhans 98, p. 10)
*Saint James Quad (7.5')

GREAT THATCH BED
Physical feature—marsh island
Suffolk—Smithtown; near the
  mouth, on the E side of
  Nissequogue River;

40°53'50"x73°12'30"
Source: (Langhans 98, p. 10)
*Saint James Quad (7.5')

GREAT WEST BAY
  see
MORICHES BAY
  Source: (Burr 124)

GREAT WONUCK
  see
ONECK
  Source: (Tooker 44, p. 290)

GREEN ACRES
Community
Nassau—Hempstead; W side of the
  town, S of Valley Stream;
  40°39'30"x73°43'
Lynbrook Quad (7.5')

GREEN CREEK
Physical feature
Suffolk—Islip; flows between Sayville
  and West Sayville;
  40°43'20"x73°5'25"
Historical: Neckapauge Creek
  (Tooker 44, p. 156), Wockakawse
  River (Pelletreau 38, facing p. 243)
Sayville Quad (7.5')

GREEN GATE POND
  see
CRUIKSHANK'S POND
  Source: (Langhans 98, p. 7)

GREEN HARBOR
Physical feature
Suffolk—Brookhaven; on the Great
  South Bay, S of West Sayville;
  40°43'10"x73°5'45"

Source: (U.S. 170, Chart No. 12352, 1980)
*Sayville Quad (7.5')

GREEN HILL
Physical feature—historical
Suffolk—Southold; in Greenport, on the E side of Main Street wharf; ca. 41°6'15"x72°21'15"
Source: (Bayles 93, p. 379)
*Greenport Quad (7.5')

GREEN ISLAND
Physical feature—marsh island
Nassau—Hempstead; in Jones Beach State Park, W of South Line Island; 40°37'x73°30'15"
Jones Inlet and West Gilgo Beach Quads (7.5')

GREEN POINT
Physical feature
Queens; in Jamaica Bay, S point of Broad Creek Marsh, W of Jo Co Marsh; 40°37'x73°48'40"
Far Rockaway Quad (7.5')

GREEN POINT
Physical feature
Suffolk—Islip; on Great South Bay; S of West Sayville, E of Nicoll Bay; 40°43'5"x73°6'20"
Sayville Quad (7.5')

GREEN SEDGE POINT
Physical feature
Nassau—Hempstead; S part of town, SE point of South Green Sedge, W of Black Banks Hassock, N of Long Beach; 40°36'15"x73°41'5"
Lawrence Quad (7.5')

GREENEVILLE
see
WEST SAYVILLE
Source: (Beers 117, p. 153)

GREENFIELD
see
PARKVILLE
Source: (Ross 39, p. 326)

GREENHILL
see
GREENPORT
Source: (Stevens 40. p. 65)

GREENLAWN
Community
Suffolk—Huntington; S of Northport Bay and Centerport; 40°52'15"x73°21'45"
Historical: Old Fields (Bailey 19, vol. 1, p. 358), Cometico (Flint 26, p. 71)
Greenlawn Quad (7.5')

GREENPOINT
Community
Kings; N side of Kings, S of Long Island City; 40°43'20"x73°57'
Historical: Cherry Point (Flint 26, p. 71)
Brooklyn Quad (7.5')

GREENPORT
Village
Suffolk—Southold; N of Shelter Island, NE of the community of Southold; 41°6'x72°22'

Historical: Sterling (Bailey 19, vol. 1,
p. 157) and (French 10, p. 639fn),
Sterling Harbour (Flint 26, p. 71),
Greenhill (Stevens 40, p. 65),
The Winter Harbor (Pelletreau 38,
p. 426), The Farms (Bailey 19, vol.
1, p. 157)
Greenport Quad (7.5')

GREENPORT HARBOR
Physical feature
Suffolk—Southold; SW of
Greenport; 41°6'x72°21'30"
Greenport Quad (7.5')

GREENS NECK
Physical feature
Suffolk—Islip; S part of Sayville;
40°43'45"x73°5'
Source: (Pelletreau 38, facing p. 243)
*Sayville Quad (7.5')

GREENVALE
Community
Nassau—North Hempstead, Oyster
Bay; NE of Roslyn, E of the S
part of Hempstead Harbor;
40°48'30"x73°37'40"
Variation: North Roslyn (Rand 154,
1977, p. 384)
Sea Cliff Quad (7.5')

GREENVILLE
see
WEST SAYVILLE
Source: (Bailey 19, vol. 1, p. 332)
and (Cram 131, p. 31)

GREENWICH
see
ROOSEVELT
Source: (Walling 172)

GREENWICH POINT
see
ROOSEVELT
Source: (Walling 172)

GREENWOLDE
Community—historical
Nassau—North Hempstead; in the
vicinity of the village of Great
Neck
Source: (Macoskey 29, p. 53)
*Sea Cliff Quad (7.5')

GUEGUIS NECK
see
LITTLE NECK
Suffolk—Babylon
Source: (Tooker 44, p. 67)

GUGGENHEIM LAKES
Physical feature
Suffolk—Babylon, Islip; N of North
Babylon, W of Bay Shore;
40°44'15"x73°18'35"
Bay Shore West Quad (7.5')

GUGGENHEIM POND
Physical feature
Nassau—Oyster Bay; in the S part of
town, in the Tobay Beach Bird and
Game Sanctuary; 40°36'30"x73°27'
Historical: Salt Pond (U.S. 5, List
No. 5904, p. 37)
Variation: Gukenheimer Pond (Ibid.)
West Gilgo Beach Quad (7.5')

GUISBERT'S ISLAND
see
CONEY ISLAND

Physical feature
Source: (Manley 30, p. 32)

GULL POND
Physical feature
Suffolk—Southold; NE of Green-
port; 41°6'50"x72°21'
Greenport Quad (7.5')

GUNNING POINT
Physical feature
Suffolk—Southampton; SE part of
Moriches Bay, S of Remsenburg;
40°47'18"x72°41'3"
Eastport Quad (7.5')

GUNNUNCK'S GARDEN
Tract of land—historical
Suffolk—East Hampton; on
Montauk Peninsula, near
Gunnuncks Swamp;
ca. 41°3'30"x71°57'20"
Source: (Tooker 44, p. 67)
*Montauk Point Quad (7.5')

GUNNUNKS SWAMP
Physical feature—historical
Suffolk—East Hampton; on
Montauk Peninsula, NW side of
North Neck, SE of Culloden Point;
41°3'30'x71°57'20"
Source: (Tooker 44, p. 67)
*Montauk Point Quad (7.5')

GUNTHERVILLE
Community—historical
Kings; S side of Kings, E of
Gravesend Bay; ca.
40°35'x73°59'15"
Source: (Beers 117, pp. 31, 32)

and (Cram's 132, p. 111)
*Coney Island Quad (7.5')

GUSCOMQUORUM
see
GREAT EAST NECK
Source: (Tooker 44, pp. 67–68)

GUT
Physical feature—channel—
historical
Queens (Nassau)—Oyster Bay; the
"channel" under Bayville Bridge;
40°54'10"x73°33'
Source: (Cocks 70, p. 6)
*Bayville Quad (7.5')

GUTHRIES CREEK
see
FROST CREEK
Source: (U.S. 6, 1977, p. 201)
and (Cocks 70, p. 3)

HABERMAN
Community
Queens; NW side of Queens, SE of
  Long Island City;
  40°43′35″x73°55′20″
Brooklyn Quad (7.5′)

HAGERMAN
Community
Suffolk—Brookhaven; NW of
  Bellport, E of Patchogue;
  40°46′15″x72°58′
Bellport Quad (7.5′)

HAGONOCK
Physical feature—historical
Suffolk—Southold, S of North
  Haven Peninsula, W of Sag Harbor
  Cove; 41°00′10″x72°19′
Source: (Hyde 147)
*Greenport Quad (7.5′)

HAINES POND
Physical feature
Suffolk—Southampton; W of
  Bridgehampton, N of Scuttlehole;
  40°56′35″x72°20′
Sag Harbor Quad (7.5′)

HAINTUCK MILL POND
  see
KENTUCK POND
  Source: (Coles 75, p. 207)

HALESITE
Community
Suffolk—Huntington; SE side of
  Huntington Harbor, W of Little
  Neck, S of the village of
  Huntington Bay; 40°53′10″x73°25′
Lloyd Harbor Quad (7.5′)

HALF HOLLOW HILLS
Community
Suffolk—Huntington; SE side of the
  town; 40°46′30″x73°20′30″
Greenlawn Quad (7.5′)

HALF HOLLOW HILLS
Physical feature
Suffolk—Huntington; E of West
  Hills, SW side of town, SE of
  Melville; 40°46′30″x73°23′15″
Historical: Massakack (Tooker 44,
  pp. 110–111)
Huntington Quad (7.5′)

HALF MILE POND
  see
PINE LAKE
  Source: (Bayles 95, p. 50)

HALF NECK
Physical feature—historical
Suffolk—Babylon; part of Amity
  Harbor; 40°39′40″x73°24′15″
Source: (Bailey 19, vol. 1, pp.
  340, 359)
*Amityville Quad (7.5′)

HALFWAY HOLLOW
Physical feature—historical
Suffolk—Riverhead; E of Wading
River, SW of Wildwood State Park;
40°57'30"x72°48'45"
Source: (U.S. 170, Chart No. 115,
1855)
*Wading River Quad (7.5')

HALLETS COVE
Community
see
ASTORIA
Source: (French 10, p. 548fn)

HALLETS COVE
Physical feature
Queens, New York County; NW
part of Queens, W of Astoria;
40°46'15"x73°56'10"
Central Park Quad (7.5')

HALLETS POINT
Physical feature
Queens; in the East River, NW
side of Queens, NW of Astoria;
40°46'40"x73°56'5"
Central Park Quad (7.5')

HALLETT'S INLET
see
HALLOCK'S GUT
Source: (Osborne 36, p. 116)

HALLOCK NECK
Physical feature—historical
Suffolk—Southold; S of the
community of Southold, W of
Town Creek
Source: (Pelletreau 38, p. 422)
*Southhold Quad (7.5')

HALLOCK'S GUT
Physical feature—historical
Suffolk—Brookhaven; in Moriches
Bay, opposite Center Moriches, W
of Moriches Inlet;
40°45'25"x72°47'
Source: (Osborne 36, p. 116). Also
known as Hallett's Inlet (Ibid.)
*Moriches Quad (7.5')

HALLOCKS POINT
see
PARADISE POINT
Physical feature
Source: (U.S. 167, Map T-68)

HALLOCKS POND
Physical feature
Suffolk—Riverhead; W of
Mattituck, SW of Jacobs Hill;
40°59'25"x72°36'
Mattituck Quad (7.5')

HALLOCKVILLE
Community—historical
Suffolk—Riverhead; NE side of
town, N of Northville;
ca. 40°51'50"x72°37'20"
Source: (Wines 112, p. 10)
*Quogue Quad (7.5')

HALLS POND
Physical feature
Nassau—Hempstead; S side of
West Hempstead, in Halls Pond
Park; 40°41'15"x73°39'40"
Lynbrook Quad (7.5')

HALSEY NECK POND
Physical feature
Suffolk—Southampton; S of the
village of Southampton;

40°52′x72°24′30″
Shinnecock Inlet and Southampton
Quads (7.5′)

HALSEY'S MANOR
Tract of land—historical
Suffolk—Brookhaven; SE side of
town, S side ranges from Carmans
River to Seatuck River,
Brookhaven-Southampton line N to
Peconic River, W to near Ridge,
and S to the mouth of the Carmans
River; ca. 40°48′x72°50′
Source: (Pelletreau 38, facing p. 259)
*Bellport, Moriches, Middle Island,
and Wading River Quads (7.5′)

HALSEY'S NECK
Physical feature
Suffolk—Southampton; SW of the
village of Southampton, E of
Taylors Creek; 40°52′x72°24′40″
Source: (Pelletreau 38, p. 292)
*Shinnecock Inlet Quad (7.5′)

HAMILTON BEACH
Community
Queens; N of Jamaica Bay, SE of
Ozone Park and Howard Beach;
40°39′10″x73°49′45″
Jamaica Quad (7.5′)

HAMILTONVILLE
Community—historical
Kings; N of Fort Hamilton
Source: (Colton 130)

HAMMEL
Community
Queens; SW side of Queens, S of
Jamaica Bay, E of Holland;
40°35′10″x73°48′35″

Variations: Hammels (Brooklyn
Quad, 15′, 1897) and (Hagstrom
142, 1976, p. 25)
Far Rockaway Quad (7.5′)

HAMPTON BAYS
Community
Suffolk—Southampton; S of Great
Peconic Bay, SE of Flanders;
40°52′30″x72°31′
Historical: Good Ground (Macoskey
29, p. 53), (U.S. 167, Map T-70)
and (Chace 127)
Mattituck Quad (7.5′)

HAMPTON BEACH
Community
Suffolk—Southampton; S of
Quogue; 40°49′15″x72°35′40″
Quogue Quad (7.5′)

HAMPTON PARK
Community
Suffolk—Southampton; N of the
village of Southampton;
40°54′35″x72°23′40″
Southampton Quad (7.5′)

HAMPTON POINT
Physical feature
Suffolk—Southampton; W side of
Shinnecock Bay, SE of East
Quogue; 40°50′10″x72°34′30″
Quogue Quad (7.5′)

HAMSTAD PLAINS
see
HEMPSTEAD PLAINS
Source: (Ryder 159)

HANDS CREEK
Physical feature
Suffolk—East Hampton; W of
Threemile Harbor;
41°1′3″x72°12′20″
Gardiners Island West Quad (7.5′)

HAPAX CREEK
Physical feature
Queens; on Rockaway Neck
Source: (Tooker 44, p. 68)
Variation: Oppeax Creek (Ibid.,
p. 169)

HAPPOGS
Locality—place of springs—historical
Suffolk—Smithtown; W of
Hauppauge;
ca. 40°49′30″x73°13′10″
Source: (Pelletreau 38, p. 232)
*Central Islip Quad (7.5′)

HARBOR ACRES
Community
Nassau—Hempstead; on Manhasset
Neck, a part of Sands Point;
ca. 40°51′15″x73°42′30″
Source: (Rand 154, 1977, p. 384)
*Sea Cliff Quad (7.5′)

HARBOR GREEN
Community
Nassau—Oyster Bay; in Massapequa
Park, S of the village, E of
Biltmore Shores; 40°39′x73°27′45″
Amityville Quad (7.5′)

HARBOR HEAD
Physical feature—historical
Suffolk—Brookhaven; NE spit of
Port Jefferson Harbor;
40°58′15″x73°5′15″

Source: (Ullitz 164, plate 4)
*Port Jefferson Quad (7.5′)

HARBOR HEIGHTS PARK
Community
Suffolk—Huntington; in the vicinity
of the community of Huntington
Source: (Rand 154, 1977, p. 384)
*Huntington and Lloyd Harbor
Quads (7.5′)

HARBOR HILL
Physical feature
Nassau—North Hempstead; E side of
the town, E of Roslyn;
40°48′x73°38′15″
Sea Cliff Quad (7.5′)

HARBOR HILLS
Community
Nassau—North Hempstead; SW of
Great Neck; 40°47′25″x73°44′45″
Sea Cliff and Flushing Quads (7.5′)

HARBOR ISLE
Community
Nassau—Hempstead; W of Island
Park, N of Long Beach;
40°36′x73°40′
Lawrence Quad (7.5′)

HARBOR OF SAGG
see
SAG HARBOR
Source: (Tooker 44, pp. 221–222)

HARD SCRABBLE
Nassau-Oyster Bay
see
FARMINGDALE
Source: (Flint 26, p. 70) and
(Thompson 41, vol. 1, inside
cover map)

HARDSCRABBLE
Community
Suffolk—East Hampton; NW of
East Hampton village;
40°58′15″x72°13′15″
East Hampton Quad (7.5′)

HARNED'S POND
Physical feature
Suffolk—Smithtown; SW of San
Remo; 40°53′35″x73°13′40″
Source: (Langhan 98, p. 10)
*Saint James Quad (7.5′)

HART COVE
Physical feature
Suffolk—Brookhaven; SW of
Eastport, N side of Moriches
Bay; 40°48′x72°45′
Historical: Incorrectly named
Tuthill's Cove (U.S. 5, List No.
5904, p. 37)
Variations: Harts Cove and Hart's
Cove (Ibid.)
Eastport and Moriches Quads (7.5′)

HASHAMOMUCK BEACH
Physical feature
Suffolk—Southold; on Long Island
Sound, NE of the community of
Southold, NW of Arshamonaque;
41°5′20″x72°25′
Southold Quad (7.5′)

HASHAMOMUCK POND
Physical feature
Suffolk—Southold; W of
Arshamonaque, NW of Shelter
Island; 41°5′x72°24′30″
Southold Quad (7.5′)

HASHAMOMUK
Locality—historical
Suffolk—Southold; "The name
originally belonged to a limited
tract of land, although early settlers
so-called the whole eastern part of
the town of Southold."
Source: (Tooker 44, p. 69)

HASHAMOMUK NECK
Physical feature
Suffolk—Southold; W of the village
of Greenport;
ca. 41°5′x72°23′15″
Source: (Tooker 44, p. 69)
Variations: Hashamamuck,
Hashshamamuck, Harshamomque,
Arshamomaque (Ibid.)
*Southold Quad (7.5′)

HASSOCK CREEK
Physical feature
Queens; in Jamaica Bay, NW of
Jo Co Marsh, S of JFK Airport;
40°37′15″x73°48′
Far Rockaway Quad (7.5′)

HASTINGS
see
ELMHURST
Source: (Ricard 86, p. 9)

HAUNTS CREEK
Physical feature—channel
Nassau—Hempstead; SE part of
town, flows between East Crow
Island and Deer Creek Marsh into
Sloop Channel;
40°36′30″x73°31′30″
Jones Inlet Quad (7.5′)

HAUPPAUGE
Community
Suffolk—Smithtown, Islip; S of the
community of Smithtown, W of
Lake Ronkonkoma;
40°50′x73°11′30″
Historical: Wingan Hoppoge,
Hoppoggs, Pleasant Springs
(Langhans 98, p. 10), Wheeler's
(Tooker 44, pp. 70–71)
Central Islip Quad (7.5′)

HAUPPAUGE NECK
Tract of land—historical
Suffolk—Smithtown; N side of
Hauppauge; 40°50′x73°11′20″
Source: (Pelletreau 38, p. 218)
*Central Islip Quad (7.5′)

HAVENS' CREEK
Physical feature—historical
Suffolk—Riverhead; flowed into
Flanders Bay
Source: (Tooker 44, p. 129)
Also known as LoPontz Creek
(Ibid.)
*Mattituck Quad (7.5′)

HAVENS' LONG POINT
see
HOG CREEK POINT
Source: (Chesebrough 128)

HAVENS POINT
Physical feature
Suffolk—Brookhaven; in Moriches
Bay, S of Eastport; 40°48′x72°44′
Historical: Captain Smith's Point
(U.S. 5, List No. 5904, p. 37)
Variations: Haven Point (Ibid.)
Eastport Quad (7.5′)

HAWKINS NECK
Physical feature—historical
Suffolk—Brookhaven; S of
Moriches, E side of Forge River;
40°47′45″x72°49′30″
Source: (Havens 97, p. 92) Also
known as Hog Neck (Ibid.) and
Littleworth Neck (Pelletreau 39,
p. 263)
*Moriches Quad (7.5′)

HAWKS NEST POINT
Physical feature
Suffolk—Southold; NW side of
Fishers Island, N of West Harbor,
NE of the community of Fishers
Island; 41°16′13″x72°0′30″
New London Quad (7.5′)

HAWLEYS LAKE
Physical feature
Suffolk—Babylon; E side of the
village of Babylon;
40°41′50″x73°19′
Bay Shore West Quad (7.5′)

HAWTREE BASIN
Physical feature
Queens; on Jamaica Bay, between
Howard Beach and JFK Airport;
40°39′10″x73°49′55″
Historical: Hawtree Creek
(Brooklyn Quad, 15′, 1897)
Jamaica Quad (7.5′)

HAY BEACH POINT
Physical feature
Suffolk—Shelter Island; N point
of Shelter Island;
41°6′27″x72°20′10″
Greenport Quad (7.5′)

HAY HARBOR
Physical feature
Suffolk—Southold; NW side of
  Fishers Island;
  41°15'45"x72°1'35"
New London Quad (7.5')

HAY HOLLOW
Physical feature
Suffolk—Smithtown; NW side of
  Nesconset; 40°51°15"x73°9'30"
Source: (Langhans 98, p. 10) and
  (Pelletreau 101, p. 361)
*Central Islip Quad (7.5')

HAYGROUND
Community
Suffolk—Southampton; N of Mecox
  Bay, SW of Bridgehampton;
  40°55'30"x72°20'
Sag Harbor Quad (7.5')

HAYGROUND COVE
Physical feature
Suffolk—Southampton; N part of
  Mecox Bay, W of West Mecox;
  40°55'x72°20'10"
Sag Harbor Quad (7.5')

HAYNES POND
see
SHORTS POND
Source: (Adams 92, p. 17)

HAYWATER COVE
Physical feature
Suffolk—Southold; N of Cutchogue
  Harbor; 41°00'35"x72°27'30"
Southold Quad (7.5')

HEAD OF BAY
Physical feature
Queens, Nassau—Hempstead; NE

side of Jamaica Bay, N of Far
  Rockaway; 40°37'30"x73°46'
Historical: The Hook (Walling 172)
Lynbrook and Far Rockaway
  Quads (7.5')

HEAD OF COW NECK
Community—historical
Queens (Nassau)—Hempstead;
  located on or near Manhasset Neck
Source: (Gordon 11, p. 639)
*Sea Cliff Quad (7.5')

HEAD OF THE CREEK
see
HEADY CREEK
Source: (Pelletreau 38, p. 292)

HEAD OF THE HARBOR
Village
Suffolk—Smithtown; W of Stony
  Brook Harbor, N of Saint James;
  40°54'x73°9'30"
Historical: formerly included what is
  now Saint James (Langhans 98,
  p. 10). Formerly known as
  Sherawoug (Ibid., p. 12)
Saint James and Central Islip
  Quads (7.5')

**HEAD OF THE NISSEQUOGUE
RIVER**
Locality—historical
Suffolk—Smithtown; an area in the
  vicinity of Hauppauge;
  ca. 40°50'x73°12'
Source: (Langhans 98, p. 10)
Variations: Head of the River (Ibid.)
*Central Islip Quad (7.5')

HEAD OF THE RIVER
see
SMITHTOWN
Community
Source: (Langhans 98, p. 11)

HEAD OF THE RIVER
MILL POND
see
PHILLIPS MILLPOND
Source: (Langhans 98, p. 26)

HEAD OF THE TIDE WATER
see
SMITHTOWN
Community
Source: (Langhans 98, p. 11)

HEADY CREEK
Physical feature—inlet
Suffolk—Southampton; E of
Shinnecock Bay, W of
Southampton village;
40°52′x72°25′20″
Historical: Head of the Creek
(Pelletreau 38, p. 292)
Shinnecock Inlet Quad (7.5′)

HECKAPAUGE
see
GREEN CREEK
Source: (Tooker 44, p. 156)

HECKSCHER CANAL
Physical feature
Suffolk—Islip; SE side of Heckscher
State Park; 40°42′25″x73°11′
Bay Shore East Quad (7.5′)

HECKSCHER PARK LAKE
Physical feature
Suffolk—Huntington; N side of the
community of Huntington, S of

Huntington Harbor;
40°52′30″x73°25′20″
Source: (Sammis 104, pp. 40–42).
Also known as Still Pond, Gaine's
Ponds, Prime's Pond (Ibid.)
*Lloyd Harbor Quad (7.5′)

HECKSCHER STATE PARK
Suffolk—Islip; SE of the community
of Islip, W of Nicoll Bay;
40°42′30″x73°10′
Historical: Deer Range Park
(Macoskey 29, p. 51)
Bay Shore East Quad (7.5′)

HEDGES BANK
Physical feature
Suffolk—East Hampton; N of
Northwest Woods, NW of Three-
mile Harbor; 41°2′30″x72°13′30″
Gardiners Island West Quad (7.5′)

HEDGES CREEK
Physical feature
Suffolk—Brookhaven; flows into
Patchogue Bay, W of Bellport;
40°44′35″x72°58′
Bellport and Howells Point
Quads (7.5′)

HEEMSTEDE
see
HEMPSTEAD
Town
Source: (Pelletreau 38, p. 83)

HEER PARK
Community—historical
Suffolk—Babylon; S of Linden-
hurst, W of the community of
Little Neck; 40°40′10″x73°22′25″
Source: (Hyde 148)
*Bay Shore West Quad (7.5′)

HEIGHTS OF GUANA
Physical feature—historical
Kings; highland area running in a
NE to SW direction
Source: (Faden 136)

HEILS CREEK
Physical feature
Suffolk—Brookhaven; W of
  Seatuck Cove, S of Eastport;
  40°48'25"x72°44'
Eastport Quad (7.5')

HELL GATE
Physical feature—channel—
historical
Queens; in Grassy Bay, between
East High Meadow and Hell Gate
Marsh, no longer exists;
40°37'55"x73°47'50"
Source: (Jamaica Quad, 7.5', AMS,
1947)
*Jamaica Quad (7.5')

HELL GATE MARSH
Physical feature—historical
Queens; in Grassy Bay, N of
  East High Meadow, NE of Broad
  Creek Marsh, no longer exists;
  40°38'x73°48'
Source: (Jamaica Quad, 7.5', AMS,
1947)
*Jamaica Quad (7.5')

HEMPSTEAD
Town
Nassau; SW part of the county
Historical: Name changed to South
  Hempstead in 1784 due to the

erection of North Hempstead town,
  readopted the name of Hempstead
  in 1796 (French 10, p. 547)
Variations: Heemstede (Pelletreau 38,
  p. 83), Hamstad (Manley 30, inside
  cover map)
Lynbrook, Lawrence, Jones Inlet and
  Freeport Quads (7.5')

HEMPSTEAD
Village
Nassau—Hempstead; N-central part
  of the town, S of Garden City;
  40°42'30"x73°37'
Lynbrook and Freeport Quads (7.5')

HEMPSTEAD BAY
Physical feature
Nassau—Hempstead; S of Merrick,
  E of Merrick Bay, N of Big Crow
  Island; 40°38'40"x73°32'30"
Source: (Hagstrom 140, 1978, p. 45)
*Freeport Quad (7.5')

HEMPSTEAD BAY
Physical feature
Nassau—North Hempstead, Oyster
  Bay; E of Manhasset Neck, W of
  Glen Cove; ca. 40°51'30"x73°40'
Source: (Hagstrom 140, 1978, p. 23)
*Sea Cliff Quad (7.5')

HEMPSTEAD BRANCH
  see
MINEOLA
  Source: (Coles 20, p. 97)

HEMPSTEAD GARDENS
Community
Nassau—Hempstead; SW of the

village of Hempstead, N of
Rockville Center;
40°41′45″x73°38′45″
Lynbrook Quad (7.5′)

HEMPSTEAD HARBOR
Physical feature
Nassau—North Hempstead, Oyster
Bay; NE side of the town of North
Hempstead, E of Manhasset Neck;
40°50′x73°39′15″
Source: (Hagstrom 140, 1978,
p. 45)
Historical: Mathagarratson's Bay
(Flint 26, p. 130)
*Sea Cliff Quad (7.5′)

HEMPSTEAD HARBOR
Village
see
ROSLYN
Source: (French 10, p. 550fn)

HEMPSTEAD LAKE
Physical feature
Nassau—Hempstead; W-central part
of the town, in Hempstead Lake
State Park; 40°40′30″x73°38′45″
Historical: Hempstead Reservoir
(Hempstead Quad, 15′, 1897)
Lynbrook Quad (7.5′)

**HEMPSTEAD LAKE STATE
PARK**
Nassau—Hempstead; S of the village
of Hempstead, N of Rockville
Centre, W of Lakeview;
40°41′x73°38′30″
Lynbrook Quad (7.5′)

HEMPSTEAD PLAINS
Locality—historical
Queens (Nassau)—Hempstead,
Oyster Bay; central part of
Hempstead town, N of Hempstead
and Jerusalem (Wantagh), S of
Success, Herricks and Jericho,
covering the EW width of the
town and across the Huntington-
Oyster Bay boundary
Source: (Burr 125). Also known as
Salisbury Plains (Manley 30, p. 181)
Variations: Hamstad Plains
(Ryder 159)
*Amityville, Freeport, Hicksville and
Huntington Quads (7.5′)

HEMPSTEAD POND
see
SOUTH POND
Source: (Hempstead Quad,
15′, 1897)

HEMPSTEAD RESERVOIR
see
HEMPSTEAD LAKE
Source: (Hempstead Quad,
15′, 1897)

HEMPSTEAD SOUTH
see
FREEPORT
Source: (Pelletreau 38, p. 102)

HENDRICK'S REEF
Physical feature—historical
Kings; within the vicinity of
Fort Hamilton, thirty acres of land

covered by water;
ca. 40°36'15"x74°2'
Source: (Thompson 41, vol. 2,
p. 196)
*The Narrows Quad (7.5')

HENDRICKSON'S PURCHASE
see
THE RIM OF WOODS
PURCHASE
Source: (Gibbs 78, p. 65)

HENDRIX CREEK
Physical feature
Kings; flows into the NW side of
Jamaica Bay, S of East New York;
40°38'50"x73°52'25"
Historical: Second Creek (Walling
172)
Brooklyn and Jamaica Quads (7.5')

HENRYS HOLLOW
Physical feature
Suffolk—Southampton; NE of East
Quogue; 40°52'10"x72°34'20"
Quogue Quad (7.5')

HERMITAGE
see
PECONIC
Source: (Bayles 93, p. 372),
(French 10, p. 640) and (Chace 127)

HERRICKS
Community
Nassau—North Hempstead; S-central
part of the town, NW of Mineola;
40°45'20"x73°40'
Sea Cliff Quad (7.5')

HERRICKS POND
Physical feature
Nassau—North Hempstead; NE side
of Herricks; 40°45'35"x73°39'35"
Sea Cliff Quad (7.5')

HET STEENRAAP
Tract of land—historical
Kings; N of Flatbush, formerly the
N part of the town of Flatbush;
ca. 40°39'30"x73°57'30"
Source: (Dilliard 23, p. 74)
*Brooklyn Quad (7.5')

HEWLETT
Community
Nassau—Hempstead; W side of the
town of Hempstead, E of
Woodmere, SW of Lynbrook;
40°38'35"x73°42'
Historical: Upper Rockaway (Wexler
90, p. 240)
Lynbrook Quad (7.5')

HEWLETT BAY
Physical feature
Nassau—Hempstead; SW part of the
town, S of East Rockaway;
40°37'30"x73°40'30"
Lawrence and Lynbrook Quads (7.5')

HEWLETT BAY PARK
Village
Nassau—Hempstead; SW part of the
town, W of Oceanside, E of
Woodmere; 40°38'x73°41'30"
Lynbrook Quad (7.5')

HEWLETT HARBOR
Village
Nassau—Hempstead; SW part of the
town, SW of East Rockaway, N of
Hewlett Bay; 40°38'10"x73°41'
Lynbrook Quad (7.5')

HEWLETT HASSOCK
Physical feature—marsh island
Nassau—Hempstead; S part of
Hewlett Bay, N of Harbor Isle;
40°37'15"x73°40'20"
Lawrence Quad (7.5')

HEWLETT NECK
Physical feature
Nassau—Hempstead; SW part of the
town, W of Hewlett Bay, E of
Cedarhurst; 40°37'15"x73°42'
Lynbrook and Lawrence Quads
(7.5')

HEWLETT NECK
Village
Nassau—Hempstead; SW part of the
town, W of Hewlett Bay, E of
Cedarhurst; 40°37'15"x73°42'
Lynbrook and Lawrence Quads
(7.5')

HEWLETT POINT
Physical feature
Nassau—North Hempstead; N point
of Great Neck, on Long Island
Sound; 40°50'15"x73°45'15"
Flushing Quad (7.5')

HEWLETTS ISLAND
see
RIKERS ISLAND
Source: (French 10, p. 548fn)

HICKS BEACH
Physical feature
Nassau—Hempstead; in Lawrence,
S part of Lawrence Marsh, on
Reynolds Channel;
40°35'30"x73°42'
Lawrence Quad (7.5')

HICKS ISLAND
Physical feature
Suffolk—East Hampton; N side of
Napeague Harbor; 41°1'x72°3'40"
Historical: Goff Island (Chace 127)
Gardiners Island East Quad (7.5')

HICKSVILLE
Community
Nassau—Oyster Bay; W-central part
of the town, N of Levittown;
40°46'x73°31'30"
Historical: Kuhl (Macoskey 29, p. 55)
Hicksville, Freeport and Huntington
Quads (7.5')

HIGH HILL
Physical feature
Suffolk—Huntington; W-central
part of the town, in the West Hills;
40°48'55"x73°25'30"
Historical: Oakley's Hill and Jayne's
Hill (Manley 30, p. 167)
Huntington Quad (7.5')

HIGH HILL CREEK OUTLET
see
ZACH'S INLET
Source: (Osborne 36, p. 116)

HIGH MEADOW
Physical feature
Nassau—Hempstead; N of Alder
Island, W of the Bay of Fundy,
SE of Middle Bay;

40°36′30″x73°35″
Jones Inlet Quad (7.5′)

HIGHLAND OF INVERCAULD
Community—historical
Suffolk—Huntington; E of the
  community of Huntington, S of
  Halesite
Source: (Ullitz 164, plate 1)
*Huntington Quad (7.5′)

HILL'S POINT
Physical feature—historical
Suffolk—Southold; on Shelter Island,
  W side of Shelter Island Heights;
  41°5′x72°21′45″
Source: (U.S. 167, Map T-69)
*Greenport Quad (7.5′)

HILLSIDE
Community
Queens; NE of Jamaica, E of
  Forest Hills, SE of Queens Village;
  40°42′15″x73°47′15″
Historical: Willow Tree (Ricard 86,
  p. 10) and (French 10, p. 548)
Jamaica Quad (7.5′)

HILLSIDE HEIGHTS
Community
Nassau—North Hempstead; in the
  vicinity of Hillside Manor;
  ca. 40°44′20″x73°40′50″
Source: (Rand 15, 1979, p. 385)
*Lynbrook Quad (7.5′)

HILLSIDE MANOR
Community
Nassau—North Hempstead; NE of
  New Hyde Park, W of Mineola;
  40°44′20″x73°40′50″
Source: (Rand 154, 1979, p. 385)
*Lynbrook Quad (7.5′)

HINGLETOWN
Community—historical
Nassau—Hempstead; NW side of
  Roosevelt, E of South Hempstead;
  40°41′x73°36′20″
Source: (Metz 82, p. 89)
*Freeport Quad (7.5′)

HINSDALE
Community—prospective village—
  historical
Queens; in Flushing (town)
Source: (Beers 117, p. 58)
*Flushing Quad (7.5′)

HITHER BROOK
Physical feature—historical
Suffolk—Smithtown; in Head of the
  Harbor, Three Sisters Hollow, E of
  the S part of Stony Brook Harbor;
  ca. 40°54′x73°10′5″
Source: (Langhans 98, p. 11),
  (Munsell 99, p. 19) and (Pelletreau
  101, p. 89)
*Saint James Quad (7.5′)

HITHER HILLS
Physical feature
Suffolk—East Hampton; SE of
  Napeague Bay, W of Montauk;
  41°2′x72°00′
Montauk Point and Gardiners
  Island East Quads (7.5′)

HITHER HILLS STATE PARK
Suffolk—East Hampton; W of Mon-
  tauk; 41°2′x72°00′
Montauk Point and Gardiners
  Island East Quads (7.5′)

HITHER PLAINS
Physical feature
Suffolk—East Hampton; SE of
   Hither Hills; S of Fort Pond Bay;
   ca. 41°1′45″x71°58′
Montauk Point Quad (7.5′)

HOBART BEACH
Physical feature
Suffolk—Huntington; SW shore of
   Eatons Neck, E side of Huntington
   Bay; 40°55′45″x73°24′15″
Lloyd Harbor Quad (7.5′)

HOCUM NECK
see
SEQUATOGUE NECK
Source: (Tooker 44, p. 71–72)

HOG CREEK
Physical feature
Suffolk—East Hampton; W of
   Whispering Woods and Fireplace,
   NE of Threemile Habor;
   41°3′x72°10′
Gardiners Island West Quad (7.5′)

HOG CREEK POINT
Physical feature
Suffolk—East Hampton; N of
   Whispering Woods, NE of Three-
   mile Harbor; 41°3′13″x72°9′40″
Historical: Haven's Long Point
   (Chesebrough 128)
Gardiners Island West Quad (7.5′)

HOG ISLAND
Nassau—Oyster Bay
see
CENTRE ISLAND
Physical feature
Source: (French 10, p. 550fn)

HOG ISLAND
Physical feature—historical
Nassau—Hempstead; N of Long
   Beach; ca. 40°36′x73°41′
Source: (Osborne 35, p. 116)
*Lawrence Quad (7.5′)

HOG ISLAND CHANNEL
Physical feature
Nassau—Hempstead; S part of town,
   N of Island Park and Harbor Isle,
   S of West Meadow;
   40°36′25″x73°39′40″
Lawrence Quad (7.5′)

HOG ISLAND INLET
see
EAST ROCKAWAY INLET
Source: (Walling 172)

HOG NECK
Nassau—Oyster Bay
see
OAK NECK
Source: (Romans 157)

HOG NECK
Suffolk—Brookhaven
see
HAWKINS NECK
Source: (Havens 97, p. 92)

HOG NECK
Suffolk—Southampton
see
NORTH HAVEN PENINSULA
Source: (Chace 127)

HOG NECK BAY
Physical feature
Suffolk—Southold; NW side
   of Little Peconic Bay;

41°2′x72°26′10″
Historical: South Harbor
(Bayles 93, p. 378)
Southold Quad (7.5′)

HOG POND
Physical feature—historical
Suffolk—Smithtown; located at
Indian Head;
ca. 40°52′20″x73°15′30″
Source: (Langhans 98, p. 11)
*Greenlawn Quad (7.5′)

HOGGENOCH
see
LITTLE HOG NECK
Source (Tooker 44, p. 72)

HOGGS NECK
Physical feature—historical
Suffolk—Brookhaven; E of
Mastic River (Forge River)
Source: (Tooker 44, p. 198)
*Moriches Quad (7.5′)

HOG'S LEG
Physical feature—point of land—
historical
Suffolk—Smithtown; on the Nisse-
quogue River, located N of the
Landing Bridge
Source: (Langhans 98, p. 11)

HOHOSBOCO CREEK
Physical feature—historical
Queens; S of Newtown, flowed
into Flushing Creek;
ca. 40°44′15″x73°53′
Source: (Tooker 44, p. 72)
*Flushing Quad (7.5′)

HOLBROOK
Community
Suffolk—Islip, Brookhaven; N of
Sayville; SE of Ronkonkoma;
40°48′40″x73°5′
Historical: Old Holbrook (Ullitz
165, index map) and (Rand 154,
1913, p. 28)
Patchogue Quad (7.5′)

HOLLAND
Community
Queens; SW part of Queens, E of
Belle Harbor, W of Arverne;
40°35′10″x73°49′
Far Rockaway Quad (7.5′)

HOLLINS ISLAND
see
EAST FIRE ISLAND
Source: (U.S. 5, List
No. 6301, p. 30)

HOLLIS
Community
Queens; SW of Queens Village,
NE of Jamaica;
40°42′45″x73°45′15″
Historical: East Jamaica
(Ricard 86, p. 10)
Jamaica Quad (7.5′)

HOLTSVILLE
Community
Suffolk—Brookhaven, Islip;
NW of Patchogue, E of Ron-
konkoma; 40°49′x73°2′40″
Historical: Waverly (Chace
127)
Patchogue Quad (7.5′)

HOMANS CREEK
Physical feature
Suffolk—Islip; flows into
 Great South Bay, S of Bay-
 port; 40°43′40″x73°3′15″
Sayville Quad (7.5′)

HOMAN'S HOLLOW
Physical feature—historical
Suffolk—Brookhaven; E side
 of Port Jefferson Harbor;
 ca. 40°57′30″x73°4′30″
Source: (Bayles 94, p. 135)
*Port Jefferson Quad (7.5′)

HOME CREEK
Physical feature
Suffolk—Brookhaven; flows into
 Moriches Bay, NE of Forge Point,
 E of Mastic Beach;
 40°46′15″x72°48′55″
Moriches Quad (7.5′)

HOME HARBOR
see
CHERRY HARBOR
Source: (Dyson 24, p. 29)

HOME POND
Physical feature
Suffolk—East Hampton; NW
 part of Gardiners Island;
 41°5′40″x72°7′10″
Gardiners Island East Quad (7.5′)

HOMECREST
Community
Kings; N of Sheepshead Bay;
 40°35′15″x73°56′40″
Source: (Rand 154, 1977, p. 385)
*Coney Island Quad (7.5′)

HOMELAND
Community—historical
Suffolk—Huntington; W side of the
 town, W of South Huntington;
 40°49′25″x73°26′45″
Source: (Hyde 148)
*Huntington Quad (7.5′)

HOMES HILL
Physical feature—historical
Suffolk—Southampton; at or near
 the community of North Sea
Source: (Tooker 44, p. 72-73)
Variations: Whomeses (Ibid.)
*Southampton Quad (7.5′)

HONE'S NECK
Physical feature—historical
Suffolk—Babylon; S side of Linden-
 hurst, possibly Little Neck;
 ca. 40°40′20″x73°21′45″
Source: (Thompson 42, p. 128)
*Bay Shore West Quad (7.5′)

HOOK CREEK
Locality—historical
Queens; NE side of JFK Airport,
 N of Head of Bay;
 ca. 40°38′45″x73°45′
Source: (Shell 161)
*Jamaica and Lynbrook
 Quads (7.5′)

HOOK CREEK
Physical feature
Nassau, Queens; flows into Head of
 the Bay, NW of Cedarhurst, SW of
 Valley Stream;
 40°38′10″x73°44′40″
Lynbrook Quad (7.5′)

HOOK POND
Physical feature
Suffolk—East Hampton; S part of
the village of East Hampton, E of
Georgica Pond; 40°57′x72°11′20″
East Hampton Quad (7.5′)

HOOPANINAK ISLAND
Physical feature
Kings; in Jamaica Bay, "an island
at Flatlands"
Source: (Tooker 44, pp. 73–74)

HOPEDALE
see
KEW GARDENS
Source: (Ricard 86, p. 11) and
(Beers 117, p. 52)

HOPPOGGS
see
HAUPPAUGE
Source: (Langhans 98, p. 10)

HORN POND
Physical feature
Suffolk—Brookhaven; E side of
the town, S of Lake Panamoka;
40°54′30″x72°50′30″
Wading River Quad (7.5′)

HORSE BEAT
Physical feature—historical
Suffolk—Smithtown; at the head
of the Nissequogue River in
Hauppauge
Source: (Pelletreau 101, p. 289)
*Central Islip Quad (7.5′)

HORSE CHANNEL
Physical feature
Kings; W side of Jamaica Bay,
between Ruffle Bar and Stony

Creek Marsh and Yellow Bar
Hassock; 40°36′10″x73°51′
Far Rockaway Quad (7.5′)

HORSE HOLLOW
Physical feature
Queens (Nassau)—Oyster Bay;
along Horse Hollow River, N
of Locust Valley, SE of Latting-
town; ca. 40°53′30″x73°35′
Source: (Cocks 70, p. 10)
*Bayville Quad (7.5′)

HORSE ISLAND
Physical feature
Suffolk—Smithtown; in the
Nissequogue River, S of Short
Beach; ca. 40°54′10″x73°13′15″
Source: (Langhans 98, p. 11)
*Saint James Quad (7.5′)

HORSE NECK
see
GREAT NECK
Nassau—North Hempstead
Source: (Flint 26, p. 71)

HORSE NECK
see
LLOYD NECK
Source: (Flint 26, p. 72)

HORSE RACE
Locality—historical
Suffolk—Smithtown; in the
vicinity of Nissequogue
village, E of Short Beach;
ca. 40°54′30″x73°12′20″
Source: (Langhans 98, p. 12)
*Saint James Quad (7.5′)

HORSESHOE COVE
Physical feature
Suffolk—Southold; NE side of
Cutchogue Harbor, W of Little
Hog Neck; 41°00′12″x72°27′20″
Southold Quad (7.5′)

HORTON LANE BEACH
Physical feature
Suffolk—Southold; NW of the
community of Southold, on
Long Island Sound;
41°4′35″x72°27′10″
Southold Quad (7.5′)

HORTON NECK
Physical feature
Suffolk—Southold; NW of the com-
munity of Southold, on Long Island
Sound; 41°5′x72°26′30″
Southold Quad (7.5′)

HORTON POINT
Community
Suffolk—Southold; NE of the com-
munity of Southold;
ca. 41°5′10″x72°26′50″
Source: (Mackoskey 29, p. 54)
*Southold Quad (7.5′)

HORTON POINT
Physical feature
Suffolk—Southold; NE of the
community of Southold, on
Long Island Sound;
41°5′10″x72°26′50″
Southold Quad (7.5′)

HOSPITAL ISLAND
Physical feature
Suffolk—Brookhaven; E part
of the Great South Bay;
40°43′55″x72°53′30″
Howells Point Quad (7.5′)

HOT WATER POND
Physical feature
Suffolk—Brookhaven; E of South
Manor; 40°51′40″x72°46′25″
Moriches Quad (7.5′)

HOUSE POND
Physical feature
Suffolk—Southampton; W of
Hampton Bays, SE of Flanders;
40°53′5″x72°33′55″
Mattituck Quad (7.5′)

HOWARD BEACH
Community
Queens; N of Jamaica Bay, SE
of Ozone Park; 40°39′30″x73°50′
Historical: Ramblersville
(Ricard 86, p. 10) and (Rand
154, 1913, p. 28)
Jamaica Quad (7.5′)

HOWELL CREEK
Physical feature
Suffolk—Babylon; flows into
the Great South Bay, E of
Amity Harbor, W of Great
Neck, S of Copiague;
40°40′15″x73°23′30″
Amityville Quad (7.5′)

HOWELL POINT
Physical feature
Suffolk—Babylon; S of Linden-
hurst, SE point of Great Neck;
40°39′30″x73°22′50″
Amityville Quad (7.5′)

HOWELLS CREEK
Physical feature
Suffolk—Brookhaven; flows into
the Great South Bay, SW part
of Bellport; 40°44′30″x72°57′15″

Bellport and Howells Point
Quads (7.5')

HOWELLS POINT
Physical feature
Suffolk—Brookhaven; S point
of Bellport;
40°44'25"x72°56'40"
Historical: Otis Point (Beers
117, p. 160)
Howells Point Quad (7.5')

HOWE'S BAY
see
MANHASSET BAY
Source: (Bailey 19, vol. 1,
p. 443)

HUBBARD CREEK
Physical feature
Suffolk—Southampton; S of
Flanders Bay, E of Flanders;
40°54'x72°34'
Historical: Red Creek, Toyonge,
Toyong, and To Youngs (Pelletreau
38, p. 382)
Mattituck Quad (7.5')

HUBBARDTOWN
Community—historical
Suffolk—Southampton; SE of
Flanders Bay, in the vicinity
of Hubbard Creek;
ca. 40°54'35"x72°34'
Source: (Bayles 93, p. 321)
*Mattituck Quad (7.5')

HUDSON CHANNEL
Physical feature
Nassau—Hempstead; SE of Free-
port, W boundary of Cow Meadow
Preserve; 40°38'x73°34'30"
Freeport Quad (7.5')

HULSES TURNOUT
see
CALVERTON
Source: (Bailey 19, vol. 1, p. 184)

HUNGRY POINT
Physical feature
Suffolk—Southold; on Fishers
Island, N of Barleyfield Cove, E
of Chocomount Cove and Brooks
Point; 41°17'5"x71°57'30"
Mystic Quad (7.5')

HUNTERS POINT
Community—historical
Queens; presently the S side
of Long Island City, N of
Greenpoint; 40°44'30"x73°57'30"
Historical: Dominies Hook
(French 10, p. 549fn), Bennett's
Point (Ricard 86, p. 10) and
(Brooklyn Quad, 15', 1897)
Source: (Brooklyn Quad, 7.5', AMS,
1947)
*Brooklyn Quad (7.5')

HUNTING TOWN
see
HUNTINGTON
Community
Source: (Dyson 24, p. 18)

HUNTINGTON
Community
Suffolk—Huntington; N central
part of the town;
40°52'30"x73°25'30"
Historical: Hunting Town
(Dyson 24, p. 18)
Lloyd Harbor and Huntington
Quads (7.5')

HUNTINGTON
Locality—historical
Suffolk—Southampton; SW of
Sag Harbor, NW of Bridge-
hampton; ca. 40°57'40"x72°18'45"
Source: (Adams 91, p. 122)
*Sag Harbor Quad (7.5')

HUNTINGTON
Town
Suffolk; NW part of Suffolk
Historical: included Babylon
town prior to 1872 (Bailey,
vol. 1, p. 337)
Lloyd Harbor, Huntington, Green-
lawn and Northport Quads (7.5')

HUNTINGTON BAY
Physical feature
Suffolk—Huntington; between
Lloyd Neck and Eatons Neck,
N of Huntington;
40°55'30"x73°25'10"
Lloyd Harbor Quad (7.5')

HUNTINGTON BAY
Village
Suffolk—Huntington; on East Neck
N of the community of Huntington;
40°54'x73°25'
Lloyd Harbor Quad (7.5')

HUNTINGTON BEACH
Community
Suffolk—Huntington; E part of East
Neck, SE of Huntington Bay;
40°53'40"x73°23'
Lloyd Harbor Quad (7.5')

HUNTINGTON CENTER
Community—historical
Suffolk—Huntington; E side of the
community of Melville;

40°47'25"x73°24'45"
Source: (Hyde 148)
*Huntington Quad (7.5')

HUNTINGTON EAST GUT
Physical feature—historical
Suffolk—Brookhaven; once existed
in the vicinity of Point O' Woods,
in the 17th Century the name stood
for Fire Island Inlet;
ca. 40°39'x73°7'45"
Source: (Osborne 36, p. 116)
*Sayville Quad (7.5')

HUNTINGTON GUT
Physical feature—historical
Suffolk—Brookhaven; between
Cedar Island and Oak Island;
ca. 40°39'x73°19'
Source: (Osbourne 36, p. 116)
*Bay Shore West Quad (7.5')

HUNTINGTON GUT
Suffolk—Islip
see
GILGO GUT
Source: (Thompson 41, vol. 1,
p. 451)

HUNTINGTON HARBOR
Physical feature
Suffolk—Huntington; W of East
Neck, N of Huntington;
40°54'x73°25'30"
Lloyd Harbor Quad (7.5')

HUNTINGTON HEIGHTS
Community
Suffolk—Huntington; E side of the
community of Huntington;
ca. 40°50'x73°25'
Source: (Hyde 148)
*Huntington Quad (7.5')

HUNTINGTON MANOR
Community
Suffolk—Huntington; S of
Huntington Station, N of South
Huntington; 40°50'30"x73°25'
Source: (Hagstrom 141, 1979, p. 24)
*Huntington Quad (7.5')

HUNTINGTON MANOR
Community—historical
see
HUNTINGTON STATION
Source: (Bailey 19, vol. 1,
p. 355)

HUNTINGTON SOUTH
Community—historical
see
BABYLON
Village
Source: (Bailey 19, vol. 1,
pp. 363–364)

HUNTINGTON SOUTH
Town
see
BABYLON
Town
Source: (Bailey 19, vol. 1, p. 337)

HUNTINGTON STATION
Community
Suffolk—Huntington; S of the
community of Huntington;
40°51'x73°24'
Historical: Fairground (Bailey
19, vol. 1, p. 355), proposed
name was Huntington Manor (Ibid.)
Huntington Quad (7.5')

**HUNTINGTON WEST NECK
SOUTH**
see

AMITYVILLE
Source: (Bailey 19, vol. 1,
p. 380)

HUNT'S POND
Physical feature
Suffolk—Smithtown; one of the
ponds along the Smithtown Branch
(Northeast Branch) of the Nisse-
quogue River;
40°50'x73°10'45"
Source: (Langhans 98, p. 12)
*Central Islip Quad (7.5')

HUTCHINSON'S CREEK
see
RICHMOND CREEK
Source: (Bayles 93, p. 372)

HYDE PARK
see
NEW HYDE PARK
Source: (French 10, p. 550fn)

IHPETONGA
see
BROOKLYN HEIGHTS
Source: (Tooker 44, p. 74)

ILANT DE GEBROKNE LANT
see
LONG ISLAND
Source: (Macoskey 29, p. 74)

ICE POND
Physical feature
Suffolk—Southold; E end of
 Fishers Island;
 41°17'20"x71°56'5"
Mystic Quad (7.5')

ICE POND
Physical feature—historical
Nassau—Hempstead; E side of
 Roosevelt; 40°41'x73°36'10"
Source: (Metz 82, p. 89)
*Freeport Quad (7.5')

IDLE HOUR
Community—historical
Suffolk—Islip; W side of
 Oakdale; 40°43'20"x73°9'
Source: (Hagstrom 141, 1969, p. 41)
*Bay Shore East Quad (7.5')

IDLEWILD
Community—historical
Queens; presently the S part
 of JFK Airport;
 40°38'5"x73°47'35"
Source: (Brooklyn Quad, 15',
 1897)
*Jamaica Quad (7.5')

INDIAN CREEK
Physical feature
Suffolk—Islip; S of West
 Sayville; 40°43'10"x73°6'
Historical: Indian Neck Creek
 (Pelletreau 38, facing p. 243)
Sayville Quad (7.5')

INDIAN FIELD
Locality—historical
Suffolk—East Hampton; E side
 of Montauk Harbor;
 ca. 41°3'45"x71°54'45"
Source: (Pelletreau 38, p. 373)
*Montauk Point Quad (7.5')

INDIAN FIELDS
Physical feature—historical
Suffolk—East Hampton; near
 Montauk Point, S of Oyster
 Pond; 41°4'x71°53'
Source: (Chace 127)
*Montauk Point Quad (7.5')

INDIAN GROUND
see
STRONGS NECK
Suffolk—Brookhaven
Source: (Pelletreau 38, p. 256)

INDIAN HEAD
Physical feature—historical
Suffolk—Smithtown; SW side of
the town; 40°52′x73°16′
Source: (Langhans 98, p. 12)
and (Ullitz 164, index map)
*Huntington Quad (7.5′)

INDIAN ISLAND
Physical feature—neck
Suffolk—Riverhead; NE part
of Flanders Bay, S of Aquebogue;
40°55′40″x72°37′
Mattituck Quad (7.5′)

INDIAN LANDING
Physical feature
Suffolk—Brookhaven; E of the
community of Brookhaven, S of
South Haven; 40°46′45″x72°53′35″
Bellport Quad (7.5′)

INDIAN NECK
Physical feature
Suffolk—Southold; NW of Little
Peconic Bay; 41°1′45″x72°27′
Southold Quad (7.5′)

INDIAN NECK
Physical feature—historical
Suffolk—Islip; bordered on the NE
by the Indian Creek, SW of
West Sayville; 40°43′30″x73°6′45″
Source: (Pelletreau 38, facing
p. 243)
*Sayville Quad (7.5′

INDIAN NECK CREEK
see
INDIAN CREEK
Source: (Pelletreau 38, facing
p. 243)

INDIAN NECK FARM
Locality—historical
Suffolk—Islip; SE part of
Heckscher State Park;
40°42′15″x73°9′45″
Source: (Ullitz 165, index map)
*Bay Shore East Quad (7.5′)

INDIAN POND
Physical feature—historical
Kings; N of Unionville, E of New
Utrecht
Source: (Walling 172)
*Coney Island Quad (7.5′)

INDIAN WELL PLAIN
see
AMAGANSETT
Source: (Tooker 44, p. 7-8)

INDIAN WELLS PLAIN
Physical feature—historical
Suffolk—East Hampton; in the
vicinity of Amagansett
Source: (Rattray 102, p. 30)
*East Hampton Quad (7.5′)

INGLESIDE
Community—historical
Queens; central part of Flushing
Source: (Hyde 147)
*Flushing Quad (7.5′)

INGLEWOOD
see
QUEENS VILLAGE
Source: (Ricard 86, p. 13)
and (Beers 117)

INGRAHAM HASSOCK
Physical feature—marsh island
Nassau—Hempstead; SW of Middle
Bay, SE of Oceanside, E of
Island Park; 40°36'x73°37'15"
Jones Inlet Quad (7.5')

INLET POINT
Physical feature
Suffolk—Southold, NE of
Arshamonaque, N of Pipes Cove,
on Long Island Sound;
41°6'55"x72°23'
Southold Quad (7.5')

INNER HARBOR
Physical feature
Nassau, Suffolk—Oyster Bay,
Huntington; S part of Cold
Spring Harbor; 40°51'45"x73°28'
Huntington Quad (7.5')

INWOOD
Community
Nassau—Hempstead; SW part of
the town, SW of Woodmere;
40°37'x73°45'
Lawrence and Far Rockaway Quads
(7.5')

IRABASH COVE
see
JABASH COVE
Source: (Tooker 44, pp. 74-75)

IRELAND
Tract of land—historical
Queens; E side of Flushing Creek,
presently the W side of Flushing;
ca. 40°45'50"x73°50'
Source: (Thompson 41, vol. 2, p. 95)
*Flushing Quad (7.5')

IRELAND'S POND
see
AVON LAKE
Source: (Hyde 148)

IRON POINT
Physical feature
Suffolk—Southampton; on Flanders
Bay, NW of Flanders;
40°55'5"x72°37'
Mattituck Quad (7.5')

ISABELLA BEACH
Physical feature
Suffolk—Southold; on Block Island
Sound, SW side of Fishers Island;
41°15'40"x71°59'30"
Mystic Quad (7.5')

ISBRANDTSEN CANAL
Physical feature
Suffolk—Islip; SW part of
Appletree Neck, S of Brightwaters;
40°41'40"x73°15'55"
Bay Shore West Quad (7.5')

ISLAND CHANNEL
Physical feature
Kings; W side of Jamaica Bay;
40°36'30"x73°52'30"
Coney Island and Far Rockaway
Quads (7.5')

ISLAND CREEK
Physical feature
Suffolk—Southampton; E of West
Neck Creek, E of Great Peconic
Bay, S of Scallop Pond;
40°56'x72°25'40"
Southampton Quad (7.5')

ISLAND CREEK
Physical feature—historical
see
LITTLE SEBONAC CREEK
Source: (Hagstrom 141, 1959, p. 51)

ISLAND OF NASSAU
see
LONG ISLAND
Source: (Macoskey 29, p. 74)
and (Bailey 19, vol. 1, p. 31)

ISLAND PARK
Village
Nassau—Hempstead; N of Long
Beach, SW of Oceanside;
40°36′x73°39′30″
Lawrence Quad (7.5′)

ISLAND PARK HARBOR
Physical feature
Nassau—Hempstead; NW of Island
Park, S of West Meadow
(island); 40°36′25″x73°39′40″
Lawrence Quad (7.5′)

ISLAND POINT
Physical feature
Suffolk—Brookhaven; E side of
Forge River;
40°47′30″x72°49′40″
Moriches Quad (7.5′)

ISLAND POND
Physical feature
Suffolk—Southold; central part
of Fishers Island;
41°16′10″x71°59′
Mystic Quad (7.5′)

ISLAND SWAMP BROOK
Physical feature
Nassau—Oyster Bay; flows N into

Dosoris Pond, NE part of North
Hempstead town and NW part of
Oyster Bay town;
40°53′40″x73°37′10″
Historical: Flagg Brook (Coles 73,
p. 11)
Bayville Quad (7.5′)

ISLE OF PATMOS
see
PLUM ISLAND
Source: (French 10, p. 639fn)

ISLE OF WIGHT
see
GARDINERS ISLAND
Source: (Tooker 44, p. 91)

ISLE PLOWDEN
see
LONG ISLAND
Source: (Bailey 19, vol. 1, p. 31)

ISLIP
Community
Suffolk—Islip; N of the NW part
of Great South Bay, E of Bay
Shore; 40°43′45″x73°12′30″
Bay Shore East Quad (7.5′)

ISLIP
Town
Suffolk; W-central part of Suffolk
Co.
Saint James, Central Islip, Bay
Shore East, Bay Shore West,
Greenlawn and Northport Quads
(7.5′)

ISLIP BAY
see
NICOLL BAY
Source: (Chace 127)

ISLIP TERRACE
Community
Suffolk—Islip; N of the community
  of Islip, SW of Lake Ronkonkoma;
  40°44'50"x73°11'40"
Central Islip and Bay Shore East
  Quads (7.5')

Chart No. 115, 1855)
Mattituck Quad (7.5 ′)

JACOBS POINT
Physical feature
Suffolk—Riverhead; N of Riverhead,
 NW of Northville, on Long Island
 Sound; 40 °58 ′50 ″x72 °39 ′
Riverhead Quad (7.5 ′)

JABASH COVE
Physical feature—historical
Suffolk—Southampton; E side
 of Shinnecock Neck;
 40 °52 ′5 ″x72 °25 ′30 ″
Source: (Tooker 44, pp. 74–75)
Variation: Irabash (Ibid.)
*Shinnecock Inlet Quad (7.5 ′)

JACOB'S WELL
Physical feature
Suffolk—Smithtown; in the vicinity
 of Head of the Harbor;
 ca. 40 °54 ′20 ″x73 °9 ′30 ″
Source: (Langhans 98, p. 12)
*Saint James Quad (7.5 ′)

JACKS HOLE CREEK
Physical feature
Queens; central Jamaica Bay, E
 of Rulers Bar Hassock;
 40 °37 ′30 ″x73 °48 ′50 ″
Far Rockaway Quad (7.5 ′)

JACQUES FARM
see
ASTORIA
Source: (Flint 26, p. 69)

JACKSON HEIGHTS
Community
Queens; NW part of Queens, E of
 Long Island City;
 40 °45 ′30 ″x73 °53 ′30 ″
Central Park Quad (7.5 ′)

JAMAICA
Community
Queens; E of Richmond Hill, NE
 of Ozone Park;
 40 °41 ′30 ″x73 °48 ′30 ″
Historical: Canarasset, Bever Pond
 (Flint 26, p. 71)

JACOBS HILL
Physical feature
Suffolk—Riverhead; W of Mattituck,
 NE of Riverhead;
 40 °59 ′30 ″x72 °35 ′45 ″
Variation: Jacobs Hills (U.S. 170,

Variations: Jamaick, Jameca,
 Jemaco, Yemacah (Tooker 44,
 p. 75), Jameco, Crafford (Ricard
 86, p. 11), Gemeco (Ross 39,
 p. 39)
Jamaica Quad (7.5 ′)

JAMAICA
Town—historical
Queens; central part of Queens
Source: (French 10, p. 547fn).
First proposed name was
Canorasset, other settlers preferred
Crawford, Dutch named it
Rusdorph, also Rustdorpe (Gordon
11, p. 637), and Rustdorp (Ricard
86, p. 11)
*Jamaica Quad (7.5 ')

JAMAICA BAY
Physical feature
Kings, Queens; SE side of Kings, S
side of Queens; 40°37 '30 "x73°50 '
Historical: Connarie See (Tooker 44,
p. 32)
Jamaica and Far Rockaway Quads
(7.5 ')

JAMAICA HEIGHTS
Community—historical
Queens—Jamaica (town); N part of
the town, proposed village in 1860
Source: (French 10, p. 548)
*Central Park Quad (7.5 ')

JAMAICA PASS
Physical feature—historical
Queens; in the vicinity of
Glendale and East New York;
ca. 40°42 '25 "x73°53 '30 "
Source: (Luke 79, p. 128)
*Brooklyn Quad (7.5 ')

JAMAICA POND
see
BAISLEY POND
Source: (Walling 172)

JAMAICA SOUTH
Community—historical
Queens; N of JFK Airport, in the
vicinity of Baisley Pond;
40°40 '25 "x73°47 '25 "
Source: (Cram 132, p. 111)
*Jamaica Quad (7.5 ')

JAMAICA SQUARE
see
SOUTH FLORAL PARK
Source: (Macoskey 29, p. 55)

JAMECO
see
JAMAICA
Community
Source: (Ricard 86, p. 11)

JAMEKO
Community—historical
Queens—Jamaica (town); S of
Jamaica South, W of Rosedale,
SE of Aqueduct
Source: (Hyde 147)
*Jamaica Quad (7.5 ')

JAMES CREEK
Physical feature
Suffolk—Southold; S of Mattituck;
40°58 '50 "x72°32 '
Mattituck Quad (7.5 ')

JAMES CREEK
Physical feature—historical
Suffolk—Smithtown; inlet on the
E side of Nissequogue River, S of
Short Beach, 40°54 '20 "x73°13 '20 "
Source: (Langhans 98, p. 12)
and Pelletreau 101, p. 63)
*Saint James Quad (7.5 ')

JAMES NECK
Physical feature
Suffolk—Smithtown; E side of
  Nissequogue River, S of Short
  Bar; 40°54′20″x73°13′15″
Source: (Langhans 98, p. 12)
  and (Pelletreau 101, p. 258)
*Saint James Quad (7.5′)

JAMESPORT
Community
Suffolk—Riverhead; NE of
  Riverhead, SW of Mattituck;
  40°57′x72°34′50″
Historical: Old Aquebogue (Chace
  127) and (U.S. 170, Chart No.
  115, 1855), Miamog, Mianrogue
  (French 10, p. 637fn)
Mattituck Quad (7.5′)

JAYNE'S HILL
see
HIGH HILL
Source: (Manley 30, p. 167)

JEFFREY BREWSTER'S SWAMP
Physical feature—historical
Suffolk—Islip; SE of East Patchogue,
  SW of Hagerman;
ca. 40°46′x72°59′30″
Source: (Pelletreau 38, p. 240)
*Bellport Quad (7.5′)

JEFFREY'S NECK
Physical feature—historical
Suffolk—Southampton; in the vicinity
  of Cow Neck and the village of
  North Sea; ca. 40°56′x72°26′
Source: (Pelletreau 38, p. 331)
*Southampton Quad (7.5′)

JEHU POND
Physical feature—historical
Suffolk—Southampton; N of
  Scuttlehole, S of Shorts Pond, NW
  of Goldfish Pond;
  40°56′43″x72°20′
Source: (Adams 92, p. 7)
*Sag Harbor Quad (7.5′)

JEKYLL ISLAND
Physical feature—historical
Nassau—Hempstead; near Oceanside
  and Island Park
Source: (Macoskey 29, p. 55)
*Lawrence Quad (7.5′)

JENNINGS POINT
Physical feature
Suffolk—Southold; NW point of
  Shelter Island; 41°4′20″x72°23′
Historical: Rocky Point, Stearns Point
  (Bailey 19, vol. 1, p. 178)
Southold Quad (7.5′)

JENNINGS POND
Physical feature—historical
Nassau—Hempstead; S of West
  Hempstead, Schodack Stream
  flowed into it; 40°41′x73°39′10″
Source: (Reifschneider 85, p. 186)
*Lynbrook Quad (7.5′)

JERICHO
Community
Nassau—Oyster Bay; N of Hicksville,
  W side of town;
  40°47′40″x73°32′10″
Historical: Lusam (Tooker 44, p. 86),
  Lusum (French 10, p. 551fn)
  The Farms (Flint 26, p. 71)
Hicksville Quad (7.5′)

JERICHO
Community
Suffolk—East Hampton; SW of East
Hampton village;
40°57′20″x72°12′15″
East Hampton Quad (7.5′)

JERICO
Community—historical
Suffolk—Riverhead; N-central part of
the town, NW of the community
of Riverhead, E of Wading River
Source: (Burr 124)

JERSEY COLONY
Community
Suffolk—Southold; E of
Hashamonaque Pond; ca.
41°5′25″x72°23′30″
Source: (Rand 154, 1977, p. 385)
*Southold Quad (7.5′)

JERUSALEM
see
WANTAGH
Source: (Marshall 80, p. 21)
and (Burr 125)

JERUSALEM BAY
Physical feature—historical
Queens (Nassau)—Hempstead; NE
side of East Bay, SW of Seaford;
ca. 40°39′15″x73°31′30″
Source: (Gordon 11, p. 635)
*Freeport Quad (7.5′)

JERUSALEM RIVER
see
SEAFORD CREEK
Source: (Pelletreau 38, p. 93)

JERUSALEM SOUTH
Community—historical
Queens (Nassau)—Hempstead;
presently part of Seaford;
40°40′x73°29′
Source: (Walling 172)
*Amityville Quad (7.5′)

JERUSALEM STATION
Community—historical
Queens (Nassau)—Oyster Bay; SE
of Hicksville, NW of Farmingdale,
presently part of Bethpage;
ca. 40°44′25″x73°28′30″
Source: (Walling 172)
*Amityville Quad (7.5′)

JESSUP NECK
Physical feature
Suffolk—Southampton; W of Noyack
Bay, E of Little Peconic Bay;
41°00′40″x72°22′30″
Historical: Great Noyack (Pelletreau
38, p. 292), Farrington Neck (U.S.
167, Map T-71), Osborn's Neck
(Chace 127)
Greenport and Southold Quads (7.5′)

JO CO CREEK
Physical feature
Queens; Jamaica Bay, E side of
Jo Co Marsh; 40°37′x73°47′15″
Far Rockaway Quad (7.5′)

JO CO MARSH
Physical feature—marsh island
Queens; E side of Jamaica Bay, N of
Arverne; 40°37′x73°47′30″
Far Rockaway Quad (7.5′)

JOBS CREEK
Physical feature
Suffolk—Southampton; on Mecox

Bay, between Sams Creek and
Swan Creek;
40°54'10"x72°18'35"
Source: (Adams 92, p. 18). Also
known as Doxeys Creek (Ibid.)
*Sag Harbor Quad (7.5')

JOCKEY CREEK
Physical feature
Suffolk—Southold; flows into
Southold Bay, S of the community
of Southold, N of Goose Creek;
41°3'30"x72°25'10"
Southold Quad (7.5')

JOHN BOYLE ISLAND
Physical feature
Suffolk—Brookhaven; E part of
the Great South Bay;
40°44'25"x72°53'55"
Howells Point Quad (7.5')

JOHN MOBY CREEK
see
BRIGHTWATERS CANAL
Source: (Babylon Quad, 15',
1903)

JOHNS NECK
Physical feature
Suffolk—Brookhaven; W side of
Narrow Bay, S of Shirley and
Mastic Bay; 40°44'45"x72°52'
Pattersquash Island and Moriches
Quads (7.5')

JOHNS NECK CREEK
Physical feature
Suffolk—Brookhaven; SW of
Moriches, flows S into Narrow
Bay; 40°44'43"x72°51'48"
Moriches Quad (7.5')

JONES BEACH STATE PARK
Nassau—Hempstead, Oyster Bay;
on the barrier beach, SE side
of the county, between Jones
Inlet and Tobay Beach;
40°35'45"x73°30'30"
Jones Inlet, Freeport, Amityville
and West Gilgo Beach Quads (7.5')

JONES CREEK
Physical feature
Nassau—Oyster Bay; borders Fort
Neck on the east, flows into
South Oyster Bay;
40°39'15"x73°27'
Amityville Quad (7.5')

JONES INLET
Physical feature
Nassau—Hempstead; S of Freeport,
E of Long Beach and Lido Beach;
40°35'x73°34'30"
Historical: New Inlet (Walling 172)
and (U.S. 170, Chart No. 119,
1844)
Jones Inlet Quad (7.5')

JONES ISLAND
Physical feature
Nassau—Hempstead; N of Sloop
Channel, S of Big Crow Island;
40°36'15"x73°32'30"
Jones Inlet Quad (7.5')

JONES POINT
Physical feature—historical
Suffolk—Smithtown; on the
Nissequogue River, NE of San
Remo; 40°53'55"x73°12'30"
Source: (Langhans 98, p. 13) and
(Pelletreau 101, pp. 60, 331)
*Saint James Quad (7.5')

JONES POND
Physical feature
Suffolk—Riverhead; NW of
  Manorville, SW of Swan Pond;
  40°52'55"x72°49'45"
Wading River Quad (7.5')

JORGKE
see
GEORGICA
Source: (Tooker 44, pp. 64–65)

JOSEPH WHITMAN'S
GREAT HOLLOW
see
WHITMAN'S HOLLOW
Source: (Langhans 98, p. 26)

JOSIAH'S NECK
Physical feature—historical
Suffolk—Babylon; SE side of
  Amityville; 40°39'45"x73°24'40"
Historical: Scurraway (Tooker 44,
  p. 229), Seascawany Neck
  (Beauchamp 7, p. 223)
*Amityville Quad (7.5')

JUDGE'S POND
Physical feature
Suffolk—Smithtown; one of the
  ponds along the Smithtown Branch
  of the Nissequogue River,
  N of Lake McKinley;
  40°50'5"x73°10'30"
Source: (Langhans 98, p. 13)
*Central Islip Quad (7.5')

JULE POND
Physical feature
Suffolk—Southampton; E of
  Southampton village, S of Flying
  Point; 40°53'10"x72°21'
Sag Harbor Quad (7.5')

JUMPING NECK
Physical feature—historical
Suffolk—Southampton; South of
  Flanders Bay, E of Flanders;
  40°54'40"x72°35'10"
Source: (Tooker 44, pp. 209–210).
  Also known as Rapahamuck Neck
  (Ibid.)
*Mattituck Quad (7.5')

JURKUM NECK
Physical feature
Suffolk—Shelter Island; S side
  of the town, E of West Neck;
  41°3'10"x72°20'45"
Source: (Hyde 147)
*Greenport Quad (7.5')

KAHAIJONGH BROOK
see
AWIXA CREEK
Source: (Tooker 44, p. 76)

KANAPAUKA KILLS
see
DUTCH KILLS
Source: (Flint 26, p. 70)

KANTUCK
Locality—historical
Queens (Nassau)—Oyster Bay; SW
 of Beaver Lake, NE of Matinecock,
 in or around Kentuck Pond;
 ca. 40°53 ′x73°34 ′15 ″
Source: (Tooker 44, p. 76)
*Bayville Quad (7.5 ′)

KANUNGUM
Community—historical
Suffolk—Riverhead; on the Peconic
 River; ca. 40°54 ′x72°44 ′
Source: (Smith 162)
*Riverhead Quad (7.5 ′)

KANUNGUM POND
see
PECONIC LAKE
Source: (Tooker 44, pp. 76–77)

KASKUTENSUKEN
see
CASTATEUM
Source: (Tooker 44, p. 35)

KATAWAMAC
see
CRAB MEADOW
Physical feature
Source: (Tooker 44, pp. 20–21, 77)

KEEMISCOMOCK BROOK
see
THOMPSONS CREEK
Source: (Tooker 44, pp. 77–78)

KEITH CANAL
Physical feature
Suffolk—Islip; on the Great South
 Bay, SW part of Islip town, E of
 Babylon Cove; 40°41 ′x73°17 ′20 ″
Bay Shore West Quad (7.5 ′)

KELLIS POND
Physical feature
Suffolk—Southampton; SW of
 Bridgehampton, N of Mecox Bay;
 40°55 ′40 ″x72°19 ′
Sag Harbor Quad (7.5 ′)

KENILWORTH
see
KILLINGWORTH
Source: (Pelletreau 38, p. 148)

KENNEL CLUB POND
see
SOUTHARDS POND
Source: (Babylon Quad, 15 ′, 1903)

KENNEYS ROAD BEACH
Physical feature
Suffolk—Southold; on Long Island
Sound, W of the community of
Southold; 41°4'10"x72°27'30"
Southold Quad (7.5')

KENSINGTON
Community
Kings; W side of Kings, SW of
Flatbush; 40°38'50"x73°58'15"
Brooklyn Quad (7.5')

KENSINGTON
Village
Nassau—North Hempstead; S of
Kings Point and Great Neck;
40°47'30"x73°43'30"
Sea Cliff Quad (7.5')

KENTUCK POND
Physical feature
Nassau—Oyster Bay; W side of the
village of Mill Neck, W of
Beaver Lake; 40°52'55"x73°34'20"
Historical: Haintuck Mill Pond
(Coles 75, p. 207)
Bayville Quad (7.5')

KESKAECHQUEREN
see
CANARSIE
Source: (Bailey 19, vol. 1, p. 29)

KESTATEUW
Physical feature—salt meadow—
historical
Kings; SE of Flatlands
Source: (Tooker 44, p. 35)
*Coney Island Quad (7.5')

KETANOMOCKE
Indian village—historical
Suffolk—Huntington; in the
vicinity of the community of
Huntington
Source: (Tooker 44, pp. 78-79).
Also known as Cutunomack (Ibid.)
*Lloyd Harbor Quad (7.5')

KETCHABONEC
Community—historical
Suffolk—Southampton; W of
Quantuck Bay on Ketchabonack
Neck
Source: (French 10, p. 638)
*Eastport Quad (7.5')

KETCHAM'S NECK
see
LITTLE NECK
Suffolk—Babylon
Source: (Beauchamp 7, p. 216)

KETCHAPONACK NECK
Physical feature—historical
Suffolk—Southampton; W of
Quantuck Bay, SW of Little Assups
Neck (Quiogue), present site of
part of Westhampton Beach;
40°48'30"x72°38'15"
Source: (Tooker 44, pp. 24, 80-81)
and (Chace 127). Also known as
Ketehapogua Neck (Burr 124)
Variations: Catchaponack,
Katchaponack, Ketchabonnack,
Ketchabonack, Catchebonnuc
(Tooker 44, pp. 80-81)
*Eastport Quad (7.5')

KETCHININCHOGE
see
KITCHAMINCHOK
Source: (Tooker 44, pp. 83-84)

KETEWOMOKE
Locality—historical
Suffolk—Huntington; in the vicinity
of the community of Huntington
Source: (Pelletreau 38, p. 172)
*Huntington and Lloyd Harbor
Quads (7.5')

KETUMPSCUT
Locality—historical
Suffolk—Southold; W end of
Fishers Island
Source: (Tooker 44, p. 81)
*New London Quad (7.5')

KEW GARDENS
Community
Queens; E of Forest Hills, N of
Richmond Hill, S of Flushing;
40°42'45"x73°49'45"
Historical: Hopedale (Ricard 80,
p. 11) and (Beers 117), Maple Grove
(Ricard 86, p. 11) and (Brooklyn
Quad, 15', 1897)
Jamaica Quad (7.5')

KILLINGWORTH
Community—historical
Nassau—Oyster Bay; in the vicinity
of Matinecock
Source: (Cocks 70, pp. 2, 4)
Variations: Cillingworth and
Kenilworth
(Pelletreau 38, p. 148)

KIMOGENER POINT
Physical feature
Suffolk—Southold; on the Great
Peconic Bay, SW of New Suffolk;
40°59'20"x72°29'
Southampton Quad (7.5')

KINGS
County—Borough (Brooklyn) of
New York City; on the SW side
of Long Island, W of Queens
Historical: part of the West Riding
of Yorkshire (French 10, p. 544fn)

KINGS CREEK
Physical feature
Suffolk—Riverhead; SW of South
Jamesport, NW side of Miamogue
Lagoon; 40°56'x72°35'
Source: (Tooker 45, p. 36)
Historical: Miamogue Creek (Ibid.)
*Mattituck Quad (7.5')

KINGS PARK
Community
Suffolk—Smithown; W-central part
of town, NW of the community of
Smithtown; 40°53'x73°16'
Historical: Sunk Meadow (Flint 26,
p. 71), St. Johnland (Langhans 98,
pp. 13, 22)
Northport Quad (7.5')

KINGS POINT
Physical feature
Nassau—North Hempstead; W side
of Great Neck, N of the village of
Kings Point; 40°50'x73°45'25"
Flushing Quad (7.5')

KINGS POINT
Village
Nassau—North Hempstead; N part
of Great Neck, NW part of the
town; 40°49'x73°44'
Sea Cliff and Flushing Quads (7.5')

KINGSTOWN
Community
Suffolk—East Hampton; E of
  Threemile Harbor;
  41°0′35″x72°9′50″
Gardiners Island West Quad (7.5′)

KISCASUTTA
Physical feature—point of trees—
historical
Nassau—Oyster Bay, Hempstead; on
  the Great Plain, NE of Hempstead,
  on the boundary between the towns
  of Hempstead and Oyster Bay
Source: (Tooker 44, pp. 82–83)
*Hicksville Quad (7.5′)

KISMET
Community
Suffolk—Islip; on Fire Island,
  SW part of Islip town, S of Islip;
  40°38′x73°12′15″
Bay Shore East Quad (7.5′)

KISSENA LAKE
Physical feature
Queens; E of Flushing Meadow
  Park, in Kissena Park;
  40°44′53″x73°48′20″
Jamaica Quad (7.5′)

KISSENA POND
Physical feature—historical
Queens; in Flushing (town)
Source: (Tooker 44, p. 83)

KITCHAMINCHOK
Physical feature—island—historical
Suffolk—Brookhaven; no longer an
  island but part of the mainland,
  S of East Moriches, N side of
  Moriches Bay;
  40°47′30″x72°45′

Source: (Tooker 44, pp. 83–84). Also
  known as Ketchininchoge,
  Kitchaminfchoke, Cochiminchoake
  and Moriches Island (Ibid.)
*Eastport and Moriches Quads (7.5′)

KNAPPS LAKE
Physical feature
Suffolk—Islip; drains into Champlin
  Creek, between Islip and East Islip;
  40°44′x73°12′5″
Bay Shore East Quad (7.5′)

KOETIES KILL
Physical feature—historical
Kings; ran through Red Hook into
  Buttermilk Channel, no longer
  exists; ca. 40°40′30″x74°1′15″
Source: (Ratzer 155)
*Jersey City Quad (7.5′)

KONKHUNGANIK
  see
FORT POND
  Source: (Tooker 44, pp. 84–85)
  Variations: Konhhonganik,
  Konk-hong-anok, Konhunganock
  (Ibid.)

KRUG'S CORNERS
  see
MINEOLA (part of)
  Source: (Macoskey 29, p. 55)

KUHL
  see
HICKSVILLE
  Source: (Macoskey 44, p. 55)

LAFARGES LANDING
Community
Suffolk—East Hampton;
S of Gardiners Bay,
NW of Threemile Harbor;
41 °2 'x72 °12 '30 "
Gardiners Island West Quad (7.5 ')

LAKE AGAWAM
see
AGAWAM LAKE
Source: (Tooker 44, p. 5)

LAKE BERYL
see
MILLERS POND
Suffolk—Smithtown
Source: (Langhans 98, pp. 5, 18)

LAKE CAPRI
Physical feature
Suffolk—Islip; flows into Willetts
  Creek, SW part of town, S part of
  West Islip; 40 °41 '45 "x73 °18 '10 "
Bay Shore West Quad (7.5 ')

LAKE GROVE
Village
Suffolk—Brookhaven; N of Lake
  Ronkonkoma;

40 °52 'x73 °7 '
Historical: Lakeville (Bayles 93,
  p. 265)
Patchogue, Port Jefferson and
  Central Islip Quads (7.5 ')

LAKE McKINLEY
Physical feature
Suffolk—Smithtown; one of the
  ponds along the Smithtown Branch
  of the Nissequogue River,
  S of Judges Pond;
  40 °44 '55 "x73 °10 '35 "
Historical: Clint Darling's Swamp
  (Langhans 98, p. 13)
*Central Islip Quad (7.5 ')

LAKE MOMOWETA
see
MARRATOOKA LAKE
Source: (Tooker 44, p. 139)

LAKE MONTAUK
Physical feature
Suffolk—East Hampton; E end of
  town, W of Montauk Point;
  41 °3 '40 "x71 °55 '20 "
Historical: Great Pond (U.S. 167,
  Map T–62), (Chace 127), and
  (Montauk Quad, 15 ', 1904),
  Lake Wyandanee (Ullitz 164, index
  map), Lake Montauk Harbor (U.S.
  5, List No. 6001, p. 42)
Montauk Point Quad (7.5 ')

LAKE MONTAUK HARBOR
see
LAKE MONTAUK
Source: (U.S. 5, List No. 6001,
  p. 42)

LAKE NOWEDONAH
see
MILL POND
Suffolk—Southampton
Source: (Tooker 44, p. 165)

LAKE PANAMOKA
Physical feature
Suffolk—Brookhaven; NE side
of town, SW of Wading River,
NE of Ridge;
40°55'25"x72°51'
Historical: Long Pond (Wading River
Quad, 7.5', 1944)
Wading River Quad (7.5')

LAKE RONKONKOMA
Community
Suffolk—Brookhaven, Smithtown;
NW of Patchogue, SW of Port
Jefferson; 40°50'x73°7'
Patchogue and Central Islip Quads
(7.5')

LAKE RONKONKOMA
Physical feature
Suffolk—Brookhaven, Islip,
Smithtown; NW of Patchogue, SW
of Port Jefferson;
40°49'40"x73°07'30"
Historical: Ronconcoma Pond,
Great Pond and Sand Pond
(Langhans 98, p. 13), Forest Lake
(Thompson 41, vol. 1, p. 448)
Variations: Raconchony,
Raconckamich, Raconkamuck,
Rockconcomuck, Ronconhama,
Ronconcoma, Ronkonkama,
Ronkonkom, Raconkumake
(Tooker 44, pp. 214–215)
Central Islip and Patchogue Quads
(7.5')

LAKE SUCCESS
Physical feature
Nassau—North Hempstead; S part of
the village of Lake Success,
N of North New Hyde Park;
40°45'50"x73°42'30"
Historical: Success Pond, Sacut
(Tooker 44, pp. 219–220),
Lake Surprise
(Oyster Bay Quad, 15', 1900)
Sea Cliff Quad (7.5')

LAKE SUCCESS
Village
Nassau—North Hempstead; SW part
of the town;
40°46'15"x73°43'
Historical: Lakeville (Walling 172),
Success (French 10, p. 550fn), and
Lake Ville (Thompson 42, p. 128)
Sea Cliff Quad (7.5')

LAKE SURPRISE
see
LAKE SUCCESS
Source: (Oyster Bay Quad, 15',
1900)

LAKE VILLE
see
LAKE SUCCESS
Source: (Thompson 42, p. 128)

LAKE WYANDANEE
see
LAKE MONTAUK
Source: (Ullitz 164, index map)

LAKELAND
Community
Suffolk—Islip; S of Lake

Ronkonkoma; 40°48′10″x73°7′10″
Patchogue and Central Islip Quads
(7.5′)

LAKEVIEW
Community
Nassau—Hempstead; central part of
the town, SW of the village of
Hempstead; 40°41′x73°38′40″
Lynbrook Quad (7.5′)

LAKEVIEW PARK
Community—historical
Suffolk—Brookhaven; in the vicinity
of Mastic
Source: (Macoskey 29, p. 55)
*Moriches Quad (7.5′)

LAKEVILLE
Nassau—North Hempstead
see
LAKE SUCCESS
Village
Source: (Walling 172)

LAKEVILLE
Suffolk—Brookhaven
see
LAKE GROVE
Source: (Bayles 93, p. 265)

LANDING
Community—historical
Queens; E of Williamsburg, SE of
Maspeth (Newtown) Creek, SE of
the village of Newtown
Source: (Burr 125)

LANES ISLAND
Physical feature
Suffolk—Southampton; S of
Hampton Bays, middle of

Shinnecock Bay;
40°50′5″x72°31′20″
Quogue Quad (7.5′)

LARKFIELD
see
EAST NORTHPORT
Source: (Macoskey 29, p. 56) and
(Northport Quad, 15′, 1901)

LATTINGTOWN
Village
Nassau—Oyster Bay; N part of
the town, NE of Glen Cove;
40°53′40″x73°36′
Bayville Quad (7.5′)

LAUGHING WATERS
Community
Suffolk—Southold; N of Little
Peconic Bay; 41°2′15″x72°25′50″
Southold Quad (7.5′)

LAUREL
Community
Suffolk—Southold; SW of Mattituck,
NE of Jamesport;
40°58′10″x72°33′50″
Historical: Franklinville (Riverhead
Quad, 15′, 1903), (U.S. 167,
Map T-55), (Chace 127), and
(U.S. 170, Chart No. 115, 1855)
Mattituck Quad (7.5′)

LAUREL CREEK
see
BRUSHS CREEK
Source: (U.S. 5, List No. 5903,
p. 42)

LAUREL HILL
Physical feature
Suffolk—Huntington; SE of
Centerport, W of East Northport;
40°52′45″x73°20′55″
Source: (Sammis 104, p. 158)
*Northport Quad (7.5′)

LAUREL HOLLOW
Village
Nassau—Oyster Bay; S of Cold
Spring Harbor, NE of Syosset;
40°51′15″x73°28′30″
Historical: Laurelton (Gibbs 27,
p. 106)
Huntington Quad (7.5′)

LAUREL LAKE
Physical feature
Suffolk—Southold; SW of Mattituck;
40°58′40″x72°33′30″
Historical: Franklinville Pond
(U.S. 167, Map T-55)
Mattituck Quad (7.5′)

LAURELTON
Nassau—Oyster Bay
see
LAUREL HOLLOW
Source: (Gibbs 27, p. 106)

LAURELTON
Community
Queens; E side of Queens, W of
Valley Stream; 40°40′10″x73°45′
Lynbrook Quad (7.5′)

LAWRENCE
Village
Nassau—Hempstead; SW part of
the town, S of Woodmere;
40°36′30″x73°43′
Lawrence Quad (7.5′)

LAWRENCE CREEK
Physical feature
Suffolk—Brookhaven; flows E of
Mastic Beach, W of Forge River,
into the Narrow Bay;
40°45′30″x72°49′10″
Moriches Quad (7.5′)

LAWRENCE CREEK
Physical feature
Suffolk—Islip; NW of Great Cove,
E side of Brightwaters;
40°42′30″x73°14′50″
Historical: Bay Shore Brook,
Thompson's Brook, Compawams
Creek, Manatuck Creek, Masquetux
Creek (Tooker 44, pp. 46, 91–92,
110), Manshtak Creek (Bayles 93,
p. 210)
Bay Shore West and Bay Shore East
Quads (7.5′)

LAWRENCE LAKE
Physical feature
Suffolk—Islip; SE part of
Brightwaters; 40°43′x73°15′20″
Bay Shore West Quad (7.5′)

LAWRENCE MARSH
Physical feature
Nassau—Hempstead; SE side of
Lawrence, W of Harbor Isle;
40°35′45″x73°41′30″
Lawrence Quad (7.5′)

LAWRENCE NECK
see
COLLEGE POINT
Physical feature
Source: (French 10, p. 546fn)

LAWRENCE POINT
Physical feature
Queens; NW point of Queens, E of
Ward Island, N of Steinway;
40°47′30″x73°54′40″
Central Park Quad (7.5′)

LAWRENCES NECK
see
COLLEGE POINT
Source: (French 10, p. 546fn)

LAWRENCEVILLE
Community—historical
Queens; village plat in the town of
Newtown, N of Maspeth
Source: (French 10, p. 549)
*Central Park Quad (7.5′)

LAZY POINT
Community—historical
Suffolk—East Hampton; near
Promised Land and Amagansett;
ca. 41°0′42″x72°3′25″
Source: (Macoskey 29, p. 56)
*Gardiners Island East Quad (7.5′)

LAZY POINT
Physical feature
Suffolk—East Hampton; NW side of
Napeague Harbor;
41°0′45″x72°3′25″
Gardiners Island East Quad (7.5′)

LE COUNT POND
Physical feature—historical
Nassau—Hempstead; S side of the
community of Lakeview, NW of
Smith Pond; 40°39′50″x73°39′30″
Source: (Hempstead Quad, 15′, 1897)
*Lynbrook Quad (7.5′)

LEADING HOLLOW
Physical feature—historical
Suffolk—Smithtown; W side of the
town, the hollow leading from
Commack to Bread and Cheese
Hollow; ca. 40°51′15″x73°17′
Source: (Langhans 98, p. 16) and
(Pelletreau 101, p. 190)
*Greenlawn Quad (7.5′)

LEEDS POND
Physical feature
Nassau—North Hempstead; SW side
of Manhasset Neck, in the vicinity
of Plandome Manor;
40°48′45″x73°42′10″
Sea Cliff Quad (7.5′)

LEISURE VILLAGE
Community—historical
Suffolk—Brookhaven; E of Middle
Island
Source: (Bayles 95, p. 51)
*Middle Island Quad (7.5′)

LEVITTOWN
Community
Nassau—Hempstead; NE side of the
town, S of Hicksville;
40°43′30″x73°30′
Freeport and Amityville Quads (7.5′)

LIBBY POINT
Physical feature
Suffolk—Brookhaven; E side of
Forge River, W of Old Neck;
40°47′10″x72°49′15″
Moriches Quad (7.5′)

LIDO BEACH
Community
Nassau—Hempstead; E of Long
  Beach city, S of Oceanside;
  40°35'15"x73°38'
  Lawrence and Jones Inlet
  Quads (7.5')

LIGONEE BROOK
Physical feature
Suffolk—Southampton; flows from
  Long Pond to Sag Harbor Cove;
  40°59'10"x72°18'
Sag Harbor Quad (7.5')

LIGONEE SWAMP
Physical feature
Suffolk—Southampton; SW of Sag
  Harbor, S of Upper Sag Harbor
  Cove; 40°59'20"x72°18'30"
Source: (Tooker 44, pp. 85–86)
Variations: Liganee, Leganee,
  Litganee (Ibid.)
*Sag Harbor Quad (7.5')

LILY POND
Community
  see
APAQUOGUE
Source: (Tooker 44, p. 15)

LILY POND
Physical feature
Suffolk—East Hampton; E of
  Georgica Pond, SW of East
  Hampton; 40°56'20"x72°12'45"
East Hampton Quad (7.5')

LILY POND
Physical feature
Suffolk—East Hampton; E part of
  Gardiners Island; 41°5'40"x72°5'
Gardiners Island East Quad (7.5')

LILY POND
Physical feature
Suffolk—Riverhead; NE of the
  community of Riverhead, S of
  Jacobs Hill; 40°59'30"x72°35'40"
Mattituck Quad (7.5')

LILY POND
Physical feature
Suffolk—Southampton; S of Sag
  Harbor; 40°58'45"x72°18'
Sag Harbor Quad (7.5')

LINDEN HILL
Community—historical
Queens; presently part of Bushwick
  Junction and Maspeth, formerly S
  of Maspeth, W of Mount Olivet
  Cemetery; ca. 40°43'x73°54'30"
Source: (Brooklyn Quad, 15', 1897)
Variation: Linden Hills (French 10,
  p. 549)
*Brooklyn Quad (7.5')

LINDENHURST
Village
Suffolk—Babylon; S-central part of
  the town, W of Babylon village;
  40°41'x73°22'30"
Historical: Breslau (Bailey 19, vol. 1,
  p. 364)
Amityville Quad (7.5')

LINUS POND
Physical feature
Suffolk—Riverhead; N of Manorville,
  W of Calverton; 40°53'30"x72°49'
Wading River Quad (7.5')

LITTLE AFRICA
Physical feature—woods—historical
Suffolk—Smithtown; NE part of the

town, S of Long Beach, N of
Porpoise Channel;
40°55'20"x73°9'45"
Source: (Langhans 98, p. 16).
Also known as The Grove (Ibid.)
*Saint James Quad (7.5')

LITTLE ASSUPS NECK
Physical feature—historical
Suffolk—Southampton; present site
of the community of Quiogue;
40°49'x72°38'
Source: (Tooker 44, p. 24).
Also known as Quiogue Neck and
Quaquanantuck (Ibid., pp. 24,
205-207)
*Eastport Quad (7.5')

LITTLE BAY
Physical feature
Queens; on the East River and Long
Island Sound, NE part of Queens,
NE of Flushing, E of Beechhurst;
40°47'30"x73°47'20"
Flushing Quad (7.5')

LITTLE BAY
Physical feature
Queens; SE part of Jamaica Bay,
NE of Arverne, NW of Edgemere;
40°36'x73°46'50"
Far Rockaway Quad (7.5')

LITTLE BAY
Physical feature
Suffolk—Brookhaven; S of Strongs
Neck, W of Setauket Harbor;
40°57'x73°6'40"
Historical: Minnoseroke, Little Neck
Bay (Flint 26, p. 71), Little Setauket
Bay (Ullitz 164, p. 22)
Port Jefferson Quad (7.5')

LITTLE BAY
Physical feature
Suffolk—Southold; E of Long Beach
Bay; 41°8'25"x72°15'20"
Orient Quad (7.5')

LITTLE BAY
Physical feature—historical
Kings; no longer exists, presently the
E side of Floyd Bennett Field;
40°35'45"x73°54'5"
Source: (Brooklyn Quad, 15', 1897)
*Coney Island Quad (7.5')

LITTLE BAY MARSH
Physical feature—marsh island
—historical
Queens; SE part of Jamaica Bay,
NE of Arverne, W of Far
Rockaway; 40°36'15"x73°47'
Source: (Brooklyn Quad, 15', 1897)
*Far Rockaway Quad (7.5')

LITTLE BEACH
see
SHORT BEACH
Source: (Langhans 98, p. 23)

LITTLE CEDAR ISLAND
Physical feature
Suffolk—Shelter Island; central part
of Shelter Island, in Coecles Inlet;
41°4'37"x72°20'10"
Greenport Quad (7.5')

LITTLE COW HARBOR
Community
see
CENTERPORT
Source: (French 10, p. 636fn)

LITTLE COW HARBOR
Physical feature
see
CENTERPORT HARBOR
Source: (Bayles 93, p. 158)

LITTLE COW NECK
see
PLANDOME
Source: (Flint 26, p. 74)

LITTLE CRABMEADOW NECK
Physical feature
Suffolk—Huntington; NE side of
town, S of Crab Meadow, NE of
Northport; 40°55′x73°19′45″
Source: (Sammis 104, p. 9)
*Northport Quad (7.5′)

LITTLE CREEK
Physical feature
Suffolk—Brookhaven; flows into
Patchogue Bay, S of Patchogue;
40°45′x73°0′25″
Patchogue and Sayville Quads (7.5′)

LITTLE CREEK
Physical feature
Suffolk—Southold; W of Little
Peconic Bay, N of Little Hog Neck;
41°1′10″x72°27′10″
Southold Quad (7.5′)

LITTLE EAST NECK
Physical feature
Suffolk—Babylon; S of Babylon,
E of Lindenhurst; 40°41′x73°20′
Historical: Anuskkummikak, Captain
Fleet's Neck (Tooker 44, p. 12–14),
Arasecoseagge (Ibid., p. 18–19)
Bay Shore West Quad (7.5′)

LITTLE EGG MARSH
Physical feature—marsh island
Queens; SW part of Queens, SW
part of Jamaica Bay, NE of Belle
Harbor; 40°35′30″x73°50′15″
Far Rockaway Quad (7.5′)

LITTLE FIRE CREEK
Physical feature
Suffolk—Brookhaven; S part of the
town, flows into the NE part of
Bellport Bay; 40°45′47″x72°53′15″
Bellport Quad (7.5′)

LITTLE FISH CREEK POND
Physical feature
Suffolk—Brookhaven; S part of the
town, NE of Bellport Bay;
40°46′x72°52′50″
Bellport Quad (7.5′)

LITTLE FRESH POND
Physical feature
Suffolk—Southampton; NW of
Southampton village, E of Big
Fresh Pond; 40°54′x72°24′35″
Historical: Nippaug (Tooker 44, pp.
159–160)
Southampton Quad (7.5′)

LITTLE GULL ISLAND
Physical feature
Suffolk—Southold; in Long Island
Sound, NE of Plum Island and
Great Gull Island;
41°12′27″x72°6′25″
Plum Island Quad (7.5′)

LITTLE HOG NECK
Physical feature
Suffolk—Southold; NE of Great
Peconic Bay; 41°00′x72°27′

Historical: Hoggenock (Tooker 44,
p. 72), Nassau Point (Bayles 93,
p. 372)
Southold and Southampton Quads
(7.5')

LITTLE INLET
Physical feature—historical
Nassau—Hempstead; once existed in
the vicinity of Atlantic Beach;
ca. 40°35'5"x73°43'
Source: (Osborne 36, p. 116)
*Lawrence Quad (7.5')

LITTLE ISLAND
Physical feature
Suffolk—Babylon; W side of Great
South Bay, S of Amity Harbor,
W of Elder Island;
40°38'35"x73°24'15"
Amityville Quad (7.5')

LITTLE LONG POND
Physical feature
Suffolk—Southampton; S of Sag
Harbor; 40°58'40"x72°17'50"
Sag Harbor Quad (7.5')

LITTLE LONG POND
Suffolk—Southampton; W of
Bridgehampton; 40°56'x72°19'20"
Sag Harbor Quad (7.5')

LITTLE MADNANS NECK
see
LITTLE NECK
Community
Queens
Source: (Ricard 86, p. 12)

LITTLE MERRIT'S POND
see

MERRITS POND
Source: (Ullitz 164, p. 29)

LITTLE NARROWS
Physical feature
Suffolk—Southampton; channel
between Sag Harbor Cove and
Upper Sag Harbor Cove;
40°59'35"x72°18'55"
Sag Harbor Quad (7.5')

LITTLE NECK
Community
Nassau—Hempstead
see
BELLMORE
Source: (French 10, p. 547)

LITTLE NECK
Community
Queens; NE side of Queens, S of
Great Neck; 40°45'50"x73°44'30"
Historical: Qaotuac (Thompson 42,
p. 128), Little Madnans Neck and
Cornbury (Ricard 86, p. 12)
Sea Cliff Quad (7.5')

LITTLE NECK
Physical feature
Queens; S of Little Neck Bay,
NE part of Queens;
40°46'30"x73°45'
Flushing and Sea Cliff Quads (7.5')

LITTLE NECK
Physical feature
Suffolk—Babylon; S side of
Lindenhurst; 40°40'20"x73°21'45"
Historical: Gueguis Neck (Tooker 44,
p. 67), Naguntatogue Neck
(Thompson 42, p. 128), Ketcham's
Neck (Beauchamp 7, p. 216)
Bay Shore West Quad (7.5')

LITTLE NECK
Physical feature
Suffolk—Huntington; on Northport
  Bay, N-central part of the town;
  40°54′x73°22′
Northport and Lloyd Harbor
  Quads (7.5′)

LITTLE NECK
Physical feature
Suffolk—Southold; S of East
  Cutchogue, N of Cutchogue
  Harbor; 41°1′x72°28′
Southold Quad (7.5′)

LITTLE NECK
Physical feature—historical
Nassau—Hempstead; S of Bellmore,
  W of Newbridge Creek;
  ca. 40°39′x73°32′15″
Source: (Pelletreau 38, p. 103)
*Freeport Quad (7.5′)

LITTLE NECK
Suffolk—Brookhaven
  see
STRONGS NECK
  Source: (Tooker 44, pp. 131–132)

LITTLE NECK BAY
Physical feature
Nassau, Queens—North Hempstead;
  NE Queens, SW of Great Neck;
  40°47′x73°44′50″
Historical: Martinnehouch Bay
  (Tooker 44, pp. 115–116), Martin
  Gerretsen's Bay (Flint 26, p. 71),
  Little York Bay (French 10, p. 549)
Sea Cliff and Flushing Quads (7.5′)

LITTLE NECK BAY
Physical feature
Suffolk—Brookhaven
  see
LITTLE BAY
  Source: (Flint 26, p. 71)

LITTLE NECK RUN
Physical feature
Suffolk—Brookhaven; flows into the
  Carmans River, N of Bellport Bay;
  40°46′40″x72°53′45″
Bellport Quad (7.5′)

LITTLE NORTHWEST CREEK
Physical feature
Suffolk—East Hampton; E of Sag
  Harbor; 41°x72°16′
Greenport and Sag Harbor Quads
  (7.5′)

LITTLE PECONIC BAY
Physical feature
Suffolk—Southampton
  see
FLANDERS BAY
  Source: (U.S. 5, List No. 5904,
  p. 37) and (Thompson 41, vol. 1,
  inside cover map)

LITTLE PECONIC BAY
Physical feature
Suffolk—Southold, Southampton;
  E of Great Peconic Bay, S of Great
  Hog Neck; 41°1′x72°25′
Southold and Southampton Quads
  (7.5′)

LITTLE PLAIN
Tract of land—historical
Suffolk—Southampton; S of the
  village of Southampton, between

Agawam Lake and Old Town Pond;
40°52'30"x72°22'30"
Source: (Pelletreau 38, p. 292)
*Southampton, Shinnecock Inlet and
Sag Harbor Quads (7.5')

LITTLE PLAINS
Community
Queens
see
QUEENS VILLAGE
Source: (Ricard 86, p. 13)

LITTLE PLAINS
Community
Suffolk—Huntington; central part of
the town, S of Greenlawn;
40°51'x73°22'
Greenlawn Quad (7.5')

LITTLE PLAINS
Physical feature
Suffolk—Huntington; N-central part
of the town, SE of the community
of Huntington;
40°51'45"x73°23'15"
Historical: Tredwell's Plain (Sammis
104, p. 197)
Huntington Quad (7.5')

LITTLE POND
Physical feature
Suffolk—East Hampton; S part of
Gardiners Island, S of Tobaccolot
Pond; 41°4'25"x72°5'50"
Gardiners Island East Quad (7.5')

LITTLE POXABOGUE POND
Physical feature
Suffolk—Southampton; NE of
Bridgehampton;
40°56'50"x72°17'30"
Sag Harbor Quad (7.5')

LITTLE QUOGUE
see
QUOGUE
Source: (Thompson 41, vol. 1,
p. 362)

LITTLE RAM ISLAND
Physical feature
Suffolk—Shelter Island; NE Shelter
Island, NE of Coecles Inlet;
41°5'x72°18'30"
Greenport Quad (7.5')

LITTLE REED POND
Physical feature
Suffolk—East Hampton; NE of
Lake Montauk;
41°4'30"x71°55'10"
Montauk Point Quad (7.5')

LITTLE RIVER
Physical feature
Suffolk—Southampton; flows into
Peconic River, S of Riverhead;
40°54'55"x72°39'50"
Riverhead Quad (7.5')

LITTLE ROUND POND
Physical feature
Suffolk—Southampton; S of Sag
Harbor; 40°59'x72°17'27"
Sag Harbor Quad (7.5')

LITTLE SEATUCK CREEK
Physical feature
Suffolk—Brookhaven; NW side of
Seatuck Cove, SW of Eastport;
40°48'50"x72°43'50"
Eastport Quad (7.5')

LITTLE SEBONAC CREEK
Physical feature
Suffolk—Southampton; SE side of
Great Peconic Bay;
40°55′30″x72°26′40″
Historical: Island Creek (Hagstrom
141, 1959, p. 51)
Southampton Quad (7.5′)

LITTLE SETAUKET BAY
see
LITTLE BAY
Suffolk—Brookhaven
Source: (Ullitz 164, p. 22)

LITTLE SWAMP
Physical feature
Suffolk—Smithtown; W side of
Nissequogue River, N of San Remo;
40°53′55″x73°13′40″
Source: (Langhans 98, p. 16)
*Saint James Quad (7.5′)

LITTLE TANNER NECK
see
TANNER NECK
Source: (Pelletreau 38, p. 341)

LITTLE WONUNK
see
WONUNKE
Source: (Tooker 44, pp. 290–291)

LITTLE YORK BAY
see
LITTLE NECK BAY
Nassau, Queens—North Hempstead
Source: (French 10, p. 549)

LITTLEWORTH
Tract of land
see

SEA CLIFF
Source: (Cocks 70, pp. 7–8)

LITTLEWORTH NECK
see
HAWKINS NECK
Source: (Pelletreau 39, p. 263)

LLOYD BEACH
Physical feature
Suffolk—Huntington; W shoreline of
parts of Lloyd Neck and West Neck;
40°54′30″x73°29′5″
Lloyd Harbor Quad (7.5′)

LLOYD HARBOR
Physical feature
Suffolk—Huntington; SE of Lloyd
Neck, N of Huntington;
40°55′x73°27′
Lloyd Harbor Quad (7.5′)

LLOYD HARBOR
Village
Suffolk—Huntington; on West Neck,
NW part of the town, NW of the
community of Huntington;
40°54′x73°27′30″
Lloyd Harbor Quad (7.5′)

LLOYD NECK
Physical feature
Suffolk—Hungtington; NW side of
the town, W of Eatons Neck;
40°56′x73°28′
Historical: Caumsett (Tooker 44,
pp. 37–38), Horse Neck (Flint 26,
p. 72)
Lloyd Harbor Quad (7.5′)

LLOYD NECK ESTATES
Community
Suffolk—Huntington; E side of

Lloyd Neck;
40°55'20"x73°27'15"
Source: (Hagstrom 141, 1965, p. 18)
*Lloyd Harbor Quads (7.5')

LLOYD POINT
Physical feature
Suffolk—Huntington; NW part of
Lloyd Neck; 40°56'45"x73°29'10"
Lloyd Harbor Quad (7.5')

LOCUST GROVE
Community
Nassau—Oyster Bay; S of Syosset,
NE of Hicksville; 40°48'30"x73°30'
Hicksville and Huntington Quads
(7.5')

LOCUST GROVE
Community—historical
Queens; in Newtown (town)
Source: (French 10, p. 549)

LOCUST MANOR
Community
Queens; SE of Jamaica, SW of
St. Albans; 40°41'x73°46'45"
Jamaica Quad (7.5')

LOCUST POINT
see
DERING POINT
Source: (Bayles 93, p. 398)

LOCUST VALLEY
Community
Nassau—Oyster Bay; NW side of
town, E of Glen Cove;
40°52'50"x73°35'30"
Historical: Buckram (Coles 75,
pp. 207, 218) and (Cocks 70, p. 8)
Bayville and Hicksville Quads (7.5')

LOFTS POND
Physical feature
Nassau—Hempstead; NE side of
Oceanside; 40°39'15"x73°37'15"
Freeport Quad (7.5')

LONE HILL
Community
Suffolk—Brookhaven; on Fire Island,
E of Fire Island Pines;
40°40'x73°4'
Source: (U.S. 170, Chart No. 12352,
1980)
*Sayville Quad (7.5')

LONELYVILLE
Community
Suffolk—Islip; on Fire Island, E of
Fair Harbor, S of Fire Islands;
40°38'25"x73°10'40"
Bay Shore East Quad (7.5')

LONG BEACH
City
Nassau; SW side of the county, E of
Atlantic Beach; 40°35'20"x73°40'
Historical: part of the city known as
West End (Macoskey 29, p. 63)
Lawrence Quad (7.5')

LONG BEACH
Physical feature
Nassau; S shoreline of the city of
Long Beach; 40°35'x73°40'
Lawrence Quad (7.5')

LONG BEACH
Physical feature
Suffolk—Smithtown; on Smithtown
Bay, N of Stony Brook Harbor;
40°55'20"x73°10'10"
Historical: Long Point (Langhans 98,
p. 16)
Saint James Quad (7.5')

LONG BEACH
Physical feature
Suffolk—Southampton; S of North
Haven Peninsula;
41°0'15"x72°19'10"
Greenport and Sag Harbor Quads
(7.5')

LONG BEACH
Physical feature
Suffolk—Southold; NE of Shelter
Island; 41°7'30"x72°17'
Greenport Quad (7.5')

LONG BEACH BAY
Physical feature
Suffolk—Southold; E of Orient;
41°8'x72°16'30"
Historical: possibly Poquatuck
(Tooker 44, p. 195)
Orient Quad (7.5')

LONG BEACH NORTH
Community
Nassau—Hempstead; the vicinity of
Island Park; ca. 40°35'20"x73°40'
Source: (Macoskey 29, p. 56)
*Lawrence Quad (7.5')

LONG BEACH POINT
Physical feature
Suffolk—Southold; S of Orient
Harbor, the W point of Orient
Beach State Park, NE of Shelter

Island; 41°6'45"x72°18'
Greenport Quad (7.5')

LONG COVE
Physical feature
Suffolk—Brookhaven; on Fire Island,
S of Patchogue Bay;
40°41'55"x72°58'30"
Howells Point Quad (7.5')

LONG COVE
Physical feature
Suffolk—Smithtown; Sunken
Meadow Creek, W of the mouth of
the Nissequogue River;
40°54'30"x73°14'15"
Source: (Langhans 98, p. 16)
*Saint James Quad (7.5')

LONG CREEK
Physical feature—channel
Nassau—Hempstead; S of Freeport,
borders Smith Meadow and High
Meadow on the E, and Pine Marsh
on the W; 40°36'45"x73°34'30"
Jones Inlet Quad (7.5')

LONG CREEK
Physical feature
Suffolk—Southold; flows into
Hashamomuck Pond, NE of
Southold, SW of Arshamonaque;
41°5'x72°24'30."
Southold Quad (7.5')

LONG CREEK
Physical feature
Suffolk—Southold; flows into
Mattituck Creek, N of Mattituck;
41°00'x72°32'25"
Mattituck and Mattituck Hills Quads
(7.5')

LONG CREEK OF SEAPONACK
see
BULLHEAD BAY
Source: (Pelletreau 38, p. 289)

LONG ISLAND
Physical feature
Kings (Brooklyn borough), Nassau,
Queens (borough), and Suffolk
counties; approximately 124 miles
long, 12-20 miles wide, extends
ENE from the mouth of the
Hudson, nearly parallel to the
Connecticut shore, from which it is
separated by Long Island Sound;
ca. 40°30'-41°12' N Lat.,
72°-74° W Long.
Historical: Island of Nassau, Ilant de
Gebrokne Lant (Macoskey 29, p.
74), Isle Plowden, Manitie, Long-
Isle, Syon (Bailey 19, vol. 1, p. 31),
Matouwacks, Matowa, Matowcas,
Mattanwake, Meitowax,
Paumanack, Seawanhacky,
Wamponomon
(Tooker 44, pp. 124-125, 182-183,
232-234, 271), Fish-shaped
Paumanok (Coles 20, p. 97),
Nassau Island (Spafford 14,
p. 291), Crooked Row (Bailey 19,
vol. 1, p. 77)

LONG ISLAND CITY
Community
Queens; NW side of Queens, S of
Astoria; 40°45'x73°56'30"
Historical: Hunter's Point,
Payntarville (Walling 172) and
(Brooklyn Quad, 15', 1897),
Bennet's Point, Domine's Hoeck
(Flint 26, p. 72)

Central Park and Brooklyn Quads
(7.5')

LONG ISLAND SOUND
Physical feature
N of Long Island, between Long
Island and Connecticut
Historical: North Sea (Flint 26,
pp. 72-73), and The Devils Belt
(Faden 136)

LONG MEADOW
Physical feature
Nassau—Hempstead; E side of Jones
Beach State Park;
40°36'15"x73°30'
Jones Inlet and West Gilgo Beach
Quads (7.5')

LONG MEADOW ISLAND
Physical feature
Nassau—Hempstead; S of Middle
Bay, W of Adler Island, NW of
Point Lookout; 40°36'x73°35'45"
Jones Inlet Quad (7.5')

LONG NECK CREEK
Physical feature—historical
Queens; no longer exists, was SW of
Springfield, JFK Airport presently
occupies the area
Source: (Walling 172)
*Jamaica Quad (7.5')

LONG POINT
Physical feature
Suffolk—Brookhaven; E part of
Bellport Bay, SE point of Fireplace
Neck; 40°45'40"x72°53'20"
Bellport Quad (7.5')

LONG POINT
Physical feature
Suffolk—Southampton; SE side of
Sag Harbor Cove, W of Morris
Cove; 40°59′35″x72°18′50″
Sag Harbor Quad (7.5′)

LONG POINT
Suffolk—Smithtown
see
LONG BEACH
Physical feature
Source: (Langhans 98, p. 16)

LONG POND
Physical feature
Suffolk—Southampton; W of
Bridgehampton
40°56′15″x72°19′40″
Sag Harbor Quad (7.5′)

LONG POND
Physical feature
Suffolk—Southampton; S of Sag
Harbor; 40°58′30″x72°17′30″
Sag Harbor Quad (7.5′)

LONG POND
Suffolk—Brookhaven
see
LAKE PANAMOKA
Source: (Wading River Quad, 7.5′,
1944)

LONG SWAMP
Community—historical
Suffolk—Huntington; between the
West Hills and Dix Hills;
ca. 40°49′x73°24′45″
Source: (Bailey 19, vol. 1, p. 356)
*Huntington Quad (7.5′)

LONGWOOD
Tract of land—historical
Suffolk—Brookhaven; NE of
Yaphank, N of Shirley;
ca. 40°51′30″x72°53′
Source: (Chace 127)
*Bellport Quad (7.5′)

LONS CREEK
Physical feature
Suffolk—Brookhaven; flows into the
W side of the Forge River, N of
Forge Neck; 40°46′40″x72°49′5″
Moriches Quad (7.5′)

LOPONTZ CREEK
see
HAVENS' CREEK
Source: (Tooker 44, p. 129)

LORDS PASSAGE
Physical feature
Suffolk—Southold; in Block Island
Sound, NE side of Southold, E of
Fishers Island;
41°17′30″x71°54′15″
Mystic Quad (7.5′)

LOTT'S LANDING
see
PORT OF HEMPSTEAD
Source: (Metz 83, p. 8)

LOTUS LAKE
Physical feature
Suffolk—Islip; NW of Bayport, NE
of Sayville; 40°44′45″x73°4′
Sayville Quad (7.5′)

LOUSE POINT
Physical feature
Suffolk—East Hampton; in

Acabonack Harbor;
41°1′10″x72°8′15″
Gardiners Island West Quad (7.5′)

LOWER BEACH
Physical feature
Suffolk—Shelter Island; NE Shelter
Island, between Little Ram Island
and Ram Island; 41°5′x72°18′
Greenport Quad (7.5′)

LOWER FRANCIS POND
Physical feature
Nassau—Oyster Bay; S of Mill Neck,
W of the community of Oyster Bay,
N of Upper Francis Pond;
40°52′20″x73°34′5″
Hicksville Quad (7.5′)

LOWER LAKE
Physical feature
Suffolk—Brookhaven; on the
Carmans River, S of Yaphank,
NW of Shirley;
40°50′5″x72°55′15″
Bellport Quad (7.5′)

LOWER LANDING
see
SAN REMO
Source: (Thompson 41, vol. 1,
inside cover map)

LOWER MELVILLE
Community
Suffolk—Huntington; SW side of the
town, E of Old Bethpage;
40°46′x73°25′20″
Huntington Quad (7.5′)

LOWER WINGANHAUPPAUGE
LAKE
Physical feature
Suffolk—Islip; N of Champlin Creek,
between Islip and East Islip;
40°43′30″x73°12′10″
Bay Shore East Quad (7.5′)

LUBBERTSEN'S NECK
Physical feature—historical
Kings; no longer exists, presently part
of Red Hook vicinity;
40°40′40″x74°00′
Source: (Stiles 66, vol. 1, p. 63).
Also known as Neck of Brookland
(Ibid.)
*Jersey City Quad (7.5′)

LUCE LANDING
Tract of land
Suffolk—Riverhead; NE of the
community of Riverhead;
40°59′10″x72°37′10″
Mattituck Quad (7.5′)

LUDLAM'S NECK
Physical feature—historical
Suffolk—Southampton; E side of
Mecox Bay, between Swan Creek
and Sams Creek;
ca. 40°54′10″x72°18′45″
Source: (Pelletreau 38, p. 322).
Also known as Miller's Land (Ibid.)
*Sag Harbor Quad (7.5′)

LUDLOWS CREEK
Physical feature
Suffolk—Islip; on Nicoll Bay, W of
Sayville; 40°43′35″x73°7′30″
Historical: Wehahamis Creek
(Tooker 44, pp. 280-281), Newton's
Creek (Pelletreau 38, p. 243)
Sayville Quad (7.5′)

LUSAM
see
JERICHO
Nassau—Oyster Bay
Source: (Tooker 44, p. 86)
Variation: Lusum (French 10,
p. 551fn)

LYNBROOK
Village
Nassau—Hempstead; W-central part
of the town, SE of Valley Stream;
40°39′30″x73°40′
Historical: Pearsalls Corner (Walling
172), Pearsalls (Beers 117, p. 106)
Lynbrook Quad (7.5′)

LYNBROOK PARK
Community
Nassau—Hempstead; within the
vicinity of Lynbrook
Source: (Macoskey 29, p. 56)
*Lynbrook Quad (7.5′)

Nassau—North Hempstead
Source: (Flint 26, p. 71)

MADNAN'S NECK
see
GREAT NECK
Nassau—North Hempstead
Source: (Tooker 44, p. 87)
and (Flint 26, p. 71)

McKAY LAKE
Physical feature
Suffolk—Riverhead; N of Swan
Pond, W of Calverton;
40°54′30″x72°47′40″
Wading River Quad (7.5′)

MACUTTERIS
Locality—marsh
Kings; in the vicinity of Flatlands
Source: (Tooker 44, pp. 86–87)
*Coney Island and Brooklyn Quads
(7.5′)

MACY CHANNEL
Physical feature
Nassau—Hempstead; E border of
Hewlett Bay Park, flows into the
N part of Hewlett Bay;
40°37′30″x73°41′15″
Lynbrook Quad (7.5′)

MAD NAN'S NECK
see
GREAT NECK
Nassau—North Hempstead
Source: (Flint 26, p. 71)

MADNACK
see

MAHCHONGITCHUGE
Physical feature—swamp—historical
Suffolk—East Hampton; on North
Neck, between Fort Pond and Lake
Montauk; 41°3′x71°56′30″
Source: (Tooker 44, pp. 87–88)
Variation: Mahchongitchigo (Ibid.)
*Montauk Point Quad (7.5′)

MAIDSTONE
see
EAST HAMPTON
Source: (Flint 26, p. 70)

MAIDSTONE PARK
Community
Suffolk—East Hampton; NE of
Threemile Harbor;
41°2′10″x72°10′40″
Gardiners Island West Quad (7.5′)

MAIDSTONE PARK BEACH
Physical feature
Suffolk—East Hampton; NE of
Threemile Harbor;
41°2′20″x72°10′50″
Gardiners Island West Quad (7.5′)

MAIN POND
Physical feature
Suffolk—Islip; the Connetquot River
flows into the pond, E of Islip
Terrace; 40°45'x73°9'
Central Islip and Bay Shore East
Quads (7.5')

MAJORS HARBOR
Physical feature
Suffolk—Shelter Island; SE side of
Shelter Island, NE of North Haven
Peninsula; 41°2'10"x72°17'
Greenport Quad (7.5')

MAJORS POINT
Physical feature
Suffolk—Shelter Island; SE part of
Shelter Island, NW of Majors
Harbor; 41°2'20"x72°17'10"
Greenport Quad (7.5')

MAKAMAH BEACH
Physical feature
Suffolk—Huntington; on Long
Island Sound, NE side of the
town, N of Crab Meadow;
40°55'40"x73°19'
Northport Quad (7.5')

MAKEOPACA
Locality—historical
Kings; in the vicinity of Gravesend,
bounded on the E by Strome Creek
Source: (Tooker 44, pp. 88–89)
*Coney Island Quad (7.5')

MALBA
Community
Queens; N side of Queens, W of
Whitestone, E of College Point;
40°47'30"x73°49'40"
Flushing Quad (7.5')

MALLOW REACH
Physical feature
Nassau—Hempstead; NW of Hewlett
Bay, SW of Bay Park;
40°37'45"x73°40'45"
Lynbrook Quad (7.5')

MALVERNE
Village
Nassau—Hempstead; W side of the
town, SW of Garden City;
40°40'30"x73°40'30"
Historical: Norwood (Reifschneider
85, p. 186) and (Macoskey 29,
p. 58), Skunk's Misery (Stevens 40,
p. 10)
Lynbrook Quad (7.5')

MAMANOCK NECK
Physical feature—historical
Suffolk—Brookhaven; SE side of
East Moriches, between Tuthill and
Hart Coves; 40°37'45"x72°45'30"
Source: (Tooker 44, pp. 89–90)
Variations: Mamanok, Mamannuck
(Ibid.)
*Moriches Quad (7.5')

MAMENKQUIAUGE
Tract of land—historical
Suffolk—East Hampton; SW side of
Montauk Harbor;
ca. 41°2'35"x71°55'50"
Source: (Pelletreau 38, p. 371)
*Montauk Point Quad (7.5')

MAMEWETA POND
see
MARRATOOKA LAKE
Source: (U.S. 5, List No. 5904,
p. 37)

MANANTIC CREEK
Physical feature
Suffolk—Shelter Island; SW side of
Shelter Island, N of West Neck
Harbor; 41°3'10"x72°20'45"
Greenport Quad (7.5')

MANANTIC NECK
Physical feature
Suffolk—Shelter Island; SW side of
Shelter Island, E of West Neck;
41°3'20"x72°21'
Source: (Tooker 44, p. 90)
*Greenport Quad (7.5')

MANATUCK CREEK
see
LAWRENCE CREEK
Suffolk—Islip
Source: (Tooker 44, pp. 91-92)
Variations: Manetuck, Manetuc,
Mantash, Manshtak, Marihtak
(Ibid.)

MANCHONACK
see
GARDINERS ISLAND
Source: (Tooker 44, pp. 90-91)
Variations: Manchonacke,
Monchongomuc, Monch O Neck,
Manchonat, Mashongonoc (Ibid.)

MANETTO HILL
Physical feature
Nassau—Oyster Bay; N of Plainview,
W of Melville; 40°47'15"x73°28'
Source: (Gibbs 76, p. 83)
*Huntington Quad (7.5')

MANETTO HILLS
Community
Suffolk—Huntington; SW part of
the town, NW of Melville;

40°47'30"x73°26'30"
Source: (Hagstrom 141, 1979, p. 26)
*Huntington Quad (7.5')

MANETUCK NECK
see
COMPOWAMS NECK
Source: (Tooker 44, pp. 91-92)

**MANHANSACK-
AHAQUATUWAMOCK**
see
SHELTER ISLAND
Source: full Indian name for Shelter
Island (Tooker 44, pp. 92-93)

MANHANSET
see
DERING HARBOR
Village
Source: (Macoskey 29, p. 56)

MANHANSETT
see
SHELTER ISLAND
Physical feature
Source: (Tooker 44, pp. 93-94)

MANHANSUCK BROOK
see
MOORES DRAIN
Source: (Tooker 44, pp. 94-95)

MANHASSET
Community
Nassau—North Hempstead; SW side
of Manhasset Neck, W of Roslyn
and Munsey Park;
40°47'50"x73°42'15"
Historical: Tan Yards (French 10,
p. 550fn), Cow Neck, Sintsinck
(Flint 26, p. 72)
Sea Cliff Quad (7.5')

MANHASSET BAY
Physical feature
Nassau—North Hempstead; N side
of town, W of Manhasset Neck;
40°50'x73°43'
Historical: Shout's Baie, Howe's Bay,
  Cow Bay (Bailey 19, vol. 1, p. 443),
  Scouts Bay (Dyson 24, p. 21)
Sea Cliff Quad (7.5')

MANHASSET HILL
Physical feature
Nassau—North Hempstead; SE part
  of Manhasset Neck;
40°47'50"x73°42'45"
Source: (Oyster Bay Quad, 15',
  1897)
*Sea Cliff Quad (7.5')

MANHASSET NECK
Physical feature
Nassau—North Hempstead; NE part
  of town; 40°50'x73°42'
Historical: Cow Neck (Tooker 44,
  p. 95) and (U.S. 170, Chart No.
  116, 1855), Sint Sink (French 10,
  p. 550fn)
Sea Cliff Quad (7.5')

MANHATTAN BEACH
Community
Kings; SW part of Kings, E of
  Coney Island and Brighton Beach;
40°34'45"x73°56'45"
Coney Island Quad (7.5')

MANITIE
see
LONG ISLAND
Source: (Bailey 19, vol. 1, p. 31)

MANITTUWOND
see
PLUM ISLAND
Source: (Tooker 44, p. 98)

MANNAHANNING
see
CONEY ISLAND
Source: (Tooker 44, p. 98)

MANNER HILLS
see
OREGON HILLS
Source: (U.S. 170, Chart No. 115,
1855)

MANNETTO HILLS
Physical feature
Nassau—Oyster Bay; E side of the
  town, NE of Hicksville;
40°48'x73°27'30"
Huntington Quad (7.5')

MANOR
see
MANORVILLE
Source: (Tooker 44, p. 199)

MANOR HILL
Physical feature
Suffolk—Southold; between the
  communities of Mattituck and
  Cutchogue; 41°00'40"x72°30'
Source: (Pelletreau 38, p. 434)
*Southold Quad (7.5')

MANOR HILLS
see
OREGON HILLS
Source: (U.S. 167, Map T–55)

MANORHAVEN
Village
Nassau—North Hempstead; NW part
  of Manhasset Neck, NW of Port
  Washington; 40°50′30″x73°43′
Sea Cliff Quad (7.5′)

MANORVILLE
Community
Suffolk—Brookhaven; E side of
  town, S of Wading River, SW of
  Riverhead; 40°52′30″x72°48′20″
Historical: Manor, Punk's Hole
  (Tooker 44, p. 199)
Moriches and Wading River Quads
  (7.5′)

MANOWTASQUOTT
see
BLUE POINT
Community
Source: (Tooker 44, p. 100)

MANOWTASSQUOT CREEK
see
NAMKEE CREEK
Source: (Tooker 44, pp. 100–101)

MANSHTAK CREEK
see
LAWRENCE CREEK
Suffolk—Islip
Source: (Bayles 93, p. 210)

MANTOOBAUGS
Tract of land—historical
Suffolk—Southold; on
  Hashamomuck Neck
Source: (Tooker 44, p. 101)
*Southold Quad (7.5′)

MANUNKQUIAUG
Locality—historical
Suffolk—East Hampton; on North
  Neck, area around the S shore of
  Lake Montauk, presently partially
  occupied by Ditch Plains;
  41°2′50″x71°55′30″
Source: (Tooker 44, pp. 101–102)
*Montauk Point Quad (7.5′)

MAPES NECK
Physical feature—historical
Suffolk—Southold; E side of
  Mattituck Creek, NW of Mattituck;
  41°00′5″x72°32′30″
Source: (Pelletreau 38, p. 434)
*Mattituck and Mattituck Hills
  Quads (7.5′)

MAPLE GROVE
see
KEW GARDENS
Source: (Ricard 86, p. 11) and
  (Brooklyn Quad, 15′, 1897)

MAPLE SWAMP
Physical feature
Suffolk—Southampton; S of
  Flanders, N of Flanders Hill;
  40°53′10″x72°36′40″
Mattituck Quad (7.5′)

MARATHON
see
DOUGLASTON
Source: (Ricard 86, p. 8)
and (Walling 172)

MARATOOKER POND
see
MARRATOOKA LAKE
Source: (U.S. 5, List No. 5904,
p. 37)

MARCONIVILLE
Community—proposed village
—historical
Suffolk—Babylon; N of the railroad
tracks in the community of
Copiague; ca. 40°41′10″x73°24′
Source: (Bailey 19, vol. 1, p. 385)
and (Hyde 148)
*Amityville Quad (7.5′)

MARECHKAWICK
Indian village—historical
Kings; in the borough of Brooklyn,
possibly part of the present site of
South Brooklyn;
ca. 40°40′30″x73°59′30″
Source: (Tooker 44, pp. 102–103)
Variations: Marchkenwikingh,
Merchkawikingh, Merechkawick,
Marechkawick, Merechkawick
(Ibid.)
*Brooklyn Quad (7.5′)

MARIGIES NECK
Physical feature—historical
Suffolk—Brookhaven; S side of
East Moriches, bounded on the
W by Terrel River (Paquetuck
River), and on the E by Tuthill
Cove, adjoins Mamanack Neck;
40°47′30″x72°46′
Source: (Tooker 44, pp. 89–90)
*Moriches Quad (7.5′)

MARION LAKE
Physical feature
Suffolk—Southold; NE of Greenport;

41°7′30″x72°20′
Historical: East Marion Lake
(Ullitz 164, plate 12)
Greenport and Orient Quads (7.5′)

MAROSSEPINCK
see
MASSAPEAQUA
Source: (Tooker 44, pp. 103–104)

MARRATOOKA LAKE
Physical feature
Suffolk—Southold; NE of Mattituck;
40°59′35″x72°31′25″
Historical: Momoweta Pond, Lake
Momoweta (Tooker 44, p. 139),
Mameweta Pond, Marratooka Pond,
Maratooker Pond, Mattituck Pond
(U.S. 5, List No. 5904, p. 37)
Mattituck Quad (7.5′)

MARRATOOKA POINT
Physical feature
Suffolk—Southold; on Great Peconic
Bay, E of Mattituck;
40°59′10″x72°30′20″
Mattituck Quad (7.5′)

MARSEY
see
MASSAPEQUA
Source: (Tooker 44, pp. 103–105)

MARSH POINT
Physical feature
Suffolk—Southold; NW of
Cutchogue Harbor;
41°0′10″x72°28′10″
Southold Quad (7.5′)

MARTIN GARRETSEN'S BAY
see
LITTLE NECK BAY
Nassau—North Hempstead
Source: (Flint 26, p. 71)

MARTINNEHOUCH BAY
see
LITTLE NECK BAY
Nassau—North Hempstead
Source: (Tooker 44, pp. 115–116)

MARTINNE-HOUCK
Indian village—historical
Suffolk—Huntington; in the vicinity
of Huntington Bay
Source: (Pelletreau 38, p. 172)
*Lloyd Harbor Quad (7.5 ')

MASHASHIMUET
Physical feature—spring—historical
Suffolk—Southampton; S of Other
Pond in the village of Sag Harbor
Source: (Tooker 44, p. 105)
*Sag Harbor Quad (7.5 ')

MASHMANOCK
see
SHINNECOCK CANAL
Source: (Tooker 44, pp. 105–106)

MASHOMACK POINT
Physical feature
Suffolk—Shelter Island; S point of
Shelter Island; 41 °1 '30 "x72 °16 '40 "
Variations: Meshomac,
Marshammock, Mashomuk,
Mashomuck (Tooker 44,
pp. 106–109)
Greenport Quad (7.5 ')

MASKACHOUNG NECK
Physical feature—historical
Nassau—Hempstead; a neck of land
in the SE part of Hempstead
Source: (Tooker 44, p. 109).
Also known as Maskutchoung
(Ibid.)
*Freeport Quad (7.5 ')

MASPETH
Community
Queens; NW side of Queens, SE of
Long Island City;
40 °43 '20 "x73 °54 '40 "
Historical: English Kills, Melvina
(French 10, p. 549fn) and
(Burr 125), Wandowenock
(Beauchamp 7, p. 179) and
(Tooker 44, pp. 272–273)
Variations: Mashpath, Mespaat,
Mespachtes Kil, Mespacht,
Mespatchis, Mespaetches
(Tooker 44, p. 127)
Brooklyn Quad (7.5 ')

MASPETH CREEK
Physical feature
Queens; flows into the SE side of
Newtown Creek, W of Maspeth;
40 °43 '25 "x73 °55 '30 "
Brooklyn Quad (7.5 ')

MASQUETUX CREEK
see
LAWRENCE CREEK
Suffolk—Islip
Source: (Tooker 44, p. 110)

MASQUETUX NECK
Physical feature—historical
Suffolk—Islip; on the Great South
Bay, between Appletree Neck and
Compowms Neck, W shore of Islip
town; ca. 40°42'20"x73°15'25"
Source: (Tooker 44, pp. 109–110) and
(Chace 127)
Variations: Missatuck, Mispotuck,
Mispatuck (Ibid.)
*Bay Shore West Quad (7.5')

MASSABARKEM
see
GRAVESEND NECK
Source: (Tooker 44, p. 110)

MASSAKACK
see
HALF HOLLOW HILLS
Source: (Tooker 44, pp. 110–111)

MASSAPEQUA
Community
Nassau—Oyster Bay; E of Wantagh
and Seaford, S of Bethpage, W of
Amityville; 40°40'45"x73°28'30"
Historical: Marossepinck (Tooker 44,
p. 111), Unkway Neck, South
Oyster Bay (Flint 26, p. 73)
Variations: Masepeage, Marsey,
Massapeage, Marsapeake,
Messepeake, Mashpeag,
Masha-peage, Matsepe, etc.
(Tooker 44, pp. 111–112, 117)
Amityville Quad (7.5')

MASSAPEQUA CREEK
Physical feature
Nassau—Oyster Bay; flows between
Massapequa and Massapequa Park,
through Massapequa Preserve and
Massapequa Lake into the NW part

of South Oyster Bay;
40°39'15"x73°36'45"
Amityville Quad (7.5')

MASSAPEQUA LAKE
Physical feature
Nassau—Oyster Bay; E side of
Massapequa, N of Biltmore Shores,
part of the Massapequa Preserve;
40°40'10"x73°28'
Amityville Quad (7.5')

MASSAPEQUA PARK
Village
Nassau—Oyster Bay; S part of the
town, E of Massapequa, NW of
Amityville; 40°41'x73°27'
Historical: part of the village known
as Wurtemberg (Hyde 147)
Amityville Quad (7.5')

MASSAPEQUA PRESERVE
Physical feature
Nassau—Oyster Bay; E side of
Massapequa; 40°41'20"x73°27'30"
Variation: Massapequa State Park
(Hagstrom 140, 1978, pp. 15, 19)
Amityville Quad (7.5')

MASSAPEQUA STATE PARK
see
MASSAPEQUA PRESERVE
Source: (Hagstrom 140, 1978,
pp. 15, 19)

MASSAPOOTUPAUG
Locality—historical
Suffolk—Southampton; SW part of
the town, possibly S of
Westhampton
Source: (Tooker 44, p. 113)

MASSEPE
see
THURSTON BASIN
Source: (Tooker 44, p. 112)

MASTIC
Community
Suffolk—Brookhaven; W of
Moriches, E of Shirley, SE part of
the town; 40°48'x72°50'30"
Historical: Paynesville (Bigelow 96,
p. 166)
Moriches Quad (7.5')

MASTIC BEACH
Community
Suffolk—Brookhaven; SE part of the
town, S of Mastic, SE of Shirley;
40°46'x72°51'
Moriches Quad (7.5')

MASTIC NECK
Physical feature
Suffolk—Brookhaven; between
Carmans River and Forge River;
40°46'15"x72°50'
Source: (Tooker 44, p. 114)
Variation: Mastic Point
(Thompson 41, vol. 1, inside cover
map)
*Moriches Quad (7.5')

MASTIC POINT
see
MASTIC NECK
Source: (Thompson 41, vol. 1,
inside cover map)

MASTIC RIVER
see
FORGE RIVER
Source: (Tooker 44, p. 114)

MASTICK NECK
Physical feature—historical
Suffolk—Brookhaven; the original
Mastic Neck, W of Forge River;
40°45'40"x72°49'15"
Source: (Pelletreau 38, p. 265)
*Moriches Quad (7.5')

MASURY POINT
Community
Suffolk—Brookhaven; in the vicinity
of Central Moriches;
ca. 40°46'35"x72°48'30"
Source: (Macoskey 29, p. 57)
*Moriches Quad (7.5')

MASURY POINT
Physical feature
Suffolk—Brookhaven; S point of
Old Neck, NW side of Moriches
Bay; 40°46'30"x72°48'30"
Moriches Quad (7.5')

MATHAGARRATSON'S BAY
see
HEMPSTEAD HARBOR
Source: (Flint 26, p. 130)

MATINECOCK
Tract of land—historical
Nassau—Oyster Bay; N part of the
town, from the Sound to the range
of hills between Glen Cove and
Oyster Bay, called the 'the hill
country' or 'land that overlooks'
Source: (Coles 75, pp. 207, 218),
(Tooker 44, pp. 115–117) and
(Cocks 70, pp. 1–11)
Variations: Matinnecock,
Matinnecoke, Matinnecogh,
Matinnekonck, Matinnecoke,
Metinicok, Montinnecok
(Tooker 44, pp. 115–117) and
(Burr 125)

MATINECOCK
Village
Nassau—Oyster Bay; NW central
part of the town, SE of Glen Cove;
40°52'x73°35'
Hicksville and Bayville Quads (7.5')

MATINECOCK ISLANDS
Physical feature—historical
Queens (Nassau)—Oyster Bay;
islands now known as East Island
and Dosoris Island;
40°53'50"x73°38'10"
Source: (Cocks 70, p. 2)
*Mamaroneck Quad (7.5')

MATINECOCK POINT
Physical feature
Nassau—Glen Cove; N point of East
Island and the city of Glen Cove;
40°54'10"x73°38'
Mamaroneck Quad (7.5')

MATINNECOCK ISLAND
see
EAST ISLAND
Nassau—Oyster Bay
Source: (Tooker 44, p. 115) and
(Thompson 41, vol. 1, p. 495)

MATONA
see
RAVENSWOOD
Source: (Ricard 86, p. 13)

MATOWCAS
Tract of land—historical
Kings; Indian name for Brooklyn,
also one of the names for Long
Island
Source: (Tooker 44, pp. 117, 124)

MATSEPE
see

MASSAPEQUA
Source: (Tooker 44, p. 117)

MATTANWAKE
see
LONG ISLAND
Source: (Tooker 44, pp. 117–118)

MATTAWOMMAX
Locality
Suffolk—Brookhaven
Source: (Tooker 44, p. 118)

MATTEMOY NECK
Physical feature—historical
Suffolk—Brookhaven; on the Great
South Bay, Johns Neck Creek
borders on the W side, SW of
Mastic Beach; 40°45'x72°52'
Source: (Tooker 44, p. 119).
Also known as Mattemog (Ibid.)
*Moriches Quad (7.5')

MATTHABANKS
see
GREAT SOUTH BEACH
Source: (Tooker 44, p. 120)

MATTITUCK
Community
Suffolk—Southold; NE of Riverhead,,
N of Great Peconic Bay;
40°59'x72°32'
Variations: Mattatuck, Matatucke,
Mattaducke, Mattatuck, Mattetuck,
Matituck (Tooker 44, pp. 120–121).
Also known as Nabiachage (Ibid.,
p. 148)
Mattituck Quad (7.5')

MATTITUCK BAY
see
MATTITUCK CREEK
Source: (Tooker 44, pp. 47, 120–121)
and (Bayles 93, p. 367)

MATTITUCK CREEK
Physical feature
Suffolk—Southold; flows into Long
Island Sound, N of Mattituck;
41°00′x72°32′50″
Historical: Mattituck Pond, W
Branch known as Waterville Creek
(U.S. 167, Map T-55), Mattituck
Bay (Tooker 44, pp. 47, 120–121)
and (Bayles 93, p. 367)
Mattituck and Mattituck Hills Quads
(7.5′)

MATTITUCK HILLS
Physical feature
Suffolk—Southold; NW of the
community of Mattituck;
41°00′15″x72°34′30″
Historical: Coopers Hills (U.S. 167,
Map T-55), Mattock Hills (Ullitz
164, plate 10)
Mattituck Hills Quad (7.5′)

MATTITUCK INLET
Physical feature
Suffolk—Southold; on Long Island
Sound, NW of Mattituck;
41°0′50″x72°33′30″
Mattituck Hills Quad (7.5′)

MATTITUCK POND
Suffolk—Southold
see
MATTITUCK CREEK
Source: (U.S. 167, Map T-55)

MATTITUCK POND
Suffolk—Southold
see
MARRATOOKA LAKE
Source: (U.S. 5, List No. 5904,
p. 37)

MATTOCK SWAMP
Physical feature—historical
Suffolk—Southampton; in the
vicinity of North Sea
Source: (Tooker 44, pp. 121–122).
Also known as Matuck Swamp
(Ibid.)
*Southampton Quad (7.5′)

MATTUCK BROOK
Physical feature
Suffolk—Brookhaven; S part of
town, E of East Moriches, flows
into the NW part of Hart Cove,
borders Watchogue Neck on the E;
40°48′10″x72°45′15″
Source: (Tooker 44, p. 122)
*Moriches Quad (7.5′)

MAYWOOD
Community
Suffolk—Babylon; SE of
Farmingdale, NW part of the town;
40°43′25″x73°25′30″
Amityville Quad (7.5′)

MEADOW GLEN
Community—historical
Suffolk—Smithtown; SE of
Middleville, N of Kings Park, S of
Sunken Meadow
Source: (Northport Quad, 15′, 1901)
*Northport Quad (7.5′)

MEADOW LAKE
Physical feature
Queens; in Meadow Park, central
part of Queens, E of Newtown;
40°44′x73°50′35″
Jamaica Quad (7.5′)

MEADOWLAND
Community—historical
Suffolk—Brookhaven; E of Coram,
W of Middle Island, S of Millers
Place; ca. 40°52′45″x72°57′
Source: (Burr 124)
*Middle Island Quad (7.5′)

MEADOWMERE PARK
Community
Nassau—Hempstead; SW part of the
town, NE of Head of Bay;
40°38′15″x73°44′15″
Lynbrook Quad (7.5′)

MEANTAUQUET
Physical feature—historical
Suffolk—East Hampton; E neck of
Long Island, the Montauk
Peninsula; ca. 41°2′30″x71°55′
Source: (Pelletreau 38, p. 369)
*Montauk Point Quad (7.5′)

MECHANICSVILLE
see
BAY SHORE
Source: (Bailey 19, vol. 1, p. 327)
and (U.S. 170, Chart No. 119,
1844)

MECHAWANIENCK
Locality—historical
Kings; near the SE side of Flatlands
Source: (Tooker 44, pp. 123–124)

MECOCK BAY
see
MECOX
Community
Source: (Burr 124)

MECOX
Community
Suffolk—Southampton; S of
Bridgehampton, E of Mecox Bay;
40°54′40″x72°18′
Historical: Mecock Bay (Burr 124)
Variations: Meacox, Meacoxe,
Mecocks, Mecoks, Meacocks,
Meecooks (Tooker 44, pp. 122–123)
Sag Harbor Quad (7.5′)

MECOX
Locality—historical
Suffolk—Southampton; between Mill
Creek and Sagaponack Pond;
ca. 40°54′40″x72°18′45″
Source: (Pelletreau 38, p. 319)
*Sag Harbor Quad (7.5′)

MECOX BAY
Physical feature
Suffolk—Southampton; E of the
village of Southampton;
ca. 40°54′x72°20′
Historical: Mecox Water (Tooker 44,
p. 122)
Variations: Meacoxe, Mecocks,
Mecoks, Meacocks, Meecooks
(Ibid.)
Sag Harbor Quad (7.5′)

MECOX WATER
see
MECOX BAY
Source: (Tooker 44, p. 122)

MEDFORD
Community
Suffolk—Brookhaven; NE of
Patchogue, SE of Port Jefferson;
40°49′15″x73°00′
Historical: Medford Station (U.S. 5,
List No. 6903, p. 22)
Bellport and Patchogue Quads (7.5′)

MEDFORD STATION
see
MEDFORD
Source: (U.S. 5, List No. 6903,
p. 22)

MEETING HOUSE BROOK
Physical feature—historical
Suffolk—Huntington; flowed into the
S side of Huntington Harbor;
40°53′x73°25′20″
Source: (Sammis 104, pp. 40–41)
*Lloyd Harbor Quad (7.5′)

MEETINGHOUSE CREEK
Physical feature
Suffolk—Riverhead; flows into the
NW part of Flanders Bay, S of
Aquebogue; 40°55′45″x72°37′
Mattituck Quad (7.5′)

MEITOWAX
see
LONG ISLAND
Source: (Tooker 44, p. 124)
Variations: Matouwac, Matouacks,
Meilowacks, Metoac, Meitowacks,
Matowcas, Mattanwake, Matowa;
it appears by these names on all
Dutch maps from about 1631 to
1775 (Ibid.)

MELVILLE
Community
Suffolk—Huntington; SW side of the
town, S of the community of
Huntington; 40°47′30″x73°25′
Historical: Sweet Hollow (French 10,
p. 636fn), Sunquams, Yaphank
(Flint 26, p. 73), Samuel Ketcham's
Hollow (Dyson 25, p. 62)
Huntington and Greenlawn Quads
(7.5′)

MELVINA
see
MASPETH (part of)
Source: (French 10, p. 549)

MEMANUSACK BROOK
see
STONY BROOK
Physical feature
Source: (Tooker 44, p. 125)
and (Langhans 98, p. 17)

MEMORIAL POND
see
ARGYLE LAKE
Source: (Bay Shore West Quad,
7.5′, 1954)

MENANTIC
Community—historical
Suffolk—Shelter Island; S of Shelter
Island Heights;
ca. 41°3′15″x72°20′30″
Source: (Macoskey 29, p. 57) and
(Hyde 147)
*Greenport Quad (7.5′)

MENANTIC CREEK
Physical feature
Suffolk—Shelter Island; SW side of
Shelter Island;
41°3'30"x72°20'40"
Greenport Quad (7.5')

MENHANSICK ISLAND
see
SHELTER ISLAND
Physical feature
Source: (Tooker 44, p. 43)

MERICOCK
see
MERRICK
Source: (Marshall 80, p. 382)

MEROCK
see
MERRICK
Source: (Pelletreau 38, p. 103)

MEROGES
see
MORICHES
Source: (Beauchamp 7, p. 216)

MEROSUCK
Physical feature—isthmus—historical
Suffolk—Southampton; the isthmus
between Shinnecock and Peconic
Bays, the Indian word means Canoe
Place; 40°53'15"x72°30'10"
Source: (Tooker 44, pp. 125-126)
*Mattituck Quad (7.5')

MERRICK
Community
Nassau—Hempstead; E of Freeport,
W of Bellmore; 40°40'x73°33'30"
Variations: Merie, Moroke, and
Merikohe (French 10, p. 547),

Mericock (Marshall 80, p. 382),
Merock (Pelletreau 38, p. 103)
Freeport Quad (7.5')

MERRICK
Physical feature—historical
Queens (Nassau); a name originally
applied to the Hempstead Plains,
meaning barren land
Source: (Tooker 44, pp. 126-127)

MERRICK BAY
Physical feature
Nassau—Hempstead; S of Merrick,
W side of East River;
40°38'25"x73°33'15"
Freeport Quad (7.5')

MERRICK CREEK
Physical feature
Nassau—Hempstead; flows through
S part of Merrick, into East Bay;
40°38'50"x73°32'40"
Freeport Quad (7.5')

MERRICK POINT
Physical feature
Nassau—Hempstead; SW point of
Merrick, W side of East Bay;
40°38'20"x73°32'45"
Freeport Quad (7.5')

MERRITTS POND
Physical feature
Suffolk—Riverhead; N side of the
community of Riverhead;
40°55'40"x72°40'
Historical: Little Merrit's Pond
(Ullitz 164, p. 29)
Riverhead Quad (7.5')

MERRYES
see

MORICHES NECK
Source: (Beauchamp 7, p. 216)

MERYCKAWICK
see
RED HOOK
Source: (Weisman 68, p. 39)

MESPAETCHES CREEK
see
NEWTOWN CREEK
Source: (Tooker 44, pp. 127–128)

MESSEMENNUCK CREEK
see
PECONIC RIVER
Source: (Tooker 44, pp. 128–130)

MESSTOPASS
Physical feature—waterhole
—historical
Queens (Nassau)—Oyster Bay; in the
vicinity of Mannetto Hills
Source: (Tooker 44, p. 130)
*Huntington Quad (7.5 ')

METROPOLITAN
Community—historical
Queens—Newtown; W side of the
town, SW of Maspeth
Source: (Hyde 147)

MEUNTAUCUT
Locality—historical
Suffolk—East Hampton; an area
from Napeague Beach, E to
Montauk Point;
ca. 41 °2 '30 "x71 °54 '45 "
Source: (Tooker 44, p. 271)
*Montauk Point Quad (7.5 ')

MEUTALEAR ISLAND
see

EAST ISLAND
Nassau—Oyster Bay
Source: (Cocks 70, p. 2)

MIAMOG
see
JAMESPORT
Source: (French 10, p. 637fn)

MIAMOGUE CREEK
see
KINGS CREEK
Source: (Tooker 45, p. 36)

MIAMOGUE LAGOON
Physical feature
Suffolk—Riverhead; S of South
Jamesport, NW part of Great
Peconic Bay; 40 °56 'x72 °35 '23 "
Mattituck Quad (7.5 ')

MIAMOGUE NECK
Physical feature
Suffolk—Riverhead; the neck on
which South Jamesport is located;
40 °55 '25 "x72 °34 '45 "
Source: (Tooker 44, p. 131)
*Mattituck Quad (7.5 ')

MIAMOGUE POINT
Physical feature
Suffolk—Riverhead; on Great
Peconic Bay, S of South Jamesport;
40 °56 'x72 °34 '40 "
Historical: Wyamaug Point (Tooker
44, p. 293)
Mattituck Quad (7.5 ')

MIDDELBURG
see
ELMHURST
Source: (Ricard 86, p. 9)

MIDDLE BROOK
Physical feature
Suffolk—Islip; between West Brook
and Rattlesnake Brook, N of
Oakdale; 40°45′x73°8′40″
Central Islip Quad (7.5′)

MIDDLE CANAL
Physical feature
Suffolk—Islip; on the Great South
Bay, one of three canals S of the
community of Islip;
40°42′30″x73°13′10″
Bay Shore East Quad (7.5′)

MIDDLE CROW ISLAND
Physical feature
Nassau—Hempstead; S of Big Crow
Island, N of Jones Island;
40°36′45″x73°32′25″
Jones Inlet Quad (7.5′)

MIDDLE FARMS POND
Physical feature
Suffolk—Southold; central part of
Fishers Island;
41°16′30″x71°58′40″
Mystic Quad (7.5′)

MIDDLE GROUND
Physical feature—shoal
Suffolk—Southold; in Long Island
Sound, W of Plum Island;
41°10′10″x72°12′50″
Plum Island Quad (7.5′)

MIDDLE ISLAND
Community
Suffolk—Brookhaven; S of Rocky
Point, NE of Coram;
40°53′x72°56′20″
Historical: Middletown and

Brookhaven (Bayles 95, p. 49)
Middle Island Quad (7.5′)

MIDDLE ISLAND
Physical feature
Nassau—Hempstead; E of Cuba
Island and Big Crow Island, S of
Deep Creek Meadow;
40°37′20″x73°31′15″
Jones Inlet Quad (7.5′)

MIDDLE ISLAND
Physical feature
Nassau—Hempstead; S of Middle
Bay, W of Alder Island;
40°35′50″x73°36′
Jones Inlet Quad (7.5′)

MIDDLE ISLAND
Physical feature—historical
Nassau—Oyster Bay
see
CENTRE ISLAND
Source: (Thompson 41, vol. 1,
p. 51)

MIDDLE NECK
Physical feature
Suffolk—Southampton; NW of
Seatuck Cove;
40°48′50″x72°44′15″
Source: (Pelletreau 38, p. 342)
*Eastport Quad (7.5′)

MIDDLE POND
Physical feature—inlet
Suffolk—Southampton; NE side of
Shinnecock Bay;
40°52′45″x72°26′50″
Southampton Quad (7.5′)

MIDDLE ROAD
Community—historical
Suffolk—Riverhead; NE of the
  community of Riverhead;
  ca. 40°56′x72°39′10″
Source: (Bayles 93, p. 299)
*Riverhead Quad (7.5′)

MIDDLE ROAD
Suffolk—Islip
see
BAYPORT
Source: (Bailey 19, vol. 1, p. 333)

MIDDLE SHOAL ROCK
Physical feature
Suffolk—Southold; in Block Island
  Sound, E of Plum Island, SW of
  Great Gull Island;
  41°11′35″x72°8′25″
Plum Island Quad (7.5′)

MIDDLE VILLAGE
Community
Queens; W side of Queens, N of
  Glendale, S of Elmhurst;
  40°43′15″x73°45′
Jamaica and Brooklyn Quads (7.5′)

MIDDLEBURG
see
NEWTOWN
Town
Source: (French 10, p. 548)

MIDDLETOWN
see
MIDDLE ISLAND
Community
Source: (Bayles 95, p. 49)

MIDDLETOWN
Community—historical
Queens—Newtown (town); SE of
  Astoria
Source: (French 10, p. 549)

MIDDLETOWN
Locality—historical
Suffolk—Brookhaven; the name is
  used in reference to the parish of
  the Presbyterian Church, NE of
  Gordon Heights;
  40°52′35″x72°57′40″
Source: (Bayles 93, p. 262)
*Middle Island Quad (7.5′)

MIDDLEVILLE
Community
Suffolk—Smithtown, Huntington;
  E of Northport, S of Fort Salonga;
  40°53′45″x73°17′50″
Historical: Slongo, Sunk Meadow
  (Bayles 93, p. 186)
Northport Quad (7.5′)

MIDHAMPTON
Community
Suffolk—East Hampton; W of East
  Hampton, NW of Georgica Pond;
  40°57′x72°14′30″
East Hampton Quad (7.5′)

MID-ROAD VILLE
see
BAYPORT
Source: (Chace 127)

MIDWAY SHOAL
Physical feature
Suffolk—Southold; in Plum Gut,
  midway between Orient Point and
  Plum Island; 41°9′40″x72°13′
Plum Island Quad (7.5′)

MIDWOUT
see
FLATBUSH
Source: (French 10, p. 372)

MILBURN
see
BALDWIN
Source: (Macoskey 29, p. 57)

MILBURN CREEK
Physical feature
Nassau—Hempstead; flows from the
central to the S part of the town,
into Baldwin Bay;
40°37′55″x73°35′45″
Variations: Millburn Creek,
Millbum Creek (U.S. 5, List No.
7002, p. 9)
Freeport Quad (7.5′)

MILBURN POND
Physical feature
Nassau—Hempstead; E side of
Baldwin and W side of Freeport;
40°39′07″x73°36′10″
Freeport Quad (7.5′)

MILEBURN
see
BALDWIN
Source: (Walling 172)

MILL BASIN
Physical feature
Kings; N of Floyd Bennett Field,
W side of Jamaica Bay, SE of
Flatlands; 40°36′15″x73°55′
Coney Island Quad (7.5′)

MILL BROOK
Physical feature
Suffolk—Islip; flows into

Connetquot River from the NW
side, S of Main Pond;
40°44′45″x73°8′5″
Source: (Town of Islip 163)
*Bay Shore East Quad (7.5′)

MILL CREEK
Physical feature
Kings; E of Gerritsen, W of Floyd
Bennet Field; 40°35′30″x73°54′50″
Coney Island Quad (7.5′)

MILL CREEK
Physical feature
Queens; NW of Flushing, SE of
College Point; 40°46′30″x73°50′
Historical: Flushing Mill Pond
(Walling 172)
Flushing Quad (7.5′)

MILL CREEK
Physical feature
Suffolk—Smithtown; flows into the
Nissequogue River, W of Saint
James; 40°52′32″x73°11′40″
Saint James Quad (7.5′)

MILL CREEK
Physical feature
Suffolk—Southampton; on Noyack
Bay, S of Noyack, W of Pine Neck;
40°59′45″x72°20′50″
Historical: Rugs Creek (Tooker 44,
p. 216)
Sag Harbor Quad (7.5′)

MILL CREEK
Physical feature
Suffolk—Southampton; NW part of
Mecox Bay, S of Water Mill;
40°54′20″x72°21′

Historical: Benedicts Creek (Adams
92, p. 18)
Sag Harbor Quad (7.5 ')

MILL CREEK
Physical feature
Suffolk—Southampton; S of Flanders
Bay, flows from Sears Pond;
40°53'55"x72°34'50"
Mattituck Quad (7.5 ')

MILL CREEK
Physical feature
Suffolk—Southold; between
Hashamomuck Pond and Shelter
Island Sound; 41°4'45"x72°24'
Historical: Tom's Creek (Pelletreau
38, pp. 415, 417, 419),
Sonnquoquas Creek (Beauchamp 7,
p. 224)
Southold Quad (7.5 ')

MILL HILLS
Physical feature
Suffolk—Smithtown; SE of San
Remo, S of Nissequogue village,
SW of Stony Brook Harbor;
40°54'x73°10'
Source: (Langhans 98, p. 17)
*Saint James Quad (7.5 ')

MILL ISLAND
Physical feature—historical
Kings; part of the mainland, SE of
Flatlands, W of Jamaica Bay;
40°36'30"x73°54'30"
Source: (Hagstrom 142, 1947, p. 23)
*Coney Island Quad (7.5 ')

MILL LAKE
see
MILL POND
Suffolk—Huntington; Centerport
Harbor
Source: (Ullitz 164, plate 1)

MILL NECK
Community
see
WATER MILL
Source: (Bayles 93, p. 333)

MILL NECK
Physical feature
Nassau—Oyster Bay; W of Oyster
Bay, S of Bayville;
40°53'15"x73°33'30"
Historical: Papequatunck (Tooker 44,
p. 176), Mill River Neck (Cocks 70,
p. 5)
Bayville Quad (7.5 ')

MILL NECK
Physical feature
Suffolk—Southampton; NW side of
Mecox Bay, the community of
Water Mill is located on the neck;
40°54'30"x72°20'45"
Source: (Bayles 93, p. 333)
*Sag Harbor Quad (7.5 ')

MILL NECK
Village
Nassau—Oyster Bay; W-central part
of Mill Neck, W of the S part of
Centre Island; 40°53'15"x73°33'20"
Bayville Quad (7.5 ')

MILL NECK CREEK
Physical feature
Nassau—Oyster Bay; S of Oak Neck
and Bayville, flows into the NE part
of Oyster Bay Harbor;
40°54'x73°33'45"
Bayville Quad (7.5')

MILL NECK STATION
Community
Nassau—Oyster Bay; SW part of
Mill Neck, SE of Beaver Lake;
40°52'50"x73°33'45"
Source: (Hagstrom 140, 1978, p. 34)
*Bayville Quad (7.5')

MILL POND
Physical feature
Nassau—Oyster Bay; W side of the
community of Oyster Bay;
40°52'25"x73°32'27"
Hicksville Quad (7.5')

MILL POND
Physical feature
Suffolk—Brookhaven; between
Center Moriches and East Moriches;
40°48'10"x72°46'30"
Moriches Quad (7.5')

MILL POND
Physical feature
Suffolk—Brookhaven, Smithtown;
SW of the community of Stony
Brook, NE of the village of Head
of the Harbor;
40°54'50"x73°8'45"
Saint James Quad (7.5')

MILL POND
Physical feature
Suffolk—Huntington; E side of West
Neck, W side of Huntington

Harbor; 40°54'x73°26'40"
Source: (Hagstrom 141, 1979, p. 22)
*Lloyd Harbor Quad (7.5')

MILL POND
Physical feature
Suffolk—Huntington; S of
Centerport Harbor, SW side of
Little Neck; 40°53'20"x73°22'15"
Historical: Mill Lake (Ullitz 164,
plate 1)
Northport Quad (7.5')

MILL POND
Physical feature
Suffolk—Islip; E of Sayville;
40°44'35"x73°4'35"
Sayville Quad (7.5')

MILL POND
Physical feature
Suffolk—Smithtown
see
NEW MILLPOND
Source: (Langhans 98, p. 17)

MILL POND
Physical feature
Suffolk—Southampton; SW part of
the town, NW of Water Mill and
Mecox Bay; 40°54'50"x72°21'30"
Historical: Lake Nowedonah
(Tooker 44, p. 165)
Sag Harbor Quad (7.5')

MILL RIVER
Physical feature
Nassau—Hempstead; flows by the E
border of East Rockaway, into East
Rockaway Channel;
40°38'10"x73°39'40"
Lynbrook Quad (7.5')

MILL RIVER HOLLOW
Physical feature—historical
Queens (Nassau)—Oyster Bay;
extended from N to S, on the E side
of Mill Neck, through East Norwich;
ca. 40°51′x73°32′30″
Source: (Cocks 70, p. 5)
*Hicksville Quad (7.5′)

MILL RIVER NECK
see
MILL NECK
Physical feature
Nassau—Oyster Bay
Source: (Cocks 70, p. 5)

MILL STONE BROOK
Physical feature—historical
Suffolk—Southampton; in the
vicinity of Sebonac Neck
Source: (Pelletreau 38, p. 332)
*Southampton Quad (7.5′)

MILLBUM CREEK
see
MILBURN CREEK
Source: (U.S. 5, List No. 7002,
p. 9)

MILLER PLACE
Community
Suffolk—Brookhaven; E of
Mt. Sinai Harbor, W of Sound
Beach; 40°57′30″x73°0′
Historical: Miller's Landing
(Stevens 40, p. 51)
Port Jefferson and Middle Island
Quads (7.5′)

MILLER PLACE BEACH
Physical feature
Suffolk—Brookhaven; on Long

Island Sound, N of Miller Place,
NE of Mt. Sinai Harbor;
40°57′55″x73°0′
Port Jefferson Quad (7.5′)

MILLER'S LANDING
see
MILLER PLACE
Source: (Stevens 40, p. 51)

MILLERS POND
Physical feature
Suffolk—Smithtown; S of
Smithtown, N of Hauppauge;
40°50′50″x73°11′40″
Historical: Lake Beryl, Brush's Pond
(Langhans 98, pp. 17-18)
Central Islip Quad (7.5′)

MILLPOND
Physical feature
Nassau—Hempstead; E side of
Bellmore, W side of Seaford, within
Millpond Park; 40°40′x73°31′10″
Freeport Quad (7.5′)

MILLS POND
Physical feature
Suffolk—Smithtown; N of Saint
James, E of the S point of Stony
Brook Harbor; 40°53′50″x73°9′
Saint James Quad (7.5′)

MILL'S POND VILLAGE
see
FLOWERFIELD
Source: (Langhans 98, pp. 7,
18, 64)

MILLSIDE
Community—historical
Suffolk—Southampton; NE of
Remsenburg, W of West Hampton;
40°49 '45 "x72°40 '25 "
Source: (Hyde 147)
*Eastport Quad (7.5 ')

MILLVILLE
Suffolk—Brookhaven
see
YAPHANK
Source: (French 10, p. 634 fn) and
(Thompson 41, vol. 1, inside cover
map)

MILLVILLE
Suffolk—Southampton
see
WATER MILL
Source: (Thompson 41, vol. 1,
inside cover map)

MINASSEROKE
see
STRONGS NECK
Source: (Tooker 44, pp. 131-132)

MINAUSSUMS
see
WINNECROSCOMS NECK
Source: (Tooker 44, p. 132)

MINEOLA
Village
Nassau—North Hempstead; S–central
part of town, S of Garden City;
40°45 'x73°38 '
Historical: Hempstead Branch (Coles
20, p. 97), part of the village called
Krug's Corners (Macoskey 29,
p. 55)
Lynbrook and Sea Cliff Quads (7.5 ')

MINNAPAUGS POND
Physical feature—historical
Suffolk—Southold; E side of
Hortons Neck, NW of the
community of Southold;
41 °5 'x72°26 '30 "
Source: (Tooker 44, p. 133)
*Southold Quad (7.5 ')

MINNELL'S CREEK
see
ARRASQUAUG BROOK
Source: (Tooker 44, pp. 178-179)

MINNESUNK POND
Physical feature—historical
Suffolk—Southampton; in the North
Sea Harbor area
Source: (Tooker 44, pp. 133-134)
*Southampton Quad (7.5 ')

MINNOSEROKE
see
LITTLE BAY
Suffolk—Brookhaven
Source: (Flint 26, p. 71)

MIRRACHTAUHACKY
see
MONTAUK
Community
Source: (Tooker 44, p. 135)

MIRROR LAKE
Physical feature
Suffolk—Islip; S part of Brightwaters;
40°42 '50 "x73°15 '50 "
Bay Shore West Quad (7.5 ')

MISPAT KIL
see
NEWTOWN CREEK
Source: (Bailey 19, vol. 1, p. 38)

MISPATUCK NECK
Physical feature—historical
Suffolk—Islip; between Appletree
Neck and Compowams Neck;
40°42′20″x73°15′25″
Source: (Tooker 44, p. 135–136)
Variations: Mispotuck, Misputuck,
Mispatuc, Masquetux, Missatuck
(Ibid.)
*Bay Shore West Quad (7.5′)

MISSATUCK BROOK
Physical feature—historical
Suffolk—Islip; flowed between
Appletree Neck and Missatuck Neck,
presently known as Thorn Canal;
40°41′50″x73°15′30″
Source: (Tooker 44, pp. 135–136)
Variation: Mispatuc Brook (Ibid.)
*Bay Shore West Quad (7.5′)

MISSATUCK NECK
see
MISPATUCK NECK
Source: (Tooker 44, p. 136)

MISSIPAUG
see
BIG FRESH POND
Source: (Tooker 44, p. 136)

MR. PAINE'S NECK
Physical feature—historical
Suffolk—Southampton; E side of
Mecox Bay, in the vicinity of Swan
Creek; ca. 40°53′55″x72°18′45″
Source: (Pelletreau 38, p. 320)
*Sag Harbor Quad (7.5′)

MITCHELLS CREEK
Physical feature
Nassau—North Hempstead;

runs through part of Kings Point,
on the NE side of Great Neck into
Manhasset Bay;
40°49′40″x73°44′20″
Sea Cliff Quad (7.5′)

MITTYVILLE
Locality—historical
Suffolk—Brookhaven; name of
settlement about halfway up the
hill between Port Jefferson and Port
Jefferson Station;
ca. 40°56′45″x73°4′
Source: (Bayles 93, p. 249)
*Port Jefferson Quad (7.5′)

MOCHGONNEKONCK
see
SHINNECOCK
Source: (Tooker 44, pp. 136–138)

MODERN TIMES
see
BRENTWOOD
Source: (French 10, p. 637)

MOEUNG
Locality—historical
Kings; Gravesend area, part of the
E end of the beach
Source: (Tooker 44, p. 138)
*The Narrows and Coney Island
Quads (7.5′)

MOGER NECK
Physical feature—historical
Suffolk—Brookhaven; S part of East
Patchogue; 40°45′x72°50′30″
Source: (Bailey 19, vol. 1, p. 269)

MOGKOMPSKUT
Physical feature—boulder—historical
Suffolk—East Hampton; W of
Threemile Harbor, near Hands Creek,
on the Hands Creek Road;
ca. 41 °1 '10 "x72 °12 '30 "
Source: (Tooker 44, p. 138)
*Gardiners Island West Quad (7.5 ')

MOHANNIS HILL
see
SAGAMORE HILL
Source: (Tooker 44, pp. 220–221)

MOHICAN
see
MONTAUK POINT
Source: (Flint 26, p. 73)

MOLASSES POINT
Physical feature
Suffolk—Brookhaven; on Fire Island,
Great South Bay side, S of Bellport;
40 °43 'x72 °55 '40 "
Howells Point Quad (7.5 ')

MOMOWETA POND
see
MARRATOOKA LAKE
Source: (Tooker 44, p. 139)

MONABAUGS CREEK
Physical feature—historical
Suffolk—Southampton; SE of the
village of Westhampton Beach;
ca. 40 °48 'x72 °38 '30 "
Source: (Tooker 44, pp. 139–140)
*Eastport Quad (7.5 ')

MONABAUGS POND
Physical feature—historical
Suffolk—Southampton; E side of the

village of Westhampton Beach;
ca. 40 °48 '10 "x72 °38 '30 "
Source: (Tooker 44, pp. 139–140)
*Eastport Quad (7.5 ')

MONABAUGS SWAMP
Physical feature—marsh—historical
Suffolk—Southampton; SE part of
the village of Westhampton Beach;
ca. 40 °48 '25 "x72 °38 '20 "
Source: (Tooker 44, pp. 139–140)
*Eastport Quad (7.5 ')

MONCORUM
see
CORAM
Source: (Tooker 44, pp. 52–53, 140)

MONEY ISLAND
Physical feature
Suffolk—Islip; one of the Fire
Islands in the Great South Bay, E of
East Fire Island, S of Heckscher
State Park; 40 °39 '25 "x73 °10 '25 "
Bay Shore East Quad (7.5 ')

MONEY POND
Physical feature
Suffolk—East Hampton; E end of
Long Island; 41 °4 '20 "x71 °52 '15 "
Montauk Point Quad (7.5 ')

MONEY POND
Physical feature
Suffolk—Southold; E end of Fishers
Island; 41 °17 '55 "x71 °55 '50 "
Mystic Quad (7.5 ')

MONEYBOQUE BAY
Physical feature
Suffolk—Southampton; SE of
Westhampton Beach, N of Reedy

Island; 40°48'x72°38'20"
Variation: Moneybogue Bay
(Hagstrom 141, 1979, p. 64)
Eastport Quad (7.5')

MONTACK POINT
see
MONTAUK POINT
Source: (Romans 157)

MONTAUK
Community
Suffolk—East Hampton; E end of
Long Island, S of Fort Pond Bay;
41°2'15"x71°57'
Historical: Mirrachtauhacky
(Tooker 44, p. 135)
Montauk Point Quad (7.5')

MONTAUK
Physical feature—peninsula
Suffolk—East Hampton; SE end of
Long Island, SE of Gardiners
Island; ca. 41°3'x71°55'
Variations: Meantaucutt, Meantaquit,
Meantquket, Meantucket,
Menataukett, Meantaukut,
Meuntaukut, Meantauk, Mantack,
etc. (Tooker 44, pp. 141-143)
Montauk Point Quad (7.5')

MONTAUK BEACH
Community
Suffolk—East Hampton; on the
Atlantic Ocean, SW of Montauk;
41°1'30"x71°58'
Montauk Point Quad (7.5')

MONTAUK HARBOR
Physical feature
Suffolk—East Hampton; NW part of

Lake Montauk, W of Star Island;
41°4'20"x71°56'30"
Source: (U.S. 170, Chart No. 13209,
1979)
*Montauk Point Quad (7.5')

MONTAUK POINT
Physical feature
Suffolk—East Hampton; NE of
Montauk, E end of Long Island;
41°4'30"x71°51'25"
Historical: Wamponamon
(Tooker 44, p. 271), Mohican,
Montaukett, Visscher's Hoeck
(Flint 26, p. 73)
Montack Point (Romans 157)
Montauk Point Quad (7.5')

MONTAUK POINT STATE PARK
Suffolk—East Hampton; on the
SE tip of Long Island; E of Lake
Montauk; 41°4'20"x71°52'
Montauk Point Quad (7.5')

MONTAUK STATION
Community
Suffolk—East Hampton; E of Fort
Pond Bay, W of Lake Montauk;
41°3'x71°57'10"
Montauk Point Quad (7.5')

MONTAUKETT
see
MONTAUK POINT
Source: (Flint 26, p. 73)

MONTCLAIR COLONY
Community
Suffolk—Shelter Island; SW part of
Shelter Island, NW of West Neck
Harbor; 41°3'10"x72°21'
Greenport Quad (7.5')

MONTROSE
Community—historical
Queens (Nassau)—North Hempstead
Source: (French 10, p. 550)

MOONEY POND
Physical feature
Suffolk—Brookhaven; W of Lake
  Ronkonkoma; 40°50′x73°5′25″
Patchogue Quad (7.5′)

MOORES DRAIN
Physical feature
Suffolk—Southold; on Pipes Cove,
  W of Greenport, E of
  Arshamonaque; 41°5′15″x72°33′
Historical: Manhansuck Brook,
  Pipe's Neck Creek (Tooker 44,
  pp. 94–95)
Southold and Greenport Quads
  (7.5′)

MORGAN ISLAND
see
EAST ISLAND
  Nassau—Oyster Bay
  Source: (Coles 72, p. 45)

MORICHES
Community
Suffolk—Brookhaven; SE side of
  town, E of Shirley;
  40°48′30″x72°50′
Historical: Meroges (Beauchamp 7,
  p. 216)
Variations: Merquices, Meritces,
  Marigies, Maritches, Moritches,
  Murichis, Meriches, etc. (Tooker 44,
  pp. 144–145)
Moriches Quad (7.5′)

MORICHES BAY
Physical feature
Suffolk—Brookhaven, Southampton;
  SE side of the town of Brookhaven
  and S side of the town of
  Southampton; 40°47′x72°45′
Historical: Great West Bay
  (Burr 124), East Bay (Chace 127)
Moriches and Eastport Quads (7.5′)

MORICHES INLET
Physical feature
Suffolk—Brookhaven; between the
  Atlantic Ocean and the Great South
  Bay, S of East Moriches, SW of
  Eastport; 40°46′x72°45′16″
Moriches and Eastport Quads (7.5′)

MORICHES ISLAND
Physical feature—historical
Suffolk—Brookhaven; no longer an
  island, now part of the mainland,
  S of East Moriches, W side of
  Moriches Bay; 40°47′30″x72°45′
Source: (Tooker 44, p. 43).
Also known as Cochiminchoake,
  Chikemenchoake, Kitchaminchok,
  Ketchininchoge (Ibid., pp. 43,
  83–84)
*Moriches and Eastport Quads (7.5′)

MORICHES NECK
Physical feature
Suffolk—Brookhaven; on Moriches
  Bay, S part of East Moriches,
  bounded on the W by Terrel River
  (formerly Paquetuck River) and on
  the E by Tuthill Cove, adjoins
  Mamanack Neck; 40°57′30″x72°46′
Source: (Tooker 44, p. 144–145)
Historical: Merquices, Meritces,
  Marigies, Maritches, Moritches,

Murichis, Meriches (Ibid.), Merryes
(Beauchamp 7, p. 216)
*Moriches Quad (7.5 ')

MORICHES STATION
see
EASTPORT
Source: (Bayles 93, p. 280)

MORMON HOLE
Physical feature—water hole
—historical
Nassau—Hempstead; on Parsonage
Creek near Oceanside;
ca. 40°38 '30 "x73 °37 '
Source: (Coghlan 71, p. 33)
*Freeport Quad (7.5 ')

MORRIS COVE
Physical feature
Suffolk—Brookhaven
see
NICOLL BAY
Source: (Beers 117, p. 153)

MORRIS COVE
Physical feature
Suffolk—Southampton; SW side of
Upper Sag Harbor Cove, W of Sag
Harbor; 40°59 '30 "x72 °18 '30 "
Sag Harbor Quad (7.5 ')

MORRIS GROVE
see
MORRIS PARK
Source: (Ricard 86, p. 12)

MORRIS PARK
Community
Queens; W of Jamaica, SE of
Richmond Hill; 40°41 '30 "x73 °49 '

Historical: Morris Grove (Ricard 86,
p. 12)
Jamaica Quad (7.5 ')

MOSCOPAS
Physical feature—hole—historical
Nassau—Oyster Bay; E side of
Plainview; 40°46 '30 "x73 °28 '
Source: (Gibbs 76, p. 83).
Also known as Muddy Hole (Ibid.)
*Huntington Quad (7.5 ')

MOSES POINT
Physical feature
Nassau—Oyster Bay; SE point of
Centre Island, W of Cove Neck, on
Oyster Bay Harbor;
40°53 '10 "x73 °31 '15 "
Bayville Quad (7.5 ')

MOSQUITO COVE
Community
see
GLEN COVE
City
Source: (French 10, p. 550fn)

MOSQUITO COVE
Physical feature
Nassau—Oyster Bay; SW of the city
of Glen Cove, NW of Sea Cliff,
NE of Hempstead Harbor;
40°51 '15 "x73 °39 '
Historical: Glen Cove (U.S. 170,
Chart No. 336, 1879 and 1905)
Variations: Mosquetah, Musceata,
Muskitoe, and Muchito (Tooker 44,
p. 145)
Sea Cliff Quad (7.5 ')

MOSQUITO NECK
Physical feature
Nassau—Oyster Bay; SW part of the
city of Glen Cove, N of Mosquito
Cove; 40°51'50"x73°38'
Source: (French 10, p. 550) and
(U.S. 170, Chart No. 366, 1879
and 1905)
*Sea Cliff Quad (7.5')

MOTT POINT
Physical feature
Nassau—North Hempstead;
NE point of Manhasset Neck;
40°51'15"x73°40'30"
Sea Cliff Quad (7.5')

MOTTS BASIN
Physical feature
Queens, Nassau; on Jamaica Bay,
N of Far Rockaway, SW of
Inwood; 40°36'40"x73°45'45"
Far Rockaway Quad (7.5')

MOTTS BROOK
Physical feature
Suffolk—Brookhaven; flows into the
NW side of Bellport Bay;
40°45'25"x72°55'40"
Historical: Osborn's Brook,
Brewster's Brook, Dayton's Brook
(Shaw 106, p. 211)
Bellport Quad (7.5')

MOTTS COVE
Physical feature
Nassau—North Hempstead; NE side
of town, NW side of Roslyn
Harbor, E shoreline of Hempstead
Harbor; 40°49'20"x73°38'45"
Sea Cliff Quad (7.5')

MOTTS CREEK
Physical feature
Nassau—Hempstead; flows through
the SW side of Valley Stream,
NW side of Woodmere, SE of
Meadowmere Park into the Head of
Bay; 40°37'55"x73°44'40"
Lynbrook Quad (7.5')

MOTTS POINT
Physical feature
Queens; on Jamaica Bay, NW of Far
Rockaway, E of Jo Co Marsh;
40°36'45"x73°46'30"
Far Rockaway Quad (7.5')

MT. BARLOW
Physical feature
Nassau—Oyster Bay; SW side of the
city of Glen Cove, N of Mosquito
Cove; 40°51'45"x73°39'
Source: (Oyster Bay Quad, 15',
1897)
*Sea Cliff Quad (7.5')

MOUNT MISERY
Physical feature—peninsula
Suffolk—Brookhaven; on Long
Island Sound, E of Port Jefferson
Harbor, W of Mt. Sinai Harbor;
40°57'30"x73°4'
Port Jefferson Quad (7.5')

MT. MISERY POINT
Physical feature
Suffolk—Brookhaven; on Long
Island Sound, N of Port Jefferson
Harbor, NW side of Mount Misery;
40°58'20"x73°4'50"
Port Jefferson Quad (7.5')

MT. MISERY SHOAL
Physical feature
Suffolk—Brookhaven; in Long
Island Sound, N of Port Jefferson
Harbor and Mt. Misery Point;
40°59'x73°5'10"
Port Jefferson Quad (7.5')

MT. PROSPECT
Physical feature
Suffolk—Riverhead; S of the
community of Rocky Point;
40°56'30"x72°55'20"
Source: (U.S. 170, Chart No. 115,
1844)
*Middle Island Quad (7.5')

MT. PROSPECT
Physical feature
Suffolk—Southold; SW side of
Fishers Island, E of the village of
Fishers Island;
41°15'20"x72°00'35"
New London Quad (7.5')

MOUNT SINAI
Community
Suffolk—Brookhaven; S of Mt.
Sinai Harbor, E of Port Jefferson;
40°56'50"x73°1'45"
Historical: Nonowantuck, Old Man's
Village, possibly Old Homes
(Tooker 44, p. 164) and (Smith 162)
Port Jefferson Quad (7.5')

MOUNT SINAI BEACH
see
CEDAR BEACH
Source: (U.S. 5, List No. 5903,
p. 42)

MT. SINAI HARBOR
Physical feature
Suffolk—Brookhaven; on Long
Island Sound, E of Mount Misery,
NE of Port Jefferson;
40°57'30"x73°2'
Historical: Old Man's Harbor
(Smith 162)
Port Jefferson Quad (7.5')

MOUNTAIN MIST SPRING
Physical feature—historical
Suffolk—Huntington; NW of High
Hill, SE of Woodbury and Cold
Spring; ca. 40°49'x73°26'15"
Source: (Northport Quad, 15', 1901)
*Huntington Quad (7.5')

MOWBRAY PATENT
Tract of land—historical
Suffolk—Islip; between Appletree
Neck and Orowoc Creek;
ca. 40°43'15"x73°15'
Source: (Pelletreau 38, p. 243)
*Bay Shore East and Bay Shore West
Quads (7.5')

MUD CREEK
Physical feature
Nassau—Hempstead; flows into
Merrick Bay, SE side of Merrick,
E boundary of Merrick Road Park;
40°38'20"x73°33'20"
Freeport Quad (7.5')

MUD CREEK
Suffolk—Babylon
see
WEST BABYLON CREEK
Source: (U.S. 6, 1977, p. 215)

MUD CREEK
Physical feature
Suffolk—Brookhaven; flows into
Patchogue Bay, W of Bellport;
40°45′x72°59′15″
Bellport and Howells Point Quads
(7.5′)

MUD CREEK
Physical feature
Suffolk—Brookhaven; flows through
part of Central Moriches into the
NW side of Moriches Bay;
40°47′x72°48′25″
Historical: West Senix Creek
(Moriches Quad, 7.5′, AMS, 1947)
Moriches Quad (7.5′)

MUD CREEK
Physical feature
Suffolk—Southampton; N of Mecox
Bay; 40°55′x72°19′15″
Sag Harbor Quad (7.5′)

MUD CREEK
Physical feature
Suffolk—Southold; flows into
Haywater Cove, N of Cutchogue
Harbor; 41°00′50″x72°27′30″
Southold Quad (7.5′)

MUD POND
Physical feature
Suffolk—Southold; E end of Fishers
Island; 41°17′50″x71°55′55″
Mystic Quad (7.5′)

MUDDY HOLE
see
MOSCOPAS
Source: (Gibbs 76, p. 83)

MUEKEBEKSUCK
Physical feature—valley—historical
Suffolk—East Hampton; in the
vicinity of Fort Pond, extends S
from Fort Pond to the beach;
ca. 41°1′45″x71°57′25″
Source: (Pelletreau 38, p. 371)
*Montauk Point Quad (7.5′)

MULFORD POINT
Physical feature
Suffolk—Southold; E of Browns
Hills, NE of Orient;
41°9′30″x72°16′45″
Orient Quad (7.5′)

MULLENER POND
Physical feature
Nassau—Hempstead; NW side of
North Merrick;
40°41′30″x73°34′30″
Freeport Quad (7.5′)

MULTEAR ISLAND
see
EAST ISLAND
Nassau—Oyster Bay
Source: (Russell 87, p. 211)

MUNCHOG ISLAND
see
STAR ISLAND
Source: (Tooker 44, pp. 145–146)

MUNCHOGUE LAKE
see
OYSTER POND
Source: (Ullitz 165, section 8)

MUNCIE ISLAND
Physical feature—marsh—historical
Suffolk—Islip; in the Great South

Bay, NW of Fire Island Inlet, no
longer exists;
ca. 40°38'45"x73°19'30"
Source: (Babylon Quad, 15', 1903)
*Bay Shore West Quad (7.5')

MUNN LAKE
Physical feature
Suffolk—Southold; N of Orient;
41°8'45"x72°18'30"
Orient Quad (7.5')

MUNNAWTAWKIT
see
FISHERS ISLAND
Source: (Tooker 44, pp. 146–147)

MUNSEY PARK
Village
Nassau—North Hempstead; S-central
of Manhasset Neck, SE of Port
Washington; 40°48'x73°40'45"
Sea Cliff Quad (7.5')

MUNSON
Community—historical
Nassau—Hempstead; presently, the
W part of Franklin Square;
40°42'30"x73°40'20"
Source: (Hempstead Quad, 15',
1897)
*Lynbrook Quad (7.5')

MURRAY HILL
see
FLUSHING (part of)
Source: (Ricard 86, p. 12)

MUSCLE ISLAND
Physical feature—historical
Kings; at the mouth of Newtown

Creek; ca. 42°44'30"x73°57'50"
Source: (Beers 120)
*Brooklyn Quad (7.5')

MUSCOTA
see
GLEN COVE
City
Source: (Flint 26, p. 71)

MUSKETA COVE
see
GLEN COVE
City
Source: (Cocks 70, p. 8)

MUSKYTTEHOOL
Locality—historical
Kings; in the vicinity of Flatlands
Source: (Tooker 44, pp. 147–148)
*Coney Island Quad (7.5')

MUSQUASH CREEK
Physical feature—historical
Suffolk—Islip; flowed from the
central part to the SW part of
Heckscher State Park, no longer
exists; 40°41'x73°11'20"
Source: (Town of Islip 163)
*Bay Shore East Quad (7.5')

MUSQUATAX CREEK
Physical feature—historical
Suffolk—Brookhaven; on Mastic
Neck, E side of Mastic, W of Forge
Point; 40°45'30"x72°49'50"
Source: (Tooker 44, p. 148)
*Moriches Quad (7.5')

MUSQUETOE COVE
see
GLEN COVE
City
Source: (Burr 125)

208

MUTTONTOWN
Village
Nassau—Oyster Bay; central part of
the town, SE of Glen Cove, N of
Syosset; 40°49′45″x73°33′
Historical: Christian Hill (Pelletreau
38, p. 154)
Hicksville Quad (7.5′)

MYERS POND
Physical feature—historical
Suffolk—Southampton; W side of
Mecox Bay, E side of Cobb, S of
Mill Creek;
ca. 40°54′x72°21′15″
Source: (Adams 92, p. 18)
*Sag Harbor Quad (7.5′)

NABIACHAGE
see
MATTITUCK
Source: (Tooker 44, p. 148)

NACHAQUATUCK
see
COLD SPRING HARBOR
Community
Source: (French 10, p. 636fn)

NACHAQUATUCK RIVER
Physical feature—historical
Suffolk, Nassau—Huntington, Oyster
Bay; river or creek which formed
the boundary between NE Nassau
and NW Suffolk, S of Cold Spring
Harbor; 40°51′10″x73°27′50″
Source: (Tooker 44, p. 149)
Variations: Nachaquetack,
Nackaquatak, Nackaquatack,
Nachquatuck (Ibid.)
*Huntington Quad (7.5′)

NAGUNTATOGUE NECK
see
LITTLE NECK
Physical feature
Suffolk—Babylon

Source: (Chace 127), (Tooker 44,
pp. 157–158) and (Thompson 42,
p. 128)

NAHICANS
Locality—historical
Suffolk—East Hampton; the E part
of Long Island, shown on a Dutch
map of 1616; a tribe of Indians
occupied what is now called
Montauk Point
Source: (Tooker 44, p. 150)

NAIECK
see
FORT HAMILTON
Military reservation
Source: (Bryant 55, p. 107)

NAJACK BAY
see
FORT HAMILTON
Community
Source: (Flint 26, p. 71)

NAMEOKE
Locality—historical
Nassau—Hempstead; in the vicinity
of Lawrence and Far Rockaway
Source: (Tooker 44, p. 150)
*Far Rockaway and Lawrence Quads
(7.5′)

NAMKEE CREEK
Physical feature
Suffolk—Islip, Brookhaven; flows
into the Great South Bay, S of Blue
Point; 40°43′50″x73°2′20″
Historical: Manowtassquot
(Tooker 44, pp. 100–101, 150–151)
Variations: Nanmicuke, Namcuke,
Namko, Namkey, Namke (Ibid.)
Sayville Quad (7.5′)

NAMMONECK LAKE
see
FRESH POND
Suffolk—East Hampton—Hither
Hills
Source: (Ullitz 165, plate 8)

NANEMOSET BROOK
Physical feature—historical
Suffolk—Brookhaven or Riverhead;
uncertain location, possibly Wading
River or one of its tributaries
Source: (Tooker 44, p. 151)

NAPEAGUE
Community
Suffolk—East Hampton; W of
Napeague Harbor;
41°00′40″x72°4′
Gardiners Island East Quad (7.5′)

NAPEAGUE
Physical feature—historical
Suffolk—East Hampton; the long
sandy and marshy beach that
connects the peninsula of Montauk
with the main part of the island;
ca. 40°59′x72°6′50″
Source: (Tooker 44, p. 156)
Variations: Neapeague, Napeag,
Napeage, Nap-pe'ag, Napeake
(Ibid.)
*Napeague Beach Quad (7.5′)

NAPEAGUE BAY
Physical feature
Suffolk—East Hampton; on Block
Island Sound, N of Hither Hills,
SE of Gardiners Island;
41°2′x71°2′
Gardiners Island East Quad (7.5′)

NAPEAGUE BEACH
Physical feature
Suffolk—East Hampton; S of Hither
Hills, SE of Napeague Harbor;
41°1′x72°00′
Napeague Beach, Gardiners Island
East, and Montauk Point Quads
(7.5′)

NAPEAGUE HARBOR
Physical feature
Suffolk—East Hampton; SW of
Napeague Bay, W of the
community of Montauk;
41°00′35″x72°3′
Gardiners Island East Quad (7.5′)

NAPEAGUE MEADOWS
Physical feature
Suffolk—East Hampton; SW of
Napeague Harbor; SE of Napeague
Bay; 40°59′50″x72°4′
Historical: Fresh Meadows (U.S. 167,
Map, T-60)
Napeague Beach Quad (7.5′)

NAPEAGUE POND
Physical feature
Suffolk—East Hampton; S of
Napeague, W of Napeague Harbor;
41°00′15″x72°4′
Gardiners Island East Quad (7.5′)

NAPEAKE
see
NAPEAGUE
Physical feature
Source: (Tooker 44, p. 156)

NAPOCK
Locality—historical
Suffolk—Brookhaven, Riverhead;
possibly the locality with the long

series of ponds that form the head waters of Peconic River
Source: (Tooker 44, p. 152)

NARRASKATUCK CREEK
Physical feature
Suffolk—Babylon; flows into the Great South Bay, part of the W boundary of Amityville; 40°39′30″x73°25′30″
Historical: Warrasketuck (Tooker 44, pp. 273-274), Clocks Creek, Clarks Creek, Narraskatucket Creek (U.S. 5, Decisions Rendered between July 1, 1940 and June 30, 1941, p. 38)
Variation: Narrasketuck (Tooker 44, p. 273)
Amityville Quad (7.5′)

NARRIOCH
see
CONEY ISLAND
Physical feature
Source: (Manley 30, p. 32)

NARRIOCH NECK
see
GRAVESEND NECK
Source: (Tooker 44, p. 153)

NARROW BAY
Physical feature
Suffolk—Brookhaven; between the Great South Bay and Moriches Bay; 40°44′45″x72°49′30″
Moriches and Pattersquash Island Quads (7.5′)

NARROW RIVER
Physical feature
Suffolk—Southold; NW of Long

Beach Bay, E of the community of Orient; 41°8′30″x72°17′
Orient Quad (7.5′)

NASHAYONSUCK BROOK
Physical feature—historical
Suffolk—Southold; a brook forming one of the boundaries of Hashamomuk Neck
Source: (Tooker 44, p. 153)
Variations: Nassayonsuck, Neshugguncer (Ibid.)
*Southold Quad (7.5′)

NASKEAGUE SWAMP
Physical feature
Suffolk—Brookhaven; in the vicinity of South Setauket
Source: (Tooker 44, p. 155)
Variations: Nesakaks, Nasakakes, Nasakeges (Ibid.)
*Port Jefferson Quad (7.5′)

NASSAKEAG
see
SOUTH SETAUKET
Source: (Tooker 44, p. 154)

NASSAU
County
W part of Long Island, between Queens County and Suffolk County; includes the towns of Hempstead, North Hempstead and Oyster Bay, cities of Long Beach and Glen Cove
Historical: part of North Riding of Yorkshire (French 10, p. 544fn).
Separated from old Queens County in 1899

NASSAU FARMS
Community
Suffolk—Southold; W of Little
Peconic Bay; 41°1′x72°27′30″
Southold Quad (7.5′)

NASSAU HEIGHTS
Community—historical
Queens; N of Glendale, W of Forest
Hills, possibly part of Middle
Village; ca. 40°43′x73°52′30″
Source: (Hagstrom 144)
*Jamaica and Brooklyn Quads (7.5′)

NASSAU ISLAND
see
LONG ISLAND
Source: (Spafford 14, p. 291)

NASSAU POINT
Community
Suffolk—Southold; S part of Little
Hog Neck;
ca. 40°59′20″x72°26′10″
Source: (Macoskey 29, p. 58)
*Southampton Quad (7.5′)

NASSAU POINT
Physical feature
Suffolk—Southold; W part of Little
Peconic Bay, S point of Little Hog
Neck; 40°59′10″x72°26′5″
Historical: Nassaw Point (Chace 127)
Southampton Quad (7.5′)

NASSAU POINT
see
LITTLE HOG NECK
Source: (Bayles 93, p. 372)

NASSAU SHORES
Community
Nassau—Oyster Bay; SE of

Massapequa Park, E of Fort Neck;
40°39′15″x73°26′15″
Amityville Quad (7.5′)

NASSAU-BY-THE-SEA
see
POINT LOOKOUT
Source: (Macoskey 29, p. 58)

NAVY YARD BASIN
Physical feature
Kings; on Wallabout Bay, NW side
of Kings, NE of Brooklyn Heights;
40°42′15″x73°58′30″
Brooklyn Quad (7.5′)

NAYACK
see
FORT HAMILTON
Military reservation
Source: (Tooker 44, p. 155)

NAYANTACAWNICK ISLAND
Physical feature—historical
Suffolk—Southold; possibly Fishers
Island or Plum Island
Source: (Tooker 44, pp. 155–156)

NEAMANS CREEK
Physical feature—historical
Suffolk—Islip; flowed into Champlin
Creek from the E, S of Lower
Winganhauppauge Lake;
40°43′15″x73°12′5″
Source: (Pelletreau 38, facing p. 243)
*Bay Shore East Quad (7.5′)

NEAR ROCKAWAY
see
EAST ROCKAWAY
Source: (Walling 172)

NECK OF BROOKLAND
see
LUBBERTSEN'S NECK
Source: (Stiles 66, vol. 1, p. 63)

NECKAPAUGE CREEK
see
GREEN CREEK
Source: (Tooker 44, pp. 156)

NEDS CREEK
Physical feature
Nassau—Hempstead; SE of Neds
  Meadow, SW of East Bay;
  40°37'30"x73°33'
Freeport and Jones Inlet Quads
  (7.5')

NEDS HOLE CREEK
Physical feature
Nassau—Hempstead; E boundary of
  North and South Green Sedge;
  40°36'45"x73°42'5"
Lawrence Quad (7.5')

NEDS MEADOW
Physical feature—marsh island
Nassau—Hempstead; S of Merrick,
  SW part of East Bay, E of False
  Channel Meadow;
  40°37'50"x73°32'55"
Freeport Quad (7.5')

NEGRO BAR CHANNEL
Physical feature
Queens, Nassau—Hempstead; E side
  of Jamaica Bay, SW part of Nassau,
  NW of Far Rockaway;
  40°36'50"x73°46'15"
Far Rockaway Quad (7.5')

NEGRO HEAD
Physical feature—historical
Suffolk—Riverhead; on the north
  shore, possibly Friars Head
Source: (Burr 124)
*Riverhead Quad (7.5')

NEGRO POINT
Physical feature—historical
Queens; N part of The Hook (Head
  of Bay);
ca. 40°38'10"x73°44'45"
Source: (Walling 172)
*Lynbrook Quad (7.5')

NEGUNTATOGUE CREEK
Physical feature
Suffolk—Babylon; flows through the
  S part of Lindenhurst into Great
  South Bay, borders Little Neck and
  Santapogue Neck;
  40°40'20"x73°21'25"
Bay Shore West Quad (7.5')

NEMAUKAK
Locality—historical
Suffolk—Brookhaven; exact location
  unknown
Source: (Tooker 44, p. 158)

NEPONSIT
Community
Queens; SW part of Queens, SW of
  Belle Harbor, SW side of Jamaica
  Bay; 40°34'20"x73°52'
Far Rockaway Quad (7.5')

NESAQUAQUE ACCOMPSETT
Locality—historical
Suffolk—Smithtown; on the W side
  of the Nissequogue River
Source: (Tooker 44, pp. 3, 158)

NESARASKE CREEK
see
PASCU-UCKS CREEK
Source: (Beauchamp 7, p. 217)

NESCONSET
Community
Suffolk—Smithtown; S of St. James,
NW of Lake Ronkonkoma;
40°51′x73°9′30″
Source: (Langhans 98, p. 18) and
(Tooker 44, pp. 154-155)
Variations: Nasseconset,
Nasseconsack, Nissequogues,
Nesatasconsett (Tooker 44,
pp. 154-155)
Central Islip Quad (7.5′)

NESTEPOL MARSH
Physical feature—marsh island
Kings; W side of Jamaica Bay, SE of
Canarsie Pol; 40°36′40″x73°52′10″
Far Rockaway Quad (7.5′)

NEW BABYLON
see
BABYLON
Village
Source: (Pelletreau 38, p. 193)

NEW BRIDGE
see
BELLMORE
Source: (Walling 172)

NEW BROOKLYN
Community—historical
Kings; in Stuyvesant, W of the
Cemetery of the Evergreens, E of
Bedford; ca. 40°41′x73°55′30″
Source: (Walling 172) and (French 10,
p. 367)
*Brooklyn Quad (7.5′)

NEW CASSEL
Community
Nassau—North Hempstead; SE side
of the town, E of Mineola, W of
Hicksville; 40°45′40″x73°34′
Historical: Westbury Station (Oyster
Bay Quad, 15′, 1900)
Hicksville Quad (7.5′)

NEW GUT
see
FIRE ISLAND INLET
Source: (Osborne 35, p. 90)

NEW HYDE PARK
Village
Nassau—North Hempstead; SW part
of the town; 40°44′x73°41′30″
Historical: Hyde Park (French 10,
p. 550fn)
Lynbrook Quad (7.5′)

NEW INLET
see
JONES INLET
Source: (Walling 172) and (U.S. 170,
Chart No. 119, 1844)

NEW LOTS
Town—historical
Kings; E side of Kings, consisted of
East New York and Cypress Hills;
ca. 40°41′x73°52′
Source: (French 10, p. 373) and
(Burr 125)
*Brooklyn and Jamaica Quads (7.5′)

NEW MADE ISLAND
Physical feature
Suffolk—Brookhaven; SE of Forge
Point and Mastic Beach, between
Narrow Bay and Moriches Bay;
40°45′25″x72°48′25″
Moriches Quad (7.5′)

NEW MILLPOND
Physical feature
Suffolk—Smithtown; SW of
  Smithtown, E of Commack;
  40°50′x73°13′30″
Historical: Mill Pond, Stump Pond,
  Blydenburgh's Pond, Weld's Pond
  (Langhans 98, p. 17)
Central Islip Quad (7.5′)

NEW MILLS
Community—historical
Suffolk—Smithtown; S of New Mill
  Pond, W of Hauppauge, along the
  S branch of the Nissequogue River;
  ca. 40°49′30″x73°14′
Source: (Bayles 93, pp. 191–192).
  Also known as Blydenburg's Mills
  (Ibid.)
*Central Islip Quad (7.5′)

**NEW PURCHASE MEADOWS
AT SOUTH**
Tract of land—historical
Suffolk—Brookhaven; marsh land
  between Carmans River and Forge
  River; 40°45′x72°52′
Source: (Pelletreau 38, p. 265)
*Bellport and Moriches Quads (7.5′)

NEW SUFFOLK
Community
Suffolk—Southold; N of Robins
  Island, SW of Cutchogue Harbor;
  40°59′30″x72°28′30″
Southampton Quad (7.5′)

NEW TOWNE
see
ELMHURST
Source: (Ricard 86, p. 9)

NEW UTRECHT
Community
Kings; W side of Kings, N of
  Bensonhurst; 40°36′50″x73°59′45″
Coney Island and The Narrows
  Quads (7.5′)

NEW UTRECHT
Town—historical
Kings; SW side of Kings
Source: (French 10, p. 373)
*Coney Island and Jersey City Quads
  (7.5′)

NEW UTRECHT BAY
Physical feature—historical
Kings; presently part of Lower New
  York Bay; 40°32′30″x74°2′30″
Source: (Thompson 41, vol. 2,
  p. 195)
*The Narrows Quad (7.5′)

NEW VENICE
see
EDGEMERE
Source: (Ricard 86, p. 9)

NEW VILLAGE
see
CENTEREACH
Source: (Bailey 19, vol. 1, p. 297),
  (Chace 127), and (Setauket Quad,
  15′, 1904)

NEWARK
see
FLUSHING
Source: (Ricard 86, p. 9)

NEWBRIDGE CREEK
Physical feature
Nassau—Hempstead; flows through

the S part of Bellmore into East
Bay; 40°38'40"x73°31'35"
Freeport Quad (7.5')

NEWBRIDGE POND
Physical feature
Nassau—Hempstead; between
Merrick and Bellmore;
40°40'x73°32'30"
Freeport Quad (7.5')

NEWEYS CANAL
Suffolk—Brookhaven; on Carmans
River, S of Squassux Landing, N of
Bellport Bay; 40°46'15"x72°53'50"
Bellport Quad (7.5')

NEWTON'S CREEK
see
LUDLOWS CREEK
Source: (Pelletreau 38, p. 243)

NEWTOWN
Community
Suffolk—Southampton; E of
Hampton Bays, W of Shinnecock
Bay; 40°52'50"x72°30'25"
Mattituck Quad (7.5')

NEWTOWN
Community—historical
Queens
see
ELMHURST
Source: (Ricard 86, p. 9) and
(Walling 172)

NEWTOWN
Town—historical
Queens; NW part of the county, it
included North and South Brothers,
Rikers, and Barrien Islands

Source: (French 10, p. 548)
Also known as Middleburg under
the Dutch (Ibid.)
*Central Park, Brooklyn and
Flushing Quads (7.5')

NEWTOWN CREEK
Physical feature
Kings, Queens; part of the N
boundary of Kings;
40°44'10"x73°57'45"
Historical: English Kills, Mispat Kil
(Bailey 19, vol. 1, p. 38),
Mespaetches Creek (Tooker 44, pp.
127–128)
Variations: Mespatchis Kil,
Mespachtes Kil, Mespacht, Mespaat,
Mespath (Ibid.)
Brooklyn Quad (7.5')

NEW-WARKE
see
FLUSHING
Source: (Ricard 86, p. 9)

NIAMUCK
see
CANOE PLACE
Source: (Tooker 44, p. 159)

NICHOLS NECK
Physical feature—historical
Suffolk—Islip; presently the SE part
of Heckscher State Park;
40°42'30"x73°9'30"
Source: (Burr 124)
*Bay Shore East Quad (7.5')

NICHOLS POINT
Physical feature
Suffolk—Shelter Island; SE part of
Shelter Island, NE of Majors
Harbor; 41°3'8"x72°16'25"

Historical: mis-named Mashamock
Point in (Romans 157)
Greenport Quad (7.5 ')

NICKS POINT
Physical feature
Nassau—Hempstead; on East Bay,
S part of Merrick, N of Big Crow
Island; 40 °38 '35 "x73 °32 '30 "
Freeport Quad (7.5 ')

NICOLL BAY
Physical feature
Suffolk—Brookhaven; in the Great
South Bay, SW side of town, E of
Heckscher State Park;
40 °42 '30 "x73 °7 '30 "
Historical: Brookhaven Bay, Islip
Bay (Chace 127), Tern's Cove
(Gordon 11, p. 714), Morris Cove
(Beers 117, p. 153), part of the Bay
known as Terrys Cove (Chace 127)
Bay Shore East and Sayville Quads
(7.5 ')

NICOLL CREEK
Physical feature
Suffolk—Islip; NE branch of
Quintuck Creek, W side of
Heckscher State Park;
40 °42 '35 "x73 °11 '10 "
Source: (Town of Islip 163).
Also known as Widows Creek
(Ibid.)
Historical: Widow's Brook,
Cantasquntah Brook (Tooker 44,
pp. 34–35)
*Bay Shore East Quad (7.5 ')

NICOLL PATENTS
Tract of land—historical
Suffolk—Islip; bordered on the W by
Orowoc Creek and N to

approximately due W of
Hauppauge, E to Namkee Creek,
and S along the Islip-Brookhaven
line to the Sunrise Highway;
40 °45 'x73 °00 '
Source: (Pelletreau 38, facing p. 238)
*Bay Shore East, Central Islip,
Sayville and Patchogue Quads
(7.5 ')

NICOLL POINT
Physical feature
Suffolk—Islip; on the Great South
Bay, SE side of the town, SE point
of Heckscher State Park;
40 °42 'x73 °9 '
Historical: Driscoll's Point
(Cram 131, p. 31)
Variations: Nicholls Point (U.S. 170,
Chart No. 119, 1844), Nichols Point
(Burr 124)
Bay Shore East Quad (7.5 ')

NICOLL'S GUT
see
FIRE ISLAND INLET
Source: (Thompson 41, vol. 1,
p. 451)

NICOLL'S RIVER
see
CONNETQUOT RIVER
Source: (Tooker 44, p. 48)

NIGGER BAR
Physical feature—marsh—historical
Nassau—Hempstead; no longer exists,
presently Negro Bar Channel;
40 °35 '55 "x73 °46 '
Source: (Brooklyn Quad, 15 ', 1897)
*Far Rockaway Quad (7.5 ')

NIGGER POINT
Physical feature—historical
Queens; no longer exists, now part of
  JFK Airport, N of East High
  Meadow; 40°38′25″x73°47′45″
Source: (Jamaica Quad, 7.5′, AMS,
  1947)
*Jamaica Quad (7.5′)

NINE MILE GUT
  see
FIRE ISLAND INLET
  Source: (Thompson 41, vol. 1,
  p. 451)

NIPPAUG
  see
LITTLE FRESH POND
  Source: (Tooker 44, pp. 159–160)

NIPSCOP
Locality—historical
Suffolk—Islip, Babylon
Source: (Tooker 44, p. 160)

NISINCKQUEGHACKY
Locality—historical
Suffolk—Smithtown; Dutch name
  for Nissequogue
Source: (Tooker 44, p. 160)
*Saint James Quad (7.5′)

NISSEQUOGUE
Village
Suffolk—Smithtown; N-central part
  of the town, W of Stony Brook
  Harbor; 40°54′15″x73°11′30″
Variations: Nasaquack, Nassaquake,
  Neesaquock, Nesaquake, Nesfquagg,
  Nesoquack, Nisinckqueghacky,
  Nisungueeghacky (Tooker 44,
  pp. 160–162)
Saint James Quad (7.5′)

NISSEQUOGUE NECK
Physical feature
Suffolk—Smithtown; E of
  Nissequogue River, NE part of the
  town
Source: (French 10, p. 637)
*Saint James Quad (7.5′)

NISSEQUOGUE POINT
Physical feature
Suffolk—Smithtown; on Smithtown
  Bay, E of Short Beach;
  40°54′35″x73°12′40″
Source: (Langhans 98, p. 18)
*Saint James Quad (7.5′)

NISSEQUOGUE RIVER
Physical feature
Suffolk—Smithtown; SW of Stony
  Brook Harbor, SE of Sunken
  Meadow State Park, flows N into
  Long Island Sound;
  40°54′x73°12′30″
Historical: Nosoquog, Wissiquack
  (Tooker 44, pp. 289–290)
Variations: Nesaquake, Nesequagg,
  Neesaquack, Nasaquack,
  Neesoquack, Nesquauk, Nesoquack,
  Nassaquake (Ibid., p. 161)
Saint James Quad (7.5′)

**NISSEQUOGUE RIVER
STATE PARK**
Suffolk—Smithtown; S of the
  community of Smithtown; N of
  Hauppauge, W of Village of the
  Branch; 40°51′x73°13′40″
Source: (Hagstrom 141, 1979, p. 36)
*Central Islip Quad (7.5′)

NOBBS CREEK
see
GOOSE CREEK
Suffolk—Southampton
Source: (Tooker 44, p. 162)

NOCCOMACK
Tract of land—historical
Suffolk—Brookhaven; W of Mastic
Neck, in the vicinity of Fire Place,
the community of Brookhaven, and
Squassux Landing;
ca. 40°46′45″x72°54′15″
Source: (Tooker 44, pp. 162-163)
Variations: Nacommock,
Necommack, Moccomack (Ibid.)
*Bellport Quad (7.5′)

NOMINICK HILLS
Physical feature—historical
Suffolk—East Hampton; in the
vicinity of Napeague
Source: (Tooker 44, pp. 163-164)
*Napeague Beach Quad (7.5′)

NONOWANTUCK
see
MOUNT SINAI
Source: (Tooker 44, p. 164)

NONOWANTUCK CREEK
see
CRYSTAL BROOK
Source: (Tooker 44, p. 164)

NORMAN'S KILL
see
BUSHWICK
Source: (Flint 26, p. 69)

NORTH AMITYVILLE
Community
Suffolk—Babylon; W side of the
town, NW of Copiague and
Lindenhurst; 40°42′x73°25′30″
Amityville Quad (7.5′)

NORTH BABYLON
Community
Suffolk—Babylon; W of Bay Shore,
E-central part of the town;
40°43′x73°19′30″
Bay Shore West Quad (7.5′)

NORTH BAY SHORE
Community
Suffolk—Islip; NW of Islip, E of
Wyandanch; 40°44′30″x73°15′40″
Bay Shore West Quad (7.5′)

NORTH BEACH
Community
Queens; NW side of Queens, SW of
Flushing Bay; 40°46′x73°52′15″
Historical: Poor Bowery, Bowery
Bay (Ricard 86, pp. 12-13), Fishers
Point (Ross 39, p. 539)
Flushing Quad (7.5′)

NORTH BELLMORE
Community
Nassau—Hempstead; SW of
Levittown, SE of the village of
Hempstead; 40°41′30″x73°32′15″
Historical: Smithville South
(Hempstead Quad, 15′, 1903)
Freeport Quad (7.5′)

NORTH BELLPORT
Community
Suffolk—Brookhaven; S-central part
of the town, N of Bellport;
40°46′20″x72°57′
Historical: Bellport Station (Bayles 93,
p. 261) and (Moriches Quad, 15′,
1903)
Bellport Quad (7.5′)

NORTH BLACK BANKS HASSOCK

Physical feature—marsh island
Nassau—Hempstead; E of Lawrence,
 W of Harbor Isle, between Broad
 Channel and Hog Island Channel;
 40°36'25"x73°40'20"
Source: (U.S. 5, List No. 8101,
 p. 13)
Historical: Black Banks Hassock
 (Lawrence Quad, 7.5', 1966)
Variations: Blackbank Hassock,
 Blacks Banks, North Black Banks
 (U.S. 5, List No. 8108, p. 13)
*Lawrence Quad)

NORTH CENTEREACH

Community
Suffolk—Brookhaven; N part of
 Centereach, SW of Terryville;
 40°53'10"x73°5'
Source: (Hagstrom 141, 1979, p. 46)
*Port Jefferson Quad (7.5')

NORTH CHANNEL

Physical feature
Nassau—Hempstead; S of Middle
 Bay, between Cinder Island and
 Middle Island; 40°36'x73°36'30"
Jones Inlet Quad (7.5')

NORTH CINDER ISLAND

Physical feature—marsh island
Nassau—Hempstead; S side of
 Middle Bay, SE of Oceanside;
 40°36'20"x73°36'45"
Jones Inlet (7.5')

NORTH DUMPLING

Physical feature—island
Suffolk—Southold; in Long Island
 Sound, NE part of Southold, N of

the W part of Fishers Island;
 41°17'18"x72°1'10"
New London Quad (7.5')

NORTH FORK

Physical feature—peninsula
Suffolk—Southold; the NE peninsula
 of Long Island;
 ca. 41°5'x72°24'
Mattituck, Mattituck Hills, Southold,
 Greenport, and Orient Quads (7.5')

NORTH GREAT RIVER

Community
Suffolk—Islip; E side of the town,
 NE of East Islip, N of Heckscher
 State Park; 40°44'45"x73°10'20"
Bay Shore East Quad (7.5')

NORTH GREEN SEDGE

Physical feature—marsh island
Nassau—Hempstead; S of Hewlett
 Neck and Hewlett Harbor;
 40°36'45"x73°41'30"
Lawrence Quad (7.5')

NORTH HAVEN

Village
Suffolk—Southampton; S-central
 part of North Haven Peninsula;
 41°1'10"x72°17'50"
Greenport Quad (7.5')

NORTH HAVEN PENINSULA

Physical feature
Suffolk—Southampton; in Shelter
 Island Sound, S of Shelter Island;
 41°1'30"x72°19'
Historical: Great Hog Neck South
 (U.S. 167, Map T-71), Hog Neck
 (Chace 127)
Greenport Quad (7.5')

NORTH HEMPSTEAD
Town
Nassau; NW side of the county
Historical: formerly part of
  Hempstead town
Sea Cliff, Mamaroneck, Hicksville
  and Lynbrook Quads (7.5 ')

NORTH HEMPSTEAD
Village—historical
Queens (Nassau)—North Hempstead;
  possibly near Mineola
Source: (French 10, p. 550)

NORTH HILL
Physical feature
Suffolk—Southold; NW side of
  Fishers Island, N of Hay Harbor;
  41 °16 '20 "x72 °1 '30 "
New London Quad (7.5 ')

NORTH HILLS
Village
Nassau—North Hempstead; S-central
  part of the town, S of Manhasset
  Neck; 40 °47 'x73 °40 '30 "
Sea Cliff Quad (7.5 ')

NORTH ISLIP
Community
Suffolk—Islip; NW of Brightwaters,
  NE of West Islip;
  40 °44 '05 "x73 °17 '30 "
Source: (Hagstrom 141, 1979, p. 31)
*Bay Shore West Quad (7.5 ')

NORTH ISLIP
  see
CENTRAL ISLIP
Source: (Chace 127) and (French 10,
  p. 637)

NORTH LINDENHURST
Community
Suffolk—Babylon; central part of the
  town, W of the village of Babylon;
  40 °42 '30 "x73 °22 '45 "
Amityville Quad (7.5 ')

NORTH LINE ISLAND
Physical feature
Nassau—Hempstead, Oyster Bay;
  W side of South Oyster Bay, E of
  Great Island, S of Goose Island;
  40 °38 'x73 °29 '
Amityville Quad (7.5 ')

NORTH LYNBROOK
Community
Nassau—Hempstead; S of Malverne,
  E of Valley Stream;
  ca. 40 °39 '45 "x73 °40 '45 "
Source: (Hagstrom 140, 1973, p. 31)
*Lynbrook Quad (7.5 ')

NORTH MANOR
Community—historical
Suffolk—Brookhaven; in the vicinity
  of Manorville
Source: (Macoskey 29, p. 58)

NORTH MASSAPEQUA
Community
Nassau—Oyster Bay; N of
  Massapequa, SE of Plainedge;
  40 °42 'x73 °27 '40 "
Source: (Hagstrom 140, 1978, p. 5)
*Amityville Quad (7.5 ')

NORTH MEADOW
Physical feature—island
Nassau—Hempstead; SW of
  Oceanside, N of Island Park;
  40 °37 'x73 °39 '30 "
Lawrence Quad (7.5 ')

NORTH MEADOW ISLAND
Physical feature
Nassau—Hempstead; in the middle
 of the Bay of Fundy;
 40°36'35"x73°33'55"
Jones Inlet Quad (7.5')

NORTH MERRICK
Community
Nassau—Hempstead; NE of Freeport,
 SE of the village of Hempstead;
 40°41'30"x73°34'
Freeport Quad (7.5')

NORTH NECK
Physical feature
Suffolk—East Hampton; between
 Fort Pond Bay and Lake Montauk,
 W of Montauk Point;
 41°3'30"x71°57'
Source: (Chace 127)
*Montauk Point Quad (7.5')

NORTH NECK
Physical feature—historical
Suffolk—Smithtown; in the vicinity
 of the NE side of the village of
 Nissequogue
Source: (Langhans 98, p. 19)
*Saint James Quad (7.5')

NORTH NEW HYDE PARK
Community
Nassau—North Hempstead; SW part
 of the town, W of Mineola;
 40°44'45"x73°41'30"
Lynbrook and Sea Cliff Quads (7.5')

NORTH PATCHOGUE
Community
Suffolk—Brookhaven; N of
 Patchogue, SE of Ronkonkoma;
 40°47'10"x73°1'
Patchogue Quad (7.5')

NORTH POND
Physical feature
Suffolk—Riverhead; N of Manorville,
 W of Swan Pond;
 40°54'15"x72°49'5"
Wading River Quad (7.5')

NORTH POND
Physical feature
Suffolk—Southampton; N of
 Quantuck Creek, NW of Quogue;
 40°50'25"x72°36'55"
Quogue Quad (7.5')

NORTH RACE
Physical feature—channel
Suffolk—Southold; in Great Peconic
 Bay, N of Robins Island;
 40°59'x72°28'20"
Southampton Quad (7.5')

NORTH RASAPEAGE
see
RASSAPEAQUE
Source: (Pelletreau 101, p. 32)

NORTH RIDING OF YORKSHIRE
see
YORKSHIRE
Source: (French 10, p. 544fn)

NORTH ROCKVILLE CENTRE
Community
Nassau—Hempstead; S of South
 Hempstead;
 ca. 40°40'50"x73°37'30"
Source: (Rand 154, 1977, p. 388),
 part of community known as
 Birchwood (Ibid., p. 381)
*Freeport Quad (7.5')

NORTH ROSLYN
see
GREENVALE
Source: (Rand 154, 1977, p. 384)

NORTH SEA
Community
Suffolk—Southampton; S of North
Sea Harbor, E of Great Peconic
Bay; 40°56′x72°25′
Southampton Quad (7.5′)

NORTH SEA
Physical feature
see
GREAT PECONIC BAY
Source: In Southampton, the name
meant the Peconic Bays, while in
the town of Southold, the name
meant Long Island Sound
(Flint 26, pp. 72–73)

NORTH SEA
Physical feature
see
LONG ISLAND SOUND
Source: In Southold, the name
meant Long Island Sound, while in
Southampton, the name meant the
Peconic Bays (Flint 26, pp. 72–73)

NORTH SEA HARBOR
Physical feature
Suffolk—Southampton; S of Little
Peconic Bay; 40°56′30″x72°25′
Southampton Quad (7.5′)

NORTH SELDEN
Community
Suffolk—Brookhaven; N part of
Selden, E of Centereach;
40°52′30″x73°2′30″
Source: (Hagstrom 141, 1979, p. 48)

*Port Jefferson and Patchogue
Quads (7.5′)

NORTH SHORE BEACH
Community
Suffolk—Brookhaven; N of Rocky
Point; 40°57′40″x72°55′45″
Source: (Hagstrom 141, 1973, p. 54)
*Middle Island Quad (7.5′)

NORTH SHORE BEACH
Physical feature
Suffolk—Brookhaven; on Long
Island Sound, N of shoreline of
Rocky Point; 40°57′45″x72°55′45″
Middle Island Quad (7.5′)

NORTH SMITHTOWN
Community
Suffolk—Smithtown; W side of the
Nissequogue River, NE of
Smithtown, SE of San Remo;
ca. 40°52′45″x73°12′
Source: (Hagstrom 141, 1979, p. 37)
*Saint James Quad (7.5′)

NORTH SWAMP
Physical feature
Suffolk—Smithtown; E side of
Nissequogue River, SE of Short
Beach, part of James Neck;
40°54′20″x73°13′15″
Source: (Langhans 98, p. 19)
*Saint James Quad (7.5′)

NORTH VALLEY STREAM
Community
Nassau—Hempstead; NW part of the
town, N of Valley Stream;
40°41′x73°42′
Lynbrook Quad (7.5′)

NORTH WADING RIVER
Community—historical
Suffolk—Riverhead; SE of Herod
Point, near Plaine Landing;
ca. 40°57'50"x72°49'
Source: (Ullitz 164, index map)
*Wading River Quad (7.5')

NORTH WANTAGH
Community
Nassau—Hempstead, E side of the
town, S of Levittown, N of Seaford;
40°41'30"x73°30'
Freeport and Amityville Quads (7.5')

NORTH WILLOW POND
see
WILLOW POND
Suffolk—Smithtown
Source: (Langhans 98, p. 26)

NORTH WOODMERE
Community
Nassau—Hempstead; W side of the
town, N of Cedarhurst;
40°39'x73°43'30"
Lynbrook Quad (7.5')

NORTHAMPTON
see
BRIDGEHAMPTON
Community
Source: (Cary 126)

NORTHEAST BRANCH
Physical feature
Suffolk—Smithtown; S of the
community of Smithtown, flows
through Millers Pond and New
Millpond into the Nissequogue
River;
Historical: Branch Brook (Langhans
98, pp. 5, 24).

Also known as Smithtown Branch
(Langhans 98, p. 19)
Central Islip Quad (7.5')

NORTHFIELD
Physical feature
Suffolk—Smithtown; a field on the
N part of Nissequogue Neck,
NW of Stony Brook Harbor;
ca. 40°54'25"x73°11'10"
Source: (Langhans 98, p. 19) and
(Pelletreau 101, p. 295)
*Saint James Quad (7.5')

NORTHFLEET
see
SOUTHOLD
Town
Source: (French 10, p. 639fn)

NORTHPORT
Village
Suffolk—Huntington; NE side of the
town, SE of Northport Bay;
40°54'x73°20'30"
Historical: Cow Harbor (Bailey 19,
vol. 1, p. 340) and (Tooker 44,
pp. 20, 37-38, 77),
Harbor (French 10, p. 636fn), To the
Harbor (Sammis 104, p. 164),
Bryant's Landing (Sammis 104,
p. 160)
Northport Quad (7.5')

NORTHPORT BASIN
Physical feature
Nassau—Oyster Bay; E of Northport
Bay, W of Crab Meadow;
40°55'30"x73°20'45"
Source: (U.S. 170, Chart No. 12365,
1979)
*Northport Quad (7.5')

NORTHPORT BAY
Physical feature
Suffolk—Huntington; on Long Island
Sound, N-central side of the town;
40°55′x73°22′
Historical: Cow Harbor (Tooker 44,
p. 77)
Northport and Lloyd Harbor Quads
(7.5′)

NORTHPORT HARBOR
Physical feature
Suffolk—Huntington; S part of
Northport Bay;
40°53′45″x73°21′30″
Historical: Great Cow Harbor
(Bayles 93, p. 160)
Northport Quad (7.5′)

NORTHVILLE
Community
Suffolk—Riverhead; N of
Aquebogue, SW of Mattituck;
40°58′15″x72°37′
Historical: Sound Avenue (Ullitz 164,
index map), Success Post Office
(Asher 116, p. 26)
Mattituck Quad (7.5′)

NORTHWEST
Community—historical
Suffolk—East Hampton; NW of the
village of East Hampton, no longer
exists
Source: (Bailey 19, vol. 1,
pp. 232–233). Also known as
Vanished Village (Ibid.)
*East Hampton Quad (7.5′)

NORTHWEST BLUFF
Physical feature
Suffolk—Huntington; W side of
Lloyd Neck; 40°55′35″x73°29′50″
Lloyd Harbor Quad (7.5′)

NORTHWEST CREEK
Physical feature
Suffolk—East Hampton; flows into
Northwest Harbor;
41°00′30″x72°15′
Gardiners Island West, Greenport
and Sag Harbor Quads (7.5′)

NORTHWEST HARBOR
Physical feature
Suffolk—East Hampton; E of North
Haven Peninsula;
41°2′x72°15′
Historical: West Harbor (U.S. 167,
Map T–72)
Gardiners Island West and Greenport
Quads (7.5′)

NORTHWEST LANDING
Community
Suffolk—East Hampton; E of
Northwest Harbor;
41°00′40″x72°14′50″
Gardiners Island West Quad (7.5′)

NORTHWEST POINT
Community
see
WESTVILLE
Source: (Beers 117, p. 118)

NORTHWEST POINT
Physical feature
Nassau—Hempstead; W side of town,
S side of the Head of Bay;
40°37′20″x73°45′50″
Far Rockaway Quad (7.5′)

NORTHWEST WOODS
Physical feature
Suffolk—East Hampton; S of
Gardiners Bay, NW of Threemile
Harbor; 41°2'20"x72°14'15"
Gardiners Island West Quad (7.5')

NORTON BASIN
Physical feature
Queens; SE side of Jamaica Bay,
W of Far Rockaway;
40°36'x73°46'30"
Historical: Norton's Creek
(Osborne 35, p. 90)
Far Rockaway Quad (7.5')

NORTON POINT
Physical feature
Kings; SW side of Kings, W point of
Coney Island; 40°34'45"x74°00'50"
The Narrows Quad (7.5')

NORTON POINT
Physical feature
Nassau—Hempstead; NE of Head of
Bay, NW of Cedarhurst, SW of
Meadowmere Park;
40°38'x73°44'45"
Lynbrook Quad (7.5')

NORTON'S CREEK
see
NORTON BASIN
Source: (Osborne 35, p. 90)

NORTON'S POINT
see
WEST END
Source: (Ross 39, p. 374)

NORWICH
see
EAST NORWICH
Source: (Walling 172), (Burr 125)
and (French 10, p. 551)

NORWOOD
Community—historical
Suffolk—Brookhaven; SE of East
Setauket, NW of Terryville;
ca. 40°55'x73°4'15"
Source: (Bayles 93, p. 241) and
(Ullitz 164, index map)
*Port Jefferson Quad (7.5')

NORWOOD
see
MALVERNE
Source: (Macoskey 29, p. 58) and
(Reifschneider 85, p. 186)

NOSH LOT
Tract of land—historical
Suffolk—Southampton; SW of the
village of Southampton, SE of Art
Village; ca. 40°52'40"x72°25'
Source: (Tooker 44, pp. 164–165)
*Southampton Quad (7.5')

NOSOQUOG RIVER
see
NISSEQUOGUE RIVER
Source: (Tooker 44, p. 289)

NOSREKA LAKE
Physical feature
Suffolk—Islip; in Brightwaters, E of
West Islip; 40°43'x73°16'
Bay Shore West Quad (7.5')

NOVA SCOTIA BAR
Physical feature
Kings; W side of Jamaica Bay, S of

Ruffle Bar, NW of Belle Harbor;
40°35′10″x73°52′
Far Rockaway Quad (7.5′)

NOYACK
Community
Suffolk—Southampton; S of Noyack
 Bay; 40°59′30″x72°20′
Variations: Noiack, Noyac, Noyak
 (Tooker 44, p. 166)
Sag Harbor Quad (7.5′)

NOYACK BAY
Physical feature
Suffolk—Southampton; N of
 Noyack, SW of North Haven
 Peninsula; 41°1′x72°20′
Greenport Quad (7.5′)

NOYACK CREEK
Physical feature
Suffolk—Southampton; SE of Jessup
 Neck, SW of Noyack Bay;
 40°59′45″x72°22′
Sag Harbor Quad (7.5′)

NUMS CHANNEL
Physical feature
Nassau—Hempstead; S of Hewlett
 Bay, SW of Nums Marsh, E of
 North Green Sedge;
 40°37′5″x73°40′40″
Lawrence Quad (7.5′)

NUMS MARSH
Physical feature
Nassau—Hempstead; in Hewlett Bay,
 E of North Green Sedge;
 40°37′10″x73°40′30″
Lawrence Quad (7.5′)

OAK BEACH
Community
Suffolk—Babylon; S part of town,
NW side of Fire Island Inlet, SW of
Oak Island; 40°38′20″x73°17′30″
Bay Shore West Quad (7.5′)

OAK ISLAND
Physical feature
Suffolk—Babylon; in the SW part of
Great South Bay, W of Captree
Island; 40°38′40″x73°18′
Bay Shore West Quad (7.5′)

OAK ISLAND INLET
Physical feature—historical
Suffolk—Babylon; once existed near
Cedar Island;
ca. 40°39′x73°19′
Source: (Osborne 36, p. 116) and
(U.S. 170, Chart No. 119, 1844)
*Bay Shore West Quad (7.5′)

OAK NECK
Physical feature
Nassau—Oyster Bay; N part of town,
N of Mill Neck; 40°54′30″x73°34′
Historical: Hog Neck (Romans 157)
Bayville Quad (7.5′)

OAK NECK
Suffolk—Islip
see
OKENOK NECK
Source: (Tooker 44, p. 169)

OAK NECK BEACH
Physical feature
Nassau—Oyster Bay; on Long Island
Sound, NE part of the shoreline of
Oak Neck and the village of
Bayville; 40°54′30″x73°34′50″
Bayville Quad (7.5′)

OAK NECK CREEK
Physical feature
Nassau—Oyster Bay; SE of Oak
Neck, flows into Mill Neck Creek
from the NE; 40°54′5″x73°34′45″
Bayville Quad (7.5′)

OAK NECK POINT
Physical feature
Nassau—Oyster Bay; N point of Oak
Neck; 40°45′x73°34′
Bayville Quad (7.5′)

OAK WOOD
see
BELLE TERRE
Source: (Chace 127)

OAKDALE
Community
Suffolk—Islip; S of Connetquot
River State Park, E of East Islip;
40°44′15″x73°8′45″
Bay Shore East Quad (7.5′)

OAKLAND GARDENS
Community
Queens; NE part of Queens, SE of
Flushing; 40°45′x73°45′

Flushing, Jamaica and Lynbrook
Quads (7.5 ')

OAKLAND LAKE
Physical feature
Queens; NE part of Oakland
Gardens, S of Little Neck Bay;
40°45 '30 "x73°45 '35 "
Flushing Quad (7.5 ')

OAKLEY'S HILL
see
HIGH HILL
Source: (Manley 30, p. 167)

OAKLEYVILLE
Community—historical
Suffolk—Brookhaven; on Fire Island,
in the vicinity of Point O' Woods;
ca. 40°39 '10 "x73°7 '30 "
Source: (Macoskey 29, p. 58)
*Bay Shore East Quad (7.5 ')

OAKVILLE
Community
Suffolk—Southampton; NW of East
Quogue; 40°51 '30 "x72°36 '20 "
Quogue Quad (7.5 ')

OCCAPOGUE
see
AQUEBOGUE
Source: (Beauchamp 7, p. 218)

OCCOMBOMOCK
see
BELLPORT
Source: (Beauchamp 7, p. 218)

OCEAN BAY PARK
Community
Suffolk—Brookhaven; on Fire Island,

SW corner of Brookhaven town,
E of Seaview; 40°39 'x73°8 '30 "
Bay Shore East Quad (7.5 ')

OCEAN BEACH
Village
Suffolk—Islip; on Fire Island, W of
Seaview, S of Heckscher State Park;
40°38 '50 "x73°9 '30 "
Bay Shore East Quad (7.5 ')

OCEANSIDE
Community
Nassau—Hempstead; S side of town,
S of Rockville Centre, SE of
Lynbrook; 40°38 '30 "x73°38 '45 "
Historical: Christian Hook
(Walling 172), (U.S. 170, Chart No.
119, 1844) and (Hempstead Quad
15 ', 1897)
Lynbrook, Freeport, Lawrence and
Jones Inlet Quads (7.5 ')

OCEANUS
Community—historical
Queens; W of Hammel, near the
present site of Holland;
40°35 '25 "x73°48 '45 "
Source: (Brooklyn Quad, 15 ', 1897)
*Far Rockaway Quad (7.5 ')

O–CO–NEE
Community—historical
Suffolk—Islip; in the vicinity of Bay
Shore and Brightwaters;
ca. 40°44 'x73°15 '25 "
Source: (Macoskey 29, p. 58)
*Bay Shore West Quad (7.5 ')

O–CO–NEE LAKE
Physical feature
Suffolk—Islip; E part of
Brightwaters; 40°44 '5 "x73°15 '30 "

Bay Shore West Quad (7.5 ')

OCQUEBAUK
see
AQUEBOGUE
Source: (Tooker 44, p. 17)

OGDEN NECK
Physical feature
Suffolk—Southampton; E of Ogden
Pond, S part of the village of
Quogue; 40°48'40"x72°35'30"
Source: (Pelletreau 38, p. 336)
*Quogue Quad (7.5 ')

OGDEN POND
Physical feature
Suffolk—Southampton; on the
Quogue Canal, S part of the village
of Quogue; 40°48'35"x72°36'
Quogue Quad (7.5 ')

OKENOK NECK
Physical feature
Suffolk—Islip; S of West Bay Shore,
SE of Babylon; 40°41'30"x73°17'
Historical: Oak Neck, Oquenock
(Tooker 44, pp. 169–170)
Bay Shore West Quad (7.5 ')

OLD AQUEBOGUE
see
JAMESPORT
Source: (Chace 127) and (U.S. 170,
Chart No. 115, 1855)

OLD BETHPAGE
Community
Nassau—Oyster Bay; E-central part
of the town, SE of Hicksville;
40°46'x73°27'15"
Huntington Quad (7.5 ')

OLD BROOKVILLE
Village
Nassau—Oyster Bay; NW part of the
town, S of Glen Cove;
40°50'x73°37'30"
Historical: Cedar Swamp (Walling
172)
Hicksville and Sea Cliff Quads (7.5 ')

OLD FIELD
Physical feature
Suffolk—Southold
see
FORT NECK
Physical feature—historical
Source: (Pelletreau 38, p. 433)

OLD FIELD
Village
Suffolk—Brookhaven; N of Stony
Brook, W of Conscience Bay;
40°57'x73°8'
Historical: Cataconnock (Tooker 44,
p. 36)
Saint James Quad (7.5 ')

OLD FIELD BAY
see
CONSCIENCE BAY
Source: (Bayles 93, p. 236)

OLD FIELD BEACH
Physical feature
Suffolk—Brookhaven; on Long
Island Sound, N of Strongs Neck
and Port Jefferson Harbor;
40°58'10"x73°6'30"
Historical: Setauket Beach (U.S. 5,
List No. 5903, p. 43)
Port Jefferson Quad (7.5 ')

OLD FIELD POINT
Physical feature

Suffolk—Brookhaven; NE side of
Old Field, N of Strongs Neck and
Conscience Bay;
40°58'35"x73°7'10"
Historical: Sharp Point (Romans 157),
Cometico (Tooker 44, p. 45)
Port Jefferson Quad (7.5')

OLD FIELDS
see
GREENLAWN
Source: (Bailey 19, vol. 1, p. 358)

OLD FORT POND
Physical feature—inlet
Suffolk—Southampton; NE part of
Shinnecock Bay;
40°52'50"x72°26'30"
Southampton Quad (7.5')

OLD GOING
see
GOING OVER
Source: (Langhans 98, p. 9)

OLD HEN
Physical feature—rock
Nassau—North Hempstead; in Long
Island Sound, N of Manhasset
Neck; 40°52'20"x73°42'50"
Sea Cliff Quad (7.5')

OLD HOLBROOK
see
HOLBROOK
Source: (Ullitz 165, index map) and
(Rand 154, 1913, p. 28)

OLD ICE POND
Physical feature
Suffolk—Southampton; N of
Quantuck Creek, NW of Quogue;

40°50'5"x72°37'
Quogue Quad (7.5')

OLD INLET
Physical feature
Suffolk—Brookhaven; on Fire Island,
S of Bellport Bay, SE of Pelican
Island; 40°43'30"x72°53'50"
Source: (Shaw 106, p. 210) and (U.S.
170, Chart 12352, 1976)
*Howells Point Quad (7.5')

OLD INLET
Physical feature—historical
Suffolk—Southampton; opposite
East Quogue, no longer exists;
ca. 40°49'x72°33'40"
Source: (Tooker 44, p. 201).
Also known as Quamuck (Ibid.)
*Quogue Quad (7.5')

OLD MAN'S HARBOR
see
MOUNT SINAI HARBOR
Source: (Smith 162)

OLD MAN'S VILLAGE
see
MOUNT SINAI
Source: (Smith 162)

OLD MILL
Physical feature—historical
Suffolk—Smithtown; one of the
earliest mills, located on the E side
of the Nissequogue River, on the
border of the village of Nissequogue;
ca. 40°52'30"x73°11'35"
Source: (Langhans 98, p. 19) and
(Pelletreau 101, p. 44)
*Saint James and Central Islip Quads
(7.5')

OLD MILL CREEK
Physical feature
Queens; SW part of Queens, NW
  part of Jamaica Bay;
  40°39'x73°51'20"
Jamaica Quad (7.5')

OLD NECK
Physical feature
Suffolk—Brookhaven; SE part of
  town, NW side of Moriches Bay;
  40°47'20"x72°48'50"
Moriches Quad (7.5')

OLD NECK CREEK
Physical feature
Suffolk—Brookhaven; flows into
  Forge River, borders Old Neck on
  the W side; 40°47'10"x72°49'10"
Moriches Quad (7.5')

OLD PURCHASE
Locality—historical
Suffolk—Huntington; a six mile
  square in the NW corner of the
  town, extended from Cold Spring
  Harbor on the W to Northport
  Harbor on the E, and S to Middle
  Country Road
Source: (Bayles 93, p. 133)

OLD RASEPEAGE
Locality—historical
Suffolk—Smithtown; W side of
  Stony Brook Harbor;
  40°54'x73°11'
Source: (Pelletreau 38, p. 226)
*Saint James Quad (7.5')

OLD RASSAPEAQUE
see
RASSAPEAQUE
Source: (Langhans 98, p. 21)

OLD SHIP POINT
Community—historical
Nassau—Oyster Bay; in the vicinity
  of the community of Oyster Bay;
  ca. 40°52'25"x73°31'15"
Source: (Macoskey 29, p. 59)
*Hicksville Quad (7.5')

OLD SILAS ROCK
Physical feature
Suffolk—Southold; E of Plum Island
  in Block Island Sound;
  41°11'30"x72°8'50"
Plum Island Quad (7.5')

OLD SOW
Physical feature—rocks
Suffolk—Brookhaven; in Long
  Island Sound, N of Rocky Point
  Landing; 40°58'5"x72°57'10"
Middle Island Quad (7.5')

OLD SWALE MARSH
Physical feature—marsh island
Kings; W side of Jamaica Bay, W of
  Ruffle Bar; 40°35'55"x73°52'10"
Far Rockaway Quad (7.5')

OLD TOWN
Community—historical
Suffolk—Southampton; E side of the
  village of Southampton;
  ca. 40°53'30"x72°22'35"
Source: (Pelletreau 38, p. 289)
*Southampton Quad (7.5')

OLD TOWN POND
Physical feature
Suffolk—Southampton; E part of the
  village of Southampton;
  40°52'45"x72°22'25"
Sag Harbor Quad (7.5')

OLD WAMPMISSIC PLACE
see
WAMPMISSIC
Source: (Ullitz 164, plate 7)

OLD WESTBURY
Village
Nassau—North Hempstead, Oyster
Bay; NW of Hicksville, NE of
Mineola; 40°47′20″x73°36′10″
Hicksville Quad (7.5′)

OLD WESTBURY POND
Physical feature
Nassau—North Hempstead; S part of
Old Westbury, N of Westbury;
40°46′55″x73°35′22″
Hicksville Quad (7.5′)

OLDSFIELD BAY
see
CONSCIENCE BAY
Source: (Flint 26, p. 73)

OLIVERS CREEK
Physical feature—historical
Suffolk—Southampton; flows
through West Mecox Village into
the E side of Hayground Cove;
40°54′55″x72°19′50″
Source: (Adams 92, p. 18)
*Sag Harbor Quad (7.5′)

OLIVERS ISLAND
Physical feature—marsh island
Nassau—Hempstead; NE part of
East Bay, SE of Bellmore, W of
Seamans Island;
40°38′20″x73°30′50″
Source: (Hagstrom 140, 1978, p. 45)
*Freeport Quad (7.5′)

OLIVERS POINT
Physical feature—historical
Queens (Nassau)—Oyster Bay; S part
of Centre Island, N of Soper's
Point; 40°53′20″x73°32′5″
Source: (Walling 172)
*Bayville Quad (7.5′)

OLYMPIC
Community—historical
Suffolk—Islip; S of the community
of Islip; ca. 40°42′45″x73°12′50″
Source: (Cram 131, p. 31)
*Bay Shore East Quad (7.5′)

OMKALOG
see
AUKABOG
Source: (Tooker 44, p. 167)

ONCHECHAUG
see
UNKECHAUG NECK
Source: (Tooker 44, p. 265–266)

ONECK
Community—historical
Suffolk—Southampton; E of
Beaverdam, SE of Westhampton;
ca. 40°48′30″x72°39′
Source: (Macoskey 29, p. 59) and
(Bayles 93, p. 314)
*Eastport Quad (7.5′)

ONECK
Physical feature—neck
Suffolk—Southampton; E side of
Moriches Bay, SW side of
Westhampton Beach;
40°48′x72°39′
Historical: Great Wonuk (Tooker 44,
p. 290)
Eastport Quad (7.5′)

ONECK DRAIN
Physical feature—creek
Suffolk—Southampton; flows into
the E side of Moriches Bay, SW of
Westhampton Beach;
40°47'55"x72°39'25"
Eastport Quad (7.5')

OOSENCE
see
ASAWSUNCE
Source: (Tooker 44, p. 22)

OOSUNK
see
ASAWSUNCE
Source: (Tooker 44, p. 167)

OPCATKONTYCKE BROOK
Physical feature—historical
Suffolk—Huntington; at the head of
Northport Harbor, NE of
Centerport; 40°53'40"x73°21'40"
Source: (Tooker 44, pp. 167-168)
Variation: Oxeatcontyck (Ibid.)
*Northport Quad (7.5')

OPERHOWESECK BROOK
Physical feature—historical
Suffolk—Huntington; possibly one of
the creeks in Crab Meadow
Source: (Tooker 44, pp. 168-169)
*Northport Quad (7.5')

OPPEAX CREEK
see
HAPAX CREEK
Source: (Tooker 44, p. 169)

OQUENOCK
see
OKENOK NECK
Source: (Tooker 44, pp. 169-170)

OQUENOCK BROOK
see
TRUES CREEK
Source: (Tooker 44, p. 169)

ORAWAC CREEK
see
OROWOC CREEK
Source: (Tooker 44, pp. 170-172)

ORCHARD NECK
Physical feature—historical
Suffolk—Brookhaven; on Moriches
Bay, W of Orchard Neck Creek,
S part of Center Moriches;
40°47'10"x72°47'45"
Source: (Pelletreau 38, p. 263)
*Moriches Quad (7.5')

ORCHARD NECK CREEK
Physical feature
Suffolk—Brookhaven; NW side of
Moriches Bay, S of Central
Moriches; 40°47'5"x72°47'30"
Moriches Quad (7.5')

OREGON
Community—historical
Suffolk—Southold; S part of the
Oregon Hills, NW of Cutchogue;
possibly Waterville;
ca. 41°1'x72°32'10"
Source: (Bayles 93, p. 369) and
(Hyde 147)
*Mattituck Hills Quad (7.5')

OREGON HILLS
Physical feature
Suffolk—Southold; N of Mattituck;
41°1'40"x72°32'20"
Historical: Manor Hills (U.S. 167,
Map T-55), Manner Hills (U.S. 170,
Chart No. 115, 1855)
Mattituck Hills Quad (7.5')

ORIENT
Community
Suffolk—Southold; E of Orient
Harbor; 41°8'20"x72°18'15"
Historical: Oyster Ponds (French 10,
p. 640)
Orient Quad (7.5')

ORIENT BEACH
Physical feature
Suffolk—Southold; S shore of Orient
Beach State Park;
41°7'50"x72°15'45"
Orient Quad (7.5')

ORIENT BEACH STATE PARK
Suffolk—Southold; E part of the
town, on Gardiners Bay, S of the
community of Orient Point;
41°7'50"x72°15'35"
Orient, Greenport and Plum Island
Quads (7.5')

ORIENT HARBOR
Physical feature
Suffolk—Southold; W of the
community of Orient;
41°8'10"x72°19'
Historical: Oyster Pond Harbor
(Thompson 41, vol. 1, p. 38)
Orient Quad (7.5')

ORIENT POINT
Community
Suffolk—Southold; NE of Orient;
40°9'x72°15'30"
Orient Quad (7.5')

ORIENT POINT
Physical feature
Suffolk—Southold; E of the
community of Orient Point;
41°9'40"x72°14'10"

Historical: Poquatuck (Tooker 44,
p. 195), Oyster Pond Point
(Thompson 41, vol. 1, p. 38)
Plum Island Quad (7.5')

ORIENT SHOAL
Physical feature
Suffolk—Southold; in Long Island
Sound, N of Truman Beach, W of
Terry Point; 41°8'50"x72°20'
Orient Quad (7.5')

OROWOC CREEK
Physical feature
Suffolk—Islip; flows from the S part
of Brentwood into the Great South
Bay; 40°43'x73°13'30"
Historical: Cachinncak Brook, Paper
Mill Brook (Tooker 44, pp. 29-30,
170-172). The lower part of the
creek was formerly known as
Doxsee's Creek (Bayles 93, p. 213)
Variations: Orawack, Orawacke,
Osawack, Orawac, Oriwic, Oriock
(Tooker 44, p. 170)
Central Islip and Bay Shore East
Quads (7.5')

OROWOC LAKE
Physical feature
Suffolk—Islip; drains into Orowoc
Creek, E of Bay Shore, W of the
community of Islip;
40°43'45"x73°13'30"
Bay Shore East Quad (7.5')

OSBORN'S BROOK
see
MOTTS BROOK
Source: (Shaw 106, p. 211)

OSBORN'S NECK
see
JESSUP NECK
Source: (Chace 127)

OSHAMAMUCKS
see
FRESH POND
Suffolk—Smithtown
Source: (Pelletreau 101, p. 172)

OTIS POINT
see
HOWELLS POINT
Source: (Beers 117, p. 160)

OTTER POND
Physical feature
Suffolk—Southampton; SW of Sag
Harbor; 40°59'30"x72°18'
Sag Harbor Quad (7.5')

OUHEYWICHKINGH
Indian village—historical
Suffolk—Brookhaven; on Mastic
Neck
Source: (Tooker 44, p. 173)
*Moriches Quad (7.5')

OVERLOOK BEACH
Physical feature
Suffolk—Islip; on the Great South
Bay, S shore of Heckscher State
Park, SE of the community of Islip;
40°41'55"x73°9'30"
Bay Shore East Quad (7.5')

OVERTON'S BROOK
Physical feature—historical
Suffolk—Brookhaven; SW of
Bellport, possibly Hedges Creek or
Howell Creek;
ca. 40°44'50"x72°57'30"

Source: (Tooker 45, p. 16)
*Howells Point and Bellport Quads
(7.5')

OVERTON'S PASS
Physical feature
Suffolk—Smithtown; an area NW of
the intersection of Moriches and
North Country Roads;
ca. 40°53'15"x73°9'45"
Source: (Langhans 98, p. 23)
Historical: Skunk Hollow (Ibid.)
*Saint James Quad (7.5')

OWENAMCHOG
Locality—Indian fishing station
—historical
Suffolk—Brookhaven; somewhere on
Great South Bay Beach
Source: (Tooker 45, p. 60)

OWLS HEAD
Physical feature—historical
Kings; W side of Bay Ridge;
40°38'30"x74°2'30"
Source: (Staten Island Quad, 15',
1898)
*Jersey City Quad (7.5')

OX PASTURE
Tract of land—historical
Suffolk—Southampton; SW of the
village of Southampton, SE of Art
Village; ca. 40°52'40"x72°24'50"
Source: (Pelletreau 38, p. 292)
*Southampton Quad (7.5')

OYSTER BAY
Community
Nassau—Oyster Bay; NE side of the
town; 40°52'x73°32'
Historical: Foleston (Flint 26, p. 73)
Hicksville Quad (7.5')

OYSTER BAY
Physical feature
Nassau, Suffolk—Oyster Bay,
Huntington; NW-NE borderline for
the counties of Suffolk and Nassau,
N of Cold Spring Harbor;
40°55′x73°30′
Bayville and Lloyd Harbor Quads
(7.5′)

OYSTER BAY
Town
Nassau; E side of the county
Bayville, Hicksville, Huntington, Freeport,
Amityville and West Gilgo Quads
(7.5′)

OYSTER BAY COVE
Village
Nassau—Oyster Bay; E of the
community of Oyster Bay, S of Oyster
Bay Harbor; 40°52′x73°30′35″
Hicksville Quad (7.5′)

OYSTER BAY HARBOR
Physical feature
Nassau—Oyster Bay; N of the
community of Oyster Bay; E of Mill
Neck; 40°52′35″x73°31′15″
Bayville Quad (7.5′)

OYSTER ISLAND
Physical feature
Suffolk—Smithtown; in the
Nissequogue River, S of Short
Beach; ca. 40°54′10″x73°13′15″
Source: (Langhans 98, p. 11) and
(Pelletreau 101, p. 424)
*Saint James Quad (7.5′)

OYSTER POND
Physical feature
Suffolk—East Hampton; E side of

Long Island, E of Lake Montauk;
41°4′20″x71°53′35″
Historical: Munchogue Lake (Ullitz
165, section 8)
Montauk Point Quad (7.5′)

OYSTER POND BEACH
see
TRUMAN BEACH
Source: (U.S. 170, Chart No. 115,
1855)

OYSTER POND HARBOR
see
ORIENT HARBOR
Source: (Thompson 41, vol. 1,
p. 38)

OYSTER POND POINT
see
ORIENT POINT
Physical feature
Source: (Thompson 41, vol. 1,
p. 38)

OYSTER POND REEF
Physical feature
Suffolk—Southold; in Plum Gut,
NE of Orient Point;
41°9′50″x72°14′
Plum Island Quad (7.5′)

OYSTER PONDS
Locality—historical
Suffolk—Southold; NE of Gardiners
Bay and Orient Harbor;
41°9′x72°17′30″
Source: (U.S. 170, Chart No. 115,
1855) and (French 10, p. 640)
*Orient Quad (7.5′)

OYSTER PONDS LOWER NECK
Physical feature—historical

Suffolk—Southold; in the vicinity
of Orient and Orient Point;
ca. 41 °8 '30 "x72 °16 "
Source: (Pelletreau 38, p. 428)
*Orient Quad (7.5 ')

OYSTER PONDS UPPER NECK
Physical feature—historical
Suffolk—Southold; in the vicinity of
East Marion;
ca. 41 °7 '30 "x72 °20 '30 "
Source: (Pelletreau 38, p. 428)
*Greenport and Orient Quads (7.5 ')

OZONE PARK
Community
Queens; W side of Queens, N of
Jamaica Bay, SW of Richmond
Hill; 40 °40 '30 "x73 °50 '45 "
Historical: South Woodhaven
(Ricard 86, p. 13)
Jamaica Quad (7.5 ')

PAERDEGAT BASIN
Physical feature
Kings; NW side of Jamaica Bay,
 SW of Canarsie;
40°37'20"x73°54'15"
Brooklyn and Coney Island Quads
 (7.5')

PAHEHETOCK
Locality—Indian village—historical
Suffolk—East Hampton; on the E
 end of Long Island, probably the
 Dutch notation for Peconic or
 Pehikkomuk, the small Indian
 village at Ucquebauge
Source: (Tooker 44, pp. 174–175)

PAHQUAHKOSSIT
see
WADING RIVER
 Physical feature
 Source: (Tooker 44, p. 175)

PAINES CREEK
Physical feature—historical
Suffolk—Southampton; NE side of
Mecox Bay, SE of Calf Creek;
 ca. 40°54'45"x72°19'45"
Source: (Adams 92, p. 18)
*Sag Harbor Quad (7.5')

PANDAGO
see
PANTIGO
Source: (U.S. 167, Map T–74)

PANOTHTICUTT RIVER
see
PENATAQUIT CREEK
Source: (Bayles 93, p. 211)

PANTIGO
Community
Suffolk—East Hampton; NE of East
 Hampton, W of Amagansett;
 40°58'15"x72°9'50"
Historical: Pandago (U.S. 167,
 Map T–4), Pantego (Tooker 44,
 p. 176)
East Hampton Quad (7.5')

PAPA-QUATUCK RIVER
see
BEAVER BROOK
Source: (Cocks 70, p. 5) and
(Tooker 44, p. 176)

PAPEQUATUNCK
see
MILL NECK
 Physical feature
 Nassau—Oyster Bay
 Source: (Tooker 44, p. 176)

PAPER MILL BROOK
see
OROWOC CREEK
Source: (Tooker 44, p. 170)

PAQUATUCK CREEK
see
TERRELL RIVER
Source: (Tooker 44, p. 177)

PAQUINAPAGOGUE
Locality—historical
Suffolk—Smithtown; exact location
  unknown
Source: (Tooker 44, p. 177)

PARADISE POINT
Community—historical
Suffolk—Southold; in the vicinity of
  the community of Southold;
  ca. 41°3′x72°23′
Source: (Macoskey 29, p. 59)
*Southold Quad (7.5′)

PARADISE POINT
Physical feature
Suffolk—Southold; NE point of
  Great Hog Neck;
  41°3′x72°23′
Historical: Hallock's Point (U.S. 167,
  Map T-68)
Southold Quad (7.5′)

PARDEES POND
Physical feature
Suffolk—Islip; between Bay Shore
  and Islip; 40°43′50″x73°13′10″
Bay Shore East Quad (7.5′)

PARISH OF SOUTHAVEN
see
SOUTH HAVEN
Source: (Manley 30, p. 275)

PARK SLOPE
Community
Kings; W side of Kings, NW of
  Flatbush; 40°40′15″x73°58′45″
Brooklyn Quad (7.5′)

PARKER ROCK
Physical feature
Suffolk—Southold; in Long Island

Sound, SW of Inlet Point, N of
  Arshamonaque; 41°6′30″x72°23′20″
Southold Quad (7.5′)

PARKSIDE
Community
Queens; W side of Queens, S of
  Forest Hills; 40°42′30″x73°51′15″
Jamaica Quad (7.5′)

PARKVILLE
Community
Kings; SW of Flatbush, S of
  Kensington; 40°38′x73°58′40″
Historical: Greenfield (Ross 39,
  p. 326)
Brooklyn Quad (7.5′)

PARSONAGE COVE
Physical feature
Nassau—Hempstead; on Middle Bay,
  S-central part of the town, NW of
  Baldwin Harbor;
  40°37′30″x73°37′
Freeport and Jones Inlet Quads
  (7.5′)

PARSONAGE CREEK
Physical feature
Nassau—Hempstead; borders
  Oceanside and Baldwin, flows into
  Parsonage Cove; 40°38′x73°37′
Freeport Quad (7.5′)

PARSONAGE ISLAND
Physical feature—marsh island
Nassau—Hempstead; SE of
  Oceanside, N of Lido Beach, W
  side of Middle Bay;
  40°36′30″x73°37′25″
Jones Inlet Quad (7.5′)

PARSONS BEACH
Physical feature
Queens; S point of Little Neck Bay;
40°46'20"x73°45'20"
Flushing Quad (7.5')

PASCU-UCKS CREEK
Physical feature—historical
Suffolk—Babylon; in the Great
South Bay, E side of Cedar Island,
S of Lindenhurst;
ca. 40°38'40"x73°20'20"
Source: (Tooker 44, pp. 177–178).
Also known as Nesaraske Creek
(Beauchamp 7, p. 217)
*Bay Shore West Quad (7.5')

PASSASQUEUNG CREEK
see
ARRASQUAUG BROOK
Source: (Tooker 44, pp. 178–179)

PATCHOGUE
Village
Suffolk—Brookhaven; NE of
Sayville, SE of Ronkonkoma;
40°46'x73°1'
Variations: Patchague, Pochoug,
Pochog (Tooker 44, pp. 179–180)
Patchogue and Sayville Quads (7.5')

PATCHOGUE BAY
Physical feature
Suffolk—Brookhaven; S of
Patchogue, E of Sayville;
40°44'30"x73°1'
Historical: Fire Place Bay (Thompson
41, vol. 1, inside cover map),
possibly Blue Point Bay (Overton 37,
p. 17)
Sayville Quad (7.5')

PATCHOGUE CREEK
see
PATCHOGUE RIVER
Source: (U.S. 5, List No. 6801,
p. 25)

PATCHOGUE RIVER
Physical feature
Suffolk—Brookhaven; flows into
Patchogue Bay, S of Patchogue;
40°44'50"x73°1'
Historical: Patchogue Creek (U.S. 5,
List No. 6801, p. 25)
Sayville Quad (7.5')

PATCHUMMUCK
Locality—historical
Suffolk—Southold; one of the
boundaries of Hashamomuk Neck,
at the head of Tom's Creek, now
known as Mill Creek
Source: (Tooker 44, p. 180)
*Southold Quad (7.5')

PATTERSQUASH CREEK
Physical feature
Suffolk—Brookhaven; flows through
Mastic Beach into Narrow Bay;
40°45'x72°50'32"
Moriches Quad (7.5')

PATTERSQUASH ISLAND
Physical feature
Suffolk—Brookhaven; in Narrow
Bay, S of Mastic Beach;
40°44'50"x72°50'20"
Variations: Patterquash, Patterquos,
Paterquas (Tooker 44, pp. 180–181)
Pattersquash Quad (7.5')

PATTERSQUASH NECK
Physical feature—historical
Suffolk—Brookhaven; S side of
 Mastic Beach, E of Johns Neck;
 40°45′x72°51′30″
Source: (Pelletreau 38, p. 264).
 Also known as Floyds Neck (Ibid.)
*Pattersquash Island and Moriches
 Quads (7.5′)

PAUCHOGUE CREEK
Physical feature—historical
Suffolk—Islip; no longer exists,
 flowed N to S from near the central
 part of what is now Heckscher State
 Park into Great South Bay;
 40°40′30″x73°9′45″
Source: (Town of Islip 163)
*Bay Shore East Quad (7.5′)

PAUCUCK
Locality—historical
Suffolk—Southampton; E of
 Beaverdam Creek, near
 Westhampton
Source: (Tooker 44, p. 14)
*Eastport Quad (7.5′)

PAUCUCKATUX CREEK
Physical feature—historical
Suffolk—Southold; on Pipes Cove,
 borders Hashamomuk Neck;
 41°5′20″x72°23′
Source: (Tooker 44, pp. 181–182)
*Southold Quad (7.5′)

PAUGANQUAQUANANTUCK
see
PONQUOGUE NECK
Source: (Pelletreau 38, p. 333)

PAUMANACK
Tract of land—historical
Suffolk; a name for the E part of
 Long Island
Source: (Tooker 44, pp. 182–183)
Variations: Pommanocc, Pamunke,
 Paumanuck, Paumanacke,
 Pamanack, Pommanock,
 Paumanacke, Paumanhacky (Ibid.)

PAUQUACUMSUCK CREEK
see
WADING RIVER
Source: (Tooker 44, pp. 184–185)

PAUTUCK
Community—historical
Suffolk—Southampton; W of
 Beaverdam Creek, SW of
 Westhampton;
 40°48′50″x72°40′10″
Source: (Bayles 93, p. 314)
*Eastport Quad (7.5′)

PAUTUCK CREEK
see
TERRELL RIVER
Source: (Tooker 44, p. 177)

PAYAQUOTUSK NECK
see
PIPE'S NECK
Source: (Tooker 44, p. 186)

PAYNES CREEK
Physical feature
Suffolk—Southampton; flows into
 Sag Harbor Cove, S of Noyack Bay;
 40°59′40″x72°19′30″
Sag Harbor Quad (7.5′)

PAYNESVILLE
see
MASTIC (N part of)
Source: (Bigelow 96, p. 166)

PAYNTARVILLE
see
LONG ISLAND CITY
Source: (Walling 172)

PEACEPUNCK BRANCH
Physical feature—historical
Suffolk—Smithtown; W branch of
the Nissequogue River;
ca. 40°51′35″x73°13′
Source: (Tooker 44, p. 186)
Variations: Pesapunk Branch,
Pessapunk (Ibid.)
*Central Islip Quad (7.5′)

PEACOCK POINT
Physical feature
Nassau—Oyster Bay; NW side of the
town, NW point of Lattingtown
40°54′5″x73°36′50″
Bayville Quad (7.5′)

PEAKEN'S NECK
Physical feature—historical
Suffolk—Southold; SE of
Hashamomuck Pond, SW of the
community of Arshamonaque;
41°4′50″x72°23′50″
Source: (Pelletreau 38, p. 417)
*Southold Quad (7.5′)

PEARSALLS
see
LYNBROOK
Source: (Beers 117, p. 106)

PEARSALLS CORNER
see
LYNBROOK
Source: (Walling 172)

PEARSALLS HASSOCK
Physical feature—marsh island
Nassau—Hempstead; S of Hewlett
Bay, E of North Green Sedge;
40°37′x73°40′
Lawrence Quad (7.5′)

PEASYS POND
Physical feature
Suffolk—Riverhead, Brookhaven;
E of Ridge, NW of Manorville;
40°54′x72°50′30″
Wading River Quad (7.5′)

PECONIC
Community
Suffolk—Southold; S of East
Cutchogue; 41°2′50″x72°28′
Historical: Hermitage (Bayles 93,
p. 372), (French 10, p. 640) and
(Chace 127)
Southold Quad (7.5′)

PECONIC LAKE
Physical feature
Suffolk—Brookhaven, Riverhead;
W of the community of Riverhead;
40°54′47″x72°42′49″
Historical: Kanungum Pond (Tooker
44, pp. 76–77)
Variations: Conungam, Conungun
(Ibid.)
Riverhead Quad (7.5′)

PECONIC RIVER
Physical feature
Suffolk—Riverhead, Southampton,
  Brookhaven; flows E into Flanders
  Bay
Historical: possibly called
  Messemennuck Creek (Tooker 44,
  pp. 128-130). Also known as River
  Aquaboug (Bailey 19, vol. 1, p. 185)
Variations: Pehik-Kanuk,
  Messememuck, Pehaconnuck,
  Peaconnock, Peheconnuck,
  Peaconnet, etc. (Ibid., pp. 186-188)
Mattituck, Riverhead and Wading
  River Quads (7.5 ')

PELICAN ISLAND
Physical feature
Kings
see
CONEY ISLAND
  Physical feature
  Source: (Manley 30, p. 32)

PELICAN ISLAND
Physical feature
Suffolk—Brookhaven; E side of the
  Great South Bay; 40°43 '35 "x72°54 '
Howells Point Quad (7.5 ')

PEMBROKE
see
GLEN COVE
  City
  Source: (Flint 26, p. 71)

PENATAQUIT
see
BAY SHORE
Source: (Tooker 44, p. 189)

PENATAQUIT CREEK
Physical feature
Suffolk—Islip; flows through Bay
  Shore and into Great Cove;
  40°42 '50 "x73°14 '20 "
Variations: Panothticutt River (Bayles
  93, p. 211), Penataquitt,
  Penettiquott (Tooker 44,
  pp. 188-189)
Bay Shore East Quad (7.5 ')

PENATAQUIT POINT
Community
Suffolk—Islip; the vicinity of Bay
  Shore; ca. 40°30 'x73°14 '10 "
Source: (Macoskey 29, p. 59)
*Bay Shore East Quad (7.5 ')

PENATAQUIT POINT
Physical feature
Suffolk—Islip; NW side of Great
  Cove, SE of Bay Shore;
  40°42 '48 "x73°14 '10 "
Bay Shore East Quad (7.5 ')

PENNIMAN COVE
Physical feature
Suffolk—Southampton; SW side of
  Shinnecock Bay, E of Quogue;
  40°49 '30 "x72°35 '
Quogue Quad (7.5 ')

PENNIMAN CREEK
Physical feature
Suffolk—Southampton; E of Quogue,
  W of Shinnecock Bay;
  40°49 '15 "x72°35 '
Quogue Quad (7.5 ')

PENNY BRIDGE
Community
Queens; NW side of Queens, on the

Newtown Creek, SE of Long Island
City; 40°43′40″x73°55′50″
Brooklyn Quad (7.5′)

PENNY ISLAND
Physical feature
Suffolk—Islip; in the Great South
Bay, E of East Fire Island, S of
Heckscher State Park,
40°39′25″x73°10′30″
Bay Shore East Quad (7.5′)

PENNY POND
Physical feature
Suffolk—Southampton; SE of
Flanders, S of Southport, W of
Squiretown; 40°53′50″x72°33′50″
Mattituck Quad (7.5′)

PENNY POND
Physical feature—inlet
Suffolk—Southampton; on
Shinnecock Bay, S of Hampton
Bays and Ponquogue;
40°51′5″x72°30′50″
Quogue Quad (7.5′)

PEQUANET NECK
Physical feature—historical
Suffolk—Southold; in the vicinity of
the community of Orient;
Source: (Tooker 44, p. 189)
Variation: Poquatuck (Ibid.)
*Orient Quad (7.5′)

PEQUASH NECK
see
FLEETS NECK
Physical feature
Source: (Tooker 44, pp. 189–190)

PESAPUNCK NECK
Physical feature—historical
Suffolk—Southold; between
Cutchogue and Mattituck;
ca. 40°59′45″x72°30′
Source: (Tooker 44, pp. 190–191)
Variations: Pessepunk, Pesapunck,
Pisapunke, Pieceapunck (Ibid.)
*Mattituck and Southold Quads
(7.5′)

PETERS NECK POINT
Physical feature
Suffolk—Southold; SE of Orient;
41°7′35″x72°17′5″
Orient Quad (7.5′)

PETER'S POND
Physical feature—marsh
Suffolk—Southampton; SE of
Bridgehampton;
40°55′5″x72°15′50″
Sag Harbor Quad (7.5′)

PETTIT MARSH
Physical feature—marsh island
Nassau—Hempstead; SE of Freeport,
S of Merrick; 40°37′30″x73°34′
Freeport Quad (7.5′)

PETTYS BIGHT
Physical feature—coastal area
Suffolk—Southold; NE of Orient;
41°9′20″x72°16′15″
Orient Quad (7.5′)

PHILLIPS CREEK
Physical feature
Suffolk—Southampton; S of East
Quogue, W part of Shinnecock Bay;
40°50′x72°35′
Quogue Quad (7.5′)

PHILLIPS MILLPOND
Physical feature
Suffolk—Smithtown; W of
Smithtown, Nissequogue River
flows into it; 40°51′10″x73°12′55″
Historical: Head of the River Mill
Pond, Phillips Pond, White's Pond
(Smithtown), (Langhans 98, p. 26)
Central Islip Quad (7.5′)

PHILLIPS POINT
Physical feature
Suffolk—Southampton; S of East
Quogue, W part of Shinnecock Bay;
40°49′50″x72°34′30″
Quogue Quad (7.5′)

PHILLIPS POND
Physical feature
Suffolk—Southampton; E of
Southampton village;
40°53′x72°21′30″
Sag Harbor Quad (7.5′)

PHILLIPS POND
Suffolk—Smithtown
see
PHILLIPS MILLPOND
Source: (Langhans 98, p. 26)

PICKET POINT
Physical feature
Suffolk—Southampton; SE side of
Moriches Bay, S of Westhampton;
40°47′35″x72°40′
Eastport Quad (7.5′)

PICKET ROCK
Physical feature
Nassau—North Hempstead; in Long
Island Sound, NW of Hempstead
Harbor, N of Mott Point;
40°51′40″x73°40′37″
Sea Cliff Quad (7.5′)

PIG CREEK
Physical feature—historical
Suffolk—Smithtown; NW of Stony
Brook Harbor, SW of Long Beach;
40°55′x73°10′55″
Source: (Langhans 98, pp. 20–21)
and (Pelletreau 101, p. 32)
*Saint James Quad (7.5′)

PIKEL HILL
Physical feature—historical
Suffolk—Brookhaven; E side of
Mount Misery;
ca. 40°57′30″x73°2′45″
Source: (Strong 108, p. 118)
*Port Jefferson Quad (7.5′)

PIKES BEACH
Physical feature
Suffolk—Southampton; on the
Atlantic Ocean, E of Moriches Inlet,
S of Eastport; 40°46′50″x72°42′
Source: (Hagstrom 141, 1979, p. 59)
and (Eastport Quad, 7.5′, AMS,
1947)
*Eastport Quad (7.5′)

PINE AIRE
Community
Suffolk—Islip; SE of Brentwood,
NE side of the town;
40°46′15″x73°16′30″
Greenlawn Quad (7.5′)

PINE CREST DUNES
Physical feature
Suffolk—Southold; W of Southold
and Great Pond;
41°4′x72°27′30″
Southold Quad (7.5′)

PINE GROVE
Community—historical
Nassau—Oyster Bay; N of Bethpage
Source: (Hyde 147)
*Huntington Quad (7.5')

PINE HOLLOW
Community—historical
Queens (Nassau)—Oyster Bay; S of
the community of Oyster Bay, N
of East Norwich;
40°52'x73°31'30"
Source: (Hyde 147)
*Hicksville Quad (7.5')

PINE ISLAND
Physical feature—peninsula—
historical
Queens (Nassau)—Oyster Bay;
between Oak Neck and Centre
Island; 40°54'20"x73°33'
Source: (Walling 172)
*Bayville Quad (7.5')

PINE ISLAND
Physical feature
Kings
see
CONEY ISLAND
Physical feature
Source: (Manley 30, p. 32)

PINE LAKE
Physical feature
Suffolk—Brookhaven; N of Coram,
SW of Wading River
40°53'15"x72°58'
Historical: Half Mile Pond (Bayles
95, p. 50)
Middle Island Quad (7.5')

PINE LOTTS
Tract of land—historical
Suffolk—East Hampton; W of
Napeague Harbor, SW of Lazy
Point; ca. 41°00'x72°4'
Source: (Rattray 102, p. 103)
*Gardiners Island East Quad (7.5')

PINE MARSH
Physical feature—marsh island
Nassau—Hempstead; S of Freeport,
E of Middle Bay, NE of Adler
Island; 40°37'x73°34'30"
Jones Inlet Quad (7.5')

PINE NECK
Community
Suffolk—Southampton; E of East
Quogue; 40°50'35"x72°33'30"
Quogue Quad (7.5')

PINE NECK
Physical feature
Suffolk—Southampton; S of Noyack
Bay, NW of Noyack;
41°00'x72°20'30"
Historical: Ruggs Neck and Rugs
Neck (Tooker 44, p. 216)
Sag Harbor Quad (7.5')

PINE NECK
Physical feature—historical
Suffolk—Brookhaven; S part of
East Patchogue, bordered by Swan
River on the W and Mud Creek on
the E; 40°45'10"x72°59'40"
Source: (Bailey 19, vol. 1, p. 269).
Also known as Moger Neck (Ibid.)
*Bellport Quad (7.5')

PINE NECK
Physical feature—historical
Suffolk—Islip; SE of East
  Patchogue, N side of Patchogue
  Bay; 40°45'x72°59'30"
Source: (Pelletreau 38, p. 238)
*Bellport and Howells Point Quads
  (7.5')

PINE NECK POINT
Physical feature
Suffolk—Southampton; W part of
  Shinnecock Bay, E of East Quogue;
  40°50'20"x72°33'10"
Quogue Quad (7.5')

PINE POINT
Physical feature
Suffolk—Southold; on Block Island
  Sound, S point of Plum Island;
  41°9'40"x72°12'
Plum Island Quad (7.5')

PINE POINT
Physical feature—historical
Suffolk—Smithtown; W side of the
  Nissequogue River, S of Sunken
  Meadow Creek;
  ca. 40°53'55"x73°13'40"
Source: (Langhans 98, p. 21) and
  (Pelletreau 101, p. 416)
*Saint James Quad (7.5')

PINELAWN
Community—historical
Suffolk—Babylon; NE of
  Farmingdale; ca.
  40°44'25"x73°25'30"
Source: (Babylon Quad, 15', 1903)
*Amityville Quad (7.5')

PINELAWN STATION
Community
Suffolk—Babylon; W of
  Wyandanch, N of North
  Lindenhurst; 40°44'40"x73°24'5"
Amityville Quad (7.5')

PINES LAKE
Physical feature—historical
Nassau—Hempstead; W of
  Hempstead Lake, NE side of
  Malverne, no longer exists;
  40°40'30"x73°40'55"
Source: (Lynbrook Quad, 7.5', 1954)
*Lynbrook Quad (7.5')

PINES POND
Physical feature—historical
Queens (Nassau)—Hempstead; no
  longer exists, formerly on the SW
  side of Hempstead, near Front
  St. and Franklin St.;
  40°42'20"x73°37'40"
Source: (Walling 172)
*Freeport Quad (7.5')

PINES STREAM
Physical feature
Nassau—Hempstead; E side of
  Malverne, flows into Mills River
  and Smith Pond;
  ca. 40°39'35"x73°39'40"
Lynbrook Quad (7.5')

PINK'S HOLLOW
see
BROOKVILLE
Source: (Flint 26, p. 69)

PIPES COVE
Physical feature
Suffolk—Southold; SW of

Greenport; 41°5'20"x72°22'30"
Greenport and Southold Quads
(7.5')

PIPE'S NECK
Physical feature
Suffolk—Southold; W of Pipes
  Cove, SE of Arshamonaque;
  41°5'20"x72°23'15"
Source: (Tooker 44, p. 186).
  Also known as Payaquotusk Neck
  (Ibid.)
*Southold Quad (7.5')

PIPE'S NECK CREEK
  see
MOORES DRAIN
Source: (Tooker 44, pp. 94–95)

PIPING ROCK
Community—historical
Nassau—Oyster Bay; in the vicinity
  of Locust Valley
Source: (Macoskey 29, p. 59)
*Bayville Quad (7.5')

PIPING ROCK
Physical feature—historical
  Nassau—Oyster Bay; in the vicinity
  of Shu Swamp
Source: (Cocks 70, p. 7)
*Bayville Quad (7.5')

PLAINEDGE
Community
Nassau—Oyster Bay; S of Bethpage,
  N of Massapeaqua, E of Levittown;
  40°43'x73°28'45"
Historical: Turkeyville
  (Flint 26, p. 74)
Amityville Quad (7.5')

PLAINEDGE
Village
Nassau—North Hempstead
  see
WESTBURY
Source: (Overton 37, p. 166)

PLAINFIELD STATION
Railroad station—historical
Suffolk—Brookhaven; E of
  Medford, S of Gordon Heights;
  40°49'10"x72°48'10"
Source: (Moriches Quad, 15', 1903)
*Bellport Quad (7.5')

PLAINVIEW
Community
Nassau—Oyster Bay; E-central part
  of the town, E of Hicksville;
  40°46'40"x73°28'15"
Huntington Quad (7.5')

PLANDOME
Village
Nassau—North Hempstead; SW side
  of Manhasset Neck, SE of
  Manhasset Bay; 40°48'20"x73°42'
Historical: Little Cow Neck
  (Flint 26, p. 74)
Sea Cliff Quad (7.5')

PLANDOME HEIGHTS
Village
Nassau—North Hempstead; SW side
  of Manhasset Neck, S of Plandome;
  40°48'10"x73°42'
Sea Cliff Quad (7.5')

PLANDOME MANOR
Village
Nassau—North Hempstead; SW side
  of Manhasset Neck, S of Port
  Washington; 40°49'x73°42'
Sea Cliff Quad (7.5')

PLANTING FIELDS ARBORETUM
State Park
Nassau—Oyster Bay; N part of the town, W of the community of Oyster Bay, S of Mill Neck; 40°51′40″x73°33′20″
Source: (Hagstrom 140, 1978, p. 34)
Historical: The State University Conference Center (Hicksville Quad, 7.5′, 1967)
*Hicksville Quad (7.5′)

PLATTSDALE
Community—historical
Queens (Nassau)—North Hempstead; W of Herricks and N of North New Hyde Park; 40°45′50″x73°41′
Source: (Walling 172)
*Sea Cliff Quad (7.5′)

PLEASANT SPRINGS
see
HAUPPAUGE
Source: (Langhans 98, p. 10)

PLUM GUT
Physical feature—channel
Suffolk—Southold; in Long Island Sound, midway between Orient Point and Plum Island; 41°10′x72°13′
Plum Island Quad (7.5′)

PLUM GUT HARBOR
Physical feature
Suffolk—Southold; SW shoreline of Plum Island; 41°10′5″x72°12′30″
Plum Island Quad (7.5′)

PLUM ISLAND
Physical feature
Suffolk—Southold; in Long Island Sound, NE of Long Island; 41°10′30″x72°12′
Historical: Manittuwond (Tooker 44, p. 98), Isle of Patmos (French 10, p. 639fn)
Plum Island Quad (7.5′)

PLUM ISLAND ROCK
Physical feature
Suffolk—Southold; in Block Island Sound, E of Plum Island; 41°10′30″x72°10′45″
Plum Island Quad (7.5′)

PLUM POINT
Physical feature
Nassau—North Hempstead; on Manhasset Neck, N point of the town, N of Kings Point; 40°50′x73°43′40″
Sea Cliff Quad (7.5′)

PLUM POINT
Physical feature
Nassau—Oyster Bay; E point of Centre Island; 40°54′5″x73°30′30″
Bayville Quad (7.5′)

PLUMB BEACH CHANNEL
Physical feature
Kings; S of Gerritsen, E of Sheepshead Bay; 40°35′5″x73°55′20″
Coney Island Quad (7.5′)

PLUMB INLET
see
GERRITSON INLET
Source: (Burr 125)

PLUMB ISLAND
see
CONEY ISLAND
Physical feature
Source: (Manley 30, p. 32)

PLUNDER'S NECK
Physical feature
Queens; SW of Flushing Bay, where
the former village of Newtown was
located; ca. 40°44'25"x73°53'
Source: (Tooker 44, p. 72)
*Central Park Quad (7.5')

POCHOUG NECK
Physical feature—historical
Suffolk—Brookhaven; the neck on
which the community of Patchogue
is located; 40°45'15"x73°1'
Source: (Tooker 44, pp.
179–180, 191–192)
*Patchogue Quad (7.5')

POINT BREEZE
Physical feature
Kings; S part of Kings, N of the
community of Rockaway Point, W
of Dead Horse Bay;
40°34'50"x73°54'50"
Coney Island Quad (7.5')

POINT LOOKOUT
Community
Nassau—Hempstead; E of Long
Beach and Lido Beach, S of
Freeport; 40°35'30"x73°34'45"
Historical: Nassau-by-the-Sea
(Macoskey 29, p. 58)
Jones Inlet Quad (7.5')

POINT O' WOODS
Community
Suffolk—Brookhaven; on Fire

Island, S of Nicoll Bay and
Oakdale, SE of Islip;
40°39'5"x73°7'30"
Historical: Pointwood (Fire Island
Quad, 15', 1903)
Bay Shore East and Sayville Quads
(7.5')

POINTWOOD
see
POINT O' WOODS
Source: (Fire Island Quad, 15',
1903)

POLLYPOD
Physical feature—bay—historical
Suffolk—Smithtown; N of New
Millpond; ca. 40°50'40"x73°13'40"
Source: (Langhans 98, p. 21)
*Central Islip Quad (7.5')

POMICHES CREEK
Physical feature
Suffolk—Brookhaven; SW side of
East Moriches, flows into Tuthill
Cove; 40°47'45"x72°45'50"
Source: (Tooker 44, p. 192)
*Moriches Quad (7.5')

POMPS POINT
Physical feature
Suffolk—Shelter Island; E part of
Shelter Island, S-central point of
Ram Island; 41°4'22"x72°17'25"
Greenport Quad (7.5')

POND BLUFF
Physical feature
Suffolk—East Hampton; SW of
Montauk Point, S of Oyster Pond,
SE of Lake Montauk; 41°3'x71°53'
Montauk Point Quad (7.5')

POND NECK
Physical feature—historical
Suffolk—Smithtown; W side of
  Stony Brook Harbor, N of Spring
  Hollow; ca. 40°54'25"x73°10'50"
Source: (Langhans 98, p. 21)
*Saint James Quad (7.5')

POND POINT
Physical feature
Suffolk—Southampton; SE side of
  Moriches Bay, S of Westhampton;
  40°47'30"x72°40'20"
Eastport Quad (7.5')

POND QUOGUE
see
PONQUOGUE NECK
Source: (Pelletreau 38, p. 333)

PONKIESBERGH
see
COBBLE HILL
Source: (Stiles 66, vol. 1, p. 252)

PONQUOGUE
Community
Suffolk—Southampton; W of
  Shinnecock Bay, S of Hampton
  Bays; 40°52'x72°30'
Historical: Bondyquogue (Tooker 44,
  pp. 29, 192–193)
Shinnecock Inlet and Quogue Quads
  (7.5')

PONQUOGUE NECK
Physical feature
Suffolk—Southampton; on
  Shinnecock Bay, S of the community
  of Ponquogue, E of Rampasture;
  40°51'x72°30'20"
Source: (Tooker 44, pp. 192–193)
Variations: Pauganquogue,

Pogenquake, Pauganquog,
Paugunquag and Pagonquag
(Ibid.), Pauganquaquanantuck and
Pond Quogue (Pelletreau 38,
p. 333)
*Shinnecock Inlet and Quogue Quads
(7.5')

PONQUOGUE POINT
Physical feature
Suffolk—Southampton; on
  Shinnecock Bay, SE of Ponquogue;
  40°50'55"x72°30'7"
Quogue Quad (7.5')

POOR BOWERY
see
NORTH BEACH
Source: (Ricard 86, pp. 12–13)

POOSPATUCK
Locality and neck—historical
Suffolk—Brookhaven; SE of Mastic,
  N of Poospatuck Creek;
  40°47'30"x72°50'
Source: (Tooker 44, pp. 193–194)
Variations: Pussp'tuck, Pusspa'tok,
  Poospatuc (Ibid.)
*Moriches Quad (7.5')

POOSPATUCK CREEK
Physical feature
Suffolk—Brookhaven; flows into the
  Forge River from the W, S of
  Moriches; 40°47'20"x72°49'40"
Moriches Quad (7.5')

POQUATUCK
see
ORIENT POINT
Physical feature
Source: (Tooker 44, p. 195)

POQUOTT
Village
Suffolk—Brookhaven; N of East
Setauket, W of Port Jefferson
Harbor; 40 °57 'x73 °5 '
Historical: Dryers Neck (Tooker 44,
p. 195)
Port Jefferson Quad (7.5 ')

PORDEGAT POND
Physical feature—historical
Kings; E of Parkville (Greenfield),
S of Flatbush; ca. 40 °38 'x73 °57 '30 "
Source: (Walling 172)
*Brooklyn Quad (7.5 ')

PORIGIES NECK
Physical feature
Suffolk—Brookhaven; SW side of
the community of Mastic Beach,
bordered on the E by Pattersquash
Creek; 40 °45 'x72 °51 '
Source: (Tooker 44, p. 195)
Variation: Porridge's Neck (Ibid.)
*Moriches Quad (7.5 ')

PORPOISE CHANNEL
Physical feature
Suffolk—Smithtown; flows into
Smithtown Bay, NE of Stony Brook
Harbor; 40 °55 'x73 °10 '
Historical: Rassapeague Bay
(Tooker 44, p. 210)
Saint James Quad (7.5 ')

PORT JEFFERSON
Village
Suffolk—Brookhaven; E of East
Setauket, S of Port Jefferson
Harbor; 40 °56 '30 "x73 °4 '
Historical: Drowned Meadow,
Souwassett, Sowassett, Sonassett
(Tooker 44, pp. 246-247)
Port Jefferson Quad (7.5 ')

PORT JEFFERSON HARBOR
Physical feature
Suffolk—Brookhaven; NW of Port
Jefferson, W of Mount Misery;
40 °57 '30 "x73 °5 '30 "
Historical: Drown Meadow Bay
(Untitled Map 171), Drown'd
Meadow Harbor (Burr 124)
and (Smith 162)
Port Jefferson Quad (7.5 ')

PORT JEFFERSON STATION
Community
Suffolk—Brookhaven; SE of the
village of Port Jefferson, SW of
Mt. Sinai; 40 °55 '50 "x73 °3 '
Historical: Comsewogue (Tooker 44,
pp. 54-55), Echo (Setauket Quad,
15 ', 1904)
Port Jefferson Quad (7.5 ')

PORT OF HEMPSTEAD
Physical feature—landing—historical
Nassau—Hempstead; SE side of
Baldwin, on Milburn Creek, above
Atlantic Avenue;
40 °38 '30 "x73 °36 '5 "
Source: (Metz 83, p. 6, 8). Also
known as Lott's Landing (Ibid.)
*Freeport Quad (7.5 ')

PORT WASHINGTON
Community
Nassau—North Hempstead; NE side
of town, W-central side of
Manhasset Neck; 40 °49 '30 "x73 °42 '
Historical: Cow Bay (Bailey 19,
vol. 1, p. 444), Cow Neck Village
(Flint 26, p. 74)
Sea Cliff Quad (7.5 ')

PORT WASHINGTON NORTH
Village
Nassau—North Hempstead; NW side
of Manhasset Neck, NE of
Manhasset Bay;
40 °50 '30 "x73 °42 '15 "
Sea Cliff Quad (7.5 ')

POST LEAD
Physical feature—channel
Nassau—Hempstead; NE side of
Lawrence, NW boundary of
Lawrence Marsh;
40 °36 '20 "x73 °41 '50 "
Lawrence Quad (7.5 ')

POST MARSH
Physical feature—marsh island
Nassau—Hempstead; E of Lawrence,
bounded by Post Lead on the S and
W, by Brosewere Bay on the N,
and Woodsburgh Channel on the E;
40 °36 '25 "x73 °41 '50 "
Source: (U.S. 5, List No. 8101,
p. 13)
*Lawrence Quad (7.5 ')

POST POINT
Physical feature
Suffolk—Brookhaven; on the N
shoreline of Bellport Bay;
40 °45 '25 "x72 °54 '45 "
Bellport Quad (7.5 ')

POT COVE
Physical feature
Queens, New York County; on Hell
Gate, N of Astoria, S of Wards
Island; 40 °46 '35 "x73 °55 '45 "
Central Park Quad (7.5 ')

POTINACK
Physical feature—a hole or deep
depression—historical
Suffolk—East Hampton; SW of
Montauk and Hither Plains;
ca. 41 °1 'x71 °59 '45 "
Source: (Tooker 44, p. 196)
*Montauk Point Quad (7.5 ')

POTUNK
Community—historical
Suffolk—Southampton; the vicinity
of Westhampton Beach;
ca. 40 °48 '30 "x72 °38 '45 "
Source: (Macoskey 29, p. 60) and
(Bayles 93, p. 314)
*Eastport Quad (7.5 ')

POTUNK NECK
Physical feature
Suffolk—Southampton; E side of
Moriches Bay, SE side of the
community of Southampton Beach;
40 °48 '15 "x72 °38 '45 "
Source: (Tooker 44, pp. 196–197)
Variations: Potunck, Potonke (Ibid.)
*Eastport Quad (7.5 ')

POTUNK POINT
Physical feature
Suffolk—Southampton; E end of
Moriches Bay;
40 °47 '50 "x72 °38 '50 "
Eastport Quad (7.5 ')

POWDER HILL
Physical feature
Suffolk—East Hampton; SE of
Northwest Harbor, SW of
Threemile Harbor;
41 °00 '20 "x72 °14 '25 "
Gardiners Island West Quad (7.5 ')

POWELL COVE
Physical feature
Queens; on the East River, N side
of Queens, W of Whitestone, E of
College Point; 40°47′30″x73°50′
Flushing Quad (7.5′)

POWELL CREEK
Physical feature
Nassau—Hempstead; NW side of the
community of Oceanside, flows into
the East Rockaway Channel;
40°38′10″x73°39′30″
Lynbrook Quad (7.5′)

POWELL POND
see
DOSORIS POND
Source: (Coles 73, p. 8)

POXABOGUE
Farming area—historical
Suffolk—Southampton; NE of
Bridgehampton, E of Poxabogue
Pond; ca. 40°56′40″x72°16′45″
Source: (Tooker 44, pp. 197-198)
Variations: Poxabog, Paugasaboug,
Pougasoboug, Pogasebogue,
Poxabog (Ibid.)
*Sag Harbor Quad (7.5′)

POXABOGUE POND
Physical feature
Suffolk—Southampton; NE of
Bridgehampton;
40°56′40″x72°17′10″
Sag Harbor Quad (7.5′)

POYHAS SWAMP
Physical feature—historical
Suffolk—Southold; in the vicinity
of Hashamomuk Neck
Source: (Tooker 44, p. 198)

PRESQUE ISLAND
see
EAST ISLAND
Nassau—Oyster Bay
Source: (Russell 87, p. 211)

PRESTONS POND
Physical feature
Suffolk—Riverhead; N of
Manorville, W of Swan Pond;
40°54′5″x72°49′5″
Wading River Quad (7.5′)

PRICE BEND
Physical feature—bay
Suffolk—Huntington; NW side of
Northport Bay; 40°55′40″x73°24′
Lloyd Harbor Quad (7.5′)

PRIME'S POND
see
HECKSCHER PARK LAKE
Source: (Sammis 104, p. 42)

PROMISED LAND
Community
Suffolk—East Hampton; SE of
Napeague Bay; 41°00′x72°5′
Gardiners Island East and
Napeague Beach Quads (7.5′)

PROSPECT
Community—historical
Suffolk—Shelter Island; possibly the
site of Shelter Island Heights;
41°5′x72°21′30″
Source: (Tooker 4, p. 40). Also
known as Prospect Grove (Cram
133, p. 36)
*Greenport Quad (7.5′)

PROSPECT GROVE
see
PROSPECT
Source: (Cram 133, p. 36)

PROSPECT HILL
Physical feature
Suffolk—East Hampton; E of Lake
Montauk; 41 °4 'x71 °54 '25 "
Montauk Point Quad (7.5 ')

PROSPECT PARK LAKE
Physical feature
Kings; S side of Prospect Park,
W of Flatbush; 40 °39 '20 "x73 °58 '
Brooklyn Quad (7.5 ')

PROSPECT POINT
Physical feature
Nassau—North Hempstead; N point
of Manhasset Neck;
40 °52 '10 "x73 °42 '50 "
Sea Cliff Quad (7.5 ')

PULPIT ROCK
Physical feature
Suffolk—Southold; in Long Island
Sound, N of West Harbor of
Fishers Island;
41 °17 '15 "x71 °59 '45 "
Mystic Quad (7.5 ')

PUMCATAWE
Tract of land—historical
Suffolk—Brookhaven; E of Mastic
River (Forge River)
Source: (Tooker 44, p. 198)
Variations: Puncatane, Puncataue,
Puencatame, Punecatone (Ibid.)

PUMPKIN PATCH CHANNEL
Physical feature
Kings, Queens; central part of

Jamaica Bay; 40 °38 'x73 °50 '
Jamaica and Far Rockaway Quads
(7.5 ')

PUMPKIN PATCH MARSH
Physical feature—marsh island
Kings; E side of Kings, central
part of Jamaica Bay
40 °37 '45 "x73 °50 '30 "
Jamaica Quad (7.5 ')

PUNG–PLUES CREEK
Physical feature—historical
Suffolk—Brookhaven; S side of East
Moriches, flows into Tuthill
Cove; ca. 40 °47 '50 "x72 °45 '50 "
Source: (Tooker 44, p. 199)
*Moriches Quad (7.5 ')

PUNK'S HOLE
see
MANORVILLE
Source: (Tooker 44, p. 199)

PURGATORY CREEK
Physical feature
Suffolk—Brookhaven; N of Blue
Point, W of Patchogue;
40 °45 'x73 °1 '55 "
Patchogue Quad (7.5 ')

PUSSYS POND
Physical feature
Suffolk—East Hampton; W of
Acabonack Harbor;
41 °1 '10 "x72 °9 '23 "
Gardiners Island West Quad (7.5 ')

QAOTUAC
see
LITTLE NECK
Community
Queens
Source: (Thompson 42, p. 128)

QUACONSIT RIVER
see
WADING RIVER
Source: (Tooker 44, p. 151)

QUADAMS HILL
Physical feature—historical
Suffolk—East Hampton; on
Montauk Peninsula, SE of Oyster
Pond; ca. 41°3′50″x71°52′45″
Source: (Tooker 44, p. 200)
*Montauk Point Quad (7.5′)

QUAGO DITCH
see
QUOGUE CANAL
Source: (Tooker 44, p. 200)

QUALICAN
Locality—historical
Suffolk—Brookhaven; on Mastic
Neck, land reserved for the
Indians' use
Source: (Tooker 44, p. 201)

QUAMUCK
see
OLD INLET
Suffolk—Southampton
Source: (Tooker 44, p. 201)

QUANCH ISLAND
Physical feature—historical
Suffolk—Brookhaven; in the Great
South Bay, near Whalehouse
Point
Source: (Tooker 44, pp. 201–202)
*Howells Point Quad (7.5′)

QUANDOEQUAREOUS BRANCH
Physical feature—historical
Queens; W of Maspeth, E side of
Newtown Creek;
ca. 40°44′x73°55′30″
Source: (Tooker 44, p. 202)
*Brooklyn Quad (7.5′)

QUANTUCK BAY
Physical feature
Suffolk—Southampton; SW of
Quogue, E of Moriches Bay;
40°48′30″x72°37′30″
Historical: Quintue Bay (Burr 124)
and (Tooker 44, pp. 202–203)
Quogue and Eastport Quads (7.5′)

QUANTUCK CANAL
Physical feature
Suffolk—Southampton; canal
between Quantuck Bay and
Moneyboque Bay; 40°48′x72°38′
Eastport Quad (7.5′)

QUANTUCK CREEK
Physical feature
Suffolk—Southampton; flows into
Quantuck Bay, W of Quogue;
40°49'x72°37'25"
Variation: Quaquantuck (Tooker 44,
pp. 202–203)
Quogue Quad (7.5')

QUANUNTOWUNK
see
FORT POND
Source: (Tooker 44, pp. 203–204)

QUAQUANANTUCK
Locality—neck—historical
Suffolk—Southampton; E of
Westhampton, NW of Quantuck
Bay; 40°x49'x72°37'30"
Source: (Tooker 44, pp. 205–206)
Variations: Quiogue Neck, Little
Assop's Neck, Quoquatuck
Meadow, Quaquanantick,
Quaquanantuck, Quagquantick,
Quaqo, Quagga, Quag (Ibid.)
*Eastport and Quogue Quads (7.5')

QUAQUANTUCK CREEK
see
QUANTUCK CREEK
Source: (Tooker 44, pp. 202–203)

QUARAPIN SWAMP
Physical feature—historical
Suffolk—Huntington; exact location
unknown
Source: (Tooker 44, p. 206)

QUASH NECK
see
FLEETS NECK
Physical feature
Suffolk—Southold
Source: (Pelletreau 38, p. 432)

QUEENS
Community
see
QUEENS VILLAGE
Source: (Ricard 86, p. 13),
(Beers 117) and (Walling 172)

QUEENS
County—Borough of New York City
W part of Long Island, between
Kings County and Nassau County
Historical: part of North Riding of
Yorkshire, except for Newtown
which was in the West Riding of
Yorkshire (French 10, p. 554fn).
Prior to 1899, included Nassau
County.

QUEENS VILLAGE
Community
Queens; NE side of Queens, W of
Floral Park; 40°43'x73°45'
Historical: Queens (Walling 172),
(Ricard 86, p. 13), (Beers 117),
Brushville (French 10, p. 584fn),
Bushville (Flint 26, p. 74),
Inglewood (Ricard 86, p. 13) and
(Beers 117), Little Plains (Ricard
86, p. 13)
Lynbrook and Jamaica Quads (7.5')

QUEENSWATER
see
LONG BEACH (part of)
City
Source: (Macoskey 29, p. 60)

QUGGALUNE
Locality—historical
Suffolk—Southampton; N part of
Quaquanantuck, near the present
site of Quiogue
Source: (Tooker 44, p. 207)
*Eastport Quad (7.5')

QUINCETREE LANDING
Physical feature
Suffolk—East Hampton; E of
Napeague Bay, N of Hither Hills
State Park; 41°1′45″x72°0′50″
Gardiners Island East Quad (7.5′)

QUINTUCK CREEK
Physical feature
Suffolk—Islip; S of East Islip,
W of Heckscher State Park;
40°42′30″x73°11′15″
Bay Shore East Quad (7.5′)

QUINTUE BAY
see
QUANTUCK BAY
Source: (Burr 124) and (Tooker 44,
pp. 202-203)

QUIOGUE
Community
Suffolk—Southampton; E of
Westhampton, W of Quogue;
40°49′x72°38′
Eastport Quad (7.5′)

QUIOGUE NECK
Physical feature
Suffolk—Southampton; NW of
Quantuck Bay, E of Westhampton;
40°49′x72°38′
Source: (Tooker 44, p. 207)
Historical: Quaquanantuck, Little
Assop's Neck (Ibid.)
*Eastport Quad (7.5′)

QUIOGUE POINT
Physical feature
Suffolk—Southampton; W side of
Quantuck Bay;
40°48′40″x73°37′32″

Source: (Eastport Quad, 7.5′, AMS,
1947)
*Eastport Quad (7.5′)

QUOGUE
Village
Suffolk—Southampton; W end of
Shinnecock Bay; 40°49′15″x72°36′
Variations: Quago, Quagga, Quoag,
Quag (Tooker 44, pp. 207-208),
Little Quogue (Thompson 41, vol.
1, p. 362)
Quogue Quad (7.5′)

QUOGUE CANAL
Physical feature
Suffolk—Southampton; channel
between Shinnecock Bay and
Quantuck Bay; 40°48′30″x72°36′
Historical: Quago Ditch (Tooker 44,
p. 200)
Variations: Quagga, Quaquanantuck
(Ibid.)
Quogue Quad (7.5′)

QUOGUE NECK
Physical feature—historical
Suffolk—Southampton; E of
Westhampton Beach, W of
Shinnecock Bay;
ca. 40°49′x72°36′
Source: (Burr 124)
*Quogue Quad (7.5′)

QUONETTQUOTT
see
CONNETQUOT RIVER
Source: (Tooker 44, p. 208)

R POINT
Community—historical
Queens (Nassau)—Hempstead;
N of Freeport, possibly Greenwich
Point
Source: (Burr 125)
*Freeport Quad (7.5 ')

RACCOON BEACH
see
SUNKEN FOREST
Source: (Tuomey 49, pp. 29–30)

RACCOON WOODS
see
CHERRY GROVE
Source: (Strong 107, p. 116)

RACE POINT
Physical feature
Suffolk—Southold; Western-most
point of Fishers Island;
41 °15 'x72 °2 '15 "
New London Quad (7.5 ')

RADIO POINT
Physical feature
Suffolk—Brookhaven; NW side of
Moriches Bay, S of East Moriches;
40 °46 '55 "x72 °45 '50 "
Moriches Quad (7.5 ')

RALPH CREEK
Physical feature
Queens, Kings; E side of Kings, N of
Jamaica Bay; 40 °39 '35 "x73 °51 '35 "
Jamaica Quad (7.5 ')

RAM HEAD
Physical feature
Suffolk—Shelter Island; NE of
Shelter Island, E point of Ram
Island; 41 °4 '40 "x72 °16 '40 "
Greenport Quad (7.5 ')

RAM ISLAND
Physical feature
Suffolk—Shelter Island; NE side of
Shelter Island, NE of Coecles Inlet;
41 °4 '40 "x72 °17 '10 "
Greenport Quad (7.5 ')

RAM ISLAND
Physical feature
Suffolk—Southampton; in Bullhead
Bay, SE of Great Peconic Bay;
40 °55 'x72 °26 '50 "
Historical: Barker's Island
(Pelletreau 38, p. 289)
Southampton Quad (7.5 ')

RAM ISLAND
Suffolk—East Hampton
see
CARTWRIGHT ISLAND
Source: (Chace 127)

RAMBLERSVILLE
see
HOWARD BEACH
Source: (Ricard 86, p. 10)
and (Rand 154, 1913, p. 28)

RAMPASTURE
Community
Suffolk—Southampton; SW of
  Hampton Bays;
40°50'30"x72°31'30"
Quogue Quad (7.5')

RAMSCAT CHANNEL
Physical feature
Nassau—Hempstead; S of Hewlett
  Bay, NW boundary of Pearsall
  Hassock; 40°37'10"x73°40'15"
Lawrence Quad (7.5')

RANDALL BAY
Physical feature—channel
Nassau—Hempstead; S part of
  Freeport, NE of Baldwin Bay;
40°38'x73°35'15"
Freeport Quad (7.5')

RANDALLVILLE
see
RIDGE
Source: (Bayles 95, p. 51)

RANGE CHANNEL
Physical feature
Suffolk—Brookhaven; S of Nicoll
  Bay in Great South Bay;
40°40'x73°8'40"
Bay Shore East Quad (7.5')

RAPAHAMUCK
Locality—historical
Suffolk—Southampton; in the
  vicinity of Birch Creek, E of
  Flanders; ca. 40°54'10"x72°35'
Source: (Tooker 45, p. 48)
*Mattituck Quad (7.5')

RAPAHAMUCK NECK
see

JUMPING NECK
Source: (Tooker 44, pp. 209-210)

RAPAHAMUCK POINT
Physical feature
Suffolk—Southampton; in the
  vicinity of Birch Creek, E of
  Flanders; ca. 40°54'45"x72°35'10"
Source: (Tooker 45, p. 48)
*Mattituck Quad (7.5')

RASAPEAGE
see
STONY BROOK HARBOR
Source: (Pelletreau 38, p. 226)

RASSAPEAQUE
Physical feature—peninsula—
  historical
Suffolk—Smithtown; NW side of the
  town, includes part of Long Beach,
  N of Stony Brook Harbor;
40°55'20"x73°10'
Source: (Pelletreau 101, p. 32) and
  Langhans 98, p. 21). Also known as
  Old Rassapeaque and North
  Rassapeaque (Ibid.)
*Saint James Quad (7.5')

RASSAPEAQUE BAY
see
PORPOISE CHANNEL
Source: (Tooker 44, pp. 210-211)

RATTLESNAKE BROOK
Physical feature
Suffolk—Islip; flows into East
  Pond which connects with
  the Connetquot River;
40°45'x73°8'35"
Central Islip Quad (7.5')

RATTLESNAKE CREEK
Physical feature
Suffolk—East Hampton; E of Sag
Harbor; 40°59'40"x72°16'10"
Sag Harbor Quad (7.5')

RATTLESNAKE NECK
see
EBWONS NECK
Source: (Tooker 44, p. 60)

RATTLESNAKE SWAMP
Physical feature
Suffolk—Smithtown; the swampy
area S of Sunken Meadow Beach;
40°54'30"x73°15'45"
Source: (Langhans 98, p. 21)
*Saint James Quad (7.5')

RATTLESNAKE SWAMP
Physical feature—historical
Suffolk—Brookhaven; N of Yaphank
and Siegfield Park, E of
Gordon Heights;
ca. 40°51'15"x72°57'
Source: (Strong 107, p. 109)
*Bellport Quad (7.5')

RAVENSCROFT
see
RAVENSWOOD
Source: (Ricard 86, p. 13)

RAVENSWOOD
Community
Queens; part of Long Island City,
SW of Astoria;
ca. 40°46'x73°56'30"
Source: (Harlem Quad, 15', 1897)
Historical: Matona, Ravenscroft
(Ricard 86, p. 13)
*Central Park Quad (7.5')

RAYNOR POND
Physical feature—historical
Queens (Nassau)—Hempstead;
corner of Front St. and Clinton
St. in the village of Hempstead,
no longer exists;
40°42'25"x73°37'10"
Source: (Walling 172)
*Lynbrook Quad (7.5')

RAYNOR SOUTH
see
FREEPORT
Source: (Gordon 11, p. 636)

RAYNORTOWN
see
FREEPORT
Source: (French 10, p. 547fn)
and (Burr 125)

RAYNORVILLE
see
FREEPORT
Source: (Pelletreau 38, p. 102)

RED BROOK
see
WADING RIVER
Source: (Bailey 19, vol. 1, p. 249)

RED CEDAR CREEK
see
RED CREEK POND
Source: (U.S. 167, Map T-70)

RED CEDAR POINT
Physical feature
Suffolk—Southampton; on Great
Peconic Bay, E of Flanders;
40°55'x72°34'10"
Mattituck Quad (7.5')

RED CREEK
Community—historical
Suffolk—Southampton; E of
Flanders, in the vicinity of
Red Creek Pond;
ca. 40°54′40″x72°33′20″
Source: (Bayles 93, p. 321)
*Mattituck Quad (7.5′)

RED CREEK
Suffolk—Brookhaven
see
WADING RIVER
Physical feature
Source: (Bailey 19, vol. 1, p. 192)

RED CREEK
Suffolk—Southampton
see
HUBBARD CREEK
Source: (Pelletreau 38, p. 382)

RED CREEK POND
Physical feature
Suffolk—Southampton; E of
Flanders, NW of Hampton Bays;
41°54′40″x72°33′15″
Historical: Red Cedar Creek
(U.S. 167, Map T-70), Fleets Pond
(Schmersal 105, p. 44)
Mattituck Quad (7.5′)

RED HOOK
Community
Kings; W side of Kings, SW of
South Brooklyn, N of Bay Ridge;
40°40′30″x74°00′40″
Historical: Merckawick (Weisman 68,
p. 39), Gerritsen's Island and
Remsen's Island, both part of Red
Hook (Ratzer 155)
Jersey City Quad (7.5′)

RED HOOK
Suffolk—Babylon
see
BABYLON
Village
Source: (Flint 26, p. 69)

RED HOOK CHANNEL
Physical feature
Kings; W side of Kings, W of Red
Hook, E part of Upper Bay;
40°40′20″x74°1′30″
Jersey City Quad (7.5′)

RED SPRING
see
GLEN COVE (part of
Source: (Macoskey 29, p. 60) and
(Hyde 147)

RED SPRING POINT
Physical feature
Nassau—Oyster Bay; W of Glen
Cove, N of Hempstead Harbor;
40°52′25″x73°39′25″
Sea Cliff Quad (7.5′)

RED-HOOK
Suffolk—Huntington
see
VERNON VALLEY
Source: (French 10, p. 636fn)

REDWOOD
Community
Suffolk—Southampton; on Brush
Neck, W of Sag Harbor;
40°59′50″x72°18′50″
Sag Harbor Quad (7.5′)

REED CHANNEL
Physical feature
Nassau—Hempstead; SW side of

Oceanside, NE Hewlett Bay,
leads into Hog Island Channel;
40°37'25"x73°39'30"
Lawrence and Lynbrook Quads
(7.5')

REED POND
see
BIG REED POND
Source: (Montauk Quad, 15',
1904)

REEDY ISLAND
Physical feature
Suffolk—Southampton; in
Moneybogue Bay, E of Moriches
Bay; 40°48'x72°38'20"
Eastport Quad (7.5')

REEL POINT
Physical feature
Suffolk—Shelter Island; SE part
of Shelter Island, SE end of
Ram Island; 41°4'10"x72°16'55"
Greenport Quad (7.5')

REEVES BAY
Physical feature
Suffolk—Southampton; W of
Flanders, SW part of Flanders Bay;
40°54'45"x72°37'
Mattituck Quad (7.5')

REEVES CREEK
Physical feature
Suffolk—Riverhead; N side of
Flanders Bay, SE of Aquebogue;
40°56'x72°36'30"
Historical: Uncawamuck Creek
(Tooker 45, p. 57) and (Tooker 44,
p. 263), Conegums Creek (Ibid.,
pp. 47–48)
Mattituck Quad (7.5')

REEVES ISLAND
Physical feature
Suffolk—Brookhaven; in Moriches
Bay, W of Moriches Inlet, S of
East Moriches;
40°46'10"x72°45'25"
Moriches Quad (7.5')

REEVES' NECK
Physical feature
Suffolk—Southold; S of Cutchogue;
40°59'45"x72°29'40"
Source: (Tooker 44, pp. 190–191)
*Southampton and Southold Quads
(7.5')

REEVES PARK
Community
Suffolk—Riverhead; NW of the
community of Riverhead;
40°58'10"x72°42'40"
Riverhead Quad (7.5')

REGO PARK
Community
Queens; W-central part of Queens,
S of Corona; 40°43'30"x73°51'15"
Jamaica Quad (7.5')

REMSEN LANDING
see
SHELLBANK BASIN
Source: (Brooklyn Quad, 15',
1897)

REMSENBERG
Community
Suffolk—Southampton; SE of
Eastport, SW part of the town;
40°48'30"x72°42'15"
Variation: Remsenburg (Hagstrom
141, 1979, p. 59)
Eastport Quad (7.5')

REMSEN'S ISLAND
Community
Kings
see
RED HOOK (part of)
Source: (Ratzer 155)

REYDON SHORES
Community
Suffolk—Southold; N part of
 Great Hog Neck;
41°2'50"x72°24'
Southold Quad (7.5')

REYNOLDS CHANNEL
Physical feature
Nassau—Hempstead; SW part of the
 town, N of Atlantic Beach and
 Long Beach; 40°35'30"x73°41'
Lawrence and Jones Inlet Quads
 (7.5')

RICHMOND CREEK
Physical feature
Suffolk—Southold; N of Indian
 Neck, flows into Hog Neck Bay;
41°2'10"x72°26'50"
Historical: Hutchinson's Creek
 (Bayles 93, p. 372)
Southold Quad (7.5')

RICHMOND HILL
Community
Queens; W side of Queens, W of
 Jamaica; 40°42'x73°50'
Historical: Part of Richmond Hill
 known as Clarenceville (Ricard 86,
 p. 13)
Jamaica Quad (7.5')

RIDDER POND
Physical feature
Nassau—North Hempstead; W part

of Herricks, N of North New
 Hyde Park;
40°45'20"x73°41'
Sea Cliff Quad (7.5')

RIDER'S POINT
Physical feature—historical
Queens; on Jamaica Bay, N of
 Hammel, W of Barbadoes Basin;
40°35'55"x73°48'40"
Source: (Walling 172)
*Far Rockaway Quad (7.5')

RIDGE
Community
Suffolk—Brookhaven; SE of Rocky
 Point; 40°53'40"x72°53°30"
Historical: Randallville (Bayles
 95, p. 51), Ridgeville (Ullitz 164,
 plate 6)
Middle Island Quad (7.5')

RIDGE ISLAND
Physical feature
Suffolk—Brookhaven; E part of
 Great South Bay;
40°43'45"x72°55'
Howells Point Quad (7.5')

RIDGEWOOD
Community
Queens; W side of Queens, S of
 Fresh Pond; 40°41'50"x73°54'15"
Historical: South Williamsburg
 (Ricard 86, p. 14), SE part known
 as Evergreen, NE part known as
 Ridgewood Heights (Hagstrom 143)
Brooklyn Quad (7.5')

RIDGEWOOD
Nassau—Hempstead
see
WANTAGH
Source: (Tooker 44, p. 273)

RIDGEWOOD HEIGHTS
see
RIDGEWOOD (NE part of)
Source: (Hagstrom 143)

RIDGEWOOD RESERVOIR
Physical feature
Queens; in Highland Park,
W side of Queens, SE of
Ridgewood; 40°41′20″x73°53′15″
Historical: Brooklyn Reservoir
(Brooklyn Quad, 15′, 1897)
Brooklyn Quad (7.5′)

RIKERS ISLAND
Physical feature
Bronx; in the East River, N of
LaGuardia Airport, formerly in
Newtown town in Queens Co;
40°47′30″x73°53′
Historical: Hewletts Island (French
10, p. 548fn)
Central Park Quad (7.5′)

RIKERS ISLAND CHANNEL
Physical feature
Queens; in the East River, NW part
of Queens, E of Rikers Island, N
of Flushing Bay; 40°47′15″x73°52′
Flushing and Central Park Quads
(7.5′)

RINNEGACKONCK
Locality—historical
Kings; in the vicinity of
Wallabout Bay;
ca. 40°42′20″x73°59′
Source: (Tooker 44, pp. 211–212)
and (Stiles 66, vol. 1, p. 47).
Later known as Walboght and
Wallabout (Bailey 19, vol. 1,
p. 36)
Variations: Rinnegachonk,
Rinnegaconck, Rennegkonc,

Rinnegachonk, Rinnegaconck, and
Runnegackonck (Tooker 44, pp.
211–212)
*Brooklyn Quad (7.5′)

RIVER AQUABOUG
see
PECONIC RIVER
Source: (Bailey 19, vol. 1,
p. 185)

RIVERHEAD
Community
Suffolk—Riverhead; E part of
Long Island, N of Westhampton;
40°55′5″x72°40′
Riverhead Quad (7.5′)

RIVERHEAD
Town
Suffolk; N-central part of
Suffolk County
Historical: part of the town
of Southold until separated in
1792 (Flint 26, p. 223)
Wading River, Riverhead and
Mattituck Quads (7.5′)

RIVERSIDE
Community
Suffolk—Southampton; S of
Riverhead, W of Flanders, N of
Quiogue; ca. 40°53′20″x73°40′
Source: (Hagstrom 141, 1979, p. 62)
*Riverhead Quad (7.5′)

ROANOKE
Community
Suffolk—Riverhead; S of Reeves
Park, NW of the community of
Riverhead; ca. 40°57′55″x72°42′30″
Source: (Hagstrom 141, 1979, p. 60)
*Riverhead Quad (7.5′)

ROANOKE POINT
Physical feature
Suffolk—Riverhead; N of Riverhead
and Centerville;
40°58'50"x72°41'10"
Riverhead Quad (7.5')

ROBBINS REST
Community
Suffolk—Islip; on Fire Island, W of
Seaview, S of Heckscher State Park;
40°38'40"x73°9'50"
Variation: Robins Rest (Hagstrom
141, 1979, p. 42)
Bay Shore East Quad (7.5')

ROBERT MOSES STATE PARK
Suffolk—Babylon, Islip; W end of
Fire Island; 40°37'30"x73°15'
Bay Shore East and Bay Shore West
Quads (7.5')

ROBERT'S ISLAND
see
ROBINS ISLAND
Source: (Tooker 44, p. 9–11)

ROBERTS POINT
Physical feature—historical
Suffolk—Brookhaven; on Narrow
Bay, NW of Pattersquash Island;
40°44'45"x72°50'50"
Source: (Chace 127)
*Pattersquash Island Quad (7.5')

ROBINS ISLAND
Physical feature
Suffolk—Southold; in the NE part
of Great Peconic Bay, N of Cow
Neck; 40°58'x72°28'
Historical: Anchannock and Robert's
Island (Tooker 44, pp. 9–11)
Southampton Quad (7.5')

ROBINS ISLAND NECK
Physical feature—historical
Suffolk—Southold; presently
occupied by the community of New
Suffolk, N of Robins Island;
40°59'50"x72°28'45"
Source: (Pelletreau 38, p. 433)
*Southampton Quad (7.5')

ROBINS REST
see
ROBBINS REST
Source: (Hagstrom 141, 1979, p. 42)

ROBINSON COVE
Physical feature
Suffolk—Brookhaven; on Fire Island
in the Great South Bay, S of
Patchogue Bay; 40°42'x72°57'55"
Howells Point Quad (7.5')

ROBINSON POND
Physical feature
Suffolk—Brookhaven; NW of
Bellport, Mud Creek flows through
it; 40°45'50"x72°58'55"
Bellport Quad (7.5')

ROCCO POINT
see
EAST MARION
Source: (Burr 124)

ROCK COVE
Physical feature
Suffolk—Smithtown; in Sunken
Meadow Creek near the mouth of
Nissequogue River;
40°54'30"x73°14'25"
Source: (Langhans 98, p. 22)
*Saint James Quad (7.5')

ROCK HILL
Physical feature
Suffolk—Brookhaven; W part of the
town, NW of Eastport;
40°51'x72°45'30"
Moriches Quad (7.5')

ROCKAWAY
Neck and Indian village—historical
Queens; name originally designated
the neck now known as Rockaway
Beach, extending from Far
Rockaway to Rockaway Point, or
the village of the Indians on the
neck, S of JFK Airport;
40°34'x73°51'
Source: (Tooker 44, pp. 213-214)
Variations: Rechouwhacky, Rechqua
Akie, Rechonhachy, Rockeway
(Ibid.)
*Far Rockaway Quad (7.5')

ROCKAWAY INLET
Physical feature
Queens, Kings; N of Rockaway
Point and Roxbury, SW part of
Jamaica Bay; 40°34'x73°54'
Coney Island and Far Rockaway
Quads (7.5')

ROCKAWAY PARK
Community
Queens; SW part of Queens, E of
Belle Harbor; 40°34'50"x73°50'
Far Rockaway Quad (7.5')

ROCKAWAY POINT
Community
Queens; S of Rockaway Inlet, SE of
Manhattan Beach;
40°33'30"x73°55'
Coney Island Quad (7.5')

ROCKAWAY POINT
Physical feature
Queens; on the Atlantic Ocean, SW
of Rockaway Inlet and Breezy
Point; 40°32'40"x73°56'30"
Coney Island Quad (7.5')

ROCKVILLE CENTRE
Village
Nassau—Hempstead; central part of
the town, E of Lynbrook, S of the
village of Hempstead;
40°39'30"x73°38'30"
Lynbrook Quad (7.5')

ROCKVILLE POND
Physical feature—historical
Queens (Nassau)—Hempstead; W of
Hempstead Pond, SW of Smith
Pond; ca. 40°40'10"x73°39'45"
Source: (Walling 172)
*Lynbrook Quad (7.5')

ROCKY HILL
Farming area—historical
Queens; in Flushing town
Source: (French 10, p. 546fn)

ROCKY POINT
Community
Suffolk—Brookhaven; on Long
Island Sound, NE part of the town;
40°57'30"x72°55'45"
Middle Island Quad (7.5')

ROCKY POINT
Community
Suffolk—Southold
see
EAST MARION
Source: (French 10, p. 640) and
(U.S. 170, Chart No. 115, 1855)

ROCKY POINT
Community—historical
Suffolk—Shelter Island; NW side of
Shelter Island, W of Shelter Island
Heights; 41°4'20"x72°22'45"
Source: (Hyde 147)
*Southold Quad (7.5')

ROCKY POINT
Physical feature
Nassau—Oyster Bay; N point of
Centre Island; 40°55'5"x73°31'25"
Historical: Centre Island Point,
Center Island Point (U.S. 5,
Decisions Rendered Between July 1,
1940 and June 30, 1941, p. 48)
Bayville Quad (7.5')

ROCKY POINT
Physical feature
Suffolk—East Hampton; W of Fort
Pond Bay, NW of Montauk;
41°2'50"x71°58'50"
Montauk Point Quad (7.5')

ROCKY POINT
Physical feature
Suffolk—Southold; NW of East
Marion; 41°8'20"x72°21'15"
Orient Quad (7.5')

ROCKY POINT
Physical feature
Suffolk—Southold
see
JENNINGS POINT
Source: (Bailey 19, vol. 1, p. 178)

ROCKY RIDGE
Physical feature—range of hills—
historical
Suffolk—East Hampton; W side
of North Neck, N of Fort Pond;

ca. 41°3'20"x71°57'10"
Source: (Tooker 44, p. 67)
*Montauk Point Quad (7.5')

ROD AND REEL POND
see
ELDA LAKE
Source: (Babylon Quad, 15', 1903)

ROD'S VALLEY
Physical feature—historical
Suffolk—East Hampton; W side of
Fort Pond Bay;
ca. 41°2'30"x71°59'30"
Source: (Rattray 102, p. 43)
*Montauk Point Quad (7.5')

ROGER'S CANOE HOLLOW
Physical feature—historical
Queens (Nassau)—Oyster Bay; in the
vicinity of the N point of Mill
Neck; 40°54'5"x73°33'
Source: (Cocks 70, pp. 5-6)
*Bayville Quad (7.5')

ROGERS POINT
Physical feature—historical
Suffolk—Islip; S tip of Compowms
Neck, S of Bay Shore;
ca. 40°42'30"x73°15'
Source: (Chace 127)
*Bay Shore West Quad (7.5')

ROHMS BAY
see
GREAT PECONIC BAY
Source: (Untitled Map 171)

RONCONCOMA POND
see
LAKE RONKONKOMA
Source: (Langhans 98, p. 13)

RONCONKOMY PLAINS
Locality—historical
Suffolk—Smithtown; W of Lake
  Ronkonkoma; ca. 40°50′x73°8′
Source: (Pelletreau 38, p. 227)
*Central Islip Quad (7.5′)

RONKONKOMA
Community
Suffolk—Brookhaven, Islip; SE of
  Lake Ronkonkoma, NW of
  Patchogue; 40°49′x73°7′30″
Patchogue and Central Islip Quads
  (7.5′)

ROOSEVELT
Community
Nassau—Hempstead; N of Freeport,
  S of Uniondale; 40°41′x73°35′
Historical: Rum Point, Greenwich,
  Greenwich Point (Walling 172)
Freeport Quad (7.5′)

ROSE GROVE
Community
Suffolk—Southampton; SE of Little
  Peconic Bay, S of Southampton;
  40°57′30″x72°23′45″
Southampton Quad (7.5′)

ROSE ISLAND
Physical feature—historical
Suffolk—Southold; NE side of Great
  Peconic Bay, S of Little Hog
  Neck, the only island within the
  area is Robins Island, possibly a
  cartographic error;
  ca. 40°57′30″x72°27′30″
Source: (Lotter 149)
*Southold Quad (7.5′)

ROSEDALE
Community
Queens; E side of Queens, W of

Valley Stream;
  40°39′50″x73°44′20″
Historical: Foster's Meadow (Ricard
  86, p. 14) and (Hempstead Quad,
  15′, 1897)
Lynbrook Quad (7.5′)

ROSLYN
Village
Nassau—North Hempstead; E-central
  part of the town, S of Hempstead
  Harbor; 40°48′x73°39′15″
Historical: Hempstead Harbor
  (French 10, p. 550fn)
Sea Cliff Quad (7.5′)

ROSLYN ESTATES
Village
Nassau—North Hempstead; W of
  Roslyn, E-central part of the town;
  40°47′40″x73°39′45″
Sea Cliff Quad (7.5′)

ROSLYN HARBOR
Village
Nassau—North Hempstead, Oyster
  Bay; NE part of the town, E of the
  SE part of Hempstead Harbor;
  40°49′x73°38′30″
Sea Cliff Quad (7.5′)

ROSLYN HEIGHTS
Community
Nassau—North Hempstead; S-central
  part of the town, S of Roslyn;
  40°47′x73°39′
Sea Cliff Quad (7.5′)

ROSLYN POND
Physical feature
Nassau—North Hempstead: central
  part of Roslyn, S of Hempstead
  Harbor; 40°47′55″x73°39′
Sea Cliff Quad (7.5′)

ROUND POND
Physical feature
Suffolk—Brookhaven; E side of
town, NE of Brookhaven National
Lab, W of Peasys Pond;
40°54'5"x72°50'45"
Wading River Quad (7.5')

ROUND POND
Physical feature
Suffolk—Southampton; S of Sag
Harbor; 40°59'10"x72°17'30"
Sag Harbor Quad (7.5')

ROUND POND
Physical feature—historical
Suffolk—Huntington; W of Melville,
near Round Swamp Road;
40°47'30"x73°26'20"
Source: (Gibbs 77, p. 126)
*Huntington Quad (7.5')

ROUND SWAMP
Physical feature
Suffolk—Huntington
see
BLANCHARD LAKE
Source: (Sammis 104, p. 181)

ROUND SWAMP
Physical feature—historical
Suffolk—Smithtown; in the
community of Nissequogue, in the
vicinity of a former landing in
Stony Brook Harbor;
ca. 40°54'x73°11'10"
Source: (Langhans 98, p. 22)
*Saint James Quad (7.5')

ROUSSEL'S NECK
see
BARCELONA NECK
Source: (U.S. 167, Map T-72)

ROXBURY
Community
Queens; SW part of Queens, E of
Rockaway Point, S of Rockaway
Inlet; 40°34'x73°53'40"
Coney Island Quad (7.5')

RUFFLE BAR
Physical feature—island
Kings; W side of Jamaica Bay, N of
Belle Harbor; 40°35'45"x73°51'30"
Far Rockaway Quad (7.5')

RUGBY
Community—historical
Kings; N of Canarsie, SE of
Brownsville;
ca. 40°38'45"x73°54'40"
Source: (Hammond 145)
*Brooklyn Quad (7.5')

RUGGS NECK
see
PINE NECK
Physical feature
Suffolk—Southampton
Source: (Tooker 44, p. 216)

RUGS CREEK
see
MILL CREEK
Suffolk—Southampton
Source: (Tooker 44, p. 216)

RUGS NECK
see
PINE NECK
Physical feature
Suffolk—Southampton
Source: (Tooker 44, p. 216)

RUGUA SWAMP
Physical feature—historical
Suffolk—Huntington (Babylon); in
the vicinity of Copiague; ca.
40°40′x73°22′30″
Source: (Tooker 44, p. 216)
*Amityville and Bay Shore West
Quads (7.5′)

RULANDS CREEK
see
BROWN CREEK
Source: (Pelletreau 38, p. 243)

RULANDS HILLS
Physical feature—historical
Suffolk—Brookhaven; E of Bald
Hill, S of Coram; ca.
40°51′x72°55′
Source: (Smith 162)
*Bellport Quad (7.5′)

RULERS BAR HASSOCK
Physical feature—marsh island
Queens; central part of Jamaica Bay;
40°37′50″x73°49′30″
Jamaica and Far Rockaway Quads
(7.5′)

RUM POINT
see
ROOSEVELT
Source: (Walling 172)

RUNGCATAMY
Tract of land—historical
Suffolk—Huntington (Babylon); at

Round Swamp
Source: (Tooker 44, p. 217)

RUSDORPH
see
JAMAICA
Town
Source: (French 10, p. 547fn)

RUSKATUX NECK
see
SEAMANS NECK
Source: (Tooker 44, pp. 217–218)

RUSSELL GARDENS
Village
Nassau—North Hempstead; W side
of the town, S of Great Neck;
40°46′50″x73°43′30″
Sea Cliff Quad (7.5′)

RUSSELL'S NECK
see
BARCELONA NECK
Source: (Tooker 44, p. 29)

RUSTDORP
see
JAMAICA
Town
Source: (Ricard 86, p. 11)

RUSTDORPE
see
JAMAICA
Town
Source: (Gordon 11, 1836, p. 637)

RUSTENBERG
Locality—historical
Kings; in the vicinity of Flatbush
Source: (Ross 39, p. 320)
*Brooklyn Quad (7.5′)

SACHEM'S NECK
Physical feature—historical
Suffolk—Shelter Island; SE neck of
Shelter Island; ca. 41°3′x72°16′30″
Source: (Tooker 44, pp. 218-219)
and (Burr 124). Also known as
Sherwood's Forest (Bailey 19, vol. 1,
p. 172)
*Greenport Quad (7.5′)

SACKHICKNEYAH CREEK
Physical feature—historical
Queens; N part of Newtown (town)
near Fish's Point, no longer exists
due to La Guardia Airport;
ca. 40°46′30″x73°52′30″
Source: (Tooker 44, p. 219)
*Flushing and Central Park Quads
(7.5′)

SABONAC NECK
see
SEBONAC NECK
Physical feature
Suffolk—Southampton
Source: (Tooker 44, pp. 235-236)

SACAPONACK LAKE
see
SAGAPONACK POND
Source: (U.S. 5, Decisions Rendered
Between July 1, 1940 and June 30,
1941, p. 49)

SACUT
see
LAKE SUCCESS
Source: (Tooker 44, pp. 219-220)

SADDLE ROCK
Village
Nassau—North Hempstead; SW side
of Great Neck, S of Kings Point,
NE of Little Neck Bay;
40°47′35″x73°45′
Flushing Quad (7.5′)

SACHEM POND
Physical feature
Nassau—Oyster Bay; in the
Tackapausha Preserve, W side of
Massapequa; 40°40′45″x73°29′
Amityville Quad (7.5′)

SACHEM'S HOLE
Locality—historical
Suffolk—East Hampton; between the
villages of Sag Harbor and East
Hampton; ca. 40°58′10″x72°14′45″
Source: (Tooker 44, p. 218)
*East Hampton Quad (7.5′)

SADDLE ROCK ESTATES
Community
Nassau—North Hempstead; N of
Great Neck Estates, E of Saddle
Rock; 40°47′30″x73°44′30″
Source: (Hagstrom 140, 1978, p. 24)
*Sea Cliff Quad (7.5′)

SAG HARBOR
Village
Suffolk—East Hampton,
Southampton; SW of Sag Harbor
Bay; 41°00′x72°17′40″
Historical: Harbor of Sagg
(Tooker 44, pp. 221-222),
Sagaponack Harbor,
Bridgehampton Bay (Adams 91, p.
148)
Sag Harbor and Greenport Quads
(7.5′)

SAG HARBOR BAY
Physical feature
Suffolk—East Hampton,
Southampton; NE of Sag Harbor,
W of Barcelona Neck;
41°0′30″x72°17′
Greenport Quad (7.5′)

SAG HARBOR COVE
Physical feature
Suffolk—Southampton; S of North
Haven Peninsula, W of Sag
Harbor; 41°00′x72°18′45″
Greenport and Sag Harbor Quads
(7.5′)

SAGAMORE COVE
Physical feature—historical
Nassau—Oyster Bay; W of
Cove Neck
Source: (Tooker 44, pp. 220-221)
Also known as Mohannis Cove
(Ibid.)
*Lloyd Harbor Quad (7.5′)

SAGAMORE HILL
Physical feature
Nassau—Oyster Bay; central part
of Cove Neck;
40°53′10″x73°30′

Historical: Mohannis Hill (Tooker
44, pp. 220-221)
Lloyd Harbor and Bayville Quads
(7.5′)

**SAGAMORE HILL NATIONAL
HISTORIC SITE**
Nassau—Oyster Bay; N part of the
town, on Cove Neck;
40°53′07″x73°30′
Bayville and Lloyd Harbor Quads
(7.5′)

SAGAPONACK
Community
Suffolk—Southampton; SE of
Bridgehampton;
40°55′30″x72°16′45″
Historical: Sagg Village (Burr 124),
Sagg (Chace 127)
Variations: Sagaponack, Sagaponach,
Sackaponock, Sagabunnuck,
Sagabonock, Sagabonnac, etc.
(Tooker 44, pp. 221-222)
Sag Harbor Quad (7.5′)

SAGAPONACK HARBOR
see
SAG HARBOR
Source: (Adams 91, p. 148)

SAGAPONACK POND
Physical feature
Suffolk—Southampton; S of
Bridgehampton, E of Mecox Bay;
40°54′30″x72°17′30″
Historical: Sagg Pond (Chace 127),
Stagg Pond, Sacaponack Lake (U.S.
5, Decisions Rendered Between July
1, 1940 and June 30, 1941, p. 49)
Sag Harbor Quad (7.5′)

SAGE
Community
Suffolk—Southold; S side of
Hashamomuck Pond, SW of
Greenport;
ca. 41°4'55"x72°24'
Source: (Rand 154, 1963, pp. 307,
319)
*Southold Quad (7.5')

SAGE POND
Physical feature
Nassau—Hempstead; SW side of
Lawrence, W of Lawrence Neck;
40°36'x73°43'25"
Lawrence Quad (7.5')

SAGG
see
SAGAPONACK
Source: (Chace 127)

SAGG POND
see
SAGAPONACK POND
Source: (Chace 127)

SAGG VILLAGE
see
SAGAPONACK
Source: (Burr 124)

SAGHTEKOOS
see
APPLETREE NECK
Source: (Tooker 44, pp. 223-224)

SAGHTEKOOS CREEK
Physical feature—historical
Suffolk—Islip; on the Great South
Bay, E boundary of Appletree

Neck; ca. 40°42'30"x73°15'20"
Source: (Tooker 44, p. 223)
*Bay Shore West Quad (7.5')

SAILS POINT HASSOCK
Physical feature—marsh island—
historical
Queens; no longer exists, was
between Old Swale Marsh and
Fishkill Hassock on the W side of
Jamaica Bay; 40°36'15"x73°52'5"
Source: (Brooklyn Quad, 15', 1897)
*Far Rockaway Quad (7.5')

ST. ALBANS
Community
Queens; E of Jamaica, S of Queens
Village and Bellaire;
40°41'50"x73°45'15"
Jamaica Quad (7.5')

ST. GEORGE'S NECK
see
GEORGE'S NECK
Suffolk—Islip
Source: (Bayles 93, p. 209)

SAINT JAMES
Community
Suffolk—Smithtown; SW of Port
Jefferson, S of Stony Brook
Harbor; 40°52'30"x73°9'30"
Historical: Boomertown, Splinter
Village (Langhans 98, p. 5),
St. Jamesville (French 10, p. 637)
Saint James and Central Islip Quads
(7.5')

ST. JAMES HARBOR
see
STONY BROOK HARBOR
Source: (Langhans 98, p. 24)

ST. JOHNLAND
see
KINGS PARK
Source: (Langhans 98, pp. 13, 22)

ST. JOHNS LAKE
Physical feature
Suffolk, Nassau—Huntington,
Oyster Bay; S of Cold Spring
Harbor; 40°51′10″x73°27′50″
Source: (Valentine 50, p. 99). Also
known as First Mill Pond (Ibid.)
*Huntington Quad (7.5′)

ST. RONANS WELL
Physical feature—island—
historical
Queens; near the head of Flushing
Bay
Source: (French 10, p. 549)
*Flushing Quad (7.5′)

SALISBURY PLAINS
see
HEMPSTEAD PLAINS
Source: (Manley 30, p. 181)

SALT POND
see
GUGGENHEIM POND
Source: (U.S. 5, List No. 5904,
p. 37)

SALTAIRE
Village
Suffolk—Islip; on Fire Island, S of
East Islip, SE of Captree Island;
40°38′15″x73°12′
Bay Shore East Quad (7.5′)

SALTAIRE HARBOR
see
CLAM POND
Source: (Hyde 148)

SAMMYS BEACH
Physical feature
Suffolk—East Hampton; N of
Threemile Harbor, S of Gardiners
Bay; 41°1′55″x72°11′50″
Historical: Copeces (Tooker 44,
p. 50)
Gardiners Island West Quad (7.5′)

SAMPAWAMS CREEK
Physical feature
Suffolk—Babylon, Islip; on
Babylon Cove, boundary for the
Towns of Babylon and Islip;
40°41′10″x73°19′10″
Historical: East Creek (Rohl 103,
p. 259)
Bay Shore West Quad (7.5′)

SAMPAWAMS NECK
Physical feature
Suffolk—Babylon; S side of the
village of Babylon;
40°41′30″x73°19′30″
Variations: Sumpawams, Sam-
pawame, Sumpwams, Sowampams,
Sumpawams, Sampaumes, Sump-
wams (Tooker 44, pp. 252-253),
Sunquams Neck (Thompson 41,
vol. 1, p. 476)
Bay Shore West Quad (7.5′)

SAMPAWAMS POINT
Physical feature
Suffolk—Babylon; on the Great
South Bay, SE point of
Sampawams Neck, SW of Babylon

Cove; 40°40'50"x73°19'
Bay Shore West Quad (7.5')

SAMS CREEK
Physical feature
Suffolk—Southampton; flows into
the E part of Mecox Bay;
40°54'10"x72°18'35"
Sag Harbor Quad (7.5')

SAMUEL KETCHAM'S HOLLOW
see
MELVILLE
Source: (Dyson 25, p. 62)

SAN REMO
Community
Suffolk—Smithtown; W of Saint
James, SE of Sunken Meadow
State Park; 40°53'x73°13'30"
Historical: Lower Landing
(Thompson 41, vol. 1, inside cover
map)
*Saint James Quad (7.5')

SAND BAR POINT
Physical feature
Nassau—Hempstead; W point of
Lawrence Marsh, S of South Green
Sedge; 40°36'x73°41'10"
Lawrence Quad (7.5')

SAND HILLS
Physical feature
Suffolk—East Hampton; in the
vicinity of East Hampton village;
ca. 40°57'x72°11'
Source: (Rattray 102, p. 76)
*East Hampton Quad (7.5')

SAND POND
see
LAKE RONKONKOMA
Physical feature
Source: (Langhans 98, p. 13)

SAND POINT
Community
Suffolk—Babylon
see
WEST GILGO BEACH
Source: (U.S. 5, List No. 5903,
p. 44)

SANDS POINT
Physical feature
Nassau—North Hempstead; NW part
of Manhasset Neck;
40°52'x73°43'45"
Sea Cliff Quad (7.5')

SANDS POINT
Physical feature
Suffolk—Brookhaven; on Moriches
Bay, W side of the mouth of the
Forge River, SW of Old Neck;
40°46'38"x72°48'55"
Moriches Quad (7.5')

SANDS POINT
Village
Nassau—North Hempstead; NW side
of Manhasset Neck;
40°51'10"x73°43'
Historical: Wampage Shores
(Macoskey 29, p. 63)
Sea Cliff Quad (7.5')

SANDY BEACH
Physical feature
Suffolk—Southold; E of Greenport;
41°6'25"x72°21'30"
Greenport Quad (7.5')

SANDY HOLLOW
Physical feature—historical
Suffolk—Smithtown; between
Commack and the ponds at the
head of Nissequogue River, along
the same line as Jericho Turnpike
Source: (Langhans 98, p. 22)
*Central Islip and Greenlawn Quads
(7.5 ')

SANDY POINT
Physical feature
Suffolk—Brookhaven; NE part of
Bellport Bay; 40°45 '45 "x72°53 '20 "
Bellport Quad (7.5 ')

SANDY POINT
Physical feature
Suffolk—Huntington; NW point of
the village of Huntington Bay;
40°54 '20 "x73°26 '
Variation: Wincoma Point (U.S. 5,
List No. 7403, p. 21)
Lloyd Harbor Quad (7.5 ')

SANDY POND
Physical feature
Suffolk—Riverhead; N of Manorville,
W of Calverton;
40°53 '40 "x72°48 '30 "
Wading River Quad (7.5 ')

SANDY POND
Physical feature
Suffolk—Riverhead; SW side of
town, W of Swan Pond, N of
Grassy Pond; 40°53 '45 "x72°50 '10 "
Wading River Quad (7.5 ')

SANFORD ISLAND
Physical feature—marsh island
Nassau—Hempstead; E part of

Jones Beach State Park, SE of
South Line Island;
40°36 '30 "x73°28 '50 "
West Gilgo Beach Quad (7.5 ')

SANFORD POINT
Physical feature—historical
Queens; presently the N part of
La Guardia Airport;
ca. 40°47 '10 "x73°52 '15 "
Source: (Harlem Quad, 15 ', 1897)
*Flushing Quad (7.5 ')

SANS SOUCI LAKES
Physical feature
Suffolk—Islip; NE of Sayville,
W of Patchogue; 40°45 'x73°3 '50 "
Sayville Quad (7.5 ')

SANTA CROIX
Physical feature—water hole—
historical
Suffolk—Smithtown; SW of the
community of Smithtown, at the
head of Bridge Branch Brook which
flows into Websters Pond, NW of
New Mill Pond, S of Jericho
Turnpike; ca. 40°50 '50 "x73°14 '25 "
Source: (Langhans 98, pp. 22–23)
*Central Islip Quad (7.5 ')

SANTAPOGUE CREEK
Physical feature
Suffolk—Babylon; flows into the
Great South Bay, E border of
Lindenhurst; 40°40 '15 "x73°20 '45 "
Bay Shore West Quad (7.5 ')

SANTAPOGUE NECK
Physical feature
Suffolk—Babylon; S of Lindenhurst,
W side of Great South Bay;

40°40′40″x73°21′5″
Variations: Santapauge, Santepaug,
Santapauge, Santepogue,
Santtapauge (Tooker 44,
pp. 224–225)
Bay Shore West Quad (7.5′)

SANTAPOGUE POINT
Physical feature
Suffolk—Babylon; on the Great
South Bay, S point of Little East
Neck, E of Great East Neck;
40°40′30″x73°20′10″
Bay Shore West Quad (7.5′)

SAPHORACKAM
Locality—historical
Kings; S part of Brooklyn
Source: (Tooker 44, p. 225)

SASSIANS
Locality—historical
Kings
Source: (Tooker 44, pp. 225–226)

SAUGUST NECK
Physical feature—historical
Suffolk—Southold; SW of
Hashamomuck Pond;
ca. 41°5′x72°24′30″
Source: Pelletreau 38, p. 417)
and (Tooker 44, pp. 226–227)
*Southold Quad (7.5′)

SAWMILL CREEK
Physical feature
Suffolk—Riverhead; flows into the
Peconic River, E of Riverhead;
40°55′20″x72°37′35″
Riverhead Quad (7.5′)

SAXTONS NECK
Physical feature—historical
Suffolk—Islip; on Great Cove,

between Bay Shore and Islip, S of
Orowoc Lake;
40°43′20″x73°13′50″
Source: (Pelletreau 38, p. 244)
*Bay Shore East Quad (7.5′)

SAYRE POND
Physical feature
Suffolk—Southampton; E of
Southampton, S of Flying Point;
40°53′5″x72°21′10″
Sag Harbor Quad (7.5′)

SAYVILLE
Community
Suffolk—Islip; SW of Patchogue;
40°44′x73°5′20″
Historical: proposed name of Seville
(Bailey 19, vol. 1, p. 331)
Sayville Quad (7.5′)

SCALLOP POND
Physical feature
Suffolk—Southampton; E of Great
Peconic Bay, NE part of
Cow Neck 40°56′30″x72°26′
Variation: Escallop (Bishop 122)
Southampton Quad (7.5′)

SCHEYER'S ISLAND
see
CONEY ISLAND
Physical feature
Source: (Flint 26, p. 70)

SCHODACK
Community—historical
Nassau—Hempstead; in the vicinity
of Schodack Brook, NE of
Malverne; ca. 40°49′x73°39′15″
Source: (Reifschneider 85, p. 186)
*Lynbrook Quad (7.5′)

SCHODACK BROOK
Physical feature
Nassau—Hempstead; S part of the
 village of Hempstead;
 40°40′15″x73°39′5″
Lynbrook Quad (7.5′)

SCHODACK POND
Physical feature
Nassau—Hempstead; W-central part
 of the town, in Hempstead Lake
 State Park;
 40°40′20″x73°39′5″
Lynbrook Quad (7.5′)

SCHOUTS
see
SYOSSET
Source: (Tooker 44, pp. 255–256)

SCOQUAMS NECK
see
SKOOKWAMS NECK
Source: (Tooker 44, pp. 227–228)

SCOTTS BEACH
Physical feature
Suffolk—Brookhaven; N shoreline
 of Sound Beach; 40°58′x72°58′30″
Middle Island Quad (7.5′)

SCOUTS BAY
see
MANHASSET BAY
Source: (Dyson 24, p. 21)

SCOW CREEK
Physical feature—channel
Nassau—Hempstead; E part of
 Middle Bay, between Smith
 Meadow and High Meadow;
 40°36′45″x73°35′
Jones Inlet Quad (7.5′)

SCOY POND
Physical feature
Suffolk—East Hampton; E of
 Northwest Harbor, W of Three-
 mile Harbor; 41°1′28″x72°14′
Gardiners Island West Quad (7.5′)

SCRECUNKAS ISLAND
see
CEDAR ISLAND
Suffolk—Babylon
Source: (Tooker 44, p. 228)
Variations: Sucrunkas, Sucrumkas,
 Seseunhas (Ibid.)

SCRETCHES RIVER
see
SENIX CREEK
Source: (Beauchamp 7, p. 223)

SCUDDERS POND
Physical feature
Nassau—Oyster Bay; SW part of
 Sea Cliff; 40°50′15″x73°39′5″
Sea Cliff Quad (7.5′)

SCURRAWAY
see
JOSIAH'S NECK
Source: (Tooker 44, p. 229)

SCUTTLE HOLE
Physical feature
Suffolk—Riverhead; NW side of
 town, SW of Deep Pond, NE of
 Lake Panamoka;
 40°55′55″x72°49′30″
Wading River Quad (7.5′)

SCUTTLE HOLE POND
see
SHORTS POND
Source: (Adams 92, p. 6)

SCUTTLEHOLE
Community
Suffolk—Southampton; NE of
Southampton, W of Bridgehampton
40°56'20"x72°20'20"
Sag Harbor Quad (7.5')

SEA CLIFF
Village
Nassau—Oyster Bay; NE part of the
town, S of Glen Cove;
40°50'45"x73°38'45"
Historical: Carpentersville (Walling
172), part of Sea Cliff was a tract
of land called Littleworth (Cocks
70, pp. 7-8)
Sea Cliff Quad (7.5')

SEA DOG CREEK
Physical feature
Nassau—Hempstead; S of Sea Dog
Island and High Meadow, N of
Alder Island; 40°36'x73°35'
Jones Inlet Quad (7.5')

SEA DOG ISLAND
Physical feature
Nassau—Hempstead; SE part of
Middle Bay, NW of Alder Island
and Point Lookout;
40°36'15"x73°35'30"
Jones Inlet Quad (7.5')

SEAFORD
Community
Nassau—Hempstead; E side of the
town, SE of Wantagh, E of
Bellmore, SW of Massapequa;
40°40'x73°29'30"
Historical: part of Seaford known as
Jerusalem South (Walling 172)
Amityville and Freeport Quads (7.5')

SEAFORD CREEK
Physical feature
Nassau—Hempstead, Oyster Bay;
part of the S boundary of
Hempstead and Oyster Bay towns,
flows into the W part of South
Oyster Bay; 40°39'x73°29'10"
Historical: Jerusalem River
(Pelletreau 38, p. 93)
Amityville Quad (7.5')

SEAFORD HARBOR
Community—historical
Nassau—Hempstead; in the vicinity
of Seaford
Source: (Macoskey 29, p. 61)
*Amityville Quad (7.5')

SEAGATE
Community
Kings; SW part of Kings, W part
of Coney Island;
40°34'45"x74°0'40"
The Narrows Quad (7.5')

SEAL ISLAND
see
FIRE ISLAND
Source: (Flint 26, p. 70)

SEAL ROCKS
Physical feature
Suffolk—Southold; in Long Island
Sound, just N of the E end of
Fishers Island;
41°17'45"x71°55'40"
Mystic Quad (7.5')

SEAMAN POND
Physical feature
Nassau—Hempstead; W side of
Wantagh, N of Wantagh Pond;
40°40'30"x73°30'55"
Freeport Quad (7.5')

SEAMANS CREEK
Physical feature
Nassau—Hempstead; flows through
Seaford into Great Island
Channel; 40°38′45″x73°29′15″
Amityville Quad (7.5′)

SEAMANS ISLAND
Physical feature
Nassau—Hempstead; S of Seaford,
SW of Massapequa;
40°38′40″x73°30′
Freeport and Amityville Quads (7.5′)

SEAMANS NECK
Physical feature
Nassau—Hempstead; SE side of
town, S of Seaford;
40°39′x73°29′30″
Historical: Ruskatux Neck
(Tooker 44, pp. 217–218)
Amityville Quad (7.5′)

SEAPONACK
Locality—historical
Suffolk—Southampton; in the
Sebonac Neck vicinity;
ca. 40°54′30″x72°27′30″
Source: (Tooker 44, pp. 235–236)
*Southampton Quad (7.5′)

SEAPOOSE
Physical feature—inlets
Suffolk—East Hampton,
Southampton; the inlets that are
open in the beaches on the
southside in the towns of East
Hampton and Southampton
Source: (Tooker 44, pp. 230–231)
Variation: Bay Poose (Adams 92,
p. 18)

SEARINGTOWN
Community
Nassau—North Hempstead; S-central
part of town, N of Mineola;
40°46′30″x73°39′15″
Sea Cliff Quad (7.5′)

SEARS POND
Physical feature
Suffolk—Southampton; SE of
Flanders; 40°53′5″x72°34′45″
Mattituck Quad (7.5′)

SEASCAWANY NECK
see
JOSIAH'S NECK
Source: (Beauchamp 7, p. 223)

SEASIDE
Community
Queens; SW part of Queens, E of
Belle Harbor and Rockaway Park;
40°35′x73°49′30″
Far Rockaway Quad (7.5′)

SEATQUAA NECK
Physical feature—historical
Nassau—Hempstead; SW side of
town, next to Rockaway Neck
Source: (Tooker 44, p. 231)

SEATUCK
see
EASTPORT
Source: (Chace 127)

SEATUCK COVE
Community—historical
Suffolk—Brookhaven, Southampton;
in the vicinity of the
community of Eastport;

ca. 40°49'10"x72°43'40"
Source: (Macoskey 29, p. 61)
*Eastport Quad (7.5')

SEATUCK COVE
Physical feature
Suffolk—Southampton, Brookhaven;
NE side of Moriches Bay, S of
Eastport; 40°48'20"x72°43'30"
Eastport Quad (7.5')

SEATUCK CREEK
Physical feature
Suffolk—Brookhaven, Southampton;
flows through Eastport into
Seatuck Cove; 40°49'x72°43'45"
Variations: Seatuck, Setuckett, Setuk,
Setuck, etc. (Tooker 44,
pp. 231–232)
Eastport Quad (7.5')

SEATUCK NECK
Physical feature
Suffolk—Southampton; W of
Seatuck Creek, SW of Eastport;
40°49'10"x72°44"
Source: (Pelletreau 38, p. 343)
*Eastport Quad (7.5')

SEAVIEW
Community
Suffolk—Islip; on Fire Island, S of
Heckscher State Park, E of Fair
Harbor; 40°38'50"x73°9'10"
Bay Shore East Quad (7.5')

SEAWANHACKY
see
LONG ISLAND
Source: (Tooker 44, pp. 232–233)

SEBONAC CREEK
Physical feature—channel
Suffolk—Southampton; connects
Great Peconic Bay with Bullhead
Bay; 40°55'x72°27'
Southampton Quad (7.5')

SEBONAC NECK
Physical feature
Suffolk—Southampton; SE of Great
Peconic Bay; 40°54'30"x72°27'30"
Variations: Seponack, Seaponack,
Sebonack, Sabonac, etc. (Tooker
44, pp. 235–236)
Southampton Quad (7.5')

SEBONACK NECK
Physical feature—historical
Suffolk—Brookhaven; S part of
Bellport; 40°46'30"x72°53'15"
Source: (Tooker 44, pp. 229–230)
Variations: Seabamuck, Sebamuck,
Seboinack, Sebonnack, Sabonack
(Ibid.)
*Bellport Quad (7.5')

SECATOGUE NECK
see
SEQUATOGUE NECK
Source: (Tooker 44, p. 234)

SECOND CREEK
see
HENDRIX CREEK
Source: (Walling 172)

SECOND NECK
Physical feature—historical
Suffolk—Southampton; E of the
village of Quogue, W side of
Shinnecock Bay;
40°49'30"x72°35'10"
Source: (Pelletreau 38, p. 336)
*Quogue Quad (7.5')

288

SECOND NECK CREEK
Physical feature
Suffolk—Brookhaven; flows into
  Forge River on the W side, SE of
  Mastic; 40°47'40"x72°50'
Moriches Quad (7.5')

SECOND PURCHASE
Tract of land—historical
Nassau—Oyster Bay; in the vicinity
  of Greenlawn and Northport;
  ca. 40°43'40"x73°21'
Source: (Bailey 18, p. 8)
*Northport Quad (7.5')

SEDGE ISLAND
Physical feature
Suffolk—East Hampton; NE part of
  Threemile Harbor;
  41°1'50"x72°11'
Gardiners Island West Quad (7.5')

SEDGE ISLAND
Physical feature
Suffolk—Southampton; SW part of
  Shinnecock Bay, E of Quogue;
  40°49'20"x72°33'40"
Quogue Quad (7.5')

SEGANUS THATCH
Physical feature
Suffolk—Babylon; in the Great
  South Bay, W end of Captree
  Island; 40°39'10"x73°17'
Bay Shore West Quad (7.5')

SELASACOTT
see
BROOKHAVEN
Town
Source: (Tooker 44, p. 234)

SELDEN
Community
Suffolk—Brookhaven; S of Port
  Jefferson, N of Farmingville;
  40°51'30"x73°2'30"
Historical: Westfield (Bayles 93,
  p. 264)
Patchogue and Port Jefferson Quads
  (7.5')

SENEKES CREEK
see
SENIX CREEK
Source: (Ullitz 165, plates 4 and 19)

SENIX CREEK
Physical feature
Suffolk—Brookhaven; flows through
  part of Central Moriches into
  Moriches Bay; 40°47'5"x72°48'10"
Historical: Senekes Creek (Ullitz
  165, plates 4 and 19), Scretches
  River (Beauchamp 7, p. 223)
Variations: Senex, Senekees,
  Seretches (Tooker 44,
  pp. 234-235)
Moriches Quad (7.5')

SEPONACK NECK
see
SEBONAC NECK
Source: (Tooker 44, pp. 235-236)
  (7.5')

SEPOOSE
Physical feature—channel—
  historical
Suffolk—Southampton; S of Water
  Mill and Flying Point, SW side
  of Mecox Bay;
  ca. 40°53'10"x72°20'15"
Source: (Pelletreau 38, p. 318)
*Sag Harbor Quad (7.5')

SEQUATOGUE BROOK
see
WILLETTS CREEK
Source: (Bayles 93, p. 209)

SEQUATOGUE NECK
Physical feature
Suffolk—Islip; on the Great South
Bay, SW side of town, SE of the
village of Babylon;
40°41'30"x73°17'30"
Historical: Hocum Neck (Tooker 44,
pp. 71-72)
Variations: Seaquetauke, Seaqutogue,
Secatake, Secatogue, Secutang,
Seguctaug, Sicketauge, Sequatak
(Ibid., p. 234)
Bay Shore West Quad (7.5')

SETAUKET
Community
Suffolk—Brookhaven; W of Port
Jefferson, NW side of town;
40°56'40"x73°7'30"
Historical: Ashford (Flint 26, p. 74),
Cromwell Bay (Thompson 41,
vol. 1, p. 433)
Variations: Seatauke, Setokett,
Setawke, Setauk, Setaket,
Seataukett, Setalcott; in town
patents: Setaulcott, Selasacott;
in Dutch, Sichteyhacky (Tooker 44,
pp. 237-238)
Saint James and Port Jefferson
Quads (7.5')

SETAUKET
Locality—historical
Suffolk—Brookhaven; the name was
derived from the Indian tribe, and
was applied to the whole territory of
the town before it was named

Brookhaven; ca. 40°50'x73°00'
Source: (Thompson 41, vol. 1,
p. 433)

SETAUKET BEACH
see
OLD FIELD BEACH
Source: (U.S. 5, List No. 5903,
p. 43)

SETAUKET HARBOR
Physical feature
Suffolk—Brookhaven; SW of Port
Jefferson Harbor, N of East
Setauket; 40°57'x73°6'
Historical: Cromwell Bay, Setauket
Bay (Flint 26, p. 74)
Port Jefferson Quad (7.5')

SETAUKET SOUTH
see
SOUTH HAVEN
Source: (Flint 26, p. 70)

SEVEN PONDS
Physical feature
Suffolk—Southampton; NE of
Southampton, NW of Mecox Bay;
40°54'50"x72°22'10"
Sag Harbor Quad (7.5')

SEVILLE
see
SAYVILLE
Source: (Bailey 19, vol. 1, p. 331)

SEXTON ISLAND
Physical feature
Suffolk—Islip; SW part of Great
South Bay, E of Captree Island;
40°39'x73°14'
Bay Shore East Quad (7.5')

SHAGAWAN POINT
see
SHAGWONG POINT
Source: (U.S. 167, Map T–62)

SHAGWANGO NECK
Physical feature—historical
Suffolk—East Hampton; the SE
peninsula of Long Island which
includes Montauk Point;
41 °3 'x71 °53 '
Source: (Beauchamp 7, p. 223)
*Montauk Point Quad (7.5 ')

SHAGWONG HILL
Physical feature
Suffolk—East Hampton; NE part of
Montauk Peninsula;
41 °5 'x71 °54 '20 "
Variations: Shagwagonock,
Shagwanack, Shagawom,
Shagwommonock, Shagwanac,
Shaugwong (Tooker 44, p. 238)
Montauk Point Quad (7.5 ')

SHAGWONG POINT
Physical feature
Suffolk—East Hampton; northern-
most point of land on the Montauk
Peninsula; 41 °5 '10 "x71 °54 '20 "
Historical: Shagawan Point
(U.S. 167, Map T–62)
Montauk Point Quad (7.5 ')

SHAGWONG REEF
Physical feature
Suffolk—East Hampton; in Block
Island Sound, N of Montauk
Peninsula and Lake Montauk;
41 °6 '50 "x71 °55 '
Montauk Point Quad (7.5 ')

SHAHCHIPPITCHUGE
Locality—historical
Suffolk—East Hampton; between
Fort Pond and Montauk Harbor;
ca. 41 °3 'x71 °56 '50 "
Source: (Pelletreau 38, p. 371)
*Montauk Point Quad (7.5 ')

SHANESOMACOCKE
Locality—historical
Kings; at Flatlands
Source: (Tooker 44, p. 239)

SHANTY BAY
Physical feature
Suffolk—Shelter Island; NE part of
Shelter Island, S of Ram Island;
41 °4 '20 "x72 °17 '
Greenport Quad (7.5 ')

SHARP POINT
see
OLD FIELD POINT
Source: (Romans 157)

SHAWANGO NECK
Physical feature—historical
Suffolk—East Hampton; E side of
Montauk Peninsula;
41 °4 'x71 °52 '30 "
Source: (Tooker 44, p. 240) and
(Burr 124)
*Montauk Point Quad (7.5 ')

SHEED NINE
Community—historical
Suffolk—Babylon; E of Maywood,
SW of West Deer Park;
40 °43 '35 "x73 °25 '10 "
Source: (Hyde 147)
*Amityville Quad (7.5 ')

SHEEP PEN CREEK
Physical feature—historical
Suffolk—Brookhaven; S of Mastic
Beach, flows into the NW part of
Narrow Bay, E of Johns Neck
Creek; 40°44'50"x72°51'50"
Source: (Tooker 44, p. 119)
*Moriches Quad (7.5')

SHEEP PEN POINT
see
GARVIES POINT
Source: (Coles 72, p. 46)

SHEEPSHEAD BAY
Community
Kings; S part of Kings, S of
Gravesend; 40°35'15'x73°56'40"
Coney Island Quad (7.5')

SHEEPSHEAD BAY
Physical feature
Kings; SW part of Kings, N of
Manhattan Beach, E of Coney
Island; 40°34'55"x73°56'30"
Coney Island Quad (7.5')

SHELL BANK CREEK
Physical feature
Kings; flows into Plumb Beach
Channel, E border of the
community of Sheepshead Bay,
W border of Gerritsen;
40°35'10"x73°55'50"
Coney Island Quad (7.5')

SHELL BEACH
Physical feature—spit
Suffolk—Shelter Island; SW part of
Shelter Island, SE part of West
Neck; 41°2'30"x72°20'45"
Greenport Quad (7.5')

SHELL CREEK
Physical feature
Nassau—Hempstead; E side of
Island Park, between Barnums
Channel and Reynolds Channel;
40°36'15"x73°38'40"
Lawrence Quad (7.5')

SHELL HARBOR
Physical feature
Nassau—Hempstead; NE of Island
Park, W of Garrett Marsh;
40°36'25"x73°38'45"
Lawrence Quad (7.5')

SHELLBANK BASIN
Physical feature—channel or canal
Queens; N of Jamaica Bay, in
Howard Beach;
40°39'15"x73°50'15"
Historical: Remsen Landing
(Brooklyn Quad, 15', 1897)
Jamaica Quad (7.5')

SHELTER ISLAND
Community
Suffolk—Shelter Island; central
part of Shelter Island;
41°4'20"x72°20'15"
Greenport Quad (7.5')

SHELTER ISLAND
Physical feature
Suffolk—Shelter Island; NE side
of Long Island;
41°4'30"x72°20'
Historical: Ahaquatuwamuck,
Cotsjewaminck, Menhansick,
Manhansack, Manhansack-
Ahaquatuwamock, Manhansett,
Unchenchie (Tooker 44, pp. 6, 43,
92-94, 264), Farret's Island,
Sylvester's Island (Flint 26, p. 74)
Greenport and Southold Quads (7.5')

SHELTER ISLAND
Town
Suffolk; E side of the county,
between the towns of Southold and
East Hampton
Greenport and Southold Quads (7.5 ')

SHELTER ISLAND HEIGHTS
Community
Suffolk—Shelter Island; NW part of
Shelter Island; 41 °5 'x72 °21 '30 "
Greenport Quad (7.5 ')

SHELTER ISLAND SOUND
Physical feature
Suffolk—Shelter Island,
Southampton, Southold; between
Shelter Island and eastern Long
Island; 41 °3 'x72 °20 '
Greenport Quad (7.5 ')

SHERAWOUG
Locality—historical
Suffolk—Smithtown; E of Stony
Brook Harbor, includes Head of the
Harbor; 40 °54 '30 "x73 °9 '40 "
Source: (Tooker 44, p. 241). Also
known as Sherrawog (Ibid.)
*Saint James Quad (7.5 ')

SHERRY HARBOR
see
CHERRY HARBOR
Source: (Dyson 24, p. 29)

SHERWOOD'S FOREST
see
SACHEM'S NECK
Source: (Bailey 19, vol. 1, p. 172)

SHINNECOCK
Locality—historical
Suffolk—Southampton; a neck of
land, a bay, and a range of hills in
the town. The name belonged
originally to the plain of which the
neck forms a part.
Source: (Tooker 44, p. 242). Also
called Mochgonnekonck by the
Dutch (Ibid., pp. 136-138)
Variations: Shinneckuke, Shinocut,
Shinnikut (Ibid., p. 242),
Shunnecock (Burr 124)
*Southampton and Shinnecock Inlet
Quads (7.5 ')

SHINNECOCK BAY
Physical feature
Suffolk—Southampton; SW of
Southampton village, S of
Shinnecock Hills;
40 °52 'x72 °28 '
Historical: Southampton Bay
(Thompson 41, vol. 1, p. 362)
Shinnecock Inlet and Southampton
Quads (7.5 ')

SHINNECOCK CANAL
Physical feature
Suffolk—Southampton; between the
SW part of Great Peconic Bay and
the NE part of Shinnecock Bay;
40 °53 '50 "x72 °30 '15 "
Historical: Mashmanock, Canoe
Place Creek (Tooker 44,
pp. 105-106)
Mattituck Quad (7.5 ')

SHINNECOCK HILLS
Community
Suffolk—Southampton; in the
Shinnecock Hills, W of
Southampton village;
40 °53 '20 "x72 °27 '50 "
Southampton Quad (7.5 ')

SHINNECOCK HILLS
Physical feature
Suffolk—Southampton; S of Great
Peconic Bay, W of Southampton
village; 40°53'20"x72°28'
Southampton Quad (7.5')

SHINNECOCK INDIAN RESERVATION
Indian Reservation
Suffolk—Southampton; on
Shinnecock Neck, E of
Shinnecock Bay; 40°52'30"x72°26'
Shinnecock Inlet Quad (7.5')

SHINNECOCK INLET
Physical feature
Suffolk—Southampton; between
Shinnecock Bay and the Atlantic
Ocean; 40°50'30"x72°28'30"
Shinnecock Inlet Quad (7.5')

SHINNECOCK NECK
Physical feature
Suffolk—Southampton; E of
Shinnecock Bay, Shinnecock
Indian Reservation occupies the
neck; 40°52'15"x72°26'
Historical: Shinnecock Plains
(Tooker 44, p. 242)
Variation: Shinecocke Playne (Ibid.)
Shinnecock Inlet and Southampton
Quads (7.5')

SHIP CHANNEL
see
FIRE ISLAND INLET
Source: (Wittlock 52, p. 165)

SHIP POINT
Physical feature—historical
Nassau—Oyster Bay; in the
vicinity of the community of
Oyster Bay;
ca. 40°52'30"x73°31'40"
Source: (Pelletreau 38, p. 131)
*Bayville Quad (7.5')

SHIRLEY
Community
Suffolk—Brookhaven; NE of Great
South Bay, SE part of the
town; 40°48'x72°52'30"
Bellport, Moriches, Howells Point
and Pattersquash Island Quads
(7.5')

SHIRLEY'S NECK
Physical feature—historical
Suffolk—Southold; W of Mattituck,
SW shoreline of Mattituck Creek;
40°59'30"x72°33'
Source: (U.S. 167, Map T-55)
*Mattituck Quad (7.5')

SHOAL ISLAND
Physical feature—historical
Suffolk—East Hampton; between the
S point of Gardiners Island and
Cartwright Island (formerly Ram
Island); 41°2'30"x72°6'
Source: (Burr 124)
*Gardiners Island East Quad (7.5')

SHOCKHEYOUNE
Tract of land—historical
Suffolk—Smithtown; W of the
mouth of Nissequogue River, from
the swamp of Sunken Meadow
Creek to Long Island Sound
Source: (Tooker 44, p. 243)
*Saint James and Northport Quads
(7.5')

SHOE SWAMP
see
SHU SWAMP
Source: (U.S. 170, Chart No. 367, 1916)

SHOO BROOK
Physical feature—historical
Queens (Nassau)—Oyster Bay; near
Shu Swamp
Source: (Cocks 70, p. 7)
*Bayville Quad (7.5 ')

SHORE ACRES
Community
Suffolk—Southold; NW of
Mattituck; 41 °00 'x72 °33 '10 "
Mattituck and Mattituck Hills Quads
(7.5 ')

SHOREHAM
Village
Suffolk—Brookhaven; E of Rocky
Point, NE part of the town;
40 °57 '30 "x72 °54 '30 "
Historical: part of Shoreham known
as Woodville Landing (Chace 127)
and (Hyde 147)
Middle Island Quad (7.5 ')

SHOREHAM BEACH
Physical feature
Suffolk—Brookhaven; on Long
Island Sound, N shoreline of
Shoreham, NE part of the town;
40 °47 '45 "x72 °54 '30 "
Middle Island Quad (7.5 ')

SHOREWOOD
Community
Suffolk—Huntington; N of
Centerport, E of Little Neck,
S of Huntington Bay;

ca. 40 °53 '45 "x73 °22 '30 "
Source: (Hagstrom 141, 1964, p. 23)
*Lloyd Harbor and Northport Quads
(7.5 ')

SHORT BEACH
Physical feature
Suffolk—Smithtown; on Smithtown
Bay, N of San Remo, W of
Nissequogue; 40 °54 '25 "x73 °14 '
Historical: East Bar, Little Beach
(Langhans 98, pp. 7, 23)
Saint James Quad (7.5 ')

SHORT BEACH
Physical feature
Suffolk—Southampton; SW coast of
North Haven Peninsula;
41 °0 '40 "x72 °19 '
Greenport Quad (7.5 ')

SHORT NECK
Physical feature—historical
Suffolk—Brookhaven; on the Great
South Bay, SW of Patchogue, E of
Blue Point; ca. 40 °45 'x73 °1 '
Source: (Pelletreau 38, p. 269)
*Sayville and Patchogue Quads (7.5 ')

SHORT NECK
Suffolk—Southampton
see
THIRD NECK
Source: (Pelletreau 38, p. 336)

SHORTS POND
Physical feature
Suffolk—Southampton; N of
Scuttlehole, NW of Bridgehampton;
40 °56 '45 "x72 °20 '
Historical: Scuttle Hole Pond,
Haynes Pond (Adams 92, pp. 6, 17)
Sag Harbor Quad (7.5 ')

SHOUT'S BAIE
see
MANHASSET BAY
Source: (Bailey 19, vol. 1, p. 443)

SHU SWAMP
Physical feature
Nassau—Oyster Bay; N part of the
town, S-central part of the village of
Mill Neck, S of Beaver Lake;
40°52′40″x73°34′
Variation: Shoe Swamp (U.S. 170,
Chart No. 367, 1916)
Bayville Quad (7.5′)

SHUNNECOCK
see
SHINNECOCK
Locality—historical
Source: (Burr 124)

SICHTEYHACKY
see
SETAUKET
Source: (Tooker 44, p. 243)

SIEKREWHACKY
see
FIRE ISLAND
Source: (Flint 26, p. 70)

SIGNAL
Community—historical
Nassau—Hempstead; SE of Carle
Place, S of Westbury, E of
Mineola; ca. 40°44′x73°35′35″
Source: (Macoskey 29, p. 62) and
(Rand 154, 1935, pp. 279, 288)
*Freeport Quad (7.5′)

SIGNAL HILL
Physical feature
Suffolk—Huntington; W part of Dix

Hills; 40°49′x73°22′10″
Greenlawn Quad (7.5′)

SILL ROCK
Physical feature
Suffolk—Brookhaven; in Long
Island Sound, NE of Shoreham;
40°58′x72°54′5″
Middle Island Quad (7.5′)

SILVER BEACH
Community
Suffolk—Shelter Island; SW part of
Shelter Island, E side of West
Neck; 41°3′x72°21′20″
Greenport Quad (7.5′)

SILVER EEL COVE
Physical feature
Suffolk—Southold; NE part of the
town, NW side of Fishers Island;
41°15′30″x72°1′50″
New London Quad (7.5′)

SILVER HOLE MARSH
Physical feature—marsh island
Queens; SE side of Jamaica Bay,
SW of Jo Co Marsh;
40°36′15″x73°48′10″
Far Rockaway Quad (7.5′)

SILVER LAKE
Physical feature
Nassau—Hempstead; W-central part
of Baldwin; 40°38′50″x73°37′
Freeport Quad (7.5′)

SILVER LAKE
Physical feature
Suffolk—Southold; NW side of
Greenport; 41°6′25″x72°22′
Greenport Quad (7.5′)

296

SIMMOND CREEK
Physical feature—canal
Nassau—Hempstead; flows from the
S-central part of Merrick into
East Bay, W of Merrick Creek;
40°38′45″x73°32′45″
Freeport Quad (7.5′)

SIMMONS HASSOCK
Physical feature—marsh island
Nassau—Hempstead; SW of Harbor
Island, N of Long Beach, SE of
Black Banks Hassock;
40°35′50″x73°40′10″
Lawrence Quad (7.5′)

SIMMONS POINT
Physical feature
Suffolk—Riverhead; SW of South
Jamesport, NE part of Flanders
Bay; 40°55′45″x72°35′25″
Mattituck Quad (7.5′)

SIMONSON POND
Physical feature—historical
Queens; formerly located NE of
Laurelton and SE of Springfield
Gardens, no longer exists;
40°40′25″x73°44′5″
Source: (Hempstead Quad,
15′, 1897)
*Lynbrook Quad (7.5′)

SIMONSONS CREEK
Physical feature—historical
Queens; E side of Queens, from
around Elmont to S of Rosedale;
ca. 40°38′45″x73°44′55″
Source: (Cram 132, p. 111)
*Lynbrook Quad (7.5′)

SINT SINCK
Locality—historical
Queens; a tract of land near Hallets

Point, including most of Hell-gate
Neck
Source: (Tooker 44, p. 244)
*Central Park Quad (7.5′)

SINT SINK
Physical feature
see
MANHASSET NECK
Source: (French 10, p. 550fn)

SINTSINCK
Community
see
MANHASSET
Source: (Flint 26, p. 72)

SIX ROADS
Community—historical
Suffolk—Southampton; presently
within the village of
Westhampton Beach;
40°48′50″x72°38′50″
Source: (Riverhead Quad, 15′, 1903)
*Eastport Quad (7.5′)

SKOOKWAMS CREEK
Physical feature
Suffolk—Islip;
flows through S part of West
Islip into Babylon Cove;
40°41′10″x73°18′40″
Bay Shore West Quad (7.5′)

SKOOKWAMS NECK
Physical feature
Suffolk—Islip; SW side of West
Islip, bounded on the W by
Sampawams Creek and on the E
by Skookwams Creek;
40°41′45″x73°19′
Source: (Tooker 44, pp. 227–228,
244–245)

Variations: Scoquams Neck,
Schookwames, Sequams,
Scoquaumes, Schoookwames (Ibid.)
*Bay Shore West Quad (7.5 ')

SKOW
see
SQUAW ISLAND
Source: (Tooker 44, p. 250)

SKUNK HOLLOW
see
OVERTON'S PASS
Source: (Langhans 98, p. 23)

SKUNK'S MISERY
see
MALVERNE
Source: (Stevens 40, p. 10)

SKUPASH CREEK
Physical feature—historical
Queens; in the vicinity of
Jamaica meadow lands
Source: (Tooker 44, p. 245)
*Jamaica Quad (7.5 ')

SKYE'S NECK
Physical feature
Suffolk—Brookhaven; on
Moriches Bay, W of Senix Creek,
E of Old Neck, SW of Center
Moriches;
40°47 '20 "x72°48 '25 "
Source: (Pelletreau 38, p. 263)
*Moriches Quad (7.5 ')

SLADE POND
Physical feature
Suffolk—Islip; N of Oakdale,
Rattlesnake Brook flows into it;
40°45 '10 "x73°8 '15 "
Central Islip Quad (7.5 ')

SLATE POND
Physical feature
Suffolk—Southampton; N of
Bridgehampton;
40°57 'x72°18 '
Sag Harbor Quad (7.5 ')

SLEIGHT'S HILL
Physical feature
Suffolk—Southampton; SE side
of the village of Sag Harbor;
40°59 '30 "x72°17 '
Source: (Adams 91, p. 29)
*Sag Harbor Quad (7.5 ')

SLONGO
Community
Suffolk—Smithtown, Huntington
see
FORT SALONGA
Source: (Langhans 98, p. 8)

SLONGO
Community
Suffolk—Smithtown, Huntington
see
MIDDLEVILLE
Source: (Bayles 93, p. 186)

SLONGO
Physical feature
see
SUNKEN MEADOW
Source: (Flint 26, p. 74)

SLOOP BAR HASSOCK
Physical feature—marsh island—
historical
Queens; E side of Jamaica Bay, N of
Mott Point, W of Inwood, no
longer exists; 40°36 'x73°46 '25 "
Source: (Brooklyn Quad, 15 ', 1897)
*Far Rockaway Quad (7.5 ')

SLOOP CHANNEL
Physical feature
Nassau—Hempstead; E of Point
Lookout, N of Jones Beach State
Park; 40°36'x73°32'30"
Jones Inlet Quad (7.5')

SMART POND
Physical feature—historical
Nassau—Hempstead; along the East
Meadow Brook, W side of
Roosevelt, N of East Meadow
Pond; 40°40'25"x73°34'20"
Source: (Hempstead Quad, 15',
1897)
*Freeport Quad (7.5')

SMITH COVE
Physical feature
Suffolk—Shelter Island; S
side of Shelter Island, E of
West Neck Harbor;
41°3'x72°18'50"
Greenport Quad (7.5')

SMITH CREEK
Physical feature
Suffolk—Southampton; on
Shinnecock Bay, S of
Hampton Bays;
40°51'5"x72°31'30"
Quogue Quad (7.5')

SMITH MEADOW
Physical feature
Nassau—Hempstead; E of Middle
Bay, N of Alder Island, S of
Freeport; 40°37'x73°35'
Jones Inlet Quad (7.5')

SMITH PATENT
Tract of land—historical
Suffolk—Brookhaven; most of the
area is presently part of
the community of Shirley;
40°45'x72°52'15"
Source: (Pelletreau 38, facing
p. 238)
*Howells Point, Bellport,
Pattersquash Island, and Moriches
Quads (7.5')

SMITH POINT
Physical feature
Suffolk—Brookhaven; E end of the
Great South Bay;
40°44'15"x72°52'30"
Howells Point Quad (7.5')

SMITH POND
Community
Nassau—Hempstead; W side of
Rockville Centre;
40°39'40"x73°39'20"
Lynbrook Quad (7.5')

SMITHFIELD
see
SMITHTOWN
Town
Source: (Dyson 24, p. 25)

SMITH'S COVE
see
TUTHILL COVE
Source: (U.S. 5, List No. 5904,
p. 38)

SMITH'S INLET
Physical feature—historical
Suffolk—Brookhaven; on Fire
Island, S of Bellport, no longer
exists; ca. 40°43'30"x72°53'50"
Source: (Osborne 36, p. 118). Also
known as Smith's Island Inlet
(Ibid.)
*Bellport Quad (7.5')

SMITH'S ISLAND INLET
see
SMITH'S INLET
Source: (Osborne 36, p. 118)

SMITH'S MEADOW
Queens
see
WINFIELD
Source: (Ricard 86, p. 15)

SMITH'S MEADOW
Suffolk
see
GREAT MEADOW
Suffolk—Southampton
Source: (Pelletreau 38, p. 324)

SMITH'S NECK
Physical feature
Suffolk—Brookhaven; on the Great
South Bay, E side of the
community of Blue Point;
ca. 40°44'45"x73°1'50"
Source: (Pelletreau 38, p. 269)
*Sayville Quad (7.5')

SMITH'S POINT
Physical feature
Suffolk—Brookhaven; SE of
Moriches, on the W side near
the mouth of the Forge River, W of
Old Neck; 40°46'45"x72°49'5"
Moriches Quad (7.5')

SMITHS TOWN
see
SMITHTOWN
Community
Source: (Langhans 98, p. 23)

SMITHTOWN
Community
Suffolk—Smithtown; SW of Saint
James, N of Hauppauge;
40°51'x73°12'
Historical: the earliest record refers
to Smithtown as Nissequogue, later
called Smithtown Branch, also
Smythfield, Smiths Town, Smyth
Town, Smith-Town (Langhans 98,
p. 23). Also known as Head of The
River and Head Of The Tide Water
(Ibid., p. 11)
Central Islip Quad (7.5')

SMITHTOWN
Town
Suffolk; in the W part of the
County; N of Islip town
Historical: Smithfield (Dyson 24,
p. 25)
Central Islip and Saint James Quads
(7.5')

SMITHTOWN BAY
Physical feature
Suffolk—Smithtown, Brookhaven;
on Long Island Sound, N part of
the town, W of Old Field;
40°57'x73°12'
Saint James Quad (7.5')

SMITHTOWN BRANCH
Community—historical
Suffolk—Smithtown; now the E part
of the community of Smithtown;
40°51'20"x73°11'20"
Source: (Setauket Quad, 15', 1904)
*Central Islip Quad (7.5')

SMITHTOWN BRANCH
Physical feature
see
NORTHEAST BRANCH
Source: (Langhans 98,
pp. 19, 24)

SMITHTOWN PATENT
Tract of land—historical
Suffolk—Smithtown; E of the
Nissequogue River, including
Stony Brook Harbor, W of Lake
Ronkonkoma, N of Hauppauge;
ca. 40°51′x73°11′
Source: (Pelletreau 38, facing
p. 238)
*Saint James and Central Islip
Quads (7.5′)

SMITHVILLE SOUTH
see
NORTH BELLMORE
Source: (Hempstead Quad, 15′,
1903), (New Century 151, p. 116)
and (Hyde 147)

SMYTHFIELD
see
SMITHTOWN
Community
Source: (Langhans 98, p. 23)

SNAKE NECK
see
EBWONS NECK
Source: (Tooker 44, pp. 289-290)

SNAKEHILL CHANNEL
Physical feature
Suffolk—Islip; in the Great
South Bay, E of Captree Island, S
of Bay Shore; 40°39′x73°15′
Bay Shore East Quad (7.5′)

SNIPE ISLAND
Physical feature—marsh island
Nassau—Hempstead; NE of Deep
Creek Meadow, NW of Jones
Beach State Park;
40°36′45″x73°30′40″
Jones Inlet Quad (7.5′)

SNOOKSVILLE
see
EASTVILLE
Source: (Bayles 93, p. 356)

SODOM
see
BAY SHORE
Source: (Bailey 19, vol. 1, p. 327)

SOMMERVILLE BASIN
Physical feature
Queens; SE part of Jamaica Bay,
N part of Arverne;
40°36′x73°47′20″
Far Rockaway Quad (7.5′)

SONNQUOQUAS
Locality—historical
Suffolk—in the vicinity of
Hashamomuk Pond and
Tom's Creek
Source: (Tooker 44, pp. 245-246)
*Southold Quad (7.5′)

SONNQUOQUAS CREEK
see
MILL CREEK
Suffolk—Southold
Source: (Beauchamp 7, p. 224)

SOPER'S POINT
see
BRICKYARD POINT
Source: (Walling 172)

SOUND AVENUE
see
NORTHVILLE
Source: (Ullitz 164, Index Map)

SOUND BEACH
Community
Suffolk—Brookhaven; E of Miller
Place, W of Rocky Point;
40°57′30″x72°58′30″
Middle Island Quad (7.5′)

SOUND VIEW
Community—historical
Suffolk—Brookhaven; in the
vicinity of Stony Brook;
ca. 40°56′30″x73°8′
Source: (Macoskey 29, p. 62)
*Saint James Quad (7.5′)

SOUTH BEACH
Physical feature
Suffolk—Southold; on Fishers
Island, S of East Harbor, NE of
Barleyfield Cove;
41°16′50″x71°56′45″
Mystic Quad (7.5′)

**SOUTH BLACK BANKS
HASSOCK**
Physical feature—marsh island
Nassau—Hempstead; E of Lawrence,
W of Harbor Isle, S of North
Black Banks Hassock between
Broad, Hog Island, and Reynolds
Channels; 40°36′x73°40′30″
Source: (U.S. 5, List No. 8101,
p. 13)
Historical: Black Banks Hassock
(Lawrence Quad, 7.5′, 1966)
Variations: Blackbank Hassock,

Black Banks, North Black Banks
(U.S. 5, List No. 8101, p. 13)
*Lawrence Quad (7.5′)

SOUTH BROOKLYN
Community
Kings; W side of Kings, S of
Brooklyn Heights;
40°41′x73°59′45″
Brooklyn and Jersey City Quads
(7.5′)

SOUTH BROTHER ISLAND
Physical feature
Queens; in the East River,
formerly in the NW part
of Queens, presently in
Bronx Co., W of Rikers Island
40°47′45″x73°54′
Central Park Quad (7.5′)

SOUTH CENTEREACH
Community
Suffolk—Brookhaven; SE of
Centereach, E of Lake
Ronkonkoma; 40°50′10″x73°5′
Source: (Hagstrom 141, 1979, p. 48)
*Patchogue Quad (7.5′)

SOUTH COMMACK
Community
Suffolk—Huntington, Smithtown;
S of Commack, N of Pilgrim State
Hospital; ca. 40°49′25″x73°17′30″
Source: (Hagstrom 141, 1979,
pp. 36, 38)
*Greenlawn Quad (7.5′)

SOUTH COW MEADOW
see
COW MEADOW RESERVE
Source: (Hagstrom 140, 1965, p. 50)

SOUTH DUMPLING
Physical feature—island
Suffolk—Southold; in Long Island
 Sound, N of the W part of
 Fishers Island; 41 °17 'x72 °1 '
New London Quad (7.5 ')

SOUTH FARMINGDALE
Community
Nassau—Oyster Bay; E of
 Levittown, NW of Amityville;
 40 °43 'x73 °27 '
Amityville Quad (7.5 ')

SOUTH FERRY
Community—historical
Suffolk—Shelter Island; W of
 Smith Cove; 41 °2 '45 "x72 °19 '15 "
Source: (Macoskey 29, p. 62)
*Greenport Quad (7.5 ')

SOUTH FLORAL PARK
Village
Nassau—Hempstead; NW part of the
 town, W of Hempstead village;
 40 °42 '45 "x73 °42 '
Historical: Jamaica Square
 (Macoskey 29, p. 55)
Lynbrook Quad (7.5 ')

SOUTH FORK
Physical feature—peninsula
Suffolk—Southampton, East
 Hampton; SE peninsula of Long
 Island, ca. 40 °52 'x72 °15 '
Shinnecock Inlet, Southampton,
 Sag Harbor, East Hampton,
 Greenport, Gardiners Island West,
 Gardiners Island East, Napeague
 Beach and Montauk Point Quads
 (7.5 ')

SOUTH GREEN SEDGE
Physical feature—marsh island
Nassau—Hempstead; E of
 Lawrence, W of Island Park;
 40 °36 '30 "x73 °41 '20 "
Lawrence Quad (7.5 ')

SOUTH GREENFIELD
Community—historical
Kings; SW of Flatlands, E of
 Mapleton; ca. 40 °36 '45 "x73 °57 '
Source: (Brooklyn Quad, 15 ', 1897)
*Coney Island Quad (7.5 ')

SOUTH HARBOR
see
HOG NECK BAY
Source: (Bayles 93, p. 378)

SOUTH HAUPPAUGE
Community
Suffolk—Islip; SE of Hauppauge,
 N of Connetquot River State
 Park; ca. 40 °48 '47 "x73 °10 '20 "
Source: (Hagstrom 141, 1979, p. 39)
*Central Islip Quad (7.5 ')

SOUTH HAVEN
Community
Suffolk—Brookhaven; W of Shirley,
 N of Bellport Bay;
 40 °48 'x72 °53 '30 "
Historical: Connecticott (Thompson
 41, vol. 1, p. 437), Fireplace
 (Flint 26, p. 70), Parish of
 Southhaven (Manley 30, p. 275),
 The Mills (Shaw 106, p. 211)
 Setauket South (Flint 26, p. 70)
Bellport Quad (7.5 ')

SOUTH HEMPSTEAD
Community
Nassau—Hempstead; central part of

the town, W of Roosevelt;
40°41'x73°37'
Freeport Quad (7.5')

SOUTH HEMPSTEAD
Town
see
HEMPSTEAD
Town
Source: (French 10, p. 547)

SOUTH HOLBROOK
Community
Suffolk—Islip; SW of Holbrook,
N of Bayport;
ca. 40°46'50"x73°5'30"
Source: (Hagstrom 141, 1979, p. 50)
*Patchogue Quad (7.5')

SOUTH HUNTINGTON
Community
Suffolk—Huntington, SW-central
part of the town, N of Melville;
40°49'30"x73°24'
Huntington Quad (7.5')

SOUTH HUNTINGTON
Village
Suffolk—Babylon
see
BABYLON
Village
Source: (Bailey 19, vol. 1,
pp. 363-364) and (Chace 127)

SOUTH JAMESPORT
Community
Suffolk—Riverhead; S of
Jamesport; 40°56'20"x72°34'45"
Historical: Jamesport (Bailey 19,
vol. 1, p. 189) and (Chace 127)
Mattituck Quad (7.5')

SOUTH LINE ISLAND
Physical feature—marsh island
Nassau—Hempstead; N of Zacks
Bay, W of South Oyster Bay;
40°37'x73°29'30"
West Gilgo Beach Quad (7.5')

SOUTH MANOR
Community
Suffolk—Brookhaven; E part of
the town, S of Manorville, N of
Moriches; 40°51'20"x72°49'
Moriches Quad (7.5')

SOUTH MEDFORD
Community
Suffolk—Brookhaven; S part of
Medford, NE of East Patchogue;
40°48'5"x72°58'50"
Source: (Hagstrom 141, 1979, p. 51)
*Bellport Quad (7.5')

SOUTH OYSTER BAY
Community
see
MASSAPEQUA
Source: (Flint 26, p. 73)

SOUTH OYSTER BAY
Physical feature
Nassau—Oyster Bay; S part of the
town, W of the Great South Bay;
40°38'30"x73°27'30"
Amityville Quad (7.5')

SOUTH OZONE PARK
Community
Queens; N of Jamaica Bay, E of
Ozone Park, S of Jamaica;
40°40'20"x73°49'
Jamaica Quad (7.5')

SOUTH POND
Physical feature
Nassau—Hempstead; W-central part
of the town, S of Hempstead Lake;
40°40'10"x73°39'5"
Historical: Hempstead Pond
(Hempstead Quad, 15', 1897)
Lynbrook Quad (7.5')

SOUTH PROVOOSTVILLE
Community, planned—historical
Suffolk—Islip; NE side of the town,
SSE of Holbrook;
ca. 40°48'30"x73°3'
Source: (Hagstrom 141, 1959, p. 31)
*Patchogue Quad (7.5')

SOUTH RACE
Physical feature—channel
Suffolk—Southold; connects Great
Peconic Bay and Little Peconic
Bay, between Cow Neck and
Robins Island;
40°57'10"x72°27'10"
Southampton Quad (7.5')

SOUTH SETAUKET
Community
Suffolk—Brookhaven; SW of Port
Jefferson, NW of Selden;
40°55'x73°6'
Historical: Nassakeag (Tooker 44,
p. 154)
Port Jefferson Quad (7.5')

SOUTH SOUND
see
GREAT SOUTH BAY
Source: (Ryder 159)

SOUTH VALLEY STREAM
Community
Nassau—Hempstead; S of Valley

Stream; 40°39'30"x73°43'
Lynbrook Quad (7.5')

SOUTH WESTBURY
see
WESTBURY SOUTH
Source: (Hagstrom 140, 1978, p. 40)

SOUTH WILLIAMSBURGH
see
RIDGEWOOD
Source: (Ricard 86, p. 14)

SOUTH WILLOW POND
see
**WEBSTER POND AND
WILLOW POND**
Suffolk—Smithtown
Source: (Langhans 98, p. 26)

SOUTH WOODHAVEN
see
OZONE PARK
Source: (Ricard 86, p. 13)

SOUTH YAPHANK
Community
Suffolk—Brookhaven; N of North
Bellport, SW of Yaphank;
40°48'5"x72°56'20"
Source: (Hagstrom 141, 1979, p. 51)
*Bellport Quad (7.5')

SOUTHAMPTON
Town
Suffolk; SE part of the county,
W of the town of East Hampton
Eastport, Riverhead, Mattituck,
Quogue, Shinnecock Inlet,
Southampton and Sag Harbor
Quads (7.5')

SOUTHAMPTON
Village
Suffolk—Southampton; SE of
Great Peconic Bay;
40°53′x72°23′
Historical: Agawam, Southton
(Flint 26, p. 74)
Southampton Quad (7.5′)

SOUTHAMPTON BAY
see
SHINNECOCK BAY
Source: (Thompson 41, vol. 1,
p. 362)

SOUTHAMPTON BEACH
Physical feature
Suffolk—Southampton; on the
Atlantic Ocean, S of Shinnecock
Bay; 40°51′30″x72°26′
Shinnecock Inlet Quad (7.5′)

SOUTHARDS POND
Physical feature
Suffolk—Babylon; N part of
Babylon village, S part of
Belmont Lake State Park;
40°42′40″x73°19′50″
Historical: Kennel Club Pond
(Babylon Quad, 15′, 1903)
Bay Shore West Quad (7.5′)

SOUTHOLD
Community
Suffolk—Southold; W side of Shelter
Island Sound, NW of Great Hog
Neck; 41°3′52″x72°25′35″
Historical: Toyong, The South Hold
(Flint 26, p. 74)
Southold Quad (7.5′)

SOUTHOLD
Town
Suffolk; E side of the county, on the
North Fork
Historical: Yennecock, Yennicock,
Northfleet, (French 10, p. 639fn),
The South Hold (Flint 26, pp. 74,
237–239), included the town of
Riverhead until 1792 (Ibid., p. 223)
Southampton, Southold, Greenport,
Orient, Plum Island, New London,
Mattituck, Mattituck Hills, and
Mystic Quads (7.5′)

SOUTHOLD BAY
Physical feature
Suffolk—Southold; in Shelter Island
Sound, SE of the community of
Southold; 41°3′30″x72°25′
Historical: Southold Harbour
(U.S. 167, Map T–68), Town
Harbor (Bayles 93, p. 378)
Southold Quad (7.5′)

SOUTHOLD HARBOUR
see
SOUTHOLD BAY
Source: (U.S. 167, Map T–68)

SOUTHPORT
Community
Suffolk—Southampton; E of
Flanders, SW of Great Peconic
Bay; 40°54′30″x72°33′
Mattituck Quad (7.5′)

SOUTHPORT BAY
Physical feature—historical
Suffolk—Southampton; "a wing of
the [Great Peconic] bay lying behind
a narrow strip of land called Red
Cedar Point"
Source: (Bayles 93, p. 321)
*Mattituck Quad (7.5′)

SOUTHTON
see
SOUTHAMPTON
Village
Source: (Flint 26, p. 74)

SOUWASSETT
see
PORT JEFFERSON
Source: (Tooker 44, pp. 246–247)

SPECTACLE POND
Physical feature
Suffolk—Smithtown; NW of Lake
  Ronkonkoma, E of Hauppauge;
  40°50′x73°8′5″
Variations: Specticul Pond, Spec's
  Pond (Langhans 98, p. 24)
Central Islip Quad (7.5′)

SPEONK
Community
Suffolk—Southampton; SE of
  of Eastport;
  40°49′10″x72°42′40″
Variations: Specunk, Speonk, Speunk
  (Tooker 44, p. 248)
Eastport Quad (7.5′)

SPEONK NECK
Physical feature
Suffolk—Southampton; site of the
  community of Speonk, SE of
  Eastport; 40°48′45″x72°44′
Source: (Tooker 44, p. 248)
*Eastport Quad (7.5′)

SPEONK POINT
Physical feature
Suffolk—Southampton; NE side of
  Moriches Bay, SE of Remsenberg
  and Eastport; 40°47′50″x72°41′40″
Eastport Quad (7.5′)

SPEONK RIVER
Physical feature
Suffolk—Southampton; flows into
  the NE side of Moriches Bay, E of
  Eastport and Remsenberg;
  40°48′15″x72°41′30″
Eastport Quad (7.5′)

SPHETONGA
see
BROOKLYN HEIGHTS
Source: (Tooker 44, p. 249)

SPLINTER VILLAGE
see
SAINT JAMES
Source: (Langhans 98, p. 5)

SPLIT ROCK LANDING
Physical feature—historical
Suffolk—East Hampton; in the
  Threemile Harbor vicinity;
  ca. 41°1′x72°17′15″
Source: (Yeager 113, p. 193)
*Gardiners Island West Quad (7.5′)

SPRING CREEK
Physical feature
Kings, Queens; E part of Kings and
  W part of Queens, NW of Jamaica
  Bay; 40°39′20″x73°51′45″
Jamaica Quad (7.5′)

SPRING HILL
Community—historical
Queens; SE of Flushing
Source: (French 10, p. 546fn)

SPRING HOLLOW
Physical feature—brook—historical
Suffolk—Smithtown; in a hollow
  spot on the W side of Stony

Brook Harbor in the village of
Nissequogue;
ca. 40°53′50″x73°10′45″
Source: (Langhans 98, p. 24) and
(Pelletreau 38, p. 357)
*Saint James Quad (7.5′)

SPRING LAKE
Physical feature
Nassau—Oyster Bay; SE part of
Mill Neck, SW of Oyster Bay
Harbor; 40°52′50″x73°32′55″
Bayville Quad (7.5′)

SPRING LAKE
Physical feature
Suffolk—Brookhaven; SW of Middle
Island, NE of Patchogue;
40°52′25″x72°57′30″
Bellport and Middle Island Quads
(7.5′)

SPRING POND
Physical feature—inlet
Suffolk—Southold; NE of
Greenport, N of Shelter Island;
41°7′10″x72°20′20″
Greenport Quad (7.5′)

SPRINGFIELD
see
SPRINGFIELD GARDENS
Source: (Brooklyn Quad, 15′, 1897)

SPRINGFIELD GARDENS
Community
Queens; E side of Queens, S of
St. Albans, NW of Valley Stream;
40°40′45″x73°45′
Historical: Springfield
(Brooklyn Quad, 15′, 1897)
Jamaica and Lynbrook Quads (7.5′)

SPRINGLAND
Community—historical
Queens; W of Valley Stream, SE
of Springfield Gardens, NE of
Laurelton; 40°40′30″x73°44′10″
Source: (New Century 151, plate 120)
*Lynbrook Quad (7.5′)

SPRINGS
Community
Suffolk—East Hampton; W of
Acabonack Harbor;
41°1′10″x72°9′35″
Historical: The Springs, Accabonac
(Manley 30, p. 38)
Gardiners Island West Quad (7.5′)

SPRINGVILLE
Community
Suffolk—Southampton; S of
Hampton Bays;
40°51′55″x72°31′40″
Quogue Quad (7.5′)

SPRINGVILLE
Community—historical
Queens; near Little Neck Bay
Source: (French 10, p. 546fn)

SQUASSUCKS
see
SQUASSUX LANDING
Source: (Tooker 44, pp. 249–250)

SQUASSUX LANDING
Community
Suffolk—Brookhaven; on the
Carmans River, E of the
community of Brookhaven;
40°46′30″x72°54′
Historical: Squassucks (Tooker 44,
pp. 249–250), Squawsucks
(Beauchamp 7, p. 224)
Bellport Quad (7.5′)

SQUAW ISLAND
Physical feature
Nassau—Oyster Bay; S part of
Oyster Bay; 40°37'37"x73°27'35"
Variation: Skow (Tooker 44, p. 250)
Amityville Quad (7.5')

SQUAW PIT PURCHASE
Tract of land—historical
Suffolk—Babylon; currently
in the NE part of the town
Source: (Bailey 19, vol. 1, p. 360)

SQUAW-HILL
Physical feature
Suffolk—Southampton; one of the
range of Shinnecock Hills, near the
Tuckahoe gate
Source: (Tooker 44, p. 250)
*Southampton Quad (7.5')

SQUAW-PIT
see
WYANDANCH
Source: (Tooker 44, p. 250)

SQUAWSUCKS
see
SQUASSUX LANDING
Source: (Beauchamp 7, p. 224)

SQUIRE POND
Physical feature—inlet
Suffolk—Southampton; SW side of
Great Peconic Bay, N of
Squiretown, E of Flanders;
40°54'x72°31'35"
Mattituck Quad (7.5')

SQUIRETOWN
Community
Suffolk—Southampton; N of

Hampton Bays, W of Shinnecock
Canal; 40°53'40"x72°31'30"
Mattituck Quad (7.5')

SQUORUMS NECK
Physical feature—historical
Suffolk—Brookhaven; on the E side
of Mastic Neck
Source: (Tooker 44, p. 250).
Also known as Waspeunk (Ibid.)
*Moriches Quad (7.5')

STADIUM PARK CANAL
Physical feature
Nassau—Hempstead; SE of Freeport,
flows into the Freeport Creek;
40°38'35"x73°34'
Freeport Quad (7.5')

STAGG POND
see
SAGAPONACK POND
Source: (U.S. 5, Decisions
Rendered Between July 1, 1940 and
June 30, 1941, p. 49)

STAR ISLAND
Physical feature
Suffolk—East Hampton; in the N
part of Lake Montauk;
41°4'15"x71°55'52"
Historical: Munchog, Munchoage
(Tooker 44, pp. 145–146) and
Munchogue Island (Ullitz 164,
index map)
Montauk Point Quad (7.5')

STARR'S NECK
Physical feature
Suffolk—Brookhaven; SW side of
Bellport; 40°45'x72°57'20"
Howells Point and Bellport Quads
(7.5')

STEARNS POINT
see
JENNINGS POINT
Source: (Bailey 19, vol. 1, p. 178)

STEEP BANKS
Physical feature—historical
Suffolk—Smithtown; E side of
the Nissequogue River, N of
Mill Creek; 40°53′x73°11′40″
Source: (Langhans 98, p. 24)
*Saint James Quad (7.5′)

STEHLI BEACH
Physical feature
Nassau—Oyster Bay; on Long Island
Sound, the NE shoreline of
Bayville; 40°54′30″x73°35′15″
Bayville Quad (7.5′)

STEINWAY
Community
Queens; NW part of Queens, NE of
Long Island City;
40°46′30″x73°54′15″
Central Park Quad (7.5′)

STEPHENS POINT
Physical feature—historical
Queens (Nassau)—Oyster Bay; NW
point of Mill Neck;
40°53′50″x73°34′5″
Source: (Cocks 70, p. 6)
*Bayville Quad (7.5′)

STEPPING STONES
Physical feature—rocks
Nassau—North Hempstead; in Long
Island Sound, NW of Great Neck;
40°49′25″x73°46′20″
Flushing Quad (7.5′)

STERLING
see
GREENPORT
Source: (Bailey 19, vol. 1, p. 157)
and (French 10, p. 639fn)

STERLING CREEK
see
STIRLING BASIN
Source: (Bailey 19, vol. 1, p. 157)

STERLING HARBOUR
see
GREENPORT
Source: (Flint 26, p. 71)

STEVENS POINT
see
COLLEGE POINT
Physical feature
Source: (Bailey 19, vol. 1, p. 39)

STEWART MANOR
Village
Nassau—Hempstead; NW part of the
town, W of Garden City;
40°43′15″x73°41′15″
Lynbrook Quad (7.5′)

STILL POND
see
HECKSCHER PARK LAKE
Source: (Sammis 104, pp. 40–41)

STILLMAN CREEK
Physical feature
Suffolk—Brookhaven; flows into
Patchogue Bay, S of Blue Point;
40°44′20″x73°2′
Sayville Quad (7.5′)

STIRLING
Community
Suffolk—Southold; N· of Greenport;
41 °7 'x72 °22 '10 "
Greenport Quad (7.5 ')

STIRLING BASIN
Physical feature
Suffolk—Southold; NE of
Greenport; 41 °6 '30 "x72 °21 '30 "
Historical: Winter Harbor and
Sterling Creek (Bailey 19,
vol. 1, p. 157)
Greenport Quad (7.5 ')

STONE CREEK
Physical feature
Nassau—Hempstead; flows between
Middle Line Island and South
Line Island; 40 °37 '25 "x73 °29 '30 "
West Gilgo Beach Quad (7.5 ')

STONE CREEK
Physical feature
Suffolk—Southampton; S of East
Quogue, on the W side of
Shinnecock Bay;
40 °49 '50 "x72 °35 '5 "
Quogue Quad (7.5 ')

STONINGTON
Community—historical
Nassau—North Hempstead; middle
of Manhasset Neck, in the vicinity
of Port Washington;
ca. 40 °50 'x73 °41 '15 "
Source: (Smith 162)
*Sea Cliff Quad (7.5 ')

STONY BROOK
Community
Suffolk—Brookhaven; W of
Setauket, E of Stony Brook

Harbor; 40 °55 '30 "x73 °8 '30 "
Historical: Wopowog (Tooker 44,
pp. 291-292)
Saint James Quad (7.5 ')

STONY BROOK
Physical feature
Suffolk—Brookhaven, Smithtown;
SW of the community of Stony
Brook, SE of Porpoise Channel;
40 °55 'x73 °9 '10 "
Historical: Cutsgunsuck,
Cussquontuck, Memanusack
(Tooker 44, pp. 58-59, 125) and
(Langhans 98, p. 7)
Saint James Quad (7.5 ')

STONY BROOK HARBOR
Physical feature
Suffolk—Smithtown; NE side of
town, between Nissequogue and
Head of the Harbor;
40 °54 '15 "x73 °10 '40 "
Historical: St. James Harbor,
Three Sister Harbour
(Langhans 98, p. 24), Rasapeage
(Pelletreau 38, p. 226)
Saint James Quad (7.5 ')

STONY CREEK MARSH
Physical feature—marsh island
Kings; SE part of Kings, W side
of Jamaica Bay, N of Ruffle Bar;
40 °36 '30 "x73 °51 '15 "
Far Rockaway Quad (7.5 ')

STONY HILL
Physical feature
Suffolk—East Hampton; S of
Kingstown, N of Amagansett;
ca. 40 °59 '45 "x72 °9 '
Source: (Hagstrom 141, 1979, p. 78)
*East Hampton Quad (7.5 ')

STONY HOLLOW
Physical feature
Suffolk—Huntington; NW to SE
hollow from Centerport to the S
side of East Northport;
40°52'40"x73°21'20"
Source: (Sammis 104, p. 28)
*Northport and Greenlawn Quads
(7.5')

STONY POINT
Physical feature
Kings; W side of Jamaica Bay, S tip
of Stony Creek Marsh;
40°36'20"x73°51'20"
Far Rockaway Quad (7.5')

STRADDLE POINT
Physical feature
Suffolk—Brookhaven; NE of
Bellport Bay, SW of Shirley;
40°46'10"x72°53'40"
Bellport Quad (7.5')

STRAIGHT CREEK
Physical feature
Queens; E side of Jamaica Bay, E
of East High Meadow, NW of
Jo Co Marsh; 40°37'25"x73°48'
Far Rockaway and Jamaica Quads
(7.5')

STRAIGHT CREEK MARSH
Physical feature—marsh island
Queens; E side of Jamaica Bay, E
of East High Meadow;
40°37'20"x73°48'
Source: (Brooklyn Quad, 15', 1897)
*Far Rockaway Quad (7.5')

STRATHMORE
Community
Nassau—North Hempstead; central

part of the town, S of Munsey
Park; 40°47'30"x73°41'
Sea Cliff Quad (7.5')

STRATTONPORT
see
COLLEGE POINT
Community
Source: (Ricard 86, p. 8)

STRATTON'S POINT
Physical feature—historical
Queens; SE side of Flushing Bay,
S of College Point;
40°46'15"x73°50'45"
Source: (Thompson 41, vol. 2, p. 95)
*Flushing Quad (7.5')

STROM KILL
see
GERRITSEN CREEK
Source: (Bailey 19, vol. 1, p. 29)

STROME CREEK
Physical feature—historical
Kings; near Gravesend, E of a large
tract of land called Makeopaca
Source: (Tookerr 44, pp. 88–89)
*Coney Island Quad (7.5')

STRONGS CREEK
Physical feature
Suffolk—Babylon; NW side of Great
South Bay, borders the NE side
of Copiague;
40°40'x73°22'5"
Bay Shore West and Amityville
Quads (7.5')

STRONGS NECK
Physical feature
Suffolk—Brookhaven; E of
Conscience Bay, W of Port
Jefferson Harbor;
40°57'30"x73°6'30"
Historical: Minasseroke, Minassouke,
Little Neck (Tooker 44,
pp. 131-132), Indian Ground
(Pelletreau 38, p. 256)
Port Jefferson Quad (7.5')

STRONGS NECK
Physical feature—historical
Suffolk—Babylon; SW of the
village of Babylon, possibly
Copiague Neck;
ca. 40°40'x73°22'20"
Source: (Thompson 42, p. 128)
*Bay Shore West Quad (7.5')

STRONGS POINT
Physical feature
Suffolk—Babylon; SE tip of
Copiague Neck, NW side of Great
South Bay;
40°39'50"x73°22'
Bay Shore West Quad (7.5')

STUMP POND
see
NEW MILLPOND
Source: (Langhans 98, p. 17)

STUYVESANT
see
BEDFORD-STUYVESANT
Source: (U.S. 5, List No. 8101,
p. 12)

SUCCED CREEK
Physical feature—historical
Nassau—North Hempstead; NW side

of Manhasset Neck; between Sands
Point and Barker Point;
40°51'15"x73°43'45"
Source: (Ross 158)
*Sea Cliff Quad (7.5')

SUCCESS
see
LAKE SUCCESS
Community
Source: (French 10, p. 550fn)

SUCCESS POND
see
LAKE SUCCESS
Source: (Tooker 44, pp. 219-220)

SUCCESS POST OFFICE
see
NORTHVILLE
Source: (Asher 116, p. 26)

SUCCESS ROCK
Physical feature
Nassau—North Hempstead; in Long
Island Sound, W of Manhasset
Neck; 40°51'20"x73°44'35"
Sea Cliff Quad (7.5')

SUCOS
see
BROOKVILLE
Source: (Tooker 44, pp. 250-251)

SUFFOLK
County
Central and E part of Long Island;
includes the towns of Babylon,
Brookhaven, East Hampton,
Huntington, Islip, Riverhead,
Shelter Island, Smithtown,
Southampton and Southold

Historical: East Riding of
Yorkshire (French 10, p. 544fn),
The Brush Plains (Flint 26, p. 74)

SUFFOLK STATION
see
CENTRAL ISLIP
Source: (Bayles 93, p. 206) and
(French 10, p. 637)

SUGAR LOAF HILL
Physical feature
Suffolk—Southampton; S side of
Shinnecock Hills, W of Far
Pond; 40°52′55″x72°28′15″
Source: (Bayles 93, p. 324)
*Southampton Quad (7.5′)

SUGGAMUCK CREEK
see
BIRCH CREEK
Source: (Tooker 44, p. 251)

SUNGIC
Locality—historical
Suffolk—Shelter Island; E side
of Shelter Island, SE of
Coecles Inlet;
ca. 41°4′x72°17′15″
Source: (Ullitz 164, plate 13)
*Greenport Quad (7.5′)

SUNGIC POINT
Physical feature
Suffolk—Shelter Island; E side
of Shelter Island, S of Ram
Island; 41°4′5″x72°17′5″
Greenport Quad (7.5′)

SUNK MEADOW
Community
Suffolk—Smithtown
see

KINGS PARK
Source: (Flint 26, p. 71)

SUNK MEADOW
Community
Suffolk—Smithtown, Huntington
see
MIDDLEVILLE
Source: (Bayles 93, p. 186)

SUNKAPOQUE CREEK
Physical feature—historical
Suffolk—Brookhaven; in the vicinity
of Mastic Neck, possibly
Musouatux Creek
Source: (Tooker 44, pp. 254–255)

SUNKEN FOREST
Physical feature
Suffolk—Brookhaven; SW of
Sayville, on Fire Island, S of
Oakdale; 40°39′20″x73°6′50″
Historical: Raccoon Beach
(Tuomey 49, pp. 29–30)
Sayville Quad (7.5′)

SUNKEN MEADOW
Physical feature
Suffolk—Smithtown; in Sunken
Meadow State Park, N of the
community of Kings Park;
40°54′30″x73°16′
Historical: Slongo, Sunk Meadow
(Flint 26, p. 74), (Langhans 98,
pp. 24-25) and (Pelletreau 101,
p. 64)
Northport Quad (7.5′)

SUNKEN MEADOW CREEK
Physical feature
Suffolk—Smithtown; N part of
Sunken Meadow State Park, N of
Kings Park; 40°54'30"x73°14'10"
Saint James and Northport Quads
(7.5')

**SUNKEN MEADOW STATE
PARK**
Suffolk—Smithtown; NW part of
the town on Long Island Sound, N
of Kings Park;
40°54'40"x73°15'35"
Northport and Saint James Quads
(7.5')

SUNNYSIDE
Community
Queens; SE of Long Island City,
W of Elmhurst;
40°44'30"x73°56'
Brooklyn Quad (7.5')

SUNQUAMS
see
MELVILLE
Source: (French 10, p. 636fn)

SUNQUAMS NECK
see
SAMPAWAMS NECK
Source: (Thompson 41, vol. 1,
p. 476)

SUNSWICK
see
ASTORIA
Source: (French 10, p. 548fn)

SUNSWICK CREEK
Physical feature—historical
Queens; flowed SE to NW into

Halletts Cove; 40°46'10"x73°56'10"
Source: (Walling 172) and
(Tooker 44, p. 255)
*Central Park Quad (7.5')

SUSCO'S WIGWAM
see
BROOKVILLE
Source: (Flint 26, p. 69)

SWAN CREEK
Physical feature
Suffolk—Southampton; flows into
the NE section of Mecox Bay;
40°54'10"x72°19'
Sag Harbor Quad (7.5')

SWAN ISLAND
Physical feature
Suffolk—Southampton; in the S part
of Moriches Bay, S of Eastport;
40°46'40"x72°43'30"
Eastport Quad (7.5')

SWAN LAKE
Physical feature
Suffolk—Brookhaven; E part of
East Patchogue;
40°46'10"x72°59'35"
Bellport Quad (7.5')

SWAN POND
Physical feature
Suffolk—Brookhaven; W of
Riverhead, S of Peconic Lake;
40°54'30"x72°43'
Riverhead Quad (7.5')

SWAN POND
Physical feature
Suffolk—Riverhead; W of
Calverton; 40°54'x72°47'40"
Wading River Quad (7.5')

SWAN RIVER
Physical feature
Suffolk—Brookhaven; flows through
part of East Patchogue into
Patchogue Bay;
40°45'x73°00'
Bellport and Howells Point Quads
(7.5')

SWAX'S HOLLOW
Dock—historical
Suffolk—Smithtown; W of the
mouth of Nissequogue River, on the
S side of Sunken Meadow Creek;
side of Sunken Meadow Creek;
ca. 40°54'25"x73°14'25"
Source: (Langhans 98, p. 25)
*Saint James Quad (7.5')

SWEDETOWN VILLAGE
Community—historical
Nassau—Oyster Bay; SE of
Hicksville, N of Bethpage;
40°46'x73°29'5"
Source: (Huntington Quad, 7.5',
AMS, 1947)
*Huntington Quad (7.5')

SWEET HOLLOW
see
MELVILLE
Source: (French 10, p. 636fn)

SWEEZEY'S HOLLOW
see
WOODHAVEN
Source: (Flint 26, p. 75)

SWEEZY POND
Physical feature

Suffolk—Southampton; S of
Riverhead, N of Wildwood Lake;
40°54'20"x72°40'20"
Riverhead Quad (7.5')

SWEGO
Locality—historical
Suffolk—Huntington
Source: (Tooker 44, p. 255)

SWEYZE
Community
Suffolk—Riverhead; SW side of the
town, N of Peconic Lake, W of the
community of Riverhead;
40°55'x72°43'15"
Riverhead Quad (7.5')

SWEZYS LANDING
Community—historical
Suffolk—Brookhaven; on the coast
of Long Island Sound
Source: (French 10, pp. 633–634)

SWIFT CREEK
Physical feature
Nassau—Hempstead; E of Hewlett
Bay, N boundary of Pearsalls
Hassock; 40°37'20"x73°40'
Lawrence Quad (7.5')

SWIFT CREEK
Physical feature
Nassau—Hempstead; flows between
Jones Island and Meadow Island;
40°36'15"x73°33'10"
Jones Inlet Quad (7.5')

SWIFT CREEK
Physical feature
Queens
see
EAST POND
Source: (Far Rockaway and
Jamaica Quads, (7.5'))

SWIFT STREAM
see
FORGE RIVER
Physical feature
Source: (Bailey 19, vol. 1, p. 272)

SYLVESTER'S ISLAND
see
SHELTER ISLAND
Source: (Flint 26, p. 74)

SYON
see
LONG ISLAND
Source: (Bailey 19, vol. 1, p. 31)

SYOSSET
Community
Nassau—Oyster Bay; NE of
  Hicksville, S of Oyster Bay Cove;
  40°50'x73'30"
Historical: East Woods (French 10,
  p. 550fn), Schouts (Tooker 44,
  pp. 255-256),
  the Oyster Bay P.O. was called
  Syosset from January 20-27, 1846
  and then changed back to Oyster
  Bay (French 10, p. 550fn)
Variations: Schout, Ciocits, Syocits
  (Tooker 44, pp. 255-256)
Hicksville and Huntington Quads
  (7.5')

'T CROMME GOUWE
see
GREAT PECONIC BAY
Source: (Flint 26, p. 73)

TACKAN
Locality—historical
Suffolk—Smithtown; a tract of land
in Smithtown on the Nissequogue
River
Source: (Tooker 44, p. 256)
*Central Islip Quad (7.5 ')

TACKAPAUSHA PRESERVE
Physical feature
Nassau—Hempstead, Oyster Bay; W
of Massapequa, SE of Wantagh, E
of Seaford; 40°40 '45 "x73°29 '
Amityville Quad (7.5 ')

TALLMAN ISLAND
Physical feature—neck
Queens; NW of Powell Cove, NE of
College Point;
40°47 '40 "x73°50 '20 "
Flushing Quad (7.5 ')

TAN YARDS
see
MANHASSET
Source: (French 10, p. 550fn)

TANGIER
Community—historical
Suffolk—Brookhaven; in the
vicinity of Mastic
Source: (Macoskey 29, p. 63)
*Bellport and Moriches Quads
(7.5 ')

TANNER NECK
Physical feature
Suffolk—Southampton; NE side of
Moriches Bay, SE of Eastport;
40°48 '20 "x72°40 '50 "
Variations: Great Tanner Neck,
Little Tanner Neck (Pelletreau 38,
p. 341)
Eastport Quad (7.5 ')

TANNER'S HOOK
Physical feature—historical
Nassau—North Hempstead; in the
vicinity of Manhasset Neck
Source: (Pelletreau 38, p. 112)
*Sea Cliff Quad (7.5 ')

TAPPEN BEACH
Physical feature
Nassau—Oyster Bay; part of the SW
shoreline of Sea Cliff, E-central
side of Hempstead Harbor;
40°50 'x73°39 '5 "
Sea Cliff Quad (7.5 ')

TARKILL POND
Physical feature
Suffolk—Brookhaven; SW of Lake
Panamoka, NE of Ridge;
40°55 'x72°51 '10 "
Wading River Quad (7.5 ')

318

TARMAN'S NECK
Physical feature—historical
Suffolk—Brookhaven; includes
Brookhaven community, N of
Bellport Bay, possibly the same
neck known as Fireplace Neck;
40°45′50″x72°54′15″
*Bellport Quad (7.5′)

TATAMUCKATAKIS CREEK
see
GREAT NECK CREEK
Source: (Tooker 44, p. 256)

TATAMUCKATAKIS NECK
see
GREAT NECK
Physical feature
Suffolk—Babylon
Source: (Tooker 44, pp. 256–257)

TAYLOR CREEK
Physical feature
Suffolk—Southampton; E of
Shinnecock Bay, S of
Southampton; 40°52′x72°24′55″
Shinnecock Inlet and Southampton
Quads (7.5′)

TERN'S COVE
see
NICOLL BAY
Source: (Gordon 11, p. 714)

TERRACE HEIGHTS
Community
Queens; SW of the community of
Queens Village, E of Forest Hills,
NE of Jamaica;
40°43′15″x73°46′15″
Jamaica Quad (7.5′)

TERRELL RIVER
Physical feature
Suffolk—Brookhaven; flows between
Central Moriches and East
Moriches into Moriches Bay;
40°47′x72°46′30″
Historical: Paquatuck, Pautuck
(Tooker 44, p. 177)
Moriches Quad (7.5′)

TERRY POINT
Physical feature
Suffolk—Southold; N of Orient
Harbor, NW of Orient;
41°8′55″x72°18′50″
Orient Quad (7.5′)

TERRYS COVE
see
NICOLL BAY
Source: (Chace 127)

TERRYS CREEK
Physical feature
Suffolk—Riverhead; NW side of
Flanders Bay, S of Aquebogue;
40°55′50″x72°37′30″
Historical: Deep Creek (U.S. 5,
List No. 5903, p. 44)
Mattituck Quad (7.5′)

TERRYS SWAMP CREEK
see
BROWN CREEK
Source: (Pelletreau 38, p. 238)

TERRYVILLE
Community
Suffolk—Brookhaven; S of Port
Jefferson; 40°55′x73°3′20″
Port Jefferson Quad (7.5′)

TERSARGE
Locality—historical
Suffolk—Smithtown; E of the town
of Huntington, on the N side of
the Island
Source: (Tooker 44, p. 258)

TERUS COVE
Physical feature—historical
Suffolk—Islip; at the mouth of the
Connetquot River;
ca. 40°43′30″x73°8′10″
Source: (Burr 124)
*Bay Shore East and Sayville Quads
(7.5′)

THATCH ISLAND
Physical feature
Suffolk—Babylon; W side of the
Great South Bay, SE of Elder
Island; 40°38′10″x73°23′
Amityville Quad (7.5′)

THATCH ISLAND
Physical feature—historical
Suffolk—Brookhaven; W side of
Port Jefferson Harbor, no longer
exists; ca. 40°57′35″x73°5′50″
Source: (Pelletreau 38, p. 239)
*Port Jefferson Quad (7.5′)

THE BAY
see
FLATLANDS
Source: (Dilliard 23, p. 67)

THE BEND OF MARECKAWIECK
Physical feature
Kings; WSW shoreline of the
Navy Yard Basin;
ca. 40°42′20″x73°58′45″
Source: (Stiles 66, vo. 1, p. 47)
*Brooklyn Quad (7.5′)

THE BRANCH
see
VILLAGE OF THE BRANCH
Source: (Langhans 98, p. 5)

THE BRUSH PLAINS
see
SUFFOLK
County
Source: (Flint 26, p. 74)

THE CLOSE
Physical feature—enclosed field or
lot—historical
Suffolk—Smithtown; SW of
Nissequogue, corner of
Nissequogue River Road and
Moriches Road; 40°54′x73°12′
Source: (Langhans 98, p. 6)
*Saint James Quad (7.5′)

THE COVE
Community—historical
Kings; near Sheepshead Bay;
ca. 40°35′x73°58′15″
Source: (French 10, p. 372)
*Coney Island Quad (7.5′)

THE COVE
Physical feature
Nassau—Oyster Bay; SE part of
Oyster Bay Harbor;
40°52′25″x73°30′30″
Hicksville Quad (7.5′)

THE COVE
Suffolk—Huntington
see
BLANCHARD LAKE
Source: (Sammis 104, p. 181)

THE CREEK BEACH
Physical feature
Nassau—Oyster Bay; part of the
N shoreline of Lattingtown;
40°54'15"x73°36'
Bayville Quad (7.5')

THE CROOKED BAY
see
GREAT PECONIC BAY
Source: (Flint 26, p. 73)

THE DEVILS BELT
see
LONG ISLAND SOUND
Source: (Faden 136)

THE DRAIN
Physical feature—channel
Nassau—Hempstead, Oyster Bay;
W side of South Oyster Bay,
S of Goose Island;
40°38'20"x73°29'
Amityville Quad (7.5')

THE DUMPLINGS
Physical feature—islands
Suffolk—Southold; in Fishers
Island Sound, N of the W part of
Fishers Island; 41°17'15"x72°1'
New London Quad (7.5')

THE FARMS
Nassau—Oyster Bay
see
JERICHO
Nassau—Oyster Bay
Source: (Flint 26, p. 71)

THE FARMS
Suffolk—Southold
see
GREENPORT
Source: (Bailey, vol. 1, p. 157)

THE FARROWS
Physical feature—historical
Suffolk—Brookhaven; a ploughed
strip running from W Yaphank to
the Granny Road;
ca. 40°50'40"x72°56'
Source: (Strong 107, pp. 109, 116)
*Bellport Quad (7.5')

THE FERRY
Community—historical
Kings; presently the NW part of
Brooklyn Heights;
40°42'20"x73°59'40"
Source: (Stiles 66, vol. 1, p. 47)
*Brooklyn Quad (7.5')

THE GLADES
Physical feature—marsh—historical
Suffolk—East Hampton; S of
Amagansett; ca. 40°58'x72°8'30"
Source: (Rattray 102, p. 81)
*East Hampton Quad (7.5')

THE GREEN
Tract of land—historical
Suffolk—Brookhaven; an open field
located between Setauket and
East Setauket;
ca. 40°56'30"x73°6'30"
Source: (Bayles 93, p. 237)
*Port Jefferson Quad (7.5')

THE GROVE
see
LITTLE AFRICA
Source: (Langhans 98, p. 16)

THE HASSOCK
Physical feature—island
Suffolk—Islip; in the Great
South Bay, NW of East Fire
Island, E of Captree Island;
40°39'40"x73°11'30"
Bay Shore East Quad (7.5')

THE HEADING
see
TOBAY HEADING
Source: (U.S. 5, List No. 5904,
p. 38)

THE HOOK
Community
Suffolk—Huntington
see
VERNON VALLEY
Source: (Sammis 104, p. 185)

THE HOOK
Physical feature
Nassau, Queens—Hempstead
see
HEAD OF BAY
Source: (Walling 172)
THE ISLE OF WIGHT
see
GARDINERS ISLAND
Source: (Tooker 44, p. 91)

THE LAGOON
Physical feature
Nassau—Hempstead; E of Island
Park, W of Garrett Marsh;

40°36'15"x73°38'50"
Lawrence Quad (7.5')

THE LAGOON
Physical feature
Suffolk—Brookhaven; S part of
Mastic Beach, N of Narrow Bay;
40°45'35"x72°50'
Moriches Quad (7.5')

THE LANDING
Community
Suffolk—Smithtown; N part of the
village of Smithtown;
40°51'45"x73°11'30"
Historical: the site and within the
vicinity previously known as
Upper Landing, Lower Landing,
Blydenburgh's Landing (Langhans
98, pp. 13–14)
*Central Islip Quad (7.5')

THE LANDING
Locality—historical
Nassau—Oyster Bay; SW side of
Glen Cove, N of Glen Cove Creek;
ca. 40°52'x73°39'
Source: (Coles 74, p. 154)
*Sea Cliff Quad (7.5')

THE LITTLE NARROWS
Physical feature
Suffolk—Southampton; channel
between Sag Harbor Cove and
Upper Sag Harbor Cove;
40°59'35"x72°18'55"
Sag Harbor Quad (7.5')

THE MANOR
Locality—historical
Suffolk—Southold; S of Oregon
Hills; 41°00'x72°32'
Source: (U.S. 167, Map T-55)
*Mattituck Hills Quad (7.5')

THE MEADOWS
Physical feature
Suffolk—East Hampton; S part of
Acabonack Harbor;
41°1′x72°8′30″
Gardiners Island West Quad (7.5′)

THE MILLS
see
SOUTH HAVEN
Source: (Shaw 106, p. 211)

THE NARROWS
Physical feature
Kings, Richmond; between Lower
Bay and Upper Bay, part of the
W boundary of Kings County;
40°37′30″x74°3′
The Narrows and Jersey City Quads
(7.5′)

THE NARROWS
Physical feature
Nassau—Hempstead; SE of Freeport,
NW side of Petit Marsh;
40°37′30″x73°34′15″
Freeport and Jones Inlet Quads
(7.5′)

THE NARROWS
Physical feature
Suffolk—Brookhaven; between
Conscience Bay and Port
Jefferson Harbor, N of Strongs
Neck; 40°58′10″x73°6′45″
Port Jefferson Quad (7.5′)

THE NORTH-WEST
Physical feature—neck—historical
Suffolk—East Hampton; W of
Threemile Harbor, E of Northwest
Harbor; 41°2′x72°13′
Source: (U.S. 167, Map T-72)
*Gardiners Island West Quad (7.5′)

THE OLD FIELD
Archeological site
Suffolk—Southold; in the Southold
Bay vicinity;
ca. 41°3′15″x72°25′
Source: (Bailey 19, vol. 1, p. 17)
*Southold Quad (7.5′)

THE PLACE
see
GLEN COVE
City
Source: (Flint 26, p. 71)

THE RAUNT
Physical feature—marsh island
Queens; in Jamaica Bay, SE of
Rulers Bar Hassock, N of Little
Egg Marsh; 40°37′15″x73°49′10″
Far Rockaway Quad (7.5′)

**THE RIM OF WOODS
PURCHASE**
Tract of land—historical
Nassau—Oyster Bay; in the vicinity
of Plainedge;
ca. 40°42′45″x73°29′
Source: (Gibbs 78, p. 65). Also
known as Hendrickson's Purchase
(Ibid.)
*Amityville Quad (7.5′)

THE RUN
Physical feature—tidal flat
Nassau—Hempstead; between Great
Island and Seamans Island, S of
Seaford; 40°38′15″x73°30′
Freeport and Amityville Quads
(7.5′)

THE SOUTH HOLD
see
SOUTHOLD
Town and Community
Source: (Flint 26, p. 74)

THE SPRINGS
see
SPRINGS
Source: (Manley 30, p. 38)

THE WILDERNESS
Physical feature—woods—historical
Suffolk—Smithtown; N side of the
village of Nissequogue, the wooded
area between Smithtown Bay and
Long Beach Road;
40°54'30"x73°12'
Source: (Langhans 98, p. 26)
*Saint James Quad (7.5')

THE WINTER HARBOR
see
GREENPORT
Source: (Pelletreau 38, p. 426)

THIRD NECK
Physical feature—historical
Suffolk—Southampton; SE of
Quogue, S of East Quogue;
40°50'x72°35'10"
Source: (Pelletreau 38, p. 336). Also
known as Short Neck (Ibid.)
*Quogue Quad (7.5')

THIXTON CREEK
Physical feature
Nassau—Hempstead; flows from the
S side of East Rockaway into the
N side of Hewlett Bay;
40°37'45"x73°40'40"
Lynbrook Quad (7.5')

THOMAS BENEDICT'S CREEK
see
MILL CREEK
Suffolk—Southold
Source: (Pelletreau 38, p. 417)

THOMAS CREEK
see
MILL CREEK
Suffolk—Southold
Source: (Pelletreau 38, p. 419)

THOMASTON
Village
Nassau—North Hempstead; W side
of the town, S of Manhasset
Bay; 40°47'10"x73°42'45"
Sea Cliff Quad (7.5')

THOMPSON STATION
Railroad Station—historical
Suffolk—Islip; W side of
Brentwood; 40°46'40"x73°15'40"
Source: (Bayles 93, p. 205)
*Greenlawn Quad (7.5')

THOMPSON'S BROOK
see
LAWRENCE CREEK
Suffolk—Islip
Source: (Tooker 44, p. 46)

THOMPSONS CREEK
Physical feature
Suffolk—Islip; flows through the
SE side of West Bay Shore, on
Appletree Neck, into the Great
South Bay; 40°41'40"x73°16'
Historical: Keemiscomock Brook and
Weepoose Brook (Tooker 44,
pp. 77-78)
Bay Shore West Quad (7.5')

THORN CANAL
Physical feature
Suffolk—Islip; E side of Appletree
Neck, S of Brightwaters;
40°41'50"x73°15'30"
Historical: formerly a stream known
as Missatuck Brook, Misatuc
Brook, Udall's Brook (Tooker 44,
pp. 135–136)
Bay Shore West Quad (7.5')

THORNE'S POINT
see
WILLET'S POINT
Source: (Flint 26, p. 75)

THREE CORNERED HASSOCK
Physical feature—marsh island
Nassau—Hempstead; SW side of
Woodburgh, S of Hewlett Neck;
40°36'50"x73°42'
Lawrence Quad (7.5')

THREE SISTER HARBOR
see
STONY BROOK HARBOR
Source: (Langhans 98, p. 24) and
(Pelletreau 101, pp. 89, 242)

THREE SISTER HOLLOW
Physical feature—landing—historical
Suffolk—Smithtown; SW side of
Head of the Harbor, SE side of
Stony Brook Harbor;
ca. 40°54'x73°10'10"
Source: (Langhans 98, p. 25) and
(Pelletreau 101, pp. 89, 242)
*Saint James Quad (7.5')

THREEMILE HARBOR
Community
Suffolk—East Hampton; E side of
Threemile Harbor;

41°1'x72°10'50"
Gardiners Island West and East
Hampton Quads (7.5')

THREEMILE HARBOR
Physical feature
Suffolk—East Hampton; S of
Gardiners Bay, N of East
Hampton village;
41°1'x72°11'40"
Gardiners Island West Quad (7.5')

THREEMILE MILL
Physical feature—marsh—historical
Queens; presently the N part of
JFK Airport; ca. 40°40'x73°47'30"
Source: (Brooklyn Quad, 15', 1897)
*Jamaica Quad (7.5')

THURSTON BASIN
Physical feature
Queens; flows into the N side of
Head of Bay; 40°38'10"x73°44'50"
Historical: possibly Massepe
(Tooker 44, p. 112)
Jamaica and Lynbrook Quads
(7.5')

THUSBY'S NECK
Physical feature—historical
Suffolk—Islip; part of the
community of Bay Shore;
40°43'15"x73°14'10"
Source: (U.S. 170, Chart No. 119,
1844)
*Bay Shore East Quad (7.5')

TIANA
Community
Suffolk—Southampton; S of Tiana
Bay, SW of Hampton Bays;
40°52'10"x72°32'15"
Quogue Quad (7.5')

TIANA BAY
Physical feature
Suffolk—Southampton; NW part of
Shinnecock Bay, SW of Hampton
Bays; 40°51'30"x72°32'30"
Variations: Tianna, Tyana, Tianah
and Tiana (Tooker 44, pp. 258-259)
Quogue Quad (7.5')

TIANA BEACH
Physical feature
Suffolk—Southampton; S of
Shinnecock Bay, W of Shinnecock
Inlet; 40°50'20"x72°30'
Quogue Quad (7.5')

TIANA CREEK
Physical feature
Suffolk—Southampton; flows into
Tiana Bay, W of Tiana, SW of
Hampton Bays;
40°52'x72°32'35"
Quogue Quad (7.5')

TIFFANY CREEK
Physical feature
Nassau—Oyster Bay; flows into The
Cove, E of Oyster Bay Cove
village; 40°52'20"x73°30'10"
Hicksville and Huntington Quads
(7.5')

TIMBER BROOK
Physical feature
Suffolk—Smithtown; NW side of the
town, NW side of Fort Salonga,
flows into the S side of
Fresh Pond; 40°55'10"x73°17'55"
Source: (Langhans 98, p. 25)
*Northport Quad (7.5')

TIMBER POINT
Physical feature
Suffolk—Islip; NW side of Nicoll

Bay, S of Oakdale;
40°43'x73°8'5"
Bay Shore East Quad (7.5')

TINNIE'S
Physical feature—hole—historical
Suffolk—East Hampton; a hole of
water on Napeague Beach, near
the Amagansett Hills
Source: (Tooker 44, p. 259)
*Napeague Beach Quad (7.5')

TO THE HARBOR
see
NORTHPORT
Source: (Sammis 104, p. 164)

TO YOUNGS CREEK
see
HUBBARD CREEK
Source: (Pelletreau 38, p. 382)

TOBACCOLOT BAY
Physical feature
Suffolk—East Hampton; E side of
Gardiners Island; 41°5'30"x72°5'
Gardiners Island East Quad (7.5')

TOBACCOLOT POND
Physical feature
Suffolk—East Hampton; E side of
Gardiners Island, W of Tobaccolot
Bay; 41°5'30"x72°5'25"
Gardiners Island East Quad (7.5')

**TOBAY BEACH BIRD AND
GAME SANCTUARY**
Physical feature
Nassau—Oyster Bay; S side of the
town, E of Jones Beach State
Park; 40°36'30"x73°27'
West Gilgo Beach Quad (7.5')

TOBAY HEADING
Physical feature—bay
Nassau—Oyster Bay; SE of South
Oyster Bay, E of Tobay Beach
Bird and Game Sanctuary;
40°36'45"x73°26'
Historical: The Heading, also
incorrectly labelled Gilgo Heading
(U.S. 5, List No. 5904, p. 38)
and (West Gilgo Beach Quad,
7.5', 1954)
West Gilgo Beach Quad (7.5')

TOILSOME
Community—historical
Suffolk—East Hampton; in the
vicinity of the village of
East Hampton
Source: (Stevens 40, p. 163)
*East Hampton Quad (7.5')

TOM'S CREEK
see
MILL CREEK
Suffolk—Southold
Source: (Pelletreau 38, p. 415)

TOMS POINT
Physical feature
Nassau—North Hempstead; NE side
of Manhasset Bay, SE of
Manorhaven; 40°50'x73°42'30"
Sea Cliff Quad (7.5')

TOWAPIONKE
Tract of land—historical
Suffolk—Brookhaven; E of Mastic
Neck
Source: (Tooker 44, p. 259)
*Moriches Quad (7.5')

TOWD
Locality—historical
Suffolk—Southampton; near
the community of North Sea;
ca. 40°54'50"x72°24'45"
Source: (Tooker 44, pp. 259-260)
Variations: Towde, Toude (Ibid.)
*Southampton Quad (7.5')

TOWD POINT
Physical feature
Suffolk—Southampton; S of
Little Peconic Bay, N of North
Sea Harbor; 40°56'55"x72°25'
Southampton Quad (7.5')

TOWN BEACH
Physical feature
Suffolk—Islip; on the Great South
Bay, S of East Islip, W of
Heckscher State Park;
40°42'30"x73°11'45"
Bay Shore East Quad (7.5')

TOWN BEACH
Physical feature
Suffolk—Islip; on the Great South
Bay, S of Islip;
40°42'30"x73°12'55"
Bay Shore East Quad (7.5')

TOWN CREEK
Physical feature
Suffolk—Southold; flows into
Southold Bay, SE of the community
of Southold; 41°3'35"x72°25'10"
Historical: Youngs Creek (Pelletreau
38, p. 422)
Southold Quad (7.5')

TOWN HARBOR
see
SOUTHOLD BAY
Source: (Bayles 93, p. 378)

TOWN HILL
Physical feature—historical
Suffolk—Huntington; in the
community of Halesite, possibly
known as Maple Hill;
ca. 40°53'10"x73°24'30"
Source: (Sammis 104, pp. 36–37)
*Lloyd Harbor Quad (7.5')

TOWN POND
see
AGAWAM LAKE
Source: (Pelletreau 38, p. 307)

TOWNSEND ISLAND
Physical feature
Nassau, Suffolk—Oyster Bay,
Babylon; E end of South Oyster
Bay; 40°38'20"x73°25'40"
Amityville Quad (7.5')

TOYONG
see
SOUTHOLD
Community
Source: (Flint 26, p. 74)

TOYONGE CREEK
see
HUBBARD CREEK
Source: (Pelletreau 38, p. 382)

TRAINS MEADOW
Physical feature—historical
Queens; N of Woodside, W of
Corona; ca. 40°45'40"x73°54'
Source: (Tooker 44, p. 219) and

(Harlem Quad, 15', 1900)
*Central Park Quad (7.5')

TREADWELL'S NECK
Physical feature—historical
Suffolk—Smithtown; NW side of the
town, from Sunken Meadow to
Fresh Pond; 40°55'x73°17'
Source: (Langhans 98, p. 25) and
(Pelletreau 101, p. 334)
*Northport Quad (7.5')

TREASURE POND
Physical feature
Suffolk—Southold; S-central part
of Fishers Island;
41°16'25"x71°58'20"
Mystic Quad (7.5')

TREDWELL'S PLAIN
see
LITTLE PLAINS
Source: (Sammis 104, p. 197)

TROUT LAKE
Physical feature—historical
Nassau—Oyster Bay, Hempstead;
on the town border, W of
Massapequa, possibly Jones
Trout Lake;
40°40'40"x73°28'55"
Source: (Walling 172)
*Amityville Quad (7.5')

TROUT POND
Physical feature
Suffolk—Southampton; W of
Noyack, S of Noyack Bay;
40°59'30"x72°21'
Sag Harbor Quad (7.5')

TRUES CREEK
Physical feature
Suffolk—Islip; flows through S
part of West Bay Shore;
40°41'25"x73°16'30"
Historical: Oquenock Brook
(Tooker 44, p. 169)
Bay Shore West Quad (7.5')

TRUMAN BEACH
Physical feature
Suffolk—Southold; NW of Orient
Harbor; 41°8'15"x72°19'40"
Historical: Oyster Pond Beach
(U.S. 170, Chart No. 115, 1855)
Orient Quad (7.5')

TUCKAHOE
Community
Suffolk—Southampton; NW of
Southampton village;
40°54'5"x72°24'30"
Southampton Quad (7.5')

TUCKER NECK
Physical feature—historical
Suffolk—Brookhaven; on the Great
South Bay, SE side of the
community of Blue Point;
ca. 40°44'45"x73°2'
Source: (Pelletreau 38, p. 269)
*Sayville Quad (7.5')

TUCKERTOWN
see
WEST SAYVILLE
Source: (Bailey 19, vol. 1, p. 332)

TUE'S NECK
see
COLLEGE POINT
Community
Source: (Ricard 86, p. 8)

TURKEY HILL
Physical feature—historical
Suffolk—Southampton; in the
vicinity of the village of Sag
Harbor
Source: (Overton 37, p. 193)
*Sag Harbor Quad (7.5')

TURKEYVILLE
see
PLAINEDGE
Community
Nassau—Oyster Bay
Source: (Flint 26, p. 74)

TURKUM NECK
Physical feature—historical
Suffolk—Shelter Island; S side of
Shelter Island, SE of Menantic
Creek; 41°3'10"x72°20'30"
Source: (Ullitz 164, plate 13)
*Greenport Quad (7.5')

TURTLE COVE
Physical feature
Suffolk—Southampton; S of
Little Peconic Bay;
40°57'5"x72°24'10"
Southampton Quad (7.5')

TURTLE HILL
Physical feature
Suffolk—East Hampton; at Montauk
Point where the lighthouse
is constructed;
41°5'20"x71°51'25"
Source: (French 10, p. 635fn)
*Montauk Point Quad (7.5')

TUTHILL
Community—historical
Suffolk—Shelter Island; S-central
part of Shelter Island;

ca. 41°2'45"x72°19'45"
Source: (Hyde 147)
*Greenport Quad (7.5')

TUTHILL COVE
Physical feature
Suffolk—Brookhaven; N side of
Moriches Bay, S of East Moriches;
40°47'30"x72°45'30"
Historical: West Cove (Moriches
Quad, 15', 1904), Bill's Cove
Hart's Cove, Smith's Cove
(U.S. 5, List No. 5904, p. 38)
Moriches Quad (7.5')

TUTHILL POINT
Physical feature
Suffolk—Brookhaven; N-central
part of Moriches Bay, S of
East Moriches;
40°47'x72°45'20"
Moriches Quad (7.5')

TUTHILLS CREEK
Physical feature
Suffolk—Brookhaven; flows into
Patchogue Bay;
40°45'x73°1'30"
Patchogue and Sayville Quads
(7.5')

TWIN PONDS
Physical feature
Suffolk—Brookhaven; NE of
Coram, SW of Rocky Point;
40°54'15"x72°57'15"
Middle Island Quad (7.5')

TWIN PONDS
Physical feature
Suffolk—Riverhead; SW side of
town, NW of Manorville;

40°53'10"x72°50'
Wading River Quad (7.5')

TWO HOLES POND
Physical feature
Suffolk—East Hampton; NW of
the village of East Hampton;
40°59'25"x72°14'35"
East Hampton Quad (7.5')

TWO PIGS
Physical feature—rocks
Suffolk—Brookhaven; in Long
Island Sound, N of Rocky Point
Landing; 40°58'15"x72°57'10"
Middle Island Quad (7.5')

TYNDAL POINT
Physical feature
Suffolk—Southampton; N point of
North Haven Peninsula;
41°2'30"x72°18'50"
Greenport Quad (7.5')

331

U

UCQUEBAAK
Locality—historical
Suffolk—Riverhead; W of Flanders
Bay, N and S of the Peconic
River; ca. 40°55′x72°37′
Source: (Pelletreau 38, p. 381)
Variations: Occabauk, Accobock,
Accobog, Agaboke, Aquabauk and
Aquebogue (Ibid.)
*Riverhead and Mattituck Quads
(7.5′)

UDALL'S BROOK
see
THORN CANAL
Source: (Tooker 44, p. 136)

UDALLS MILLPOND
Physical feature
Nassau—North Hempstead; SW side
of Great Neck;
40°47′55″x73°44′50″
Sea Cliff Quad (7.5′)

UNCAWAMUCK CREEK
see
REEVES CREEK
Source: (Tooker 45, p. 57) and
(Tooker 44, p. 263)

UNCHACHOGUE CREEK
Physical feature
Suffolk—Brookhaven; flows into
Narrow Bay, SE side of Shirley,
W of Johns Neck Creek;
40°44′30″x72°52′30″
Moriches and Pattersquash
Island Quads (7.5′)

UNCHENCHIE
see
SHELTER ISLAND
Physical feature
Source: (Tooker 44, p. 264)

UNCLE DANIELS POINT
Physical feature
Nassau—Hempstead; NW of
Cedarhurst, SW of Meadowmere
Park, N side of Head of Bay;
40°37′50″x73°44′45″
Lynbrook Quad (7.5′)

UNION CHAPEL
Community
Suffolk—Southampton; S
of Noyack Bay, W of Noyack;
40°59′25″x72°21′30″
Sag Harbor Quad (7.5′)

UNION PLACE
Community—historical
Queens; in the vicinity of
Flushing
Source: (French 10, p. 546fn)

UNION PLACE
Community—historical
Suffolk—Southampton; SW of
Westhampton;
ca. 40°48′30″x72°41′45″
Source: (Bayles 93, p. 313)
*Eastport Quad (7.5′)

UNIONDALE
Community
Nassau—Hempstead; N-central part
of the town, E of the village of
Hempstead, N of Roosevelt;
40°42'x73°35'30"
Freeport Quad (7.5')

UNIONVILLE
Community—historical
Kings; no longer exists, S of
Bensonhurst, W of Gravesend;
ca. 40°35'30"x73°59'30"
Source: (Walling 172) and (Brooklyn
Quad, 15', 1897)
*Coney Island Quad (7.5')

UNIVERSITY GARDENS
Community
Nassau—North Hempstead; W side
of the town, S of Great Neck;
40°46'40"x73°43'15"
Sea Cliff Quad (7.5')

UNKAWA NECK
Physical feature—historical
Nassau—Oyster Bay; SE-most neck
of Oyster Bay town, E of Nassau
Shores; 40°39'45"x73°25'45"
Source: (Burr 125) and (Tooker 44,
p. 265)
Variations: Unqua, Unkaway (Ibid.)
*Amityville Quad (7.5')

UNKECHAUG NECK
Physical feature—historical
Suffolk—Brookhaven; a neck of land
in the Manor of St. George
Source: (Tooker 44, pp. 265-266)
Variations: Unquachack, Unkachauk,
Unkechage, Unkechake,

Onchechaug (Ibid.)
*Moriches and Pattersquash Island
Quads (7.5')

UNKWAY NECK
see
MASSAPEQUA
Source: (Flint 26, p. 73)

UNQUA POINT
Physical feature
Nassau—Oyster Bay; NE part of
South Oyster Bay, SE point of
Nassau Shores, S of the mouth
of Carman Creek;
40°39'x73°25'45"
Amityville Quad (7.5')

UNSHEMAMUCK
see
FRESH POND
Suffolk—Smithtown
Source: (Tooker 44, pp. 266-268)

UPLAND PURCHASE
Tract of land—historical
Nassau—Oyster Bay; SE side of
town; ca. 40°44'x73°21'
Source: (Bailey 18, p. 8)
*Amityville Quad (7.5')

UPPER AQUEBOGUE
see
AQUEBOGUE
Source: (U.S. 170, Chart No. 115,
1855)

UPPER BEACH
Physical feature
Suffolk—Shelter Island; NE part of
Shelter Island, E of Dering Harbor;
41°5'30"x72°19'20"
Greenport Quad (7.5')

UPPER BROOKVILLE
Village
Nassau—Oyster Bay; N-central
part of the town, SE of Glen Cove;
40°50′30″x73°33′50″
Hicksville Quad (7.5′)

UPPER FRANCIS POND
Physical feature
Nassau—Oyster Bay; S of Mill Neck
and Lower Francis Pond, W of the
community of Oyster Bay;
40°52′10″x73°34′5″
Hicksville Quad (7.5′)

UPPER LAKE
Physical feature
Suffolk—Brookhaven; NE of
Siegfield Park, S of Middle Island,
NW of Yaphank;
40°50′30″x72°56′20″
Bellport Quad (7.5′)

UPPER LANDING
see
THE LANDING
Community
Source: (Langhans 98, pp. 13–14)

UPPER ROCKAWAY
see
HEWLETT
Source: (Wexler 90, p. 240)

UPPER SAG HARBOR COVE
Physical feature
Suffolk—Southampton; W of the
village of Sag Harbor;
40°59′40″x72°18′30″
Sag Harbor Quad (7.5′)

UPPER WILLOW BROOK
Physical feature
Suffolk—East Hampton; N part of
Gardiners Island, S of Bostwick
Creek; 41°6′34″x72°6′50″
Source: (Gardiners Island East
Quad, 7.5′, AMS, 1947)
*Gardiners Island East Quad (7.5′)

**UPPER WINGANHAUPPAUGE
LAKE**
Physical feature
Suffolk—Islip; on Champlin Creek,
between Islip and East Islip;
40°43′45″x73°12′10″
Bay Shore East Quad (7.5′)

UPTON
Community
Suffolk—Brookhaven; S of Ridge,
within the boundaries of the
Brookhaven National Laboratory;
ca. 40°52′15″x72°52′50″
Historical: Camp Upton Military
Reservation (Moriches Quad, 7.5′,
AMS, 1944) and (Bellport Quad,
7.5′, AMS, 1944)
Bellport Quad (7.5′)

UPTON STATION
Railroad Station
Suffolk—Brookhaven; SE of
Brookhaven National Laboratory,
W of Manorville;
40°51′15″x72°51′10″
Moriches Quad (7.5′)

UTOPIA
Community
Queens; SE of Flushing, SW of
Queens Village;
40°43′40″x73°47′20″
Jamaica Quad (7.5′)

VAIL POND
Physical feature
Suffolk—Smithtown; SW of the
community of Smithtown, NW of
Hauppauge; 40°50′50″x73°13′35″
Central Islip Quad (7.5′)

VAIL'S BROOK
see
CHAMPLIN CREEK
Source: (Thompson 42, p. 129)

VAILEY GROVE
see
EATONS NECK
Community
Source: (Macoskey 29, pp. 52, 63)

VALLEY STREAM
Physical feature
Nassau—Hempstead; on the W side
of the town, flows through Valley
Stream State Park, the village of
Valley Stream and North
Woodmere; 40°39′10″x73°43′15″
Historical: Clear Creek (Cram 132,
p. 111), Watts Creek (Lynbrook
Quad, 7.5′, AMS, 1947)
Lynbrook Quad (7.5′)

VALLEY STREAM
Village
Nassau—Hempstead; W part of the
town, W of Rockville Centre;
40°40′x73°42′30″
Lynbrook Quad (7.5′)

VALLEY STREAM POND
Physical feature
Nassau—Hempstead; in Valley
Stream State Park, N part of the
village of Valley Stream;
40°40′10″x73°42′
Source: (Hempstead Quad,
15′, 1897)
*Lynbrook Quad (7.5′)

VALLEY STREAM STATE PARK
Nassau—Hempstead; W part of the
town, N part of Valley Stream, W
of Malverne; 40°40′x73°42′
Lynbrook Quad (7.5′)

VALMONT VILLAGE PARK
Park
Suffolk—Smithtown; SW part of the
town; 40°49′30″x73°17′
Greenlawn Quad (7.5′)

VAN BRUNT'S NECK
see
DRYERS NECK
Source: (Flint 26, p. 70)

VAN BRUNT'S POINT
Physical feature—historical
Kings; S of Bay Ridge Dock
and Bennetts Point;
40°37′50″x74°2′30″
Source: (Walling 172)
*Jersey City Quad (7.5′)

VAN TWILLER'S BOWERY
Physical feature—historical
Kings; in the vicinity of
 Gerritsen, S of Flatlands
Source: (Ross 39, p. 775)
*Coney Island Quad (7.5 ')

VANDYKES MILL POND
see
ERIE BASIN
Source: (Field 138)

VANISHED VILLAGE
see
NORTHWEST
Source: (Bailey 19, vol. 1, p. 232)

VEKHIES NECK
Physical feature—historical
Suffolk—Brookhaven; W of Wading
 River; ca. 40°57 '30 "x72°51 '50 "
Source: (Pelletreau 38, p. 255)
*Wading River Quad (7.5 ')

VENETIAN SHORES
Community—historical
Suffolk—Babylon; the vicinity of
 Lindenhurst, on Santapogue Neck;
 40°40 '40 "x73°21 '20 "
Source: (Macoskey 29, p. 63) and
 (Hyde 148)
*Bay Shore West Quad (7.5 ')

VERNAM BASIN
Physical feature
Queens; SE side of Jamaica Bay,
 NW of Arverne, NE of Hammel;
 40°35 '40 "x73°48 '20 "
Far Rockaway Quad (7.5 ')

VERNON VALLEY
Community—historical
Suffolk—Huntington; NE side of

town, SE of Northport;
 ca. 40°51 '15 "x73°17 '45 "
Source: (French 10, p. 636). Also
 known as Red-Hook (Ibid.) and
 The Hook (Sammis 104, p. 185)
*Greenlawn Quad (7.5 ')

VILLAGE OF THE BRANCH
Village
Suffolk—Smithtown; E of
 Smithtown, SW of Saint James;
 40°51 '10 "x73°11 '
Historical: known also as The
 Branch, geographically part of what
 was formerly called Smithtown
 Branch (Langhans 98, p. 5)
Central Islip Quad (7.5 ')

VISCHERS ISLAND
see
FISHERS ISLAND
Physical feature
Source: (French 10, p. 636fn)

VISSCHER'S HOECK
see
MONTAUK POINT
Source: (Flint 26, p. 73)

VLISSINGEN
see
FLUSHING
Source: (Ricard 86, p. 9)

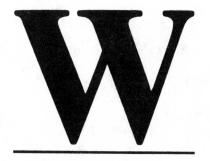

WADING RIVER
Community
Suffolk—Riverhead; NW side of
town, E of Rocky Point and
Shoreham; 40°57′20″x72°51′
Historical: Westhold (Bailey 19,
vol. 1, p. 197)
Wading River Quad (7.5′)

WADING RIVER
Physical feature
Suffolk—Brookhaven, Riverhead;
flows into Long Island Sound, N
boundary between Brookhaven and
Riverhead; 40°57′55″x72°52′
Historical: Quaconsit River,
Pahquahkossit, and
Pauquacumsuck (Tooker 44,
pp. 151, 175, 184), Red Creek
and Red Brook (Bailey 19, vol. 1,
pp. 192, 249), Weading Kreek
(Pelletreau 38, p. 381)
Wading River Quad (7.5′)

WAGASPOR CREEK
Physical feature—historical
Kings; in Flatland meadows
Source: (Tooker 44, p. 268)

WAINSCOTT
Community
Suffolk—East Hampton; E of
Bridgehampton; 40°56′x72°14′30″
Historical: Wayumscutt (Flint 26,
p. 74)
Sag Harbor and East Hampton
Quads (7.5′)

WAINSCOTT BEACH
Physical feature
Suffolk—East Hampton; on the
Atlantic Ocean, SE of Wainscott,
SW part of the town;
40°55′30″x72°14′30″
East Hampton Quad (7.5′)

WAINSCOTT POND
Physical feature
Suffolk—East Hampton; SE of
Wainscott, SW corner of the town;
40°55′50″x72°14′30″
East Hampton Quad (7.5′)

WALBOGHT
see
WALLABOUT BAY
Source: (Bailey 19, vol. 1, p. 36)

WALKING DUNES
Physical feature
Suffolk—East Hampton; E of
Napeague Harbor, W side of
Hither Hills State Park;
ca. 41°1′x72°2′10″
Source: (Rattray 102, p. 102)
*Gardiners Island East Quad (7.5′)

WALLABOUT
Community—historical
Kings; E of Wallabout Bay;
ca. 40°42′30″x73°57′45″
Source: (French 10, p. 367). Also
known as East Brooklyn (Ibid.)
and Rinnegackonck (Bailey 19,
vol. 1, p. 36)
*Brooklyn Quad (7.5′)

WALLABOUT BAY
Physical feature
Kings; on the East River, NNW of
Navy Yard Basin;
40°42′30″x73°58′30″
Variation: Walboght (Bailey 19,
vol. 1, p. 36)
Brooklyn Quad (7.5′)

WALLAGE
see
WESTBURY
Source: (Tooker 44, p. 269)

WALLEYS
Community—historical
Suffolk—Southampton; NE of North
Sea village; possibly the
present site of Rose Grove;
40°57′35″x72°23′45″
Source: (Cram 131, p. 37)
*Southampton Quad (7.5′)

WALNUT NECK
Physical feature
Suffolk—Huntington; W part of
Eatons Neck, in Duck Island
Harbor; 40°56′10″x73°23′
Lloyd Harbor Quad (7.5′)

WAMPAGE SHORES
see

SANDS POINT
Village
Source: (Macoskey 29, p. 63)

WAMPANAMON
see
LONG ISLAND
Source: (Bailey 19, vol. 1, p. 31)

WAMPMISSIC
Physical feature—tract of land and
large swamp—historical
Suffolk—Brookhaven; near what is
now Brookhaven National Lab,
between Yaphank and Manor
Stations on the Long Island
Railroad; ca. 40°52′x72°53′
Source: (Tooker 44, pp. 270–271)
and (Chace 127). Also known as
Old Wampmissic Place (Ullitz 164,
plate 7)
*Bellport Quad (7.5′)

WAMPONAMON
see
MONTAUK POINT
Source: (Tooker 44, pp. 271)

WAMSER ISLAND
see
WANSERS ISLAND
Source: (U.S. 5, List No. 7001,
p. 13)

WANASQUATTAN
Locality—historical
Suffolk—Huntington (Babylon);
near Amityville
Source: (Tooker 44, p. 272)
*Amityville Quad (7.5′)

WANDOWENOCK
see

MASPETH
Source: (Beauchamp 7, p. 179)
and (Tooker 44, pp. 272–273)

WANSERS ISLAND
Physical feature
Suffolk—Babylon; SW side of town,
 S of Amityville, NW of Gilgo
 Island; 40°38′10″x73°25′15″
Historical: Warren Island
 (Hempstead Quad, 15′, 1897) and
 (Hagstrom 140, 1965, p. 58),
 Wamser Island (U.S. 5, List No.
 7001, p. 13)
Amityville Quad (7.5′)

WANTAGH
Community
Nassau—Hempstead; E side of
 town, N of Seaford, S of
 Levittown; 40°41′x73°30′
Historical: Jerusalem (Marshall 80,
 p. 21) and (Burr 125), Ridgewood
 (Tooker 44, p. 273)
Freeport and Amityville Quads (7.5′)

WANTAGH POND
Physical feature
Nassau—Hempstead; W side of
 Wantagh, NE of Bellmore, W of
 Seaford; 40°40′25″x73°31′
Freeport Quad (7.5′)

WARDEN CLYFFE
Community—historical
Suffolk—Riverhead; E of the
 community of Rocky Point
Source: (Ullitz 164, index map)

WARDS POINT
Physical feature
Suffolk—Shelter Island; S part of

Shelter Island;
 41°2′40″x72°19′50″
Greenport Quad (7.5′)

WARISHONE
see
ARESHUNK NECK
Source: (Tooker 44, p. 20)

WARNER ISLAND
Physical feature
Suffolk—Southampton; SW part of
 Shinnecock Bay, S of Ponquogue;
 40°51′x72°29′50″
Shinnecock Inlet Quad (7.5′)

WARRASKETUCK CREEK
see
NARRASKATUCK CREEK
Source: (Tooker 44, pp. 373–374)

WARRATTA NECK
Physical feature
Suffolk—Brookhaven; S part of
 Center Moriches, bordered on the E
 by the Terrell River and on the
 W by Senix Creek;
 40°47′30″x72°47′
Source: (Tooker 44, p. 274)
Variations: Waracto, Warracta (Ibid.)
*Moriches Quad (7.5′)

WASHINGTON SHOAL
Physical feature
Suffolk—East Hampton; in Block
 Island Sound, N of Montauk
 Peninsula and Shagwong Point;
 41°6′10″x71°54′37″
Montauk Point Quad (7.5′)

WASPEUNK NECK
Physical feature—historical
Suffolk—Brookhaven; E side of
Mastic Neck, also known as
Squorums
Source: (Tooker 44, p. 275)
*Moriches Quad (7.5 ')

WATCH HILL
Physical feature
Suffolk—Brookhaven; on Fire
Island, E of Davis Park, W of
Long Cove; 40°40'40"x72°59'15"
Source: (U.S. 170, Chart No. 12352,
1976)
*Howells Point Quad (7.5 ')

WATCHOGUE CREEK
Physical feature
Suffolk—Islip; NW part of the
Great South Bay, flows into Great
Cove, S of Bay Shore;
40°42'50"x73°14'30"
Variation: West Creek (U.S. 6, 1977,
p. 213)
Bay Shore East Quad (7.5 ')

WATCHOGUE NECK
Physical feature
Suffolk—Islip; on the Great South
Bay, bounded on the E by
Watchogue Creek and on the W by
Lawrence Creek; 40°43'x73°14'40"
Source: (Tooker 44, pp. 46, 92, 275)
*Bay Shore East Quad (7.5 ')

WATCHOGUE NECK
Physical feature—historical
Suffolk—Brookhaven; SE part of
East Moriches;
40°47'30"x72°45'30"
Source: (Tooker 44, p. 275)
*Moriches Quad (7.5 ')

WATER ISLAND
Community
Suffolk—Brookhaven; on Fire
Island, S of Blue Point, SE of
Sayville; 40°40'30"x73°1'50"
Sayville Quad (7.5 ')

WATER MILL
Community
Suffolk—Southampton; NW of
Mecox Bay; 40°54'30"x72°21'
Historical: Mill Neck (Bayles 93,
p. 333), Millville (Thompson 41,
vol. 1, inside cover map)
Sag Harbor Quad (7.5 ')

WATERMILL BEACH
Physical feature
Suffolk—Southampton; on the
Atlantic Ocean, E of Southampton,
SW of Mecox Bay;
40°53'10"x72°20'30"
Sag Harbor Quad (7.5 ')

WATERS CHAPEL
Community
Suffolk—East Hampton; NE of
East Hampton, E of Amagansett;
40°58'25"x72°10'20"
East Hampton Quad (7.5 ')

WATERSIDE PARK
see
CRAB MEADOW
Community
Source: (Rand 154, 1977, p. 382)

WATERVILLE
Community
Suffolk—Southold; N of the
community of Mattituck;
41°00'40"x72°32'15"
Mattituck Hills Quad (7.5 ')

WATERVILLE
Locality—historical
Suffolk—Brookhaven; formerly the
 E part of Eastport;
 ca. 40°49′30″x72°43′50″
Source: (Bayles 93, p. 280)
*Eastport Quad (7.5′)

WATERVILLE CREEK
see
MATTITUCK CREEK
Source: (U.S. 167, Map T-55)

WATTS CREEK
see
VALLEY STREAM
Physical feature
Source: (Lynbrook Quad, 7.5′,
 AMS, 1947)

WATTS POND
Physical feature—historical
Nassau—Hempstead; S side of the
 village of Valley Stream;
 ca. 40°39′40″x73°42′40″
Source: (Lynbrook Quad, 7.5′,
 AMS, 1947)
*Lynbrook Quad (7.5′)

WATTUQUASSET NECK
Physical feature—historical
Suffolk—East Hampton; SW side
 of Lake Montauk;
 41°3′10″x71°55′25″
Source: (Tooker 44, p. 276)
*Montauk Point Quad (7.5′)

WAUBHEAG CREEK
Physical feature—historical
Queens; W side of Rockaway Neck
Source: (Tooker 44, pp. 276–277)

WAUWEPEX
see
COLD SPRING HARBOR
Physical feature
Source: (Bayles 93, p. 139)

WAVE CREST
Community
Queens; SE part of Queens,
 S of Far Rockaway, N of
 Edgemere; 40°35′50″x73°46′
Far Rockaway Quad (7.5′)

WAVE CREST INLET
see
EDGEMERE INLET
Source: (Osborne 36, p. 117)

WAVERLY
see
HOLTSVILLE
Source: (Chace 127)

WAWEPEX GROVE
Physical feature—swamp—historical
Suffolk—Huntington; W of the
 community of Huntington,
 E of Cove Neck;
 ca. 40°53′x73°28′10″
Source: (U.S. 170, Chart No. 367,
 1916)
*Lloyd Harbor Quad (7.5′)

WAYUMSCUTT
see
WAINSCOTT
Source: (Flint 26, p. 74)

WEADING KREEK
see
WADING RIVER
Physical feature
Source: (Pelletreau 38, p. 381)

WEBBVILLE
Community—historical
Suffolk—Southold; in the vicinity of
Greenport
Source: (Rand 154, 1963, p. 322)

WEBSTER POND
Physical feature
Suffolk—Smithtown; SW of
Smithtown, NW of Hauppauge;
40°50'55"x73°13'50"
Historical: South Willow Pond
(Langhans 98, p. 26)
Central Islip Quad (7.5')

WECKATUCK NECK
Physical feature—historical
Suffolk—Southampton; NE part of
Noyack, SE of Noyack Bay;
40°59'35"x72°19'45"
Source: (Tooker 44, pp. 277–278)
Variations: (Weeckatuck, Weckatuck
(Ibid.)
*Sag Harbor Quad (7.5')

WEEKEWACKMAMISH CREEK
see
MILL CREEK
Suffolk—Southampton
Source: (Tooker 44, p. 279)

WEEKS PONT
Physical feature
Nassau—Oyster Bay; NW of the city
of Glen Cove; 40°52'33"x73°39'20"
Mamaroneck Quad (7.5')

WEEKS POINT
Physical feature
Nassau—Oyster Bay; SE side of
Oyster Bay Harbor, W of The
Cove, NE of the community of
Oyster Bay; 40°52'28"x73°30'30"
Hicksville Quad (7.5')

WEEKS POND
Physical feature
Suffolk—Brookhaven; SE of
Yaphank; 40°49'45"x72°54'45"
Bellport Quad (7.5')

WEEPOOSE BROOK
see
THOMPSONS CREEK
Source: (Tooker 44, pp. 77–78)

WEESUCK CREEK
Physical feature
Suffolk—Southampton; NE of East
Quogue, W side of Shinnecock
Bay; 40°50'50"x72°34'40"
Historical: Achabachawesuck and
Wesuck (Tooker 44, pp. 3–4)
Quogue Quad (7.5')

WEGONTHOTAK RIVER
see
FORGE RIVER
Source: (Tooker 44, p. 280)
Variations: Wanungatuck,
Waunungtatuck, Wegonthotuck,
Wenunguetuck, Wongattack (Ibid.)

WEHAHAMIS CREEK
see
LUDLOWS CREEK
Source: (Tooker 44, pp. 280–281)

WELD'S POND
see
NEW MILLPOND
Source: (Langhans 98, p. 17)

WELLS CREEK
Physical feature
Suffolk—Southampton; on

Shinnecock Bay, S of
Ponquogue and Hampton Bays;
40°51'10"x72°31'10"
Quogue Quad (7.5')

WELLS NECK
Physical feature—historical
Suffolk—Southampton; E of the
community of Flanders, SE side of
Flanders Bay;
40°54'30"x72°34'30"
Source: (Pelletreau 38, p. 382)
*Mattituck Quad (7.5')

WEST AMAGANSETT
Community
Suffolk—East Hampton; NW of
Amagansett, S of Threemile
Harbor; ca. 40°58'45"x72°10'
Source: (Hagstrom 141, 1979, p. 78)
*East Hampton Quad (7.5')

WEST AMITYVILLE
Community
Nassau—Oyster Bay; W of
Amityville, E of East
Massapequa; 40°39'40"x73°25'45"
Source: (Hagstrom 140, 1978, p. 52)
*Amityville Quad (7.5')

WEST BABYLON
Community
Suffolk—Babylon; central part of the
town, N of Lindenhurst;
40°43'x73°22'
Bay Shore West Quad (7.5')

WEST BABYLON CREEK
Physical feature
Suffolk—Babylon; S part of
Babylon, on the E side of Great
East Neck; 40°40'30"x73°20'15"

Historical: Mud Creek (U.S. 6, 1977,
p. 215)
Bay Shore West Quad (7.5')

WEST BAY SHORE
Community
Suffolk—Islip; SW part of the town,
E of Babylon; 40°42'30"x73°17'
Bay Shore West Quad (7.5')

WEST BEACH
Physical feature
Suffolk—Huntington; SW part of
Eatons Neck, separating Huntington
Bay and Northport Bay;
40°55'15"x73°24'25"
Lloyd Harbor Quad (7.5')

WEST BEACH
Physical feature
Suffolk—Islip; on the Great South
Bay, SW shoreline of Heckscher
State Park, SE of Islip;
40°42'x73°10'10"
Bay Shore East Quad (7.5')

WEST BELLPORT
Community
Suffolk—Brookhaven; E of
Patchogue, NE side of Patchogue
Bay, W of Bellport;
ca. 40°45'20"x72°58'20"
Source: (Hagstrom 141, 1979, p. 53)
*Bellport Quad (7.5')

WEST BRIGHTON
Community—historical
Kings; central part of Coney
Island, W of Brighton Beach;
40°34'30"x73°58'
Source: (Ross 39, p. 375). Also
known as Cables (Ibid.)
*Coney Island Quad (7.5')

344

WEST BROAD CHANNEL
Physical feature
Kings, Queens; in Jamaica Bay,
extends SW from the community
of Broad Channel to Runway
Channel, W of Far Rockaway;
40°36'x73°50'
Source: (U.S. 5, List No. 8101, p.
13)
*Far Rockaway Quad (7.5')

WEST BROOK
Physical feature
Suffolk—Islip; flows into East
Pond, E of Main Pond;
40°45'x73°8'40"
Central Islip Quad (7.5')

WEST BROOK
Physical feature
Suffolk—Islip; flows through the
Bayard Cutting Arboretum into
West Brook Pond, W of Connet-
quot Brook; 40°45'x73°9'30"
Central Islip Quad (7.5')

WEST BROOK POND
Physical feature
Suffolk—Islip; West Brook flows
into the pond, E of Islip Terrace,
NW of Oakdale;
40°44'50"x73°9'30"
Bay Shore East Quad (7.5')

WEST BROOKLYN
Community—historical
Kings; S of Greenwood Cemetery,
W of Kensington;
ca. 40°38'35"x73°59'15"
Source: (Brooklyn Quad, 15', 1897)
*Brooklyn Quad (7.5')

WEST CANAL
Physical feature
Suffolk—Islip; on the Great South

Bay, one of three man-made canals,
S of Islip; 40°42'30"x73°13'20"
Bay Shore East Quad (7.5')

WEST CONNECTICUT RIVER
see
CONNETQUOT RIVER
Source: (Tooker 44, p. 48)

WEST COVE
Physical feature
Suffolk—Brookhaven; N part of
Bellport Bay, E of Fire Place
Neck; 40°45'45"x72°53'45"
Bellport Quad (7.5')

WEST COVE
Suffolk—Brookhaven; on Moriches
Bay
see
TUTHILL COVE
Source: (Moriches Quad, 15', 1904)

WEST CRABMEADOW NECK
Physical feature
Suffolk—Huntington; the community
of Crab Meadow occupies the neck,
N of Northport; 40°55'10"x73°20'
Source: (Sammis 104, p. 9)
*Northport Quad (7.5')

WEST CREEK
Suffolk—Babylon
see
CARLLS RIVER
Source: (Sammis 104, p. 252)

WEST CREEK
Suffolk—Islip
see
WATCHOGUE CREEK
Source: (U.S. 6, 1977, p. 213)

WEST CROW ISLAND
Physical feature
Nassau—Hempstead; NW of Jones

Island, SE of Pettit Marsh and of
Big Crow Island;
40 °36 '50 "x73 °33 '10 "
Jones Inlet Quad (7.5 ')

WEST DEER PARK
see
WYANDANCH
Source: (Bailey 19, vol. 1, p. 364)

WEST END
Community
see
LONG BEACH (part of)
City
Source: (Macoskey 29, p. 63)

WEST END
Locality—historical
Kings; W section of Coney Island;
40 °34 '45 "x74 °00 '40 "
Source: (Ross 39, p. 374). Also
known as Norton's Point (Ibid.)
*Coney Island Quad (7.5 ')

WEST FIRE ISLAND
Physical feature
Suffolk—Islip; in the Great South
Bay, E of Captree Island, S of
East Islip; 40 °39 '30 "x73 °12 '
Historical: West Island (U.S. 5,
List No. 6301, p. 31)
Bay Shore East Quad (7.5 ')

WEST FLUSHING
see
CORONA
Source: (Ricard 86, p. 8))

WEST FORT
Fort—historical
Suffolk—Huntington; SW side of
Lloyd Neck, SE of Northwest
Bluff; 40 °55 'x73 °29 '10 "
Source: (U.S. 170, Chart No. 367,
1916)
*Lloyd Harbor Quad (7.5 ')

WEST FORT SALONGA
Community
Suffolk—Huntington; W of Fort
Salonga, N of Vernon Valley,
NE of Northport;
40 °54 '45 "x73 °19 '
Source: (Hagstrom 141, 1979, p. 34)
*Northport Quad (7.5 ')

WEST FOX CREEK
Physical feature
Suffolk—Babylon; W part of Cedar
Island in the SW part of the Great
South Bay; 40 °38 '20 "x73 °22 '
Bay Shore West Quad (7.5 ')

WEST GILGO
see
WEST GILGO BEACH
Source: (U.S. 5, List No. 5903,
p. 44)

WEST GILGO BEACH
Community
Suffolk—Babylon; SW corner of the
town, S of Amityville;
40 °36 '45 "x73 °25 '20 "
Historical: Sand Point, West Gilgo,
West Gilgo Heading (U.S. 5, List
No. 5903, p. 44)
West Gilgo Beach Quad (7.5 ')

WEST GILGO HEADING
see
WEST GILGO BEACH
Source: (U.S. 5, List No. 5903,
p. 44)

WEST HARBOR
Physical feature
Suffolk—Southold; on Long Island
Sound, NW side of Fishers Island,
NE of the community of Fishers
Island; 41°16'x72°00'25"
New London and Mystic Quads
(7.5')

WEST HARBOR
Suffolk—East Hampton
see
NORTHWEST HARBOR
Source: (U.S. 167, Map T-72)

WEST HEMPSTEAD
Community
Nassau—Hempstead; N-central part
of the town; 40°42'15"x73°39'
Lynbrook Quad (7.5')

WEST HILLS
Community
Suffolk—Huntington; W of South
Huntington, N of Melville;
ca. 40°49'x73°26'15"
Huntington Quad (7.5')

WEST HILLS
Physical feature
Suffolk—Huntington; SW-central
part of the town; 40°49'x73°26'
Huntington Quad (7.5')

WEST HUNTINGTON
Community
Suffolk—Huntington; on the W side
of the town, W of South
Huntington, E of Woodbury;
40°49'30"x73°25'55"
Source: (Hagstrom 141, 1979, p. 24)
*Huntington Quad (7.5')

WEST ISLAND
Physical feature
Nassau—Oyster Bay; E part of
South Oyster Bay;
40°38'x73°26'35"
Amityville Quad (7.5')

WEST ISLAND
Queens (Nassau)—Oyster Bay
see
DOSORIS ISLAND
Source: (Walling 172)

WEST ISLAND
Suffolk—Islip
see
WEST FIRE ISLAND
Source: (U.S. 5, List No. 6301,
p. 31)

WEST ISLIP
Community
Suffolk—Islip; SW part of the town,
E of Babylon; 40°42'30"x73°18'20"
Bay Shore West Quad (7.5')

WEST LAKE
Physical feature
Suffolk—Brookhaven; W of
Patchogue, N of Blue Point;
40°45'50"x73°1'45"
Patchogue Quad (7.5')

WEST MEADOW
Physical feature—island
Nassau—Hempstead; N of Harbor
Isle, SE of Pearsalls Hassock;
40°36'45"x73°39'50"
Lawrence Quad (7.5')

WEST MEADOW
Physical feature—marsh
Suffolk—Brookhaven; N of Stony
  Brook, W of Setauket, E of
  Smithtown Bay; 40°56'x73°8'35"
Saint James Quad (7.5')

WEST MEADOW BEACH
Physical feature
Suffolk—Brookhaven; W part of
  West Meadow, E shoreline of
  Smithtown Bay; 40°56'x73°8'45"
Saint James Quad (7.5')

WEST MEADOW CREEK
Physical feature
Suffolk—Brookhaven; flows through
  West Meadow into Porpoise
  Channel, W of Stony Brook;
  40°56'30"x73°8'55"
Saint James Quad (7.5')

WEST MECOX VILLAGE
Community
Suffolk—Southampton; N of Mecox
  Bay; 40°55'x72°19'50"
Sag Harbor Quad (7.5')

WEST MIDDLE ISLAND
see
CENTEREACH
Source: (Bayles 93, p. 265)

WEST MILLPOND
Physical feature
Suffolk—Brookhaven; E of Mastic,
  N of Forge River;
  40°48'30"x72°50'10"
Moriches Quad (7.5')

WEST NECK
Physical feature
Suffolk—Huntington; NW part of

the town, S of Lloyd Neck;
  40°54'30"x73°27'30"
Lloyd Harbor Quad (7.5')

WEST NECK
Physical feature
Suffolk—Shelter Island; SW part of
  Shelter Island; 41°3'20"x72°22'
Greenport Quad (7.5')

WEST NECK
Physical feature—historical
Suffolk—Babylon; SW part of
  Amityville, W of Amity Harbor and
  Amityville Creek;
  40°39'45"x73°25'15"
Source: (Tooker 44, p. 18). Also
  known as Araca, Arace (Ibid.)
*Amityville Quad (7.5')

WEST NECK
Village
see
AMITYVILLE
Source: (French 10, p. 636fn)

WEST NECK BAY
Physical feature
Suffolk—Shelter Island; W part of
  Shelter Island, S of Shelter Island
  Heights; 41°3'50"x72°21'45"
Greenport Quad (7.5')

WEST NECK BEACH
Physical feature
Suffolk—Huntington; W shoreline of
  West Neck, on Cold Spring Harbor;
  40°54'10"x73°28'50"
Lloyd Harbor Quad (7.5')

WEST NECK CREEK
Physical feature—channel
Suffolk—Southampton; connects
Little Sebonac Creek with Scallop
Pond; 40°55'45"x72°26'10"
Southampton Quad (7.5')

WEST NECK HARBOR
Physical feature
Suffolk—Shelter Island; on Shelter
Island Sound, S part of Shelter
Island; 41°2'50"x72°20'45"
Greenport Quad (7.5')

WEST NECK HARBOR
Physical feature—historical
Suffolk—Southampton; SSW of
West Neck, S of Robins Island,
NW of the village of Southampton;
40°54'55"x72°26'10"
Source: (Geographia 139, p. 51)
*Southampton Quad (7.5')

WEST NECK POINT
Physical feature
Suffolk—Shelter Island; end of
West Neck, SW side of Shelter
Island; 41°2'30"x72°20'50"
Greenport Quad (7.5')

WEST POINT
Physical feature
Suffolk—Southampton; on Tiana
Bay, S of Tiana; 40°51'x72°32'15"
Quogue Quad (7.5')

WEST POND
Physical feature
Queens; on Rulers Bar Hassock
in Jamaica Bay, NW of Far
Rockaway;
40°37'05"x73°49'52"

Source: (U.S. 5, List No. 8101,
p. 14)
*Far Rockaway Quad (7.5')

WEST POND
Physical feature—inlet
Nassau—Glen Cove; in the NW part
of the city of Glen Cove;
40°53'20"x73°38'15"
Mamaroneck Quad (7.5')

WEST RIDING OF YORKSHIRE
see
YORKSHIRE
Source: (French 10, p. 544fn)

WEST SAINT JAMES
Community
Suffolk—Smithtown; NW of Saint
James, SW of the village of
Nissequogue;
ca. 40°52'50"x73°10'30"
Source: (Hagstrom 141, 1979, p. 37)
*Saint James Quad (7.5')

WEST SAYVILLE
Community
Suffolk—Islip; SW of Patchogue,
W of Sayville; 40°44'x73°6'
Historical: Tuckertown, Greenville
(Bailey 19, vol. 1, p. 332),
Greenville (Cram 131, p. 31) and
Greeneville (Beers 117, p. 153)
Sayville Quad (7.5')

WEST SENIX CREEK
see
MUD CREEK
Suffolk—Brookhaven; on
Moriches Bay
Source: (Moriches Quad, 7.5',
AMS, 1947)

WEST TIANA
Community
Suffolk—Southampton; N of the W
  part of Shinnecock Bay, W of
  Tiana Bay; 40°51′45″x72°32′50″
Quogue Quad (7.5′)

WEST WILLISTON
Community
Nassau—North Hempstead; W of
  Williston Park, E of Herricks;
  40°45′30″x73°39′25″
Source: (Hagstrom 140, 1978, p. 27)
*Sea Cliff Quad (7.5′)

WEST YAPHANK
Community
Suffolk—Brookhaven; NW of
  Yaphank, W of Carmans River;
  40°50′45″x72°56′30″
Source: (Hagstrom 141, 1979, p. 51)
*Bellport Quad (7.5′)

WESTBURY
Village
Nassau—North Hempstead; SE side
  of town, E of Mineola;
  40°45′30″x73°35′30″
Historical: Wallage (Tooker 44,
  p. 269), Woodedge, Plainedge
  (Overton 37, p. 166)
Hicksville and Freeport Quads (7.5′)

WESTBURY SOUTH
Community
Nassau—Hempstead; SE of
  Westbury; 40°45′x73°33′35″
Variation: South Westbury
  (Hagstrom 140, 1978, p. 40)
Hicksville Quad (7.5′)

WESTBURY STATION
see
NEW CASSEL
Source: (Oyster Bay Quad, 15′,
  1900)

WESTFIELD
see
SELDEN
Source: (Bayles 93, p. 264)

WESTHAMPTON
Community
Suffolk—Southampton; E of
  Eastport, NE of Moriches Bay;
  40°49′20″x72°39′40″
Historical: Beaverdam (Pelletreau
  38, p. 340)
Eastport Quad (7.5′)

WESTHAMPTON BEACH
Physical feature
Suffolk—Southampton; on the
  Atlantic Ocean, SE of Moriches
  Bay; 40°47′25″x72°39′30″
Eastport and Moriches Quads (7.5′)

WESTHAMPTON BEACH
Village
Suffolk—Southampton; E end
  of Moriches Bay; SE of Eastport;
  40°48′10″x72°37′
Eastport and Quogue Quads (7.5′)

WESTHOLD
see
WADING RIVER
Community
Source: (Bailey 19, vol. 1,
  p. 197)

WESTMORELAND
Community
Suffolk—Shelter Island; W side
of Shelter Island;
41 °3 '30 "x72 °22 '
Greenport Quad (7.5 ')

WESTVILLE
Community—historical
Queens (Nassau)—Hempstead;
SW side of the town, NE of Far
Rockaway, in the vicinity of
Inwood; ca. 40 °37 '30 "x73 °44 '50 "
Source: (Beers 117, p. 118). Also
known as Northwest Point
(Ibid.), Woodedge and Bung
(Flint 26, p. 75)
*Lynbrook Quad (7.5 ')

WHALE CREEK
Physical feature
Kings; NW part of Kings, flows into
Newtown Creek from the south
side; 40 °44 '10 "x73 °56 '50 "
Brooklyn Quad (7.5 ')

WHALE HILL
Physical feature
Suffolk—East Hampton; E side of
Gardiners Island, N of
Tobaccolot Pond;
41 °6 'x72 °5 '30 "
Gardiners Island East Quad (7.5 ')

WHALE NECK
Physical feature
Nassau—Hempstead; on East Bay,
SE of Merrick; 40 °38 '20 "x73 °32 '
Source: (Pelletreau 38, p. 103)
*Freeport Quad (7.5 ')

WHALEHOUSE POINT
Physical feature
Suffolk—Brookhaven; on Fire
Island, in the Great South Bay, S of
Bellport; 40 °42 '55 "x72 °56 '20 "
Howells Point Quad (7.5 ')

WHALENECK POINT
Physical feature
Nassau—Hempstead; on East Bay,
SE point of Merrick, N of Cuba
Island; 40 °38 '15 "x73 °32 '
Freeport Quad (7.5 ')

WHEAT NECK
Physical feature—historical
Nassau—North Hempstead; in the
vicinity of Manhasset Neck
Source: (Pelletreau 38, p. 112)
*Sea Cliff Quad (7.5 ')

WHEATLEY
Community
Nassau—Oyster Bay; part of Old
Westbury; 40 °48 '20 "x73 °35 '
Historical: Wheatley Hills (Macoskey
29, p. 64), Wheatly Hills (Hyde 147)
Hicksville Quad (7.5 ')

WHEATLEY HILLS
see
WHEATLEY
Source: (Macoskey 29, p. 64)

WHEATLY HILLS
see
WHEATLEY
Source: (Hyde 147)

WHEELER'S
see
HAUPPAUGE
Source: (Tooker 44, pp. 70–71)

WHEELERS CORNER
Community—historical
Suffolk—Huntington; S of
Centerport
Source: (Ullitz 164, plate 1)
*Northport Quad (7.5 ')

WHEELERS DITCH
Physical feature—canal
Suffolk—Islip; E branch of
Quintuck Creek;
40 °42 '35 "x73 °11 '10 "
Source: (Town of Islip 163)
*Bay Shore East Quad (7.5 ')

WHIG INLET
Physical feature
Suffolk—Islip; on the Great South
Bay, SE side of Captree Island;
40 °38 '50 "x73 °15 '
Bay Shore East Quad (7.5 ')

WHITE BEACH
Physical feature
Suffolk—Brookhaven; on Long
Island Sound, N shoreline of
Mount Misery; 40 °58 'x73 °4 '
Port Jefferson Quad (7.5 ')

WHITE BROOK
Physical feature
Suffolk—Southampton; flows into
the Peconic River, SE of the
community of Riverhead, W of
Flanders; 40 °55 'x72 °38 '40 "
Source: (Pelletreau 38, p. 317)
*Riverhead Quad (7.5 ')

WHITE POINT
Physical feature
Nassau—Hempstead; on East Bay, S

point of Bellmore;
40 °38 '20 "x73 °31 '20 "
Freeport Quad (7.5 ')

WHITEPOT
see
FOREST HILLS
Source: (Ricard 86, p. 9) and (Cram
132, p. 111)

WHITE'S POND
see
PHILLIPS MILLPOND
Source: (Langhans 98, p. 26)

WHITESTONE
Community
Queens; N of Flushing, W of
Beechhurst; 40 °47 '40 "x73 °49 '
Historical: Cookie Hill, Clintonville
(French 10, p. 546fn)
Flushing Quad (7.5 ')

WHITESTONE POINT
Physical feature
Queens; on the East River, N point
of Whitestone, N of Flushing;
40 °48 'x73 °49 '10 "
Flushing Quad (7.5 ')

WHITEWOOD POINT
Physical feature
Suffolk—Huntington; W part of
Lloyd Neck; 40 °55 '20 "x73 °29 '50 "
Lloyd Harbor Quad (7.5 ')

WHITMAN STREAM
Physical feature
Suffolk—Smithtown; flows into
Willow Pond from the N, SW
of the community of Smithtown;
40 °51 '10 "x73 °13 '40 "
Source: (Langhans 98, p. 26)
*Central Islip Quad (7.5 ')

WHITMAN'S HOLLOW
Physical feature—historical
Suffolk—Smithtown, Huntington;
a broad hollow near Commack
Source: (Langhans 98, p. 26)
Variations: Whitmans Hollow,
Whitmansdale, Joseph Whitman's
Great Hollow (Ibid.) and
Whitmansdale (Burr 124)
*Greenlawn Quad (7.5 ')

WHITMANSDALE
see
WHITMAN'S HOLLOW
Source: (Langhans 98, p. 26)
and (Burr 124)

WHITNEY LAKE
Physical feature
Nassau—North Hempstead; S of
Manhasset Bay, E of Thomaston,
W part of Manhasset;
40°47'15"x73°42'20"
Sea Cliff Quad (7.5 ')

WIANDANCE
see
WYANDANCH
Source: (Tooker 44, p. 250)

WIBORG'S
Physical feature—historical
Suffolk—East Hampton; area
between East Hampton,
Amagansett and the ocean;
ca. 40°57'50"x72°9'
*East Hampton Quad (7.5 ')

WICKAPOGUE
Community
Suffolk—Southampton; E of the
village of Southampton, W of

Flying Point; 40°52'50"x72°21'55"
Source: (Hagstrom 141, 1979, p. 71)
*Sag Harbor Quad (7.5 ')

WICKAPOGUE
Locality—historical
Suffolk—Southampton; W of Mecox
Bay, in the vicinity of Flying
Point; ca. 40°53'40"x72°21'30"
Source: (Tooker 44, p. 282)
Variations: Weekapaug, Wecapoug,
Wickapogue, and Wickapog (Ibid.)
*Sag Harbor Quad (7.5 ')

WICKAPOGUE POND
Physical feature
Suffolk—Southampton; E of the
village of Southampton;
40°52'50"x72°22'
Sag Harbor Quad (7.5 ')

WICKHAM CREEK
Physical feature—inlet
Suffolk—Southold; NW of
Cutchogue Harbor;
41°0'30"x72°28'35"
Southold Quad (7.5 ')

WICOPESSET ISLAND
Physical feature
Suffolk—Southold; in Long Island
Sound, NE part of Southold, NE
of Fishers Island;
41°17'40"x71°54'50"
Mystic Quad (7.5 ')

WICOPESSET PASSAGE
Physical feature
Suffolk—Southold; in Long Island
Sound, between the E end of
Fishers Island and Wicopesset
Island; 41°17'30"x71°55'10"
Mystic Quad (7.5 ')

WIDOW'S BROOK
see
NICOLL CREEK
Source: (Tooker 44, pp. 34–35)

WIDOWS CREEK
see
NICOLL CREEK
Source: (Town of Islip 163)

WIGWAGONOCK
Locality—historical
Suffolk—East Hampton; the
E side of the village of
Sag Harbor;
41°0'x72°29'45"
Source: (Tooker 44, pp. 283–285)
*Sag Harbor Quad (7.5')

WIGWAM SWAMP
see
COLLEGE POINT
Physical feature
Source: (Flint 26, p. 69)

WIGWAME
Physical feature—swamp—historical
Suffolk—Huntington; near the
former community of Cold Spring,
S of Cold Spring Harbor;
ca. 40°50'x73°47'15"
Source: (Tooker 44, p. 285)
*Huntington Quad (7.5')

WILDERNESS POINT
Physical feature
Suffolk—Southold; SW side of
Fishers Island, SE of Mt.
Prospect; 41°15'10"x72°0'15"
New London Quad (7.5')

WILDWOOD
Community
Suffolk—Riverhead; NE of the
community of Wading River;
40°57'30"x72°49'
Wading River Quad (7.5')

WILDWOOD LAKE
Physical feature
Suffolk—Southampton; S of the
community of Riverhead;
40°53'40"x72°40'30"
Historical: Great Pond (Chace 127)
Riverhead Quad (7.5')

WILKENS NECK
Physical feature—historical
Queens; W side of Little Neck Bay,
S of Little Bay, includes present-day
Fort Totten and parts of Bayside;
40°47'x73°46'45"
Source: (Burr 125)
*Sea Cliff Quad (7.5')

WILLETS PATENT
Tract of land—historical
Suffolk—Islip; S side of West Islip,
E of Sampawams Creek and W of
Trues Creek;
ca. 40°41'30"x73°17'45"
Source: (Bayles 93, p. 198)
*Bay Shore West Quad (7.5')

WILLET'S POINT
Physical feature
Queens; NE of Little Bay;
40°47'45"x73°46'50"
Historical: Thorne's Point
(Flint 26, p. 75)
Flushing Quad (7.5')

WILLETTS CREEK
Physical feature
Suffolk—Islip; flows through West
Islip into Babylon Cove;
40°41'10"x73°18'10"
Historical: Sequatogue or
Secatogue Brook (Bayles 93, p. 209)
Bay Shore West Quad (7.5')

WILLETTS POINT
Physical feature
Suffolk—Islip; on the Great
South Bay, SW part of the town,
E of Babylon Cove;
40°41'x73°17'20"
Bay Shore West Quad (7.5')

WILLIAMS PURCHASE
Tract of land—historical
Queens (Nassau)—Oyster Bay;
included Hicksville, Plainview,
Jericho, Woodbury and part of
Syosset
Source: (Bailey 19, vol. 1, p. 457)

WILLIAMSBURG
Community
Kings; NW part of Kings, S of Long
Island City, NE of Brooklyn
Heights; 40°42'45"x73°57'15"
Brooklyn Quad (7.5')

WILLIAMSBURG
Town—historical
Kings; NW part of Kings, N of
Wallabout Bay
Source: (French 10, p. 367). Formed
from the town of Bushwick in
1840, incorporated as a city in
1851, annexed to the city of
Brooklyn in 1854 (Ibid.)

WILLISTON PARK
Village
Nassau—North Hempstead; S part of
the town, N of Mineola;
40°45'40"x73°39'
Sea Cliff Quad (7.5')

WILLOW BROOK
Physical feature
Suffolk—East Hampton; NE side of
Gardiners Island, flows into
Tobaccolot Pond;
41°5'35"x72°5'25"
Gardiners Island East Quad (7.5')

WILLOW HILL
Physical feature
Suffolk—Southold; W side of the
community of Southold;
41°3'20"x72°26'10"
Southold Quad (7.5')

WILLOW LAKE
Physical feature
Queens; in Meadow Park, central
part of Queens, NE of Forest
Hills, S of Flushing;
40°43'30"x73°50'
Jamaica Quad (7.5')

WILLOW POND
Physical feature
Nassau—Hempstead; N part of the
village of Hewlett Bay Park;
40°38'20"x73°41'30"
Lynbrook Quad (7.5')

WILLOW POND
Physical feature
Suffolk—Smithtown; W of the
community of Smithtown, S of
San Remo; 40°51'5"x73°13'35"

Historical: North Willow Pond,
South Willow Pond (Langhans 98,
p. 26)
Central Islip Quad (7.5 ')

WILLOW TREE
see
HILLSIDE
Source: (Ricard 86, p. 10)
and (French 10, p. 548)

WIN
see
WINFIELD
Source: (Rand 154, 1941, p. 273)

WINANTSVILLE
Community—historical
Queens—Newtown (town); in the
vicinity of Maspeth;
ca. 40°43'50"x73°54'20"
Source: (French 10, p. 549)
*Central Park Quad (7.5 ')

WINCOMA
Community
Suffolk—Huntington; W part of the
village of Huntington Bay, NW part
of East Neck; 40°54'10"x73°25'30"
Lloyd Harbor Quad (7.5 ')

WINCOMA POINT
see
SANDY POINT
Suffolk—Huntington
Source: (U.S. 5, List No. 7403,
p. 21)

WINCORAM
see
CORAM
Source: (Tooker 44, pp. 52–53)

WINDSOR TERRACE
Community—historical
Kings; in the vicinity of
Parkville (formerly Greenfield)
Source: (Ross 39, p. 326)
*Brooklyn Quad (7.5 ')

WINFIELD
Community—historical
Queens; N of Maspeth, NW of
Newtown; ca. 40°44'30"x73°53'45"
Source: (Walling 172). Earlier known
as Smith's Meadow (Ricard 86,
p. 15). Also known as Win (Rand
154, 1941, p. 273)
*Brooklyn Quad (7.5 ')

WINFIELD JUNCTION
Community—historical
Queens; SE of Woodside, NE of
Maspeth; ca. 40°44'20"x73°54'
Source: (Brooklyn Quad, 15', 1897)
*Brooklyn Quad (7.5 ')

WINGAN HOPPOGE
see
HAUPPAUGE
Source: (Langhans 98, p. 10)
Variations: Winganhappauge,
Winganheppoge (Ibid.)

WINGANHAUPPAUGE BROOK
see
CHAMPLIN CREEK
Source: (Tooker 44, p. 286)

WINGANHAUPPAUGE NECK
Physical feature—historical
Suffolk—Islip; S side of the
  community of Islip;
  40°42′45″x73°12′45″
Source: (Tooker 44, pp. 286–288)
Variations: Wingan Hauppauge,
  Winghanhoppog, and Wingatt (Ibid.)
*Bay Shore East Quad (7.5′)

WINHOLE CHANNEL
Physical feature
Queens; E side of Jamaica Bay, W
  of Jo Co Marsh;
  40°36′45″x73°48′30″
Far Rockaway Quad (7.5′)

WINHOLE HASSOCK
Physical feature—marsh island
Queens; E side of Jamaica Bay, W
  of Silver Hole Marsh, N of
  Hammel; 40°36′25″x73°48′35″
Far Rockaway Quad (7.5′)

WINHOLE POINT
Physical feature
Queens; E side of Jamaica Bay, S
  tip of East High Meadow, W of
  Jo Co Marsh; 40°36′45″x73°48′20″
Far Rockaway Quad (7.5′)

WINIPPAGUE
see
BERGEN BEACH
Source: (Tooker 44, p. 288)

WINKLE POINT
Physical feature
Suffolk—Huntington; S side of
  Eatons Neck; 40°55′22″x73°23′20″
Lloyd Harbor Quad (7.5′)

WINNECOMAC
see
COMMACK
Source: (Tooker 44, pp. 288–289)

WINNECOMAC PATENT
Tract of land—historical
Suffolk—Smithtown; SW corner of
  the town; ca. 40°49′x73°15′
Source: (Pelletreau 38, p. 229,
  map on p. 228)
*Greenlawn and Central Islip
  Quads (7.5′)

WINNECROSCOMS NECK
Physical feature—historical
Suffolk—Brookhaven; part of Mastic
  Neck, SE of the community of
  Mastic Beach, NE of Pattersquash
  Island; 40°45′40″x72°50′
Source: (Tooker 44, pp. 289–290).
  Also known as Minaussums (Ibid.,
  p. 132)
*Moriches Quad (7.5′)

WINTER HARBOR
Physical feature
see
STIRLING BASIN
Source: (Bailey 19, vol. 1, p. 157)

WINTER HARBOR
Village
see
GREENPORT
Source: (Pelletreau 38, p. 426)

WINTHROP PATENT
Tract of land—historical
Suffolk—Brookhaven; E of Namkee
  Creek and N along the Islip-
  Brookhaven line to the middle

of the island, W of Bellport and N up to the middle of the island; ca. 40°47′x73°00′
Source: (Pelletreau 38, p. 268)
*Sayville, Patchogue, Bellport and Howells Point Quads (7.5′)

WINTHROP'S ISLAND
see
FISHERS ISLAND
Source: (Manley 30, p. 220)

WISQUOSUCKS POINT
Physical feature
Suffolk—Brookhaven; W side of Carmans River at Squassux Landing; 40°46′30″x72°53′45″
Source: (Tooker 44, p. 290)
Variations; Squassucks, Wisquosuck, Wesquasesac, Wisquassuck (Ibid.)
*Bellport Quad (7.5′)

WISSIQUACK
see
NISSEQUOGUE RIVER
Source: (Tooker 44, p. 290)

WOCKAKAWSE RIVER
see
GREEN CREEK
Source: (Pelletreau 38, facing p. 243)

WOLF HILL
Physical feature—historical
Suffolk—Huntington; in the vicinity of the West Hills
Source: (Dyson 25, p. 70)
*Huntington Quad (7.5′)

WOLF PIT LAKE
Physical feature
Suffolk—Southold; N of Mattituck; 41°0′10″x72°32′
Mattituck Hills Quad (7.5′)

WOLVER HOLLOW
see
BROOKVILLE
Source: (Cocks 70, p. 6) and (Burr 125)

WOLVERHAMPTON
see
BROOKVILLE
Source: (Cocks 70, p. 6)

WONUKE
Physical feature—neck—historical
Suffolk—Southampton; two necks of land E of Beaverdam Creek, Great Wonunk (Oneck) and Little Wonunk; ca. 40°48′15″x72°39′
Source: (Tooker 44, pp. 290–291)
Variations: Onuck, Wounk, Wononck, Wonnonch, Wononke, Wonock, Onuck, Onach (Ibid.)
*Eastport Quad (7.5′)

WOOD HOLLOW
Physical feature—depression—historical
Suffolk—Huntington; S of Northport Basin, NE of Bluff Point, S of Eatons Neck Road; 40°55′3″x73°20′45″
Source: (Sammis 104, p. 182).
Also known as Deep Hollow, Deep Hole (Ibid.)
*Northport Quad (7.5′)

WOOD LAWN
Locality—historical
Suffolk—Brookhaven; SE of
Yaphank, NW of South Haven;
ca. 40°49'45"x72°53'45"
Source: (Chace 127)
*Bellport Quad (7.5')

WOOD TICK ISLAND
Physical feature
Suffolk—East Hampton; in
Acabonack Harbor, E of Threemile
Harbor; 41°1'20"x72°8'25"
Gardiners Island West Quad (7.5')

WOODBURY
Community
Nassau—Oyster Bay; E-central
part of the town of Oyster Bay,
S of Cold Spring Harbor;
40°49'30"x73°28'15"
Huntington Quad (7.5')

WOODCHOPPERS POND
Physical feature
Suffolk—Brookhaven; E side of
town, S of Lake Panamoka, NW of
Manorville; 40°53'50"x72°50'30"
Wading River Quad (7.5')

WOODCLIFF CANAL
Physical feature
Nassau—Hempstead; S side of
Freeport, E of Baldwin Bay;
40°38'x73°34'55"
Historical: Woodcliff Bay (Freeport
Quad, 7.5', AMS, 1947)
Freeport Quad (7.5')

WOODCLIFF PARK
Community
Suffolk—Riverhead; NW of Baiting

Hollow; 40°58'x72°45'
Wading River Quad (7.5')

WOODEDGE
Nassau—Hempstead
see
WESTVILLE
Source: (Flint 26, p. 75)

WOODEDGE
Nassau—North Hempstead
see
WESTBURY
Source: (Overton 37, p. 166)

WOODFIELD
Community—historical
Nassau—Hempstead; S of West
Hempstead, part of Lakeview;
ca. 40°41'15"x73°39'
Source: (Reifschneider 85, p. 186)
*Lynbrook Quad (7.5')

WOODHAVEN
Community
Queens; W side of Queens, NW of
Ozone Park; 40°41'30"x73°51'30"
Historical: Sweezey's Hollow (Flint
26, p. 75), Woodville (Ricard 86,
p. 15)
Jamaica Quad (7.5')

WOODHAVEN JUNCTION
Community—historical
Queens; NE of Woodhaven, NW of
Ozone Park, SW of Richmond Hill;
ca. 40°41'25"x73°50'30"
Source: (Brooklyn Quad, 15', 1897)
*Jamaica Quad (7.5')

WOODHULL PARK
Community—historical
Queens; presently in the area of

Hillside, E of Jamaica;
ca. 40°42'20"x73°47'20"
Source: (Brooklyn Quad, 15', 1897)
*Jamaica Quad (7.5')

WOODMERE
Community
Nassau—Hempstead; W side of
town, NE of Cedarhurst;
40°38'x73°42'
Lynbrook and Lawrence Quads
(7.5')

WOODMERE CHANNEL
Physical feature
Nassau—Hempstead; S part of
Woodmere, flows into Brosewere
Bay; 40°36'50"x73°42'30"
Lawrence Quad (7.5')

WOODS CREEK
Physical feature
Suffolk—Babylon; flows into the
Great South Bay, SE boundary
of Amityville, W of Amity Harbor;
40°39'30"x73°24'25"
Amityville Quad (7.5')

WOODS HOLE POND
Physical feature
Suffolk—Brookhaven; SW of
Shirley, NE of Bellport Bay;
40°46'43"x72°52'46"
Bellport Quad (7.5')

WOODSBURGH
Village
Nassau—Hempstead; SW part of the
town, partly on Hewlett Neck;
40°37'45"x73°42'30"
Lawrence and Lynbrook Quads
(7.5')

WOODSBURGH CHANNEL
Physical feature
Nassau—Hempstead; SE of
Woodsburgh, W boundary of North
Green Sedge; 40°36'40"x73°41'40"
Lawrence Quad (7.5')

WOODSIDE
Community
Queens; SW of Jackson Heights,
NW of Elmhurst;
40°44'45"x73°54'15"
Brooklyn Quad (7.5')

WOODTOWN
see
BUSHWICK
Source: (Bayles 93, p. 16)

WOODVILLE
see
WOODHAVEN
Source: (Ricard 86, p. 15)

WOODVILLE LANDING
see
SHOREHAM (part of)
Source: (Chace 127) and
(Hyde 147)

WOOLEY POND
Physical feature—inlet
Suffolk—Southampton; S of
Little Peconic Bay;
40°57'15"x72°24'
Southampton Quad (7.5')

WOOLSEY'S ISLAND
see
EAST ISLAND
Nassau—Oyster Bay
Source: (Cocks 70, p. 2)

WOORUSKHOUSE
Locality—historical
Suffolk—Babylon; about three miles
from West Neck, in the vicinity of
Lindenhurst-Santapogue Neck;
ca. 40°41'x73°21'15"
Source: (Tooker 44, p. 291)
*Bay Shore West Quad (7.5')

WOPOWOG
see
STONY BROOK
Community
Source: (Tooker 44, pp. 291-292)

WRECK ISLAND
Physical feature
Suffolk—Southold; in Block Island
Sound, S of the E part of Fishers
Island; 41°16'55"x71°55'55"
Mystic Quad (7.5')

WRECK LEAD
Community—historical
Nassau—Hempstead; in the vicinity
of Island Park;
ca. 40°36'15"x73°39'55"
Source: (Macoskey 29, p. 64) and
(Rand 154, 1938, p. 286)
*Lawrence Quad (7.5')

WRECK LEAD CHANNEL
Physical feature
Nassau—Hempstead; between Long
Beach, and Harbor Isle and
Island Park;
40°35'45"x73°39'30"
Lawrence Quad (7.5')

WUCHEBEHSUCK VALLEY
Physical feature—historical
Suffolk—East Hampton; in the
Montauk area, E side of North
Neck, W of Lake Montauk;
41°3'45"x71°56'15"
Source: (Tooker 44, pp. 292-293)
*Montauk Point (7.5')

WURTEMBERG
see
MASSAPEQUA PARK (part of)
Source: (Hyde 147)

WYAMAUG POINT
see
MIAMOGUE POINT
Source: (Tooker 44, p. 293)

WYANDANCH
Community
Suffolk—Babylon; N-central part
of the town, E of Farmingdale;
40°45'x73°21'45"
Historical: West Deer Park (Bailey
19, vol. 1, p. 364), Wiandance,
Squaw-Pit, Squam-Pit (Tooker 44,
p. 250)
Variations: Weandance, Wiantanse,
Wiantance, Weyrinteynich,
Waindance, Wyandance,
Wyandack, Wayandanch,
Waiandance, etc. (Ibid.,
pp. 294-295)
Bay Shore West and Greenlawn
Quads (7.5')

(French 10, p. 634fn), East Middle
Island (Thompson 41, vol. 1,
p. 440)
Variations: Yemkhamp, Yamphank
(Tooker 44, pp. 295-296)
Bellport Quad (7.5 ')

YAPHANK
Suffolk—Huntington
see
MELVILLE
Source: (Flint 26, p. 73)

YAMPHANK NECK
Physical feature—historical
Suffolk—Brookhaven; S of South
Haven, NE of the community of
Brookhaven; 40°47 '30 "x72°53 '45 "
Source: (Pelletreau 38, p. 266)
*Bellport Quad (7.5 ')

YATAMUNTITAHEGE RIVER
Physical feature—historical
Suffolk—Babylon; W of Copiague
Neck, possibly Great Neck Creek
Source: (Beauchamp 7, p. 226)
*Amityville Quad (7.5 ')

YANKEE CHANNEL
Physical feature
King; W side of Jamaica Bay,
N of Neponsit;
40°35 'x73°51 '45 "
Far Rockaway Quad (7.5 ')

YELLOW BAR HASSOCK
Physical feature—marsh island
Kings; SE part of Kings, W side of
Jamaica Bay, NE of Ruffle Bar;
40°36 '30 "x73°50 '30 "
Far Rockaway Quad (7.5 ')

YAPAHANK CREEK
Physical feature
Suffolk—Brookhaven; flows into the
Carmans River, SW of Shirley, NE
of the community of Brookhaven;
40°46 '55 "x72°53 '45 "
Historical: Yamphanke, Barteau's
Creek (Bailey 19, vol. 1, p. 255)
Bellport Quad (7.5 ')

YELLOW HOOK
Community—historical
Kings; S of Red Hook, on the Bay,
W of Bar Ridge;
ca. 40°37 '50 "x74°2 '15 "
Source: (Spafford 14, p. 62) and
(Burr 125)
*Jersey City Quad (7.5 ')

YAPHANK
Community
Suffolk—Brookhaven; NW of
Shirley, S of Middle Island, N of
Bellport; 40°50 '10 "x72°55 '
Historical: Millville, Brookfield

YENNICOCK
see
SOUTHOLD
Town
Source: (Tooker 44, pp. 296–297)
Variations: Yennycok, Yennicok,
Yenycott, Yennicock, Yenicott,
Yeanocock, Yannocock,
Yeannecock (Ibid.)

YORK
Locality—historical
Suffolk—Smithtown; between the
communities of Smithtown and
Hauppauge;
ca. 40°50′45″x73°11′30″
Source: (Langhans 98, p. 27)
*Central Islip Quad (7.5′)

YORKSHIRE
Administrative district—historical
"By a convention held at Hempstead
in 1665, Long Island, Staten Island,
and a part of Westchester County
were erected into a shire called
'Yorkshire,' for the purpose of
holding courts and administer-
ing justice. This was subdivided
into 'Ridings' known as 'East
Riding' (Suffolk County), 'West
Riding' (Kings County, Staten
Island, and Newtown) and 'North
Riding' (Queens County except
Newtown).''
Source: (French 10, p. 544fn)

YOUNGS CREEK
see
TOWN CREEK
Source: (Pelletreau 38, p. 422)

YOUNGS ISLAND
Physical feature
Suffolk—Smithtown; in Stony Brook

Harbor, in the middle of Porpoise
Channel, S of Long Beach;
40°55′20″x73°9′10″
Historical: Goose Island
(Langhans 98, p. 9)
Saint James Quad (7.5′)

YOUNGS POINT
Physical feature
Suffolk—Southold; E of Greenport;
41°6′25″x72°21′
Greenport Quad (7.5′)

YOUNGSPORT
see
GREAT RIVER
Suffolk—Islip
Source: (Bailey 19, vol. 1, p. 324)

ZACHS BAY
Physical feature
Nassau—Hempstead; SE part of the
  town, SE part of Jones Beach
  State Park; 40°36′x73°29′15″
West Gilgo Beach and Jones Inlet
  Quads (7.5′)

ZACHS INLET
Physical feature—historical
Nassau—Hempstead; once existed in
  the vicinity of Zachs Bay;
  ca. 40°36′30″x73°29′
Source: (Pearsall 100, p. 18). Also
  known as High Hill Creek Outlet
  (Osborne 36, p. 116)
*West Gilgo Beach Quad (7.5′)

ZEEKS POND
Physical feature
Suffolk—Brookhaven; NW of
  Manorville; 40°52′40″x72°50′30″
Wading River Quad (7.5′)

BIBLIOGRAPHY

GENERAL

1   American Name Society. *Names: Journal of the American Name Society.* Vol. 1— 1953-.

2   Sealock, Richard, and Seely, Pauline A. *Bibliography of Place-Name Literature: United States and Canada.* 2nd ed. Chicago: American Library Association, 1967. Updated periodically in *Names* 1968-.

3   Stewart, George R. *American Place-Names.* New York: Oxford University Press, 1970.

4   *Names on the Globe.* New York: Oxford University Press, 1975.

5   U.S. Board on Geographic Names. *Decisions on Geographic Names in the United States.* Decision List No.- 1953-; *Decisions of United States Board on Geographical Names,* Decisions Rendered [Between] July 1, 1940–June 30, 1941. Washington, D.C.: Government Printing Office.

6   U.S. National Ocean Survey. *United States Coast Pilot* 2; Atlantic Coast: Cape Cod to Sandy Hook. Washington, D.C.: U.S. National Oceanic and Atmospheric Administration, 1918-. From 1918–1970 issued by the Survey under its earlier name, U.S. Coast and Geodetic Survey.

NEW YORK STATE

7   Beauchamp, William M. "Aboriginal Place Names of New York," *New York State Museum Report* 60 (1906) 5–333.

8   Disturnell, John. *A Gazetteer of the State of New York.* 2nd ed. Albany, NY: C. Van Benthuysen, 1843.

9   Flick, Alexander C. "New York Place Names," *History of the State of New York* 10 (1962) 291–332.

10   French, John H. *Gazetteer of the State of New York.* 10th ed. Syracuse, NY: R.P. Smith, 1860.

11   Gordon, Thomas F. *Gazetteer of the State of New York.* Philadelphia: Thomas F. Gordon, 1836.

12   Hale, Edward Everett, Jr. "Dialectical Evidence in the Place-Names of Eastern New York," *American Speech* 5 (December 1929) 154–167.

13   Hough, Franklin B. *Gazetteer of the State of New York.* Albany, NY: A. Boyd, 1872.

14   Spafford, Horatio G. *A Gazetteer of the State of New York.* Albany, NY: B.D. Packard, 1824.

15   Swaen, A.E.H. "Dutch Place-Names in Eastern New York," *American Speech* 5 (June 1930) 400.

16   Werner, Edgar A., compiler. "Obsolete Towns and Villages," in *The New York Civil List.* Albany, NY: 1888.

LONG ISLAND

17   Armbruster, Eugene L. "Gazetteer of Long Island." 7 vols. Manuscript held by late author's family, Brookyn, NY.

18   Bailey, Paul. *Early Long Island, its Indians, Whalers and Folklore Rhymes.* Westhampton Beach, NY: Long Island Forum, 1962.

19   Bailey, Paul, ed. *Long Island: A History of Two Great Counties, Nassau and Suffolk.* 3 vols. New York: Lewis Historical Publishing Company, [1949].

20   Coles, Robert R. "Indian and Other Place-Names," *Long Island Forum* 34 (May 1971) 94–97.

21   "Long Island's Indian Names," *Long Island Forum* 20 (August 1957) 145–146.

22   DeKay, James E. *Indian Names of Places on Long Island.* New York: Holman and Gray, Book and Job Printers, [1851].

23   Dilliard, Maud E. "The Dutch Settle Long Island," *Long Island Historical Society Quarterly* 3 (January 1941) 67–76.

24   Dyson, Verne. *Anecdotes and Events in Long Island History.* Port Washington, NY: Ira J. Friedman, 1969.

25 Dyson, Verne. *The Human Story of Long Island.* Port Washington, NY: Ira J. Friedman, 1969.
26 Flint, Martha B. *Early Long Island; A Colonial Study.* New York: G.P. Putnam's Sons, 1896.
27 Gibbs, Alonzo, and Gibbs, Iris. "Moving Day," *Long Island Forum* 36 (June 1973) 105-107.
28 "In the Driftway," *Nation* 124 (April 20, 1927) 421-422.
29 Macoskey, Arthur R. *Long Island Gazetteer: A Guide to Historic Places.* New York: The Eagle Library, Inc., 1939.
30 Manley, Seon. *Long Island Discovery.* Garden City, NY: Doubleday & Company, 1966.
31 Minton, Arthur. "Names of Real-Estate Developments: Part I," *Names* 7 (September 1959) 129-153.
32 "Names of Real-Estate Developments: Part II," *Names* 7 (December 1959) 233-255.
33 "Names of Real-Estate Developments: Part III," *Names* 9 (March 1961) 8-36.
34 "Names of Places on Long Island and Their Derivations," *Historical Magazine* 9 (January 1865) 31.
35 Osborne, Chester G. "South Shore Inlets and Place Names," *Long Island Forum* 33 (May 1970) 88-90.
36 "South Shore Inlets and Place Names," *Long Island Forum* 33 (June 1970) 116-118.
37 Overton, Jacqueline. *Long Island's Story.* Garden City, NY: Doubleday, Doran, 1932.
38 Pelletreau, William Smith. *A History of Long Island.* Vol. 2. New York: Lewis Publishing Co., 1903.
39 Ross, Peter. *A History of Long Island.* Vol. 1. New York: Lewis Publishing Company, 1903.
40 Stevens, William O. *Discovering Long Island.* New York: Dodd, Mead & Co., 1939.
41 Thompson, Benjamin F. *The History of Long Island.* 2 vols. New York: Gould, Banks & Company, 1843.
42 "Indian Names of Long Island," *New York Historical Society Proceedings* (1845) 125-131.
43 Tooker, William W. *Indian Names for Long Island, With Historical and Ethnological Notes.* The Algonquian Series, No. 4. New York: F.P. Harper, 1901.
44 *The Indian Place-Names on Long Island and Islands Adjacent.* New York: G.P. Putnam's Sons, 1911.
45 *Some Indian Fishing Stations Upon Long Island.* The Algonquian Series, No. 7. New York: F.P. Harper, 1901.
46 "Some Indian Names of Places on Long Island, NY and Their Correspondence in Virginia, as Mentioned by Capt. John Smith and Associates," *Magazine of New England History* 1 (July 1891) 154-158.
47 "Some Supposed Indian Names of Places on Long Island," *Long Island Magazine* 1 (May 1893) 51-54.
48 Trumbull, James H. "Indian Names of Places on Long Island, Derived from Esculent Roots," *Magazine of American History* 1 (June 1877) 386-387.
49 Tuomey, Douglas. "What's in a Name," *Long Island Forum* 23 (February 1960) 29-30.
50 Valentine, Andrus T., and Valentine, Harriet G. "Wood's Tide Mill Grist Book," *Long Island Forum* 34 (May 1971) 98-101.
51 Wilson, Rufus R. *Historic Long Island.* New York: Berkeley Press, 1902.
52 Wittlock, Lavern A. "Conjecture on Origin of 'Fire Island'," *Long Island Forum* 36 (September 1973) 165.

KINGS COUNTY

53   Armbruster, Eugene L. *Bruijkleen Colonie, 1638-1918.* New York: By the Author, 1918.
54   Blumengarten, Jeannette G. "Flatbush Place-Names." M.A. Thesis, Brooklyn College, 1960.
55   Bryant, Margaret M. "Some Indian and Dutch Names Reflecting the Early History of Brooklyn," *Names* 20 (June 1972) 106-110.
56   "City Draws Borders for 87 Neighborhoods," *New York Times,* July 16, 1962, p. 25.
57   Field, Thomas W. "Indian, Dutch and English Names of Localities in Brooklyn," in *Manual of the Common Council of the City of Brooklyn,* pp. 459-470. Brooklyn, NY: Common Council, 1868.
58   Haber, Richard. "Gravesend Place-Names," M.A. Thesis, Brooklyn College, 1964.
59   Marlowe, Nicholas. "Bedford-Stuyvesant Place-Names." M.A. Thesis, Brooklyn College, 1963.
60   Minsky, Pearl G. "Canarsie Place-Names." M.A. Thesis, Brooklyn College, 1963.
61   Pearlman, Archie. "East New York Place-Names." M.A. Thesis, Brooklyn College, 1967.
62   Rashkin, Henry. "Bay Ridge Place Names." M.A. Thesis, Brooklyn College, 1960.
63   Rubel, Tamara K. "Place Names in Brooklyn Heights." M.A. Thesis, Brooklyn College, 1963.
64   Sherman, Herman. "Red Hook Place-Names." M.A. Thesis, Brooklyn College, 1965.
65   Shulman, David. "Coney Island's Name," *New York Times,* September 26, 1938, p. 16.
66   Stiles, Henry R. *A History of the City of Brooklyn.* New York: Publication by Subscription, 1867-70.
67   Tooker, William W. *Indian Names of Places in the Borough of Brooklyn with Historical and Ethnological Notes.* The Algonquian Series, No. 2. New York: F.P. Harper, 1901.
68   Weisman, Carl M. "Brooklyn from Breukelen and Bruijkleen," *Names* 1 (March 1953) 39-40.
69   Williams, John D. "Place Names in Sea Gate, Coney Island, Brighton Beach and Manhattan Beach." M.A. Thesis, Brooklyn College, 1964.

NASSAU AND QUEENS COUNTIES

70   Cocks, George W. "Old Matinecock," *Nassau County Historical Journal* 22 (Fall 1961) 1-11.
71   Coghlan, William R. "The Parsonage Farm," *Long Island Forum* 37 (February 1974) 32-33.
72   Coles, Robert R. "The American Revolution: Incidents at Glen Cove," *Long Island Forum* 38 (March 1975) 44-47.
73   "The Ghosts of Dosoris," *Long Island Forum* 34 (January 1971) 8-11.
74   "A Road to Yesteryear," *Long Island Forum* 37 (August 1974) 154-160.
75   "Some Matinecock Place-Names," *Long Island Forum* 17 (November 1954) 207, 218.
76   Gibbs, Alonzo, and Gibbs, Iris. "About Pond and Hill," *Long Island Forum* 38 (May 1975) 83.
77   "The Bethpage Purchase—Part X: The Carpenter Claim," *Long Island Forum* 38 (July 1975) 126-127.
78   "Local History and the Law," *Long Island Forum* 37 (April 1974) 65-67.
79   Luke, Myron H. "Battle of Long Island," *Long Island Forum* 39 (July 1976) 126-129, 144-147.
80   Marshall, Bernice S. *Colonial Hempstead; Long Island Life Under the Dutch and English.* 2nd ed. Port Washington, NY: Ira J. Friedman, 1962.
81   "Metropolitan Area Loses One of Its Central Parks," *New York Times,* October 3, 1936, p. 2.
82   Metz, Clinton E. "The Ice Ponds of Hingletown," *Long Island Forum* 39 (May 1976) 89-90.

83   "What Ever Happened to Milburn?" *Long Island Forum* 36 (January 1973) 6–12.

84   Pearsall, Louis P. "Hog Island Inlet," *Long Island Forum* 39 (April 1976) 79.

85   Reifschneider, Felix E. "Villages That Have Disappeared," *Long Island Forum* 41 (August 1978) 186.

86   Ricard, Herbert F. "The Origin of Community Names in Queens Borough," *Queens (Borough) Historian* 1 (1944) 5–15.

87   Russell, Daniel E. "The Mills of Glen Cove," *Long Island Forum* 38 (November 1975) 208–211.

88   "Sea-Cove Beach Renamed," *New York Times,* February 26, 1956, p. 65.

89   Verity, Wilbur R. "The Party Boat Salnada," *Long Island Forum* 39 (September 1976) 202.

90   Wexler, Jeffrey. "Colonel Richard Hewlett, Tory," *Long Island Forum* 39 (November 1976) 238–243.

SUFFOLK COUNTY

91   Adams, James T. *History of the Town of Southampton.* Bridgehampton, NY: Hampton Press, 1918.

92   *Memorials of Old Bridgehampton.* Port Washington, NY: Ira J. Friedman, 1962.

93   Bayles, Richard M. *Historical and Descriptive Sketches of Suffolk County.* Port Jefferson, NY: By the Author, 1874.

94   Bayles, Thomas R. "Ships Built in Port Jefferson," *Long Island Forum* 36 (July 1973) 135.

95   "Some Brookhaven History," *Long Island Forum* 37 (March 1974) 48–52.

96   Bigelow, Paul W. "Old Long Island Decoys," *Long Island Forum* 36 (September 1973) 166–169.

97   Havens, Barrington S. "The Archibald Havens Papers," *Long Island Forum* 37 (May 1974) 90–95.

98   Langhans, Rufus B. *Place Names in the Town of Smithtown: Their Location and Meaning.* Smithtown Library-Handley Series No. 2. Smithtown, NY: Smithtown Library, 1961.

99   Munsell, William W. *History of Suffolk County.* New York: W.W. Munsell & Co., 1882.

100   Pearsall, Louis P. "Gilgo Station Washed Away," *Long Island Forum* 37 (January 1974) 18–20.

101   Pelletreau, William Smith, ed. *Records of the Town of Smithtown, Long Island, NY.* [Huntington, NY: Long-Islander Print,] 1898.

102   Rattray, Everett T. *The South Fork: The Land and the People of Eastern Long Island.* New York: Random House, 1979.

103   Rohl, Kenneth K. "The Legend of John Lee Baldwin," *Long Island Forum* 39 (December 1976), 256–262.

104   Sammis, Romanah. *Huntington-Babylon Town History.* Huntington, NY: Huntington Historical Society, 1937.

105   Schmersal, Emma E. "Surrey Ride to Red Creek," *Long Island Forum* 40 (March 1977) 44–47.

106   Shaw, Edward Richard. *Legends of Fire Island Beach and the South Side.* New York: Lovell, Coryell & Co., 1895.

107   Strong, Kate Wheeler. "Some Strange Old Place-Names," *Long Island Forum* 15 (June 1952) 109, 116.

108   "Some Strong Family Tales," *Long Island Forum* 38 (June 1975) 118–119.

109   Sugrue, Francis. "Joy in Babylon: U.S. Approves Sampawams as Name of Creek," *New York Herald Tribune,* October 28, 1948, p. 27.

110   Tooker, William W. *Indian Place-Names in East-Hampton Town, Long Island with Their Probable Significations.* Sag Harbor, NY: J.H. Hunt, 1889.

111   Valentine, Andrus T., and Valentine, Harriet G. "Farming from Wood's Records," *Long Island Forum* 39 (April 1976) 72–77.

112   Wines, Virginia. "A Brief History of Hallockville," *Long Island Forum* 41 (January, 1978) 10–13.

113   Yeager, Edna Howell. "Dunnage Wood," *Long Island Forum* 36 (October 1973) 190–194.
114   "Harvesting Ice—A Local Industry," *Long Island Forum* 37 (January 1974) 10–15.
115   Young, Thomas T. "Fyke Fisherman," *Long Island Forum* 39 (February 1976) 28–30.

MAPS AND ATLASES

116   *Asher & Adams' New Topographical Atlas and Gazetteer of New York.* New York: Asher & Adams, [1871].
117   Beers, F.W. *Atlas of Long Island.* New York: Beers, Comstock & Cline, 1873.
118   *Atlas of the Towns of Babylon, Islip and South Part of Brookhaven Suffolk Co., in New York.* New York: Wendelken & Co., 1888.
119   *New Map of Kings and Queens Counties.* New York: Beers & Co., 1886.
120   Beers, J.B. *Farm Line Map of the City of Brooklyn, NY.* New York: Beers & Co., 1874.
121   *Map of the City of Brooklyn.* New York: Beers & Co., 1874.
122   Bishop, H.F. *Building Zone Map for the Town of Southampton, Suffolk Co., NY.* Westhampton Beach, NY: Town of Southampton, 1957. (Revised to 1967).
123   Blunt, Edmund. *Long Island Sound from New York to Montock Point.* Scale 1:1,000,000. New York: E. & G.W. Blunt, 1828–30.
124   Burr, D.H. *Map of the County of Suffolk, NY.* New York: D.H. Burr, 1829.
125   *Map of the Counties of New York, Queens, Kings and Richmond.* New York: D.H. Burr, 1829.
126   Cary, John. *A New Map of Part of the United States of North America.* Scale 1:2,787, 840. London: J. Cary, 1806.
127   Chace, J. Jr. *Map of Suffolk County, Long Island, New York.* Philadelphia: John Douglass, 1858.
128   Chesebrough, Ephraine. *A New and Correct Chart of the Eastern End of Long Island Sound from Oyster Point to Montaug and from Watch Hill to Black Point.* New Haven, CT: A. Doolittle, 1811–14.
129   Colton, J.H. *Travellers Map of Long Island, New York.* New York: J.H. Colton, 1843.
130   *Colton's Road Map of the Counties of Kings & Queens, State of New York.* Scale 1:252, 130. New York: G.W. & C.B. Colton & Co., 1893.
131   *Cram's Standard American Railway System Atlas of the World.* Chicago: George F. Cram, 1899.
132   *Cram's Superior Atlas of the World.* Chicago: George F. Cram, 1901.
133   *Cram's Unrivaled Family Atlas of the World.* Chicago: George F. Cram, 1883.
134   Dripps, M. *Map of Kings and Part of Queens Counties, Long Island, NY.* Scale 1:19, 800. New York: M. Dripps, 1852.
135   *Map of Kings County with Parts of Westchester, Queens, New York and Richmond Counties.* Scale 1:22,400. New York: M. Dripps, [1872].
136   Faden, William. *A Map of the Province of New York.* London: Wm. Faden, 1776. Facsimile published under the title *New York at the Time of Ratification of the Constitution, from 1776 and 1787.* Originals in the Library of Congress at Washington. Washington, D.C.: U.S. Geological Survey, 1976.
137   *Farm Line Map of the City of Brooklyn...* Section 4. New York: J.B. Beers & Co., 1874.
138   Field, Thomas W. *Plan of the Positions and Movement of the British and American Army on the 26th and 27th of August 1776 on Long Island,* in *The Battle of Long Island, with connected Preceeding Events, and the Subsequent American Retreat.* Vol. 2. Brooklyn, NY: Long Island Historical Society, 1869.
139   Geographia Map Company, Inc. *Geographia Atlas of Suffolk County, New York.* Hoboken, NJ: Geographia Map Co., 1973.
140   Hagstrom Company, Inc. *Hagstrom Atlas; Nassau County.* New York: Hagstrom Company, 1957– . (Title varies.)
141   *Hagstrom Atlas; Suffolk County.* New York: Hagstrom Company, 1961– . (Title varies.)
142   *Hagstrom's Atlas of the City of New York; Five Boroughs.* New York: Hagstrom Company, 1941– . (Title varies.)

143   *Hagstrom's Map of Queens.* New York: Hagstrom Co., 1928.

144   *Hagstrom's Map of Queens.* New York: Hagstrom Co., [1930].

145   *Hammond's Large Scale Map of Brooklyn.* Scale 1:18,000. New York: C.S. Hammond & Co., [1929].

146   *Higginson's Map of Kings and a Large Part of Queens Counties.* Scale 1:63,360. New York: J.H. Higginson, 1860.

147   Hyde & Company. *Map of Long Island, New York.* 2nd ed. New York: Hyde & Company, 1897.

148   Hyde, E. Belcher. *Real Estate and Reference Map of Suffolk County, Long Island, NY.* Westerly Part, First Section. Scale 1:24,000. New York: E. Belcher Hyde, Inc., 1931.

149   Lotter, Mathew A. *A Map of the Provinces of New York and New Jersey.* Augsburg: Mathew Albert Lotter, 1777.

150   *Map of Huntington-Smithtown Townships, LI, NY.* Boston: Map Corporation of America, [1967].

151   *New Century Atlas of Counties of the State of New York.* New York: Everts Publishing Co., 1911.

152   Perrish, William. *Kings* [Portion]. Scale 1:3,960. 4 sheets. New York: Wm. Perrish & J.H. Higginson, 1855.

153   Rand, McNally and Company. *Business Atlas.* Chicago: Rand, McNally, 1880.

154   *Commercial Atlas and Marketing Guide.* Chicago: Rand, McNally, 1911– .

155   Ratzer, B. *Plan of the Town of Brooklyn and Part of Long Island, 1776–1777,* in Henry R. Stiles' *A History of the City of Brooklyn,* Vol. 1, p. 63. New York: Publication by Subscription, 1867–70.

156   Rogers, Paul Jr. *A Chart of Long Island Sound...* Scale 1:130,000. New London, CT: By the Author, 1857.

157   Romans, Bernard. *Connecticut and Parts Adjacent.* Scale 1:316,800. New Haven, CT: Bernard Romans, 1777.

158   Ross, Don. *Historic Map of Cow Neck.* 1940. In Bailey, Paul, ed., *Long Island; A History of Two Great Counties, Nassau and Suffolk,* Vol. 1. New York: Lewis Historical Publishing, 1949. p. 450.

159   Ryder, Robert. [Facsimile map of] Long Inland Siruaide, 1675. Scale 1:320,000. Meriden, CT: Meriden Gravure Company, [1950].

160   [Map of Long Island as far east as Wading River.] Scale ca. 1:950,400. 1670.

161   *[Shell] Street Guide of Brooklyn-Queens.* Chicago: H.M. Gousha Co., 1942.

162   Smith, J. Calvin. *Map of Long Island with the Environs of New-York and the Southern Part of Connecticut.* Scale 1:158,400. New York: J.H. Colton & Co., 1836.

163   *Town of Islip, Suffolk County, NY. Streets & Zoning.* Islip, NY: Town of Islip, Engineering Dept., 1959.

164   Ullitz, H. and others. *Atlas of Suffolk County, Long Island, New York, Sound Shore.* Vol. 2. New York: E. Belcher Hyde, 1909.

165   *Atlas of Suffolk County, Long Island, New York, South Shore.* Vol. 1. New York: E. Belcher Hyde, 1902.

166   U.S. Army Map Service. *A.M.S. Topographic Series V821.* Scale 1:24,000. Washington, D.C.: Army Map Service, 1943–1969; became U.S. Army Topographic Command, 1969–1972; became U.S. Defense Mapping Agency, 1972– .

167   U.S. Coast Survey. *Topographic Surveys.* Washington, D.C.: U.S. Coast Survey Office, 1838–46.

168   U.S. Geological Survey. *National Topographic Series.* Scale 1:24,000. Reston, VA: U.S. Geological Survey, 1947– .

169   *National Topographic Series.* Scale 1:62,500. Reston, VA: U.S. Geological Survey, 1879– .

170 U.S. National Ocean Survey. *Nautical Charts.* Riverside, MD: National Ocean Survey, 1970– ; earlier U.S. Coast & Geodetic Survey, 1878–1969; earlier U.S. Coast Survey, 1836–1878.

171 [Untitled Map Showing Eastern Portion of Long Island and the Coast of Connecticut.] Photostat from manuscript in French. 1 in. = 7 geographical miles on original. French Archives 135 bis-10-2 (17–). Located at Library of Congress, G & M Division.

172 Walling, H.F. *Topographical Map of the Counties of Queens and Kings.* New York: W.E. & A.A. Baker, 1859.

USGS 7.5′ TOPOGRAPHIC QUADRANGLE MAPS OF LONG ISLAND
(WITH DATES OF EDITIONS USED IN PLACE NAME ENTRIES)

Amityville, N.Y.	1969		Mamaroneck, N.Y.-Conn.	1967
Bay Shore East, N.Y.	1967		Mattituck, N.Y.	1956
Bay Shore West, N.Y.	1969		Mattituck Hills, N.Y.	1956
Bayville, N.Y.-Conn.	1967		Middle Island, N.Y.	1967
Bellport, N.Y.	1967		Montauk Point, N.Y.	1956
Brooklyn, N.Y.	1967		Moriches, N.Y.	1967
Central Islip, N.Y.	1967		Mystic, Conn.-N.Y.-R.I.	1958
Central Park, N.Y.	1966		Napeague Beach, N.Y.	1956
Coney Island, N.Y.-N.J.	1966		The Narrows, N.Y.-N.J.	1966
East Hampton, N.Y.	1956		New London, Conn.-N.Y.	1970
Eastport, N.Y.	1956		Northport, N.Y.	1967
Far Rockaway, N.Y.	1969		Orient, N.Y.	1956
Flushing, N.Y.	1966		Patchogue, N.Y.	1967
Freeport, N.Y.	1969		Pattersquash Island, N.Y.	1967
Gardiners Island East, N.Y.	1956		Plum Island, N.Y.	1954
Gardiners Island West, N.Y.	1956		Port Jefferson, N.Y.	1967
Greenlawn, N.Y.	1967		Quogue, N.Y.	1956
Greenport, N.Y.	1956		Riverhead, N.Y.	1956
Hicksville, N.Y.	1967		Sag Harbor, N.Y.	1956
Howells Point, N.Y.	1967		Saint James, N.Y.	1967
Huntington, N.Y.	1967		Sayville, N.Y.	1967
Jamaica, N.Y.	1966		Sea Cliff, N.Y.	1968
Jersey City, N.J.-N.Y.	1967		Shinnecock Inlet, N.Y.	1955
Jones Inlet, N.Y.	1967		Southampton, N.Y.	1956
Lawrence, N.Y.	1966		Southold, N.Y.	1956
Lloyd Harbor, N.Y.-Conn.	1967		Wading River, N.Y.	1967
Lynbrook, N.Y.	1969		West Gilgo Beach, N.Y.	1967

Map III

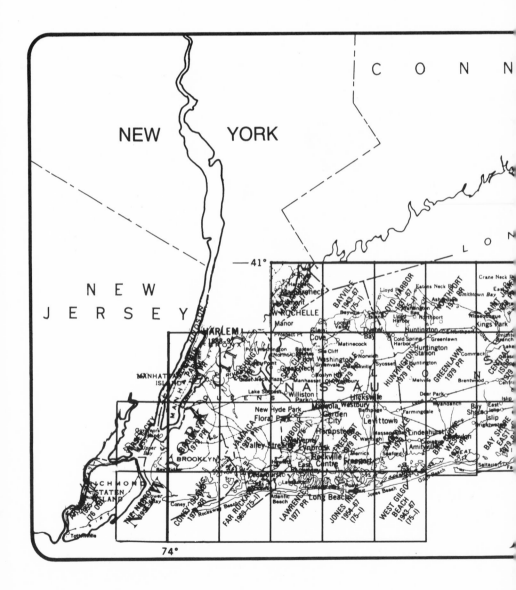